HYPERTEXT '89
Proceedings

Graphic design by Helen DeAndrade
Index by Rosemary Simpson

November 5 – 8 • Pittsburgh, Pennsylvania

The Association for Computing Machinery
11 West 42nd Street
New York, New York 10036

ISBN 0-89791-339-6

Additional copies may be ordered prepaid from:

ACM Order Department
P.O. Box 64145
Baltimore, MD 21264

Price:
Members $23.00
All others $30.00

ACM Order Number: 608891

Welcome to Hypertext '89

Two years ago, Hypertext '87 — the first ACM Conference on Hypertext — was organized to bring together researchers and practitioners in the just-emerging field of hypertext. That conference was a success; over 250 people attended, but unfortunately, an equal number had to be turned away because of lack of space.

With the continued blossoming of interest in hypertext, we thought it was time for a second ACM Conference on Hypertext. With Hypertext '89, we are trying to provide a forum for assessing the state of the field and for thinking about where it might go from here. Conference participants include people who develop hypertext tools, build and use application systems based on those tools, and publish databases of materials in hypertext form — as well as those doing research on hypertext. We hope that their differing perspectives will make for some enlightened (and maybe heated!) discussions.

If this conference succeeds, it will be because of all the effort that the Committee members have poured into it. For instance, in July the program committee met in Pittsburgh for several marathon days of reviewing papers and panels. They ended up selecting 28 papers and 5 panels from the 119 papers and 9 panels that were submitted. Then, they put together four new panels to round out the technical content of the conference. I would like to thank Frank Halasz for the excellent job he has done as Program Chair. I would also like to thank the other conference committee members; their areas of responsibility (proceedings, publications, industry, demos, courses, and student volunteers) benefitted greatly from the considerable effort they invested.

The conference committee would like to thank ACM for its continued support. In particular, the three sponsoring SIGS — SIGIR, SIGOIS, and SIGCHI — were instrumental in funding and promoting this conference. We would also like to thank the conference's corporate sponsors, which include Apple Computer, IBM, and Texas Instruments, whose additional financial support was very helpful during the planning stages of the conference.

Finally, the committee members also thank their employers and sponsors for their support, cooperation, and patience. We hope the success of the conference more than compensates for any disruption created by the committee members' volunteer efforts.

Interest in hypertext continues to grow rapidly. Journals, conferences, work-shops, and papers seem to sprout at every turn. As the field matures, events such as this conference are a good opportunity to share knowledge with each other and perhaps to influence the future directions of the field. We'd like to hold another ACM conference on hypertext; please let us know when and where it should be held.

We hope you enjoy the paper sessions, panels, demos, courses, and other events on the Hypertext '89 program. However, as conference organizers we could only do so much, we're now counting on you to provide the extra magic — the spirited discussion and camaraderie that are the real reasons for attending a conference.

Rob Akscyn
Conference Chair

Conference Committee

Donna Harman
Treasurer
National Institute of Standards and Technology

Frank Halasz
Program Chair
Xerox PARC

Mary Laplante
Publicity Chair
Consultant

John Leggett
Demonstrations Co-Chair
Texas A&M University

Norman Meyrowitz
Proceedings Chair
Brown University

Tim Oren
Industry Chair
Apple Computer

Amy Pearl
Demonstrations Co-Chair
Sun Microsystems

Maria Wadlow
Student Volunteers
Carnegie-Mellon University

Jan Walker
Courses Chair
Digital Equipment

Nicole Yankelovich
Publications Chair
Brown University

Elise Yoder
Executive Administrator
Knowledge Workshop

The Hypertext '89 Program

Welcome to Hypertext' 89, the "Second" ACM Conference on Hypertext. The first ACM "Conference" on Hypertext was the Hypertext 87 WORKSHOP held in Chapel Hill during November of 1987. The Chapel Hill Workshop was a watershed event. Hypertext was just coming of age, breaking out of the research labs and garage shop operations into widespread attention (and considerable hype) in the computer world. Hypertext' 87 was the first chance for many of us to develop a sense that there was a hypertext community. People who had been working on related issues but in relative isolation, sometimes for many years, had a chance to meet and exchange their ideas and experiences for the very first time. I know that for myself, Hypertext 87 brought me into a whole new world of colleagues and compatriots.

Perhaps the most exciting aspect of Hypertext' 87 was its interdisciplinary nature. Hypertext is a crossroads where many disparate interests meet. Some of us in the hypertext community are computer scientists and technologists interested in exploring hypertext as a class of computing systems. Some of us are application builders whose interest is in providing tools to help people manage and represent information. Some of us are writers and artists who see hypertext as a new and liberating medium in which to express our ideas.

The world of hypertext has changed quite a bit in the last two years. In both the research and commercial worlds, interest in the field has expanded tremendously. Despite these changes, I hope that Hypertext' 89 will foster the same level of excitement, of new ideas, of interdisciplinary interchange, and of sense of community that we found in Chapel Hill.

Our goal in putting together the Hypertext' 89 program was to provide a forum for the leading edge in research and thinking about hypertext and hypermedia. We tried hard to balance the program among the various facets of our community. Although the program is heaviest at the technology end of the spectrum, it also includes an ample sampling of research into the applications of hypertext ideas. Fortunately, the program also includes a small but fascinating representation from the artistic community.

Hypertext' 89 is a research oriented conference. The program was carefully selected to maintain the scholarly approach prevalent at Hypertext' 87. One entailment of this is that commercially-oriented presentations of hypertext implementations, application, and services were specifically excluded from the program. There are other forums for such commercial presentations. Hypertext' 89 is an opportunity to take at look at new ideas, many of which will be the basis for commercial presentations 2, 5, or 7 years down the line.

I want to thank the members of the program committee who put in many hours of effort in evaluating submissions and in shaping the program for this conference. Altogether there were 119 papers and 9 panel proposals submitted. In a marathon session in July, we selected 28 papers and 5 panels for presentation at the conference. Four additional panels were solicited to help balance the program. Our selection criteria were varied; not only were we looking for leading-edge research and thinking that would be of interest to a broad segment of the hypertext community, but we were also looking to provide a balanced program in which no single topic or point-of-view dominated the presentations. Given the time-constraints imposed by a 2.5-day conference, we unfortunately had to turn away many excellent papers and panels.

In addition to the papers and panels, the program consists of eleven tutorial courses and two sessions dedicated to hands-on demos of systems and applications. The courses are intended to provide an opportunity for you to explore in detail some more specialized hypertext topics and technologies. Many, many thanks go to Jan Walker, who did an incredible job in organizing these courses.

The demos will give you a chance to see and to play with various systems and applications. We hope that they will bring to life the necessarily abstract descriptions that will populate the rest of the program. The demo session was absolutely the best part of Hypertext' 87. I encourage you to help make it as big a success in '89. Special thanks go to John Leggett and Amy Pearl for their efforts in organizing the demo track.

I hope that you enjoy the Hypertext' 89 program. I also hope that you will learn a great deal from the conference. But most of all I hope that you will take the opportunity to meet and to interchange your ideas and excitement with other members of the hypertext community. It is this interchange that will keep our field interesting and vital in the years to come.

Frank Halasz
Program Chair

Program Committee

Mark Bernstein
Eastgate Systems

Tim Oren
Apple Computer

Jeff Conklin
MCC

Roy Pea
Institute for Research on Learning

Steven Feiner
Columbia University

Darrell Raymond
University of Waterloo

Edward Fox
VPI & SU

Walter Scacchi
University of Southern California

Mark Frisse
Washington University

Mayer Schwartz
Tektronix Laboratories

George Landow
Brown University

Ben Shneiderman
University of Maryland

John Leggett
Texas A&M University

John Smith
University of North Carolina

Norman Meyrowitz
Brown University

Randy Trigg
Aarhus University

Elli Mylonas
Harvard University

Jan Walker
Digital Equipment

Jakob Nielsen
Technical University of Denmark

Nicole Yankelovich
Brown University

Contents

Navigation in Context

Hypertext Engineering

Knowledge Representation

Implementations and Interfaces

Applications

Information Retrieval I

Usability, Links, and Fiction

Information Retrieval II

Applications in Writing

Panels

Scripted Documents:
A Hypermedia Path Mechanism

Polle T. Zellweger

Xerox Palo Alto Research Center
3333 Coyote Hill Road
Palo Alto, California 94304

ABSTRACT

The concept of a *path*, or ordered traversal of some links in a hypertext, has been a part of the hypertext notion from its early formation. Although paths can help to solve two major problems with hypertext systems, namely user disorientation and high cognitive overhead for users, their value has not been recognized. Paths can also provide the backbone for computations over a hypertext, an important issue for the future of hypertext. This paper constructs a framework for understanding path mechanisms for hypertext and explores the basic issues surrounding them. Given this framework, it reviews path mechanisms that have been provided by other hypertext systems. Finally, it describes the Scripted Documents system, which has been developed to test the potential of one powerful path mechanism.

1. INTRODUCTION

Hypertext is a valuable contribution to the information age, allowing readers to access related information through machine-supported links. However, current hypertext systems have several well-recognized problems. Two of the most significant are *user disorientation* in hypertext networks and the additional *cognitive overhead* needed to create, manage and choose among links [Conk87a, Conk87b]. Moreover, the browsing paradigm offered by most hypertext systems does not meet the needs of readers who are unfamiliar with the material being presented [Hamm88]. An important component of the information conveyed by an author to a reader in a traditional setting is the order in which the material appears. In most current hypertext systems, readers may fail to understand the material presented because they view it in the wrong order, or they may simply comprehend it less well.

The concept of a path, or ordered traversal of some links in a hypertext, can help solve these problems. Users are less likely to feel disoriented or lost when they are following a pre-defined path rather than browsing freely, and their cognitive overhead is reduced because the path either makes or narrows their choices. Paths allow authors to determine an appropriate order of presentation for a given audience. In addition, paths can provide the backbone for computations over a hypertext, one of Halasz's seven issues for the next generation of hypermedia systems [Hala88].

Although paths have been a part of the hypertext notion from its early formation [Bush45], few current hypertext systems provide paths, and in fact the path concept has not been examined systematically. As we shall see, paths need to become first-class citizens in hypertext systems. Systems should provide path mechanisms that make all kinds of paths easy to create, to find, and to follow.

Paths are not intended to supplant browsing as a hypertext navigation paradigm, but rather to augment it. Obviously paths can reduce the readers' flexibility as well. The challenge is to provide paths that are expressive and/or are an integrated adjunct to other links within a hypertext network.

This paper constructs a framework for understanding path mechanisms for hypertext and explores the basic issues surrounding them. Given this framework, it reviews path mechanisms that have been provided by other hypertext systems. The final section describes the Scripted Documents system, which has been developed to test the potential of one powerful path mechanism.

2. A FRAMEWORK FOR EFFECTIVE PATH MECHANISMS

There is more to providing paths than merely allowing authors to specify sequences of nodes or links. This section presents a framework for understanding and evaluating path mechanisms.

An effective path mechanism must satisfy three major requirements. It must bring expressive power to authors, help authors create and modify paths, and help readers find paths and follow them in flexible ways. Furthermore, it should provide for efficient storage and execution.

2.1 Expressive power of paths

By a path, we mean a presentation of successive entries, ordered such that most or all of the decisions about the order of presentation are made by the author in advance, rather than by the reader during path playback. The expressive power of a path is determined by two things: the sequencing model that the path uses to order entries and the characteristics of the entries that can appear along the path. We discuss each in turn.

We define several different sequencing models, ranging from simple sequential paths to more complex paths that are essentially programs.

A *sequential path* is an ordered sequence of entries. Sequential paths can be used to present an ordered progression or merely to collect an unordered set of entries. Most existing implementations allow an entry to appear repeatedly in a path.

A *branching path* contains branches from which the reader must manually choose, and thus acts as a smaller subnetwork of the hypertext network. Although branches provide options to allow readers to customize a path for their interests, they also increase the cognitive overhead required to follow the path.

A *conditional path* contains branches at which the system evaluates author-specified tests to determine which direction to go next. For example, conditional paths can be used to tailor presentations to a given class of readers, to adapt to particular hardware constraints such as lack of color or audio output devices, or to provide information appropriate to the current time. A path may also be able to examine its previous history. A conditional path that asks the reader questions can provide control similar to branching paths.

Extending the simple idea of conditionals to a more complete programming paradigm can provide more expressive power. Several significant types of paths appear along this progression:

- *procedural paths*, which allow a path to appear as an entry of another path, and thus ease a script author's job by supporting modularity and re-use;
- *programmable paths*, which are conditional paths that can store values in variables to form indexed loops or record information for later use;
- *variable paths*, which are conditional paths that contain variable links, in which the next entry to be presented is located dynamically, perhaps

computed by an earlier entry or perhaps involving a search through the hypertext; and

- *parallel paths*, which are paths that can execute simultaneously and may be able to fork, join, or synchronize with activities on another branch.

We call the items that are linked together along a path *entries*. Their purpose is to provide the content, while the path provides the sequencing.

In its simplest form, an entry is (or refers to) a node in the underlying hypertext, and the path provides a way to display a sequence of nodes.[1] However, we note that hypertext systems have offered users a wide range of addressing granularity for links, from points or regions within a node to collections of nodes [Conk87a, Trig88]. A path mechanism may offer the user the same entry granularity as the underlying hypertext system, or it may offer a different one (typically coarser). Notice that although link endpoints have asymmetric granularity in most current hypertext systems (e.g., point source and node destination), each path entry acts as both a link source and a link destination.

An entry may thus be a separate object that shares some of the features of a node or link in the underlying hypertext. It may refer to a point or region within a node, a node, or a collection of nodes. It may also have additional fields that modify or add to the behavior of the underlying node(s).

We call entries that can perform actions *active entries*. For example, an active entry might animate a picture, play back voice, perform a computation, or construct part of an output document. Combining active entries with paths is particularly appropriate, because the paths can provide the ordering for the actions performed at each entry, thus creating sequences of actions that flow across the hypertext network. A path mechanism that incorporates active entries should allow a flexible association between entry locations and entry actions, so that a path (or possibly different paths) can visit the same location repeatedly and perform different actions.

2.2 Creating and editing paths

Although paths can be created manually using only conditional links, this process is quite tedious and error-prone. A path mechanism should include a path editor that allows authors to create and edit paths from path-level views. They should be able to link existing material into paths quickly and easily. They should also be able to edit paths by rearranging, adding or deleting entries. These editing operations may take different forms depending on the physical representation of the path.

Paths can be represented as sequences, as directed graphs, or as "programs" (linear text), as shown in Figure 1. Sequences and programs have no explicit links. Instead, implicit links are formed respectively by their adjacency relationships and interpretation rules.

2.3 Visualization and navigation support

Visualization tools help authors maintain paths and help readers find them.

Because paths form a meta-level above the underlying material, they must be kept consistent when authors edit that material. The responsibility for this maintenance rests jointly on the author and the path mechanism, but the path mechanism must at least alert the author when paths cross an item that is being edited. For example, if an author

---

[1]A path could also consist of a sequence of links. However, this imposes a much stricter consistency requirement on the author or the path editor: the destination of entry i must equal the source of entry $i+1$.

deletes material from the underlying hypertext network, any corresponding entry should also be removed from all paths in which it participates. Ideally, the author would be alerted appropriately *before* the material is deleted. If a corresponding entry has actions, the author should also be informed that the computational semantics of the path may be in jeopardy. Edits to the underlying material may also cause the opposite problem, in which an edited entry remains a member of a path to which it is no longer relevant. Moving or copying underlying material may also cause difficulties for some path mechanisms.[2]

Readers must be able to find relevant paths easily, just as they must be able to view and select among hypertext links. Ideally, this means that readers would be shown that paths start from or traverse the current location. However, local indicators are not sufficient, because readers may never stumble on places that are members of relevant paths. Thus there must also be global ways to locate relevant paths. Both local and global methods must be robust and easy to use, because their intended audience is the reader who is unfamiliar with the material and/or the hypertext network.

2.4 Playback control

A path mechanism must also allow readers to play back or display a path.[3] We describe several possible methods that provide readers with varying playback control. A system may provide more than one method.

A system with *single-stepping control* allows the reader to start a path and then issue a "next" command repeatedly to traverse it in order.

A system with *automatic control* allows the reader to start a path and have it continue automatically to successive entries. Such systems must allow authors to specify timing to indicate when the next link should be traversed. In addition, readers must be able to stop a path that is executing and possibly resume later. An ideal system would further allow the reader to adjust the playback speed to his or her liking.

In addition, a system may provide *browsing control*, to permit a user to visit entries in a path in an arbitrary order by selecting them individually from a path-level view.[4] This provides a level of mixed initiative that can be useful as the expertise of a reader increases [Hamm88].

However, combining programmable paths or active entries with browsing control can be dangerous. In particular, the actions earlier in a path may be necessary pre-conditions for either the branching decisions or the actions at a later step of the path. For example, earlier actions may open a window that a later entry wishes to write in, or they may record a reader's preference that will be used later to direct the specific path. Devising flexible methods for ensuring that all pre-conditions have executed before a reader may jump to a new point in a path remains a topic for further research.[5] In addition,

---

[2]Many of these situations could damage corresponding links as well, especially in systems that allow some links to be invisible, such as Intermedia [Yank88].

[3]A path could be presented spatially rather than temporally, by concatenating the entries in the path to form a single linear view. Playback control is not really relevant in this case.

[4]We consider that a path mechanism that provides only browsing control is not really a path mechanism, because it provides no path interpreter.

[5]A generalization of Textnet's *prerequisite* and *must-follow* tags on links [Trig86] might prove useful here.

designing paths to permit the maximum reader flexibility is a significant challenge for path authors.

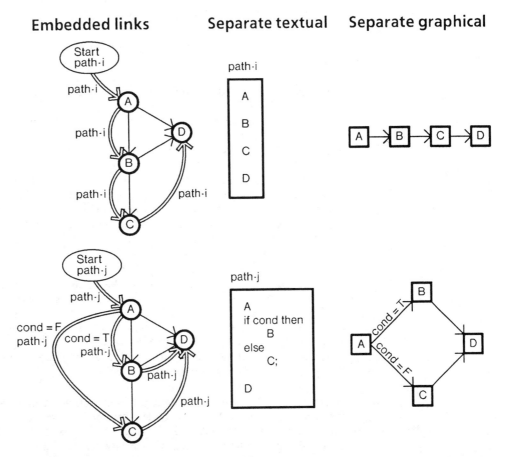

Figure 1. Alternative path representations. Three different representations of paths are shown for linear (top) and conditional (bottom) paths. On the left, circles represent hypertext nodes, while double-line arrows represent path links embedded in the hypertext network.

2.5 Path storage

Issues of where hypertext systems should store their links are currently being debated within the hypertext community. Paths present similar issues. A path mechanism can store its path links with other hypertext links, or it can store its path links separately. In either case, the information stored must support path playback and path visualization. Figure 1 displays two paths expressed in three ways: as embedded links, as a separate textual path, and as a separate graphical path.

Path links that are stored with other hypertext links must be distinguishable from them to permit playback. Furthermore, as the sequencing model increases in complexity, more information must be stored on each link to determine the next entry during playback. Although embedded links make it easy to discover what paths cross a given location, they do not directly support finding the start of a path.

When paths are stored separately, the path specification either names or refers to entries. These "forward links" are required to support path playback. In addition, to support path visualization, it is important to provide "back links" from the entries to the path specification. The back links may be actual links, or they may be indices into a path database. If no back links are provided, readers cannot readily discover existing paths.

3. DESCRIPTION OF OTHER SYSTEMS WITH PATHS

Using the framework developed in the previous section, we now examine other systems that have provided paths.

Memex trails. Vannevar Bush argued convincingly that his memex should support *trails*, or sequences of links that scientists would construct and consult while working [Bush45]. Any location could appear in multiple trails; each trail acted in essence as a new book.

Textnet paths. Textnet paths are simply ordered lists of nodes; these are separately-stored paths that a user can modify by adding or deleting nodes from the list [Trig86]. Thus Textnet provides sequential paths whose entries are entire nodes. The contents of a path are shown to the user as a single linear concatenation of text from each node, with small markers at each node boundary, rather than as a temporally ordered sequence of visits to the nodes. Textnet paths are used to generate multiple different linear documents from a single hypertext network, especially as formatted hardcopy, although it is unclear how readers learn of the existence of alternate paths.

HyperCard scripts. HyperCard's HyperTalk language allows an author to construct programmable or even variable paths, for example as a button script for some card [Good87]. However, although HyperCard does provide the necessary raw functionality, it provides no tools for creating, maintaining, finding, or playing back paths as distinguished objects. An implementor would have to provide these separately. According to Trigg, Elli Mylonos has extended HyperCard with a path card that can store and play back a linear sequence of cards [Trig88].

Guided tours in NoteCards. NoteCards is an authoring or idea management system [Hala87]. Its path mechanism, called *guided tours*, was developed as a way of communicating the organization of a NoteCards filebox to other users [Trig88]. Guided tours provide branching paths whose entries are a special kind of node, namely spatially-organized collections of cards called *tabletops*. Tours store their path links as ordinary links of type *GuidedTour* among tabletop nodes. Each tabletop node can display its GuidedTour links on request, but individual nodes cannot tell if they are part of a tabletop node. Thus navigational support for maintaining tours is weak in this respect. Authors create and edit a graphical view of a guided tour. In fact, a tour need not have a single starting point. Readers have both single-stepping and browsing control over the resulting graph, but no automatic control. The reader is given visual history feedback in the form of highlighting on links and nodes that have been traversed in this session.

Hammond & Allinson's guided tours. Hammond and Allinson used a "travel holiday" metaphor to study a variety of navigation methods in educational materials [Hamm88]. For users unfamiliar with the material being taught, their experiments demonstrated the utility of conditional paths (also called *guided tours*) over maps, keyword indices and browsing . Each multimedia node (called a *frame*) can include text, graphics, sound, time-delayed items and animation. Their procedural, conditional paths permit sub-tours (called *excursions*) and branches based on reader response or prior activity. A user has only single-stepping control through a tour, although he or she can suspend the tour at any time and return to it later. Tours always return the reader to the starting point. Their local maps, which show the connectivity of some subpart of the network, are a completely separate mechanism. These maps are quite similar to GuidedTour cards in NoteCards, except that they provide only browsing control (i.e., no path interpreter).

Petri nets in αTrellis. Stotts and Furuta model a hypertext as a Petri net that defines all possible transitions through the hypertext [Stot88]. The strengths of this unconventional hypertext representation are that it can express prerequisite relationships between entries well, and it can formally synchronize the simultaneous viewing of multiple locations. While it is true that a Petri net is a generalization of hypertext link structures, a Petri net is less powerful as a path mechanism than a programmable path. Furthermore, the ability of authors to learn to construct such hypertexts (which depends largely on what Petri net construction tools are provided) has not yet been shown, especially for the more complex Petri nets. Programs are familiar to more potential authors.

4. PATHS IN SCRIPTED DOCUMENTS

The Scripted Documents system extends the previous mechanisms to address several key issues: conditional and programmable paths; automated path playback; navigational support for authors and readers; active entries with a wide range of actions; and multiple media, including voice.

The primary goal of Scripted Documents is to explore the role of hypermedia sequencing and action in a variety of uses of online multimedia documents, including idea organization, interpersonal communication, user documentation, programming tasks, memoranda, and audio-visual presentations. Scripted Documents is a bit unusual as a hypertext system, because it provides paths as its sole linking mechanism. The Scripted Documents system is implemented in the Cedar programming environment [Swin86] at Xerox PARC. Scripted Documents runs on Dorado personal workstations [Lamp81] in a distributed environment connected by Ethernet.

This paper concentrates on the path mechanism available in Scripted Documents. An earlier paper provides many examples of scripts and discusses the object-oriented approach to underlying documents that permits smooth integration with existing editors [Zell88b]. A longer report also details the consistency operations needed to maintain scripts that traverse existing files that users continue to move, copy, and edit [Zell89].

4.1 Overview of Scripted Documents

Briefly, a script is an active directed path through one or more documents that need not follow the linear order of the documents. Each entry in a script consists of a document location, together with an associated action and timing. A script is typically played back with automatic control, displaying the location of the first entry and performing its action, then continuing automatically to the second entry, and so on.

As a simple example, consider the following use of scripts to review a manuscript. Each reviewer prepares a script for the manuscript, including voice annotations as well as branches through supporting reference documents. Each script follows an arbitrary path through the document to collect related points. The author plays the scripts back later to hear what the reviewers have said. This use provides much of the value of a face-to-face interaction between a reviewer and the author, in which the reviewer makes comments while flipping back and forth through the manuscript and other documents to substantiate those comments.

As a result of the efforts of the Etherphone project, recorded and synthesized voice are widely available in the Cedar environment [Zell88a]. A major motivating goal behind Scripted Documents was to be able to collect and order related voice annotations to form narrations of one or more documents. The essential sequentiality of narrations led directly to our exploration of paths.

4.2 Expressive power of scripts

Scripted Documents provides procedural, programmable paths with active entries, called *scripts*. A script has three parts:

- A set of *documents*, which are typically pre-existing files of various types, such as text, 2D or 3D illustrations, VLSI diagrams, database entries, or combinations thereof.

- A set of *script entries*, which associate locations or objects within those documents with actions and timing information. Entries can perform arbitrary actions, ranging from issuing system commands to manipulating variables via an interpreter. Sample actions might be to play back a previously-recorded voice annotation, send text to a text-to-speech synthesizer, animate a picture, or query a database. Although actions can be forked while the path continues, there are no script-level primitives for synchronization among the resulting forks.

- A *path specification*, also known as a *script header*, which is a program written in the Cedar language, a Pascal-like language that is the major programming language for the Cedar programming environment [Swin86]. These programs can be as simple or as complex as the author needs to express his or her sequencing constraints. A sequential script appears as a textual list of script entries. More complex scripts can call other scripts, add conditions or loops, declare variables, or manipulate the environment in an arbitrary way.

4.3 Creating and editing scripts

The author edits script headers and entries via form-based tools, as shown in Figure 2.

Script headers. Sequential paths can be created by direct manipulation: the author selects a document region and clicks a menu button in the script header tool. The system creates a new entry and adds it to the script at the current insert point, which is typically positioned at the end of the script. To create a programmable or procedural path, the author uses a text editor to add loops, conditionals, or calls to other scripts. The text editor is also used to copy entry names from other scripts and rearrange or delete entries. Although using a text editor is convenient for the author, it has drawbacks: it provides opportunities for creating scripts with syntactic errors or references to nonexistent entries or scripts. These errors are detected either by playing a script or by *verifying* it.

Script entries. The author specifies the action, timing or other fields of a script entry by filling in the fields of a script entry tool. The author can name a script entry or provide keywords, if desired. The system provides a unique identifier for each script entry and records the creator and create time. Narrative entries can be created without forms: the default action is to play back all voice annotations at the location, if any, and the default timing is to continue when the action completes. The system also provides a library of commands for interacting with the user to ask questions, and for manipulating windows and buttons on the display so that arbitrary applications can be controlled from a script.

4.4 Visualization and navigation support

Local visualization and navigation help authors maintain scripts by alerting them when changes to an underlying document might damage a script. They also help readers find scripts of possible interest. At the document content level, each scripted location is distinctively marked. Textual scripted locations are marked with a surrounding rectangle; other scripted objects may be marked differently. The marker indicates the presence of one or more script entries at that location, which may appear at multiple places in multiple scripts. Navigation commands display all scripts or script entries that include that scripted location.

In addition, an author who wishes to change an entry must be able to discover the associated document location and all scripts that the entry appears in. Similarly, authors must be able to discover what scripts include calls to a given script. Menu commands are provided for these operations in script header and entry tools.

```
ScriptHeader: Greeting
STOP!  Save  AddTagged  AddAbsolute  AddSearched  PlayScript
PlayEntry  RemoveScript  RemoveEntry  OpenEntry  OpenScript
EntryToLoc  LocToEntries  LocToScripts  RemoveTagsFromLoc
Pause  Resume  PrevStep  NextStep


SID:    0AAS1016SH#675942101
FirstFile    []<>Users>PolleZ.pa>scripteddocs>Greetings.tioga
MapAction:
Name:    Greeting
Desc:    Greet the user according to the time of day and offer to read his or her mail.
SequencingInfo:    &time ← BasicTime.Unpack[BasicTime.Now[]];
                   IF &time.hour < 12 THEN %Morning
                   ELSE IF &time.hour < 18 THEN %Afternoon
                   ELSE %Evening;
                   %Name
                   %CheckMail
                   IF PopUpMenu.TorF["Read mail now?"] THEN
                       %ReadMail   >>
```

```
ScriptEntry: Name
STOP!  Save  PlayEntry  EntryToLoc  EntryToScripts  ChangeRange
MoveEntryTo[Tag|Abs]  RemoveEntry  RemoveEntryFromLoc

    Entry is in scripts: Greeting


EID:    0AAS1016SH#675943129
File:    []<>Users>PolleZ.pa>scripteddocs>Greetings.tioga
Class:    $Tioga
Location:    224 2
Type:    $Tagged
MapAction:
Name:    Name
Desc:    Speak the user's name using the Etherphone system's text-to-speech synthesizer server.
PauseBefore:    0
PauseAfter:    0
Action:    ← FinchSynthesizer.SpeakText[UserCredentials.Get[].name]
```

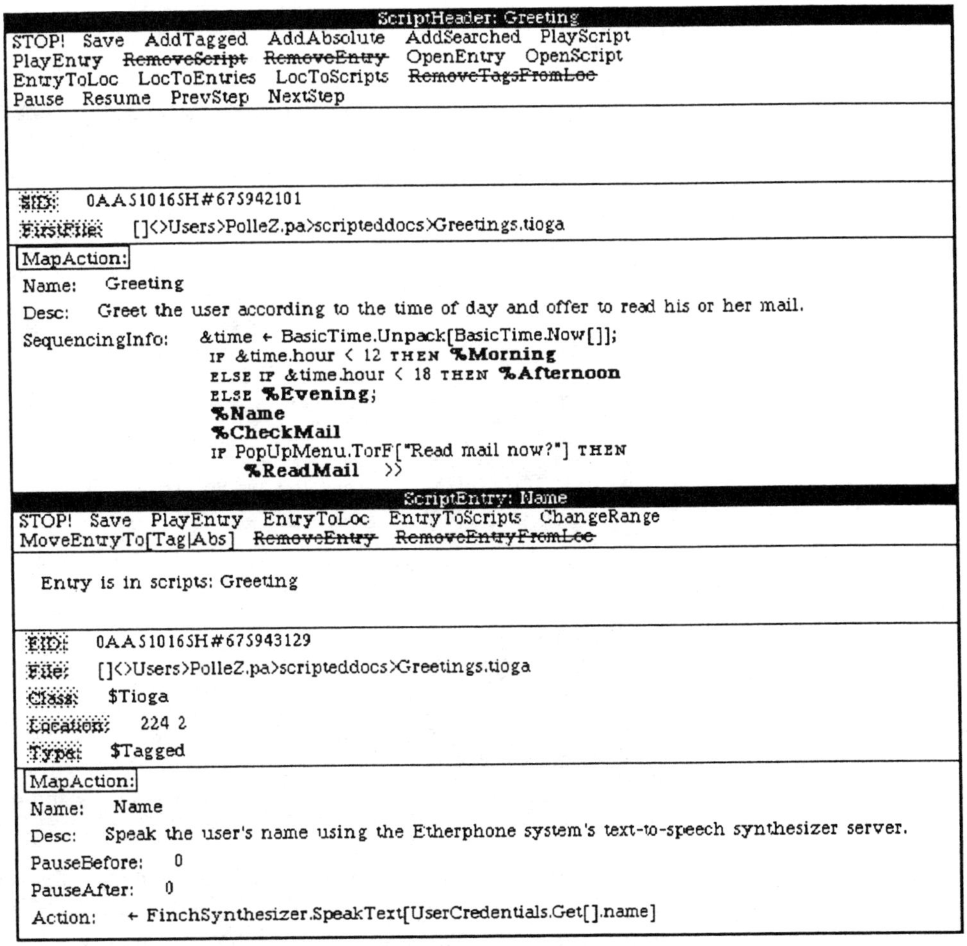

Figure 2. Script header and entry tools. Each tool has four parts: the top section has a menu of script operations, the second section is a feedback area, the third section displays read-only fields that the system manages, and the bottom section has user-editable fields. The upper window shows a script header tool that contains a programmable path. The path, displayed in the SequencingInfo: field, refers to entries as %<entry name> (translated from internal unique identifiers by the user interface). Sequential parts of the path appear as lists (e.g. %Name %CheckMail). Double brackets ">>" mark the current insert point. The lower window shows an entry tool for the Name entry.

Other methods for finding scripts are more global. The Scripts button in a document header displays a list of all scripts that start in or cross that document and allow the user to create a script header to edit or play back a script. A user can also access a script by name or by browsing the script database for keywords, descriptions, or other script fields.

Assorted visualization mechanisms help to orient the user. Because script headers show a textual program representation of a path, users can get a feel for how long the script is (at least in steps, if not in time), how complex it is, and what entries it visits. The system also displays playback feedback: the entry currently being executed is highlighted in the script header. This provides a valuable percent-done indicator [Myer85]. Finally, the system provides a form of dynamic location visualization: the user can inhibit the execution of the actions and play the script, which will then traverse all of its locations at a controllable speed.

Figures 3 and 4 illustrate several visualization and navigation mechanisms in Scripted Documents.

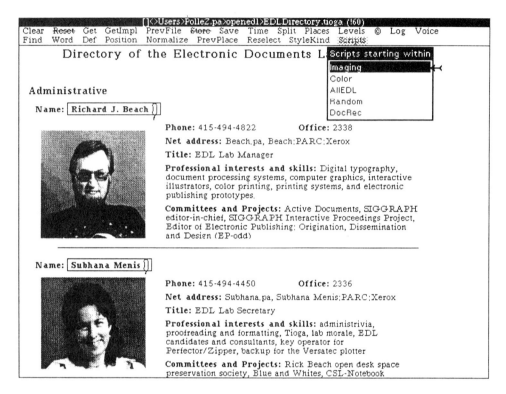

Figure 3. Finding scripts. This multimedia document contains color photos (reproduced here in black and white), formatted text, and voice annotations describing the staff of PARC's Electronic Documents Laboratory. Voice annotations are indicated by small "voice balloons" after each person's name. Several scripts traverse the document to show members of various projects and play back their voice descriptions of themselves; some people are on multiple projects. The user has just clicked the Scripts button in the document header, which has created a menu of scripts that start in this document. Script entries are shown as boxes around text.

4.5 Playback control

Scripted Documents provides rich playback control: automatic control, single-stepping control and browsing control. The PlayScript command plays an entire script from the beginning, proceeding automatically from one location to the next, executing the associated actions with the associated timings. This feature is particularly useful for narrations, presentations, and document processing situations. Readers can also pause, resume, stop, or single-step forward or backward (which consults a history of the current execution). In addition, readers can browse a script by selecting and playing individual entries. As discussed earlier, active entries and programmable scripts make browsing control potentially dangerous. Scripted Documents does not currently protect readers from executing entries without their prerequisites.

The Scripted Documents system does not take over the entire screen. Users can perform other tasks simultaneously while interacting with Scripted Documents. Unfortunately,

4.6 Script storage

Script entries and headers are stored separately from the documents, in a simple database. This design has several advantages.

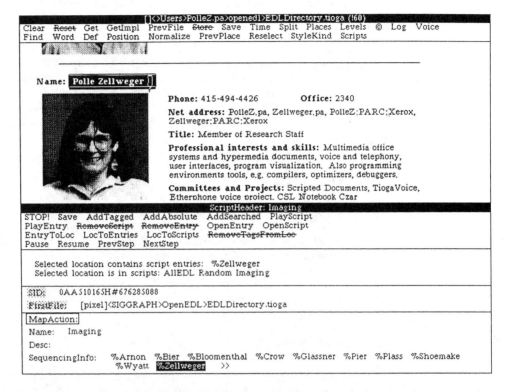

Figure 4. Script navigation and playback. These two windows show the playback of the last entry in the sequential Imaging script. In the document in the upper window, the location of the Zellweger script entry is highlighted and the voice annotation is being played. The lower window shows the script's header tool (created by the Scripts button click in Figure 3). To indicate playback progress, the Zellweger entry is also highlighted in the SequencingInfo: field. In addition, the tool's feedback area shows the result of two earlier navigational queries regarding the text "Polle Zellweger" in the document.

First, separating script entries from script headers allows multiple actions or timings to be associated with the same document location, even in a purely sequential script. Entries can also be re-used in multiple scripts.

Second, separating script information from documents allows existing documents to be involved in scripts without requiring authors to copy information into a closed hypertext system. Aside from the inconvenience of an extra copying step, copying presents two other problems: it removes the information from its original context (within the document and/or within the file system), and it requires authors to maintain both copies across future changes.

Finally, storing script information in a database provides rich query capabilities to support visualization and navigation aids for script users. The default script database resides on a centralized server to permit sharing scripts among users. Users can also specify private databases to replace or supplement the public database.

4.7 Experience with scripts

We have created educational scripts consisting of multiple narrations for language lessons; scripts that provide narrative reviews of manuscripts; several versions of slide presentations for short, medium and long talks; and user documentation that demonstrates the execution of an application on examples.

Scripts have also proven useful in software engineering tasks, such as task management, debugging, system documentation, and testing. Scripts can mark unfinished routines or questionable sections that should be re-examined. They can also collect groups of program locations to form sets of potential breakpoints that will be automatically maintained by the system throughout the program's lifecycle. Breakpoints can be set or cleared at a given group of locations by playing back the appropriate script. Script narrations can provide system documentation, and scripts can execute software tests and record results and timing information.

4.8 Future work

Although Scripted Documents has already demonstrated the power of scripts, much work remains to be done. Scripts currently have no versioning mechanism, they provide only minimal support for collaboration and sharing among users, and they do not support the synchronization of multiple simultaneous branches along a path. In addition, we would like to provide better visualization of scripts for both script readers and writers, including browsing tools and visual displays of script sequencing (such as a graphical document-level view of a script's path, or a view that embeds the entries' actions in the path specification program).

5. CONCLUSIONS

Simple sequential paths can collect locations, order them (such as for printing), or perform sequential activities. Indeed, if authors provide enough sequential paths, the resulting structures begin to approximate the computational power of conditional or branching paths. However, the issues involved in managing and presenting to the reader a large forest of paths argues strongly for fewer, more powerful paths.

Paths are particularly valuable when combined with multiple media and actions, as in the Scripted Documents system. Attaching audio actions to visual entries provides authors with easily understood synchronization between audio and visual material.

Paths should become first-class citizens of their hypertext systems. When a reader is lost in hypertext, it is important to be able to recognize nearby paths. Maps or overviews of paths, particularly situated overviews (such as thumbnails or a similar representation), are also helpful.

Finally, paths provide expressive power to authors. Complex paths allow great flexibility in creating presentations specifically tuned to readers, thus reducing their cognitive load. These paths will not be trivial to create, but with the appropriate tools the creative effort will continue to outweigh the technical effort.

ACKNOWLEDGMENTS

Cecelia Buchanan implemented the programmable paths in Scripted Documents, as well as the user interaction library. Rok Sosic improved the playback control. Other Etherphone project members, including Dan Swinehart, Doug Terry, and Stephen Ades, contributed to the voice substrate and helped hone the script concept. Jock Mackinlay and Rick Beach improved the organization and presentation of this paper.

REFERENCES

[Bush45]   Bush, V. As we may think. *The Atlantic Monthly*, July 1945: 101-108. Reprinted in Adele Goldberg (editor), *A History of Personal Workstations*, ACM Press, New York, 1988, 237-247.

[Conk87a]   Conklin, J. Hypertext: an introduction and survey. *IEEE Computer*, **20**, 9, (September 1987), 17-41.

[Conk87b]   Conklin, J. *A survey of hypertext*. MCC Technical Report STP-356-86, Rev. 2, December 1987.

[Good87]   Goodman, D. *The Complete HyperCard Handbook*. Bantam Books, New York, 1987.

[Hamm88]   Hammond, N. & Allinson, L.   Travels around a learning support environment: rambling, orienteering or touring? *Proc. ACM CHI'88 Conf.*, Washington, DC, May 15-19, 1988, 269-273.

[Hala87]   Halasz, F., Moran, T. & Trigg, R. NoteCards in a nutshell. *Proc. ACM CHI+GI'87 Human Factors in Computing Systems and Graphics Interface Conf.*, Toronto, Canada, April 5-9, 1987, 45-52.

[Hala88]   Halasz, F. Reflections on NoteCards: seven issues for the next generation of hypermedia systems. *CACM*, **31**, 7, (July 1988), 836-852.

[Myer85]   Myers, B. The importance of percent-done progress indicators for computer-human interfaces. *Proc. ACM CHI'85 Conf.*, San Francisco, CA, April 14-18, 1985, 11-17.

[Lamp81]   Lampson, B. and Pier, K.; Lampson, B., McDaniel, G., & Ornstein, S.; Clark, D., Lampson, B., & Pier, K. *The Dorado: a high performance personal computer, three papers*. Xerox PARC Report CSL-81-1, 1981.

[Stot88]   Stotts, P.D. & Furuta, R. Adding browsing semantics to the hypertext model. *Proc. ACM Document Processing Systems Conf.*, Santa Fe, NM, December 5-9, 1988, 43-50.

[Swin86]   Swinehart, D., Zellweger, P., Beach, R. & Hagmann, R. A structural view of the Cedar programming environment, *ACM Trans. Prog. Lang. and Syst.*, **8**, 4, (October 1986), 419-490.

[Trig86]   Trigg, R. & Weiser, M. TEXTNET: a network-based approach to text handling. *ACM Trans. Office Info. Syst.* **4**, 1, (January 1986), 1-23.

[Trig88]   Trigg, R. Guided tours and tabletops: tools for communicating in a hypertext environment. *ACM Trans. Office Info. Syst.* **6**, 4, (October 1988), 398-414.

[Yank88]   Yankelovich, N., Haan, B., Meyrowitz, N., and Drucker, S. Intermedia: The concept and the construction of a seamless information environment, *IEEE Computer*, **21**, 1, (January 1988), 81-96.

[Zell88a]   Zellweger, P., Terry, D. & Swinehart, D. An overview of the Etherphone system and its applications, *Proc. 2nd IEEE Computer Workstations Conf.*, Santa Clara, CA, March 8-10, 1988, 160-168.

[Zell88b]   Zellweger, P. Active paths through multimedia documents. In J.C. van Vliet (editor), *Document Manipulation and Typography,* Proc. Int'l Conference on Electronic Publishing, Document Manipulation and Typography, Nice (France), April 20-22, 1988. Cambridge University Press, 1988, 19-34.

[Zell89]   Zellweger, P. *Scripted Documents.* Xerox PARC Report, in preparation.

Guided Tours and On-Line Presentations: How Authors Make Existing Hypertext Intelligible for Readers

Catherine C. Marshall
Peggy M. Irish

Systems Sciences Laboratory
Xerox Palo Alto Research Center
3333 Coyote Hill Road
Palo Alto, California 94304

ABSTRACT

Hypertext systems like NoteCards provide facilities for authoring large networks. But they provide little support for the associated task of making these networks intelligible to future readers. Presentation conventions may be imported from other related media, but because the conventions have not yet been negotiated within a community of hypertext readers and writers, they provide only a partial solution to the problem of guiding a reader through an existing network of information. In this paper, we will discuss how a recent facility, Guided Tours, has been used to organize hypertext networks for presentation. The use of Guided Tours in NoteCards has exposed a set of authoring issues, and has provided us with examples of solutions to the problems associated with on-line presentations.

1. INTRODUCTION

Hypertext can be a valuable interactive medium for presenting semi-structured information on-line; it gives the reader the opportunity to traverse links according to interest, level of understanding, and other individually determined factors. But constructing a network of information is not the same task as authoring an intelligible on-line presentation of an existing network. Just as readers often find it difficult to interpret on-line hypermedia presentations [Char87], authors find it difficult to create them. System support for guided navigation does not ensure the future intelligibility of hypertext. Thus it is important to investigate methods for authoring audience-directed hypertext and to initiate a dialog between readers and writers in order to establish presentation conventions for this new medium.

Because hypertext borrows characteristics from a variety of other media, it inherits a confluence of authoring problems. The ultimate linearity resulting from link traversal brings with it a need to create coherence, manage transitions, and supply context as in traditional written forms. Problems associated with screen layout require the skills and conventions of graphic design. Techniques derived from computer-supported cooperative work for implementing remote gesture and reference are helpful in the construction of the narrative explicating a hypertext network. Hypertext's potential for interactivity also poses questions addressed in fields such as computer-aided instruction. Then too, hypertext traversal has certain dynamic qualities suggesting the characteristics and associated difficulties of film-making or animation.

Other authoring problems arise from the task of presenting existing hypermedia networks. Guiding a reader through a semi-structured maze of information has an inherent quality of "aboutness" that obliges the author to bring in large quantities of metainformation to explain what she is doing and why. Constraints imposed by the particular hypertext system may compound the authoring problem further by preventing the application of obvious strategies for presenting information on-line.

In short, authors of hypertext presentations are expected to solve problems derived from many different media, as well as others brought to the table by hypertext itself. Our experiences show that conventions and techniques for coping with these problems may be imported from related domains, or invented by authors on the fly. The hypertext authoring problem is complicated by the fact that conventions for this new communication medium are still to be negotiated within a community of readers and writers; authoring and navigational experiences have yet to be brought together and closely examined.

In this paper, we explore the problem of presenting an existing hypertext network through the use of a set of examples created using the NoteCards Guided Tour facility. But first we discuss the underlying hypertext technology and provide a brief history of on-line presentations in NoteCards.

2. BACKGROUND

NoteCards is a second generation hypertext system intended to be a tailorable vehicle for performing a variety of idea processing tasks [Hala88]. NoteCards users are provided with mechanisms for building networks of electronic *cards* connected by typed *links*. The contents of the cards are displayed in windows on the screen; we will therefore use the terms cards and windows interchangeably throughout this paper. Multiple cards may be displayed at any given time. Cards are brought to the screen by traversing links represented by *link icons*, usually boxed titles; users button the mouse on these link icons to retrieve the destination card. They may then read or edit the card. NoteCards maintains its database of cards in a *notefile*.

Several types of cards are of particular relevance to this discussion. *Text* cards and *sketch* cards are the usual vehicles for writing and illustration. *Fileboxes* allow a user to impose a hierarchical structure on the network. *Browsers* are computed, editable overviews of the network that display cards as graph nodes and links as edges drawn in different dashing styles. For more information on NoteCards, see [Hala87].

Our focus here is on NoteCards' presentational facilities, whose need has been clear from the earliest uses of NoteCards. Over the course of NoteCards' development, members of the user community have evolved techniques for presenting their notefiles to future readers, including various means of guiding traversal, annotating both substance and structure, presenting slide shows, addressing notes to the reader, and constructing hierarchies oriented toward reader traversal. They based their strategies on a set of assumptions regarding how readers approach and understand unfamiliar networks.

Experiences with these early on-line presentations fostered the development of the *Guided Tours* facility, which in turn provides computational support for communication between the author of a NoteCards network and its future readers. This graph-based interactive facility explicitly represents the presentational structure of a NoteCards network; the author and the reader interact with the tour through the same representation. Figure 1 shows an example of a guided tour. An author constructs a tour as a graph whose nodes are the stops on the tour and whose edges are *GuidedTour links* connecting the stops. The author uses a graph-based editor to lay out the stops and label the tour branches, although the layout can also be performed automatically by the system.

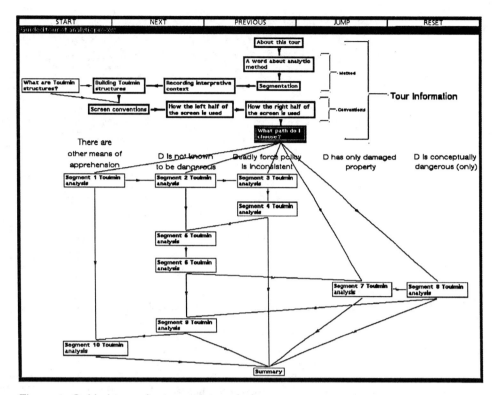

Figure 1. Guided tour of a transcript analysis.

The tour stops are *tabletops*, or screenfuls of cards whose layouts have been designated by the author; an example of a tabletop is shown in Figure 2. A tabletop captures various characteristics of the layout, including card window shapes, screen positions, scrolling locations, and order of window opening. As the reader moves from stop to stop, the current tabletop is automatically closed down and the next one brought up.

To run a guided tour, the reader makes use of the five buttons appearing at the top of the guided tour card (Figure 1). They allow her to start the tour at its beginning, move to the next stop, move to a previously visited stop, jump to any stop on the tour, and reset the tour. If there is more than one "next" stop, ie. a branch point, the reader chooses one of the possible stops from a menu. The graph structure shown in the guided tour card provides indications of the reader's place in the tour and recent traversal history. The node in the graph whose tabletop is currently open is highlighted, while the nodes for tabletops already visited have dark borders. Also, the edges corresponding to the path followed using the NEXT command are displayed with darker lines. In the tour in Figure 1, a reader has used the NEXT button to follow the tour from the starting stop, *About this tour*, to the current stop, *What path do I choose?*.

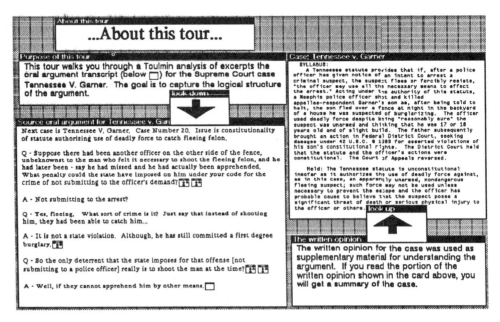

Figure 2. Introductory tabletop.

Since guided tours are themselves nodes in the hypertext network, they are part of the same database they are presenting. The tabletop cards which make up a tour may have other links connecting them to other parts of the network. Therefore, a guided tour is a subgraph of the subnetwork containing those cards. See [Trig88] for a full description and historical perspective of guided tours and tabletops.

Subsequent to [Trig88], the Guided Tours facility has been used by the authors and other members of the user community to create a number of tours; these attempts to author on-line hypermedia presentations have brought further issues to light. The tour we use as our primary example in this paper organizes a hypertext-based argument analysis of a Supreme Court oral transcript for presentation to two different audiences - readers interested in argument analysis and representation, and readers interested in the content of the argument. Details of the application are described in [Mars89].

3. ISSUES FOR ON-LINE PRESENTATION TOOLS

Experience has shown that authoring on-line hypertext presentations is a substantially more complex activity than Guided Tours, coupled with existing authoring conventions, alone supports. In our attempts at creating and reading guided tours, we have uncovered a set of issues that designers and users of on-line hypertext presentation tools should consider. They include the functions of metainformation in structuring on-line hypertext presentations, problems with narration and reference, and how coherence is maintained in a medium that promotes fragmentation. In discussing these issues, we provide examples of metainformation added to improve tour intelligibility, methods for providing absentee narration, and strategies for maintaining coherence and providing context. The examples are from a guided tour, illustrated in Figure 1, that explains a hypertext analysis of a courtroom transcript.

3.1 Information versus metainformation

Metainformation is the material added to an existing hypermedia network to make the information in the network intelligible and to help the reader avoid disorientation. We have found the following kinds of metainformation in guided tours:

- expository text referring to the original network

- instructions to the reader on how to interpret the screen layout

- descriptions of the structure of the tour

- textual and annotative devices that offset the effects of fragmentation.

Figure 2 shows an example of what we mean by metainformation. Two of the cards displayed, *Source oral argument for Tennessee v. Garner* and *Case: Tennessee v. Garner*, are part of the original network created during the course of the argument analysis. The remaining five cards, *About this tour*, *Purpose of this tour*, *The written opinion*, and the two cards containing arrows, comprise metainformation with respect to the original network.

The expository text necessary to explain the content of the original network forms a significant category of metainformation. The exposition added to the original network inherits many of the problems of traditional linear forms such as presentation order and tone. Expository text early in the tour discussing how and why the network was created can help readers anticipate the content of the tour and ascertain its relevance to their own interests. Figure 2 provides a limited example of an introductory tabletop containing expository text. It describes the goal in creating the original network and captions a sample of the material used in the analysis of the case. Often the expository text used to annotate the original network for the tour has a quality analogous to a figure caption in linear text. But, unlike linear text, there are no set spatial relationships to connect the caption with the figure; devices like drawn arrows and links are needed to call the reader's attention to the relationship between the caption and the piece of the original network.

Two other categories of metainformation arise from the need to discuss presentation conventions. Our experience with the NoteCards Guided Tours facility has shown that because hypermedia presentation conventions have yet to be negotiated in the user community, they need to be made explicit; conventions imported from other domains or invented for an individual tour must be explained. In time, such conventions will evolve and become internalized by readers and authors. But, for the time being, readers need to be given information about how to interpret the screen layout and and the tour structure.

Relevant metainformation about screen layout conventions may include: significance of font size, conventions of gestural and pointing devices, divisions of screen space, and assumptions about the reader's on-line environment (such as screen size and system parameter settings). We have found that explaining these conventions allows the reader to focus on the content of the tour and avoid having to uncover and possibly misunderstand the author's conventions. In our example, the convention-explaining tabletops are labelled in the guided tour card, so that the reader can locate them in the beginning and refer back to them when necessary. A screen conventions tour stop is shown in Figure 3; it provides a schematic view of the typical "content" tabletop; two other stops, *How the left half of the screen is used* and *How the right half of the screen is used*, describe details of screen use conventions and show abstract version of cards in the original network that will appear in later tabletops. Without schematic views of the kinds of cards in the network and how they are organized on the screen, readers find it difficult to interpret the kinds of complex displays an author typically creates using the Guided Tours facility.

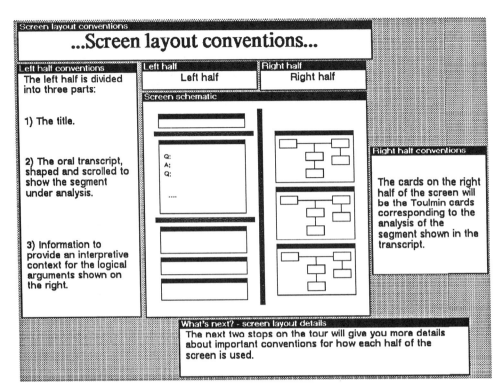

Figure 3. Abstract view showing tabletop conventions.

In addition to providing metainformation for interpreting the screen, the author is also faced with the task of discussing the tour's structure and how it relates to the interests of the intended audiences; readers must have a good idea of the author's intentions if they are going to make choices appropriate to their level of knowledge, experience and interest at branch points. Metainformation about tour structure has been provided in several ways in our example tour. The author has annotated the Guided Tour card shown in Figure 1 with metainformation concerning tour structure by labelling the tour with headings and subheadings such as *Tour Information, Method*, and *Conventions*. These labels, in conjunction with tour stop titles, tell the reader which stops describe the tour content, screen layout conventions, and path organizations. The reader is also given a labelled overview of the tour's topic structure showing the different lines of argument found in the analysis; these annotations function much like section headings in a paper.

Besides annotating the tour card, the author discusses the tour's structure within various stops as the tour progresses. For example, in Figure 4, the reader has been given an overview of the available paths. The author has drawn abstract maps of the paths, along with descriptions of the information presented along each path. In this case, she addresses both audiences, those interested in the analysis, and those interested in the argument's development.

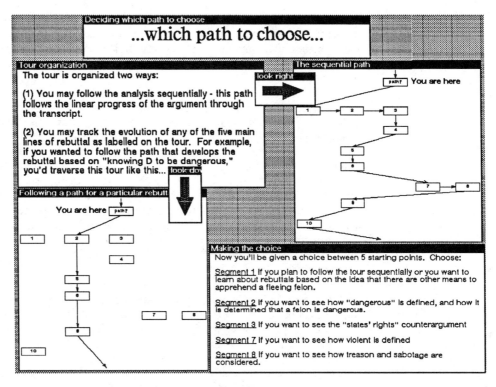

Figure 4. Tabletop showing map of tour structure.

Since hypertext displays are often complicated and non-linear, an author may also supply metainformation in the form of textual and annotative devices to cope with fragmentation and complexity. Some of the fragmentation an author introduces through the NoteCards Guided Tour facility is a consequence of creating multi-card displays. Thus metainformation to group cards on the screen helps simplify the reader's interpretive task. A second kind of fragmentation occurs between tour stops. Metainformation such as the "What's next?" card shown at the bottom right hand corner of Figure 3 attempts to reduce this kind of fragmentation. Section 3.3 discusses other techniques for maintaining coherence and context.

3.2 Narration

Guided tours of existing networks have been observed as having a quality of "aboutness," in part created by the multiple functions of the artifact and the dual roles of the author. The original network in our example served as the analytic medium; the network augmented by metainformation now acts as a presentation vehicle. Since a guided tour, like any text, involves an absentee narrator, an author may wish to provide a sense of the narrative voice and indicate her perspective on the work. Some hypermedia systems geared mainly to the task of presentation solve the narrative problem with an explicit narrator [Salo89]. In NoteCards however, most on-line presentations rely on an implicit presence, as in more conventional literary forms. To establish a narration in our example, the tour author distinguishes metainformation from text already in the network through visual cues. In Figure 2, the use of a larger bold font indicates narration. It may also help readers understand this distinction if the original network can be given a consistent appearance as viewed from the tour. One of our readers had trouble interpreting the the introductory tabletop shown in Figure 2 because the original analytic material appeared in two different fonts.

Another complexity in providing narration to present an existing network arises from the disparate goals of the narration. On one hand, the author may be discussing the content of network, and on the other, properties of the medium. It is difficult to adopt a consistent tone and level of formality when expository text is mixed with a variety of other types of metainformation, including instructions to the reader to "do this" and discussions of the medium. In our example tour, the author tended toward formality in the expository text, and toward informally addressing the reader when network content was not under discussion.

Tour authors also must confront the problem of reference, since they are not present to point and gesture during the reading process. In our experience, graphical arrows, asterisks, and other reference devices have been used to serve as stand-ins for the narrator's gestures and emphasis. Arrows are used to indicate the reading order of cards in a tabletop (Figure 2); they are also used to attach text to figures (Figure 3). In Figure 5, the arrows are annotated by the title of the window containing them, providing additional discourse cues. See [Trig88] for a more thorough discussion of deictic reference in guided tours. Arrows used in this manner illustrate an important distinction between narrative reference and the hypertext notion of reference. By using arrows instead of links, information and metainformation can be kept distinct; the tour remains an adjunct to the original information. The narrative reference is only available in the appropriate context for interpretation.

Reference embedded in text creates another set of problems for the author. It is very difficult to delineate (and interpret) the scope of a given reference in this presentation medium. Scope can vary wildly; a phrase like "The cards on the right half of the screen" can refer to cards within a single tabletop, across multiple tabletops, or in every tabletop of the tour. References to specific pieces of information can refer to a card that's on the screen now, a card the reader has seen in a previous tabletop, or a card at the end of a link. Our readers were disturbed by these questions of unresolved reference and tended to want to flip back and forth between tabletops.

3.3 Maintaining coherence and context

Although methods for maintaining coherence are more or less settled for conventional forms of writing, hypertext violates many of the assumptions underlying these methods. It is important to examine the characteristics of on-line presentations that distinguish them from conventional writing. One important aspect of conventional forms absent from hypertext is the transitional text that helps the reader maintain a sense of the material's coherence. The fragmentation characteristic of hypertext may also lead to a lack of interpretive context [Land87]. Therefore, authors of on-line presentations need to be particularly aware of strategies for promoting coherence, and ways of providing context to the reader.

In our example, sequential stops discuss either the same topic or closely related topics. To convey a sense of continuity and coherence across these stops, the tour makes use of *persistent cards*, cards that remain on the screen across a series of stops. Spatial cues are used to the same end; related tabletops have similar cards in the same (or almost the same) places. The use of persistent cards, combined with similar window layouts in the stops, allows the reader to anticipate material and relate it to previous stops.

Figures 5 and 6 show an example of this strategy. The argument card, *A: It is reasonable to use deadly force to apprehend a dangerous fleeing felon*, and its annotation, *Question: where's the dividing line?*, persist through the successive tabletops defining the notion of "dangerous felon." Figures 5 and 6 also illustrate the idea of *persistent gestures*; the "grey line" dividing dangerous and not dangerous moves across the screen in the two presentations. The author can assume at this point in the tour that the reader understands such higher level graphical metaphors.

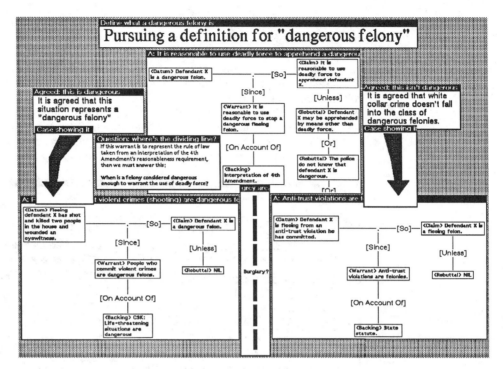

Figure 5. Use of persistent cards and gestures - part 1.

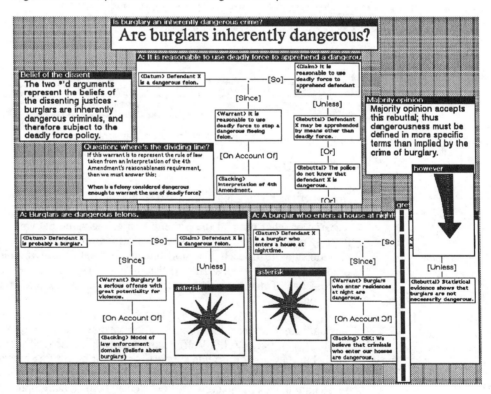

Figure 6. Use of persistent cards and gestures - part 2.

The coherence of a section of a tour can also be maintained using the notion of *spines*. A tour spine (indicated by layout or labels in the guided tour card) is a primary path through the tour with minimal branching. For example, the main portion of the tour shown in Figure 1 has several spines organized by the different argument strategies represented in that series of tabletops, such as the one labeled *D is not known to be dangerous*. Side trips are defined relative to a spine; they can be taken according to interest, and readers can easily find their way back to the spine.

One complication in the maintenance of coherence and context comes from the inherent interactivity of hypertext. In our task domain, where there is considerable information that falls outside of the tour, readers can make unplanned forays into the network, sometimes resulting in complex and confusing screen layouts. This raises the issue of screen management in touring situations. For example, in Figure 7 the tour author encourages readers to explore the network from a tour stop, but there is currently no way for the author to prevent readers from opening too many cards and getting lost.

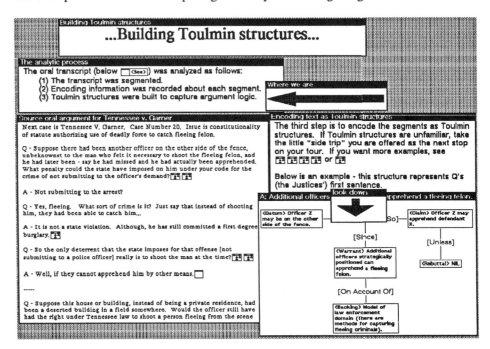

Figure 7. Encouraging readers to explore the network.

4. CONCLUSIONS

Our experience with guided tours and ad hoc on-line presentations in NoteCards highlights a need to distinguish between the formulation of a hypertext network for a user's own research or other use and the presentation of the same network to an audience. Because these two very different processes are easily confounded in hypertext, it is necessary to provide support for each. The trail-blazing and path-following metaphors that have been proposed in earlier work such as [Bush45] and [Trig86] may be insufficient for a reader to make sense of another's path in the absence of context-creating metainformation and narration.

Mechanisms that provide representations for guiding a future reader through a network [Stot88], [Trig88], [Zell88] offer partial solutions, especially from the reader's point of view, but they do not provide support for authoring on-line presentations. Since we have found that considerable metainformation is necessary to structure a network for presentation, we need to consider how we can help an author provide this audience-directed narration. Future support for authoring guided tour-like presentations should include frameworks for:

- Annotated graphical overviews.

- Tour stops that explicate layout conventions.

- Integrating expository text with other types of metainformation.

- Context-sensitive reference.

- Persistent gestures and cards.

- Tools to support activities from other disciplines.

- Examples of successful presentation strategies.

As the hypertext community's experience with on-line presentations grows, an increased appreciation of what it means to produce an intelligible network will emerge. Furthermore, as a wider community of readers and writers begins to communicate about the content of existing networks, conventions will continue to evolve for hypertext as a presentation medium.

5. ACKNOWLEDGMENTS

Many thanks to Frank Halasz, Susan Newman, and Randy Trigg for invaluable discussions and comments on drafts of this paper. Thanks too to Susan Newman and Richard Southall for sharing their experiences as tour-takers.

6. REFERENCES

[Bush45]   Bush, V. "As We May Think," *The Atlantic Monthly*, August, 1945.

[Char87]   Charney, D. "Comprehending Non-Linear Text: The Role of Discourse Cues and Reading Strategies," *Hypertext '87 Papers*, Chapel Hill, North Carolina, November 13-15, 1987.

[Hala88]   Halasz, F.G. "Reflections on Notecards: Seven Issues for the Next Generation of Hypermedia Systems," *Communications of the ACM*, 31(7), pp. 836-852, July 1988.

[Hala87]   Halasz, F.G., Moran, T.P., Trigg, R.H. "Notecards in a Nutshell," *Proceedings of the ACM CHI+GI Conference*, pp. 45-52, Toronto, 1987.

[Land87]   Landow, G.P. "Relationally encoded links and the rhetoric of hypertext," *Hypertext '87 Papers*, Chapel Hill, North Carolina, November 13-15, 1987.

[Mars89]   Marshall, C.C. "Representing the Structure of a Legal Argument," *Proceedings of the Second International Conference on AI and Law*, Vancouver, British Columbia, June 14-16, 1989.

[Salo89]   Salomon, G., Oren T., Kreitman, K. "Using Guides to Explore Multimedia Databases," *Proceedings of HICSS '89*, January 3-6, 1989.

[Stot89]   Stotts, P.D., Furuta, R. "Petri Net Based Hypertext: Document Structure with Browsing Semantics," to be published in *ACM Transactions on Office Information Systems*.

[Trig88]   Trigg, R. H. "Guided Tours and Tabletops: Tools for Communicating in a Hypertext Environment," *ACM Transactions on Office Information Systems*, 6(4), pp 398-414, October 1988.

[Trig87]   Trigg, R.H., Irish, P.M. "Hypertext Habitats: Experiences of Writers in NoteCards," *Hypertext '87 Papers*, Chapel Hill, North Carolina, November 13-15, 1987.

[Trig86]   Trigg, R.H., Weiser M. "TEXTNET: A Network-Based Approach to Text Handling," *ACM Transactions on Office Information Systems*, 4(1), 1986.

[Zell88]   Zellweger, P. "Active paths through multimedia documents," *Proceedings of the EP '88 Conference on Electronic Publishing, Document Manipulation, and Typography*, Nice, France, April 20-22, 1988.

Programmable Browsing Semantics in Trellis

Richard Furuta* and P. David Stotts**

Department of Computer Science
University of Maryland
College Park, MD 20742

INTRODUCTION

Different researchers have different ideas about how a hypertext should be navigated. Each new implementation of a hypertext browser works slightly differently from previous ones. This is due both to variations in personal taste and to discoveries of new, useful ways to organize and present information.

In this report we outline a technique by which a hypertext system can offer flexible, programmable browsing behavior, or *browsing semantics*. Differences in the way documents are to be browsed can be specified by an author on a document-by-document basis, or by a style designer for an entire class of documents. The ability to specify and modify how a browser presents information is an important and useful property in general. We first discuss the issues involved in programmable browsing semantics, and then we present one method of providing them within the context of the Trellis project at the University of Maryland.

The Trellis model of hypertext [Stot88, Stot89b] is a notational and analytical framework in which two critical aspects of a hypertext are unified: the logically linked information structure, and the experience a reader has when browsing the structure. The unifying formalism in Trellis is net theory, specifically that of place/transition nets, or Petri nets [Pete81, Reis85]. Petri nets have an easily exploited dualism that naturally facilitates this two-way specification. Represented as bipartite graphs, they describe links among information elements just as well as directed graphs do, without any loss of expressive power. Being automata as well, their execution properties can be used to specify restrictions and conditions on how information fragments are to be visited. These are the browsing semantics that are the focus of this report.

Net theory provides a mathematically rich and notationally flexible basis for hypertext. First, a Petri net is a process model, and browsing a hypertext is a process. Secondly, a Petri net is inherently a concurrency model, so it provides a simple notation and semantics for expressing simultaneous display of multiple information elements. Thirdly, in the twenty years since their creation, a large body of Petri net analysis techniques has been developed that can be directly applied to problems in the hypertext domain. Together these points allow expression of, and reasoning about, the experience a reader will have while navigating a document. These capabilities include synchronization of simultaneous traversals of separate paths through a hypertext (including multiple

* Supported in part by a grant from the National Science Foundation, CCR-8810312.

** Supported in part by the University of Maryland Institute for Advanced Computer Studies.

readers), as well as access control and other security considerations (specifying nodes that can be proven accessible only to certain classes of reader).

At the most abstract level, this work can be viewed as exploring an analogy between structured programming and hypertext authoring. The analogy appears to provide solutions not only to the problem of specifying and implementing variable browsing semantics, but to the problem of how to perform disciplined construction of (very) large hypertext documents as well. Our report on what we have learned from this analogy is presented in the three major sections. Section 2 first presents an overview of browsing primitives in Petri net-structured hypertext and explains how an author can customize and vary the browsing behavior of such documents. It includes a brief introduction to Petri nets and the Trellis model for readers not already familiar with these topics. Section 3 then discusses constrained document classes and develops the structured programming analogy for hypertext authoring. It also presents the authoring language Alpha as one example of how to write structured hypertexts. Alpha is a textual authoring language for construction of structured hyperdocuments in the αTrellis system. The Alpha language encourages hypertext authors to employ top-down design instead of simply assembling document components from the bottom up. Finally, Section 4 discusses other systems with browsing flexibility, and presents some extensions being made to the Trellis model that will add even greater flexibility to its semantic programmability.

2. TRELLIS AND BROWSING SEMANTICS

We have developed αTrellis, a prototype hypertext browsing and authoring system based on the Trellis model. The details of αTrellis have been presented elsewhere [Stot89c], but for completeness of the ensuing discussion on browsing semantics we will first summarize its major points, along with a brief description of Petri nets and the Trellis model on which the system is built. Readers already familiar with these topics can skip directly to Section 2.2.

2.1. Petri nets, Trellis, and αTrellis

Figure 1 shows a screen from αTrellis. It presents a visible browsing environment in which many different elements may be viewed at a given point in time. While browsing, the reader selects buttons from menus, thereby causing the display to change as target elements become visible and the source elements are removed from view. The current implementation operates on Sun-3 workstations under the SunView window package. αTrellis is intended as an experimental platform and a proof-of-principle vehicle. As such, we have focussed on implementing the Petri net document representation with associated browsing semantics, rather than worrying initially about important user interface issues such as window placement, use of highlighting, and incorporation of graphics. Based on our experience with αTrellis, we now are developing an expanded version called χTrellis for the workstation-independent X windows system that will incorporate a more realistic and state-of-the-art user interface.

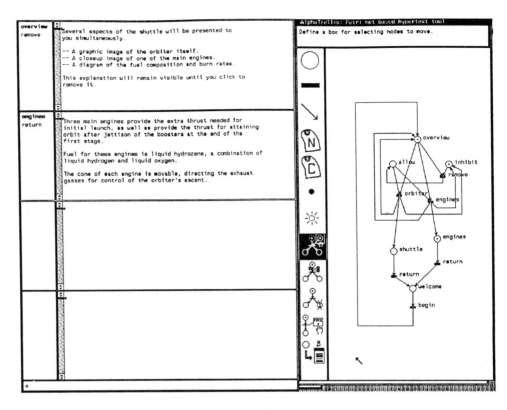

Figure 1: Screen from the αTrellis hypertext system

αTrellis allows both construction and viewing of a Petri net hyperdocument. Physically, the αTrellis screen is divided into two main parts. On the right side is a Petri net editor and simulator, derived from Molloy's SPAN [Moll86]. Petri nets are represented as bipartite graphs in which the circular nodes are called *places* and the bar nodes are called *transitions*.[1] A dot in a place is called a *token*, and it represents the realization of some condition associated with the place. A place containing one or more tokens is said to be *marked*. When each place incident on a transition is marked that transition is *enabled*. An enabled transition may *fire* by removing one token from each of its input places and putting one token into each of its output places. The full token distribution among places is the *state* of the net and is termed a *net marking*. One transition firing causes one state change.

The left side of the αTrellis screen contains the hypertext browser, subdivided into four text windows. In the Trellis hypertext model, an information element is associated with each Petri net place, and when a place is marked its element is displayed in one of these text windows. The model also associates with each transition a user-selectable *button*, which is not visible until the transition is enabled. When a transition is enabled, its button is displayed in a menu to the left of the window for each of the transition's input places. Selection of a button in the browser causes its transition to fire, changing the net state and thereby causing a change in the information elements that are displayed in the text windows.

---

[1]Readers unfamiliar with Petri net theory can find a thorough exposition in the books by Reisig [Reis85] and Peterson [Pete81].

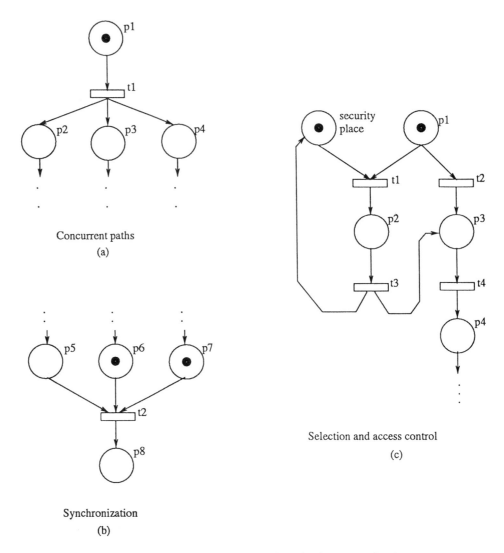

Figure 2: Trellis primitives: concurrency, synchronization, security, buttons

It also should be noted that the Trellis model incorporates hierarchy. This means that the contents of a place can be either an information fragment or another complete hypertext, one level deeper in the hierarchy. One of the main ways in which the Alpha language (see Section 3) controls document complexity is by constructing this hierarchy using a notation similar to procedural abstraction in programming.

2.2. Variable browsing semantics

By having a formal definition and implementation based on a process model with inherent execution semantics, the αTrellis system provides a facility for tailoring the manner in which information is presented to the reader of a hypertext. An author can construct a document relying only on the primitive browsing actions in αTrellis, or he can compose these actions into more complex "higher-level" behaviors and alter the default presentation of a document's contents.

In the Trellis hypertext model, the browsing semantics are closely tied to the actions that occur during Petri net execution. The primitive actions are *sequencing, selection, concurrency, synchronization, access control, display/undisplay button,* and *display/undisplay element.* These actions are provided collectively by the net fragments and interconnections, the execution rules for nets, and the mappings of information elements to net nodes. Figure 2 illustrates several of these basic Trellis operations.

Sequencing is provided via directional arcs from nodes to successors. Display element (associated with a place) occurs when a token moves into a place, and undisplay element occurs when a token moves out of a place. Display button (associated with a transition) occurs when ever a transition is enabled; undisplay button occurs whenever a transition ceases to be enabled (either by itself firing, or by some other transition firing and removing one of its input tokens). Part (a) of Figure 2 shows creation of concurrent browsing paths. In this net, transition t_1 is enabled and its button is therefore visible. When selected by a reader, t_1 fires and places a token in *each* of its output places, thereby creating three tokens and causing three elements to be concurrently displayed. Part (b) shows synchronization of browsing paths at transition t_2. Its button will not be visible for selection until a token appears in each of its input places, indicating that a reader has browsed to the end of each concurrent path. When this happens, t_2 may fire, causing a single token to move on to place p_8.

Part (c) of Figure 2 shows selection and access control. Transition t_2 is enabled, and its button is visible in the display for the element associated with place p_1. In addition, transition t_1 is also enabled, so its button is also visible in the same display. A reader viewing this information has a choice of next element corresponding to the two selectable buttons.[2] The place labeled *security place* provides access control to the information associated with place p_2. If there were no token in the security place, then a reader would have no choice in the window for p_1. The only selectable button would be the one for transition t_2. By convention in αTrellis, a place used like this for access control can be designated as having *null* contents, and nothing will be displayed when a token is present in it.

Self-spawn browsing behavior

By allowing flexible composition of these simple actions, the Trellis model provides authors with variable browsing semantics. The net shown in Figure 1 is a simple illustration of this concept. This small net was specifically constructed to provide browsing behavior in which the text element called "overview" is *not* removed when the buttons in its panel ("orbiter" and "engines") are selected, as is the case with the base-level αTrellis behavior. Instead, when a button is selected, the following panel will be displayed and the "overview" panel will remain visible. In addition, a new button (labeled "remove") becomes visible in "overview" so the reader may manually remove that panel from view at his convenience. This form of presentation can be termed "self-spawn," since selection of a button causes (in Trellis terms) an indefinite redisplay of its information panel. Analysis of this net reveals that in addition to allowing a reader to keep a panel around after reading it, the structure is synchronized to prevent a reader from passing through the panel a second time *without* disposing of the display from the first pass.

---

[2]Although this is not shown, a button will appear in the display window for each of the input places of an enabled transition. Thus, one transition can be fired by selecting one of perhaps several buttons. This feature is useful in a distributed viewing environment.

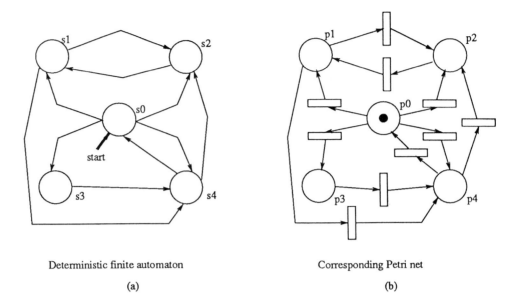

Deterministic finite automaton

(a)

Corresponding Petri net

(b)

Figure 3: Common "DFA" browsing behavior with Trellis

An author desiring the "self-spawn" presentation for hypertext elements can write a base-level Trellis document and then augment the net by adding similar redisplay and synchronization structures in between the appropriate places and transitions. This can obviously be a tedious and error prone undertaking if all elements were to be presented this way (as opposed to just a select few). Section 3 below provides a solution that avoids this problem for such large-scale changes to base-level browsing semantics.

DFA-like browsing

Many hypertext systems exhibit one of the simplest forms of browsing behavior, which can be classified as "DFA-like." The structure of such a hypertext can be thought of as the transition diagram of a DFA, with each state of the automaton representing an information node in the hypertext and with the arcs between states representing the hypertext links. Browsing behavior in a DFA-like system is then defined by the execution rules for DFAs. Browsing begins in the start state and ends if a final state is ever reached. Only one state may be visited at a time. From each state, selecting a link causes traversal of an arc and a change of state. Thus one screen of information is visible at a time and a reader traces a single path through the transition diagram.

DFAs are a proper subclass of Petri nets, so any DFA-like hypertext structure can be created in Trellis with the simple transformation shown in Figure 3, parts (a) and (b). Each node in the hypertext becomes a place in the Petri net, and a transition is placed on each arc. No concurrency appears in this form of browsing, so every transition will have one input and one output.

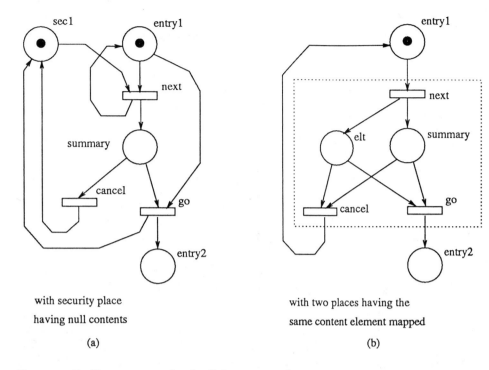

with security place
having null contents

(a)

with two places having the
same content element mapped

(b)

Figure 4: Trellis representation for link summary feature

Link summaries

Hyperties [Shne87] provides an interesting extension to DFA-like browsing, in that a reader who selects an arc first gets a short summary of the information at the other end. A second click will produce the full entry, whereas another selection will cancel the whole investigation of that link. This is still conceptually DFA-like browsing behavior, but with some extra activity possible at each node. The two net fragments shown in Figure 4 demonstrate how a form of link summary similar to that of Hyperties can be provided in a Trellis document.[3] Here a limited form of concurrent browsing appears, in that two text frames are sometimes displayed simultaneously (an entry and a link summary), represented by the fact that two tokens can appear in the net at some points. Notice that in part (a) the desired browsing effects are obtained using the security place "sec1," which has null contents and so will not have a display. The element "entry1" will remain displayed when transition "next" is fired, popping up the "summary" element as well, but the security place prevents the "next" from being fired again until after either "cancel" or "go" has been selected. In part (b) the same effect has been obtained using the content mapping feature of Trellis. Here, selecting button "next" causes the element "entry1" to be undisplayed, since a token is removed from its place. However, the same information content is associated with place "elt" as with place "entry1," thus making it visible both before and during the "summary" display. This second form is perhaps easier to envision as an abstraction of a link, since as the dotted box shows, the extra net components can easily be viewed as a complex version of the transition "next".

---

[3]To limit the complexity of the graphs in this example, the behavior of our link summary implementation is a bit simpler than the actual behavior of Hyperties.

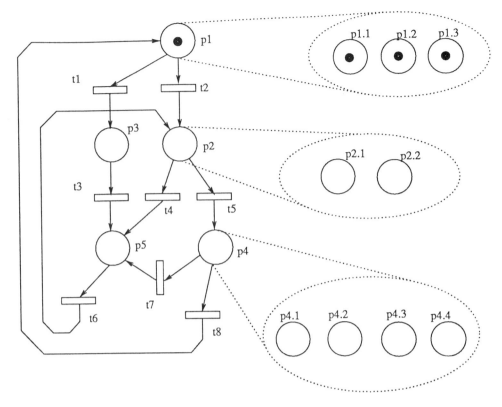

Figure 5: Trellis representation for a NoteCards guided tour

Concurrent sets browsing

Concurrency appears in a number of hypertext systems. One recently introduced form is *guided tours* [Trig88] in Xerox's NoteCards system [Hala88]. In guided tours, a number of sets of concurrently displayed elements, called *tabletops*, are constructed and linked together with DFA-like browsing behavior. This can be created in Trellis by letting each node in a DFA transition diagram represent one tabletop. Figure 5 shows this construction. The hierarchy feature of Trellis is used to represent a tabletop. All the elements of one tabletop form the lower level net that is the collective content of one high-level place. In the figure, a place that is not expanded is assumed to have a single element in its tabletop.

To summarize this section, there are many differing views about how information elements can, or should, be presented during hypertext browsing. We can simulate other people's ideas of "good," "necessary," or "appropriate" behaviors with the base level primitive actions (concurrency, synchronization, sequencing, display and undisplay of elements and buttons, access control) inherent in Petri net execution. One system, then, built on the Trellis model, can satisfy the tastes of a wide range of hypertext authors and readers. For any specific hypertext, its author can tailor the presentation of its information to suit his particular requirements for reader/document interaction. In the next section we discuss how to generate tailored browsing behavior for an entire class of documents instead of on a document-by-document basis.

3. STRUCTURED PROGRAMMING ANALOGY FOR AUTHORING

We believe that writing some types of hypertext can be viewed as a form of programming. Specification of the structure of a document and the manner in which it is to be browsed can be done in a disciplined way, much as large and complex software systems can be successfully constructed with a methodical approach. One method of programming is the graphical construction just discussed, in which the manner of presentation of node is encoded in the net structure of a document on a node-by-node basis. Another method, discussed in this section, is to use a textual language, like a traditional programming language, that generates appropriate net fragments for its "control structures." In a recent paper, van Dam discussed the need for such a disciplined approach to hypertext authoring, stating:

> My point of view is that in a sense hypertext gives us a **goto**, and a **goto**, as we all know, produces spaghetti. At most we have invented the **if-then-else-if**, with hierarchy. That's our one structured flow-of-control concept ... we need to discover what the equivalent of other constructs are [vanD88, page 894].

Our work in Trellis is an attempt to define this approach to hypertext construction. The analogy to structured programming seems to be a fruitful one with the promise of several solutions from software engineering (notably, procedural abstraction for complexity control), being directly applicable to the hypertext problem domain.

In the following sections, we discuss one technique for "programming" a hypertext, that of authoring with *Single-Input/Single-Output* Petri net structures, or *SISO* structures. The browsing semantics discussed in section 2.2 are useful to apply by direct construction only if they are needed in a document at scattered and infrequent locations. If all nodes must be surrounded by complex net structures, then the process of direct document definition is tedious and error prone. The solution is a language feature that succinctly expresses the desired browsing semantics and then automatically generates the appropriate net fragments. Interconnection of net fragments is then easily accomplished by creating appropriate links between the inputs and outputs of the structures.

3.1 SISO net structures

A SISO structure is a net fragment that has one input place and one output transition. Two SISO structures that are to be interconnected are always linked by creating an arc from the output of one to the input of the other.[4] As examples of SISO net structures, we show the semantics of the control mechanisms in the Alpha language (discussed in section 3.2).

We start the composition of a hypertext with atomic SISO structures, each of which is simply a single place followed by a single transition. The transition represents "half a link," to be connected to another place to complete the link. An atomic SISO represents a single element (text, graphics, etc.) for display. Given these, more complex SISO structures are produced via particular compositions:

---

[4]The choice of beginning and ending nodes for the SISO definition and their linking follows the structural rules of Petri nets, requiring that every arc must be between a place and a transition, or *vice versa*.

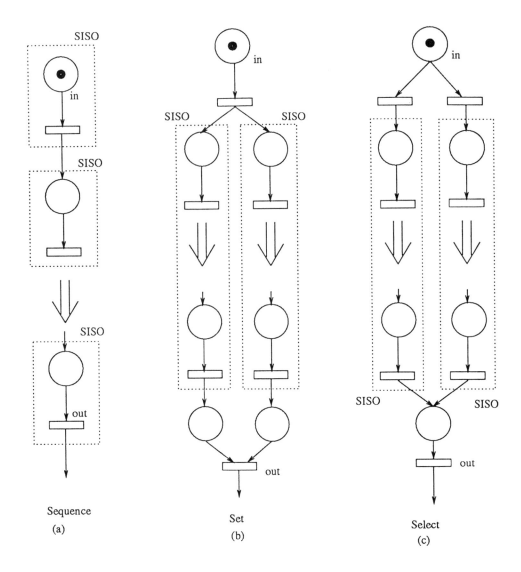

Figure 6: Single-input/single-output hypertext components (I)

- Figure 6, part (a), shows *sequencing*, the simplest interconnection mechanism. The output transition of one SISO is linked to the input place of another, forming a complete link.

- Figure 6, part (b), shows the *set* structure, the basic unit of browsing concurrency. Here, several arbitrary SISO structures are composed for concurrent presentation by tying together all their inputs with a new input place and a token-multiplying transition. Their outputs all feed into a terminating structure formed from one new place per SISO and a single synchronizing transition. The meaning of a set is that all the SISOs will be concurrently browsed, and that no browsing can proceed past the set until browsing is completed in each SISO.

- Figure 6, part (c), shows the *select* structure, the basic unit of branching. Here, several arbitrary SISO structures are linked by a new input place with several output transitions, one per SISO. The terminating structure is a single new place and a single new output transition. The meaning of a select structure is similar to a Pascal "case" statement, in that only one of the component SISOs will be browsed, depending which link (transition) the reader chooses.

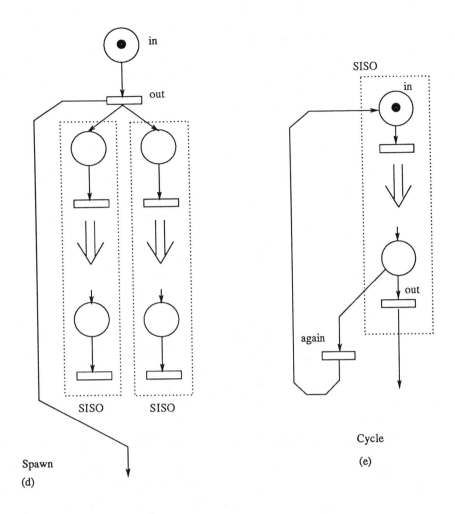

Figure 7: Single-input/single-output hypertext components (II)

- Figure 7, part (d), shows the *spawn* structure, an alternate form of browsing concurrency. Here, several arbitrary SISOs are composed by creating a new input place followed by a new output transition as shown, and linking the SISO inputs to the new output. The meaning of a spawn is that concurrent browsing of all SISOs is initiated, but no synchronization is prescribed for their terminations. A spawn essentially creates concurrently existing browsing activities with indefinite relative lifetimes.

- Figure 7, part (e), shows the *cycle* structure, the main unit of repetition. Here, an arbitrary SISO is installed as the body of a loop by creating a new transition and linking it back to the input of the SISO. The input and output of the new SISO are the same as those of the body. The meaning of a cycle is that a reader can read the body once and then either repeat it or continue on to the following portion of the hypertext.

```
TITLE_PANEL {
    Space Shuttle Engine Diagram:
    The accompanying picture shows an external posterior view of the main
    engines used on the space shuttle.  Many of the wires and supply lines
    have been excluded to simplify the presentation of the major
subsystems.
    The diagram will remain visible as you browse the accompanying
discussion
    of the individual components.
}

CLOSING_PANEL {
    Please log your session before leaving with the database editor in the
    other window.  Information on other NASA projects can be found in the
    section entitled "Current Activities" in the main collection.  Consult
    the article entitled "Help with Hypertext" for further assistance in
    using this system.
}

extern directional_control(), failure_detection();
extern throttle(), fuel_delivery();

engine_components ( p1 ) { -- p1 specifies default initially visible
elements
  cycle -> more {
    p1: `Details are available on the follow subsystems:' ;
    set group -> options { -- all choices are externally defined subnets
      p2:  directional_control ( ) ;
      p3:  failure_detection ( ) ;
      { p4:  throttle ( ) ;
        p5:  fuel_delivery ( ) ; }
} } }

extern engine_pic_1
extern in_flight_operation(), subsystem_details(), browser_log();

main shuttle_engines (g1) { -- g1 specifies default initially visible
elements
  set g1 -> t1 {              -- elements p1, p2, p3 are shown concurrently
    p1: engine_pic_1 ;        -- graphics in external file
    p2: TITLE_PANEL ;         -- named text definition from above
    p3: engine_components ( ) ; -- invoke subnet with default initial
marking
  }
  p5: in_flight_operation ( ) ;    -- invoke subnet with default init
marking
  cycle -> again {
    p4: subsystem_details ( ) ;    -- subnet contents found in external
file
    p8: `Select "again" to rebrowse the details.' ;
  }
  set log -> done {
    p6: CLOSING_PANEL ;       -- named text definition from above
    p7: browser_log ( ) ;     -- external subnet, database editor
} }
```

Figure 8: A simple hypertext specification in Alpha

When a token is in a place, the content element associated with that place will be displayed. As mentioned earlier, αTrellis recognizes a convention in which a place with null contents generates no display. We use this convention to make SISO composition practical from the point of view of a hypertext reader. When composing SISOs, many of the automatically generated places forming input and output structures are created simply to provide synchronization and linkage points in the net; they serve no informative purpose. Thus they must have null contents to avoid spurious displays. In fact, the only places in a composed hypertext that have visible contents are ones in atomic SISOs.

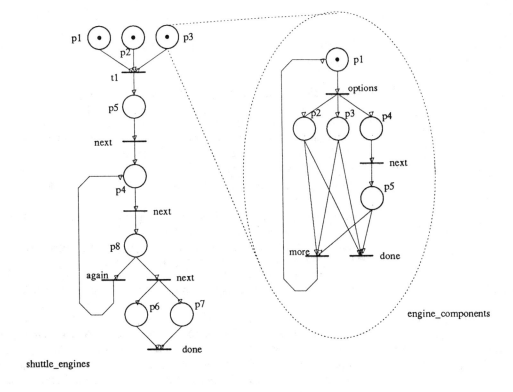

Figure 9: Petri net hypertext structure generated from Alpha specification in Figure 8

Null contents, though, create an interesting problem. If a place has null contents, no window is displayed for that place. If all the places into a transition have null contents, then there is no window in which to display the associated button when the transition is enabled, so it cannot be fired. The synchronizing structure at the end of a set, for example, exhibits this problem. We have remedied the situation by allowing such transitions to fire automatically whenever they become enabled.[5] Thus the the null places do not create unnatural displays and they do not hinder the smooth flow of information. An alternative to using automatic events is to postprocess the Petri net generated by SISO composition and "optimize" its structure, essentially removing the null-content places and shifting the links accordingly.

3.2. The Alpha authoring language

Under the assumption that hypertext authoring can be a programming activity, we have created Alpha (*Author Language for Petri-net-based Hypertext, α version*), our first language for constructing hypertexts via structured composition. Its syntax is essentially C-like, with some alterations to keywords and some additions to enhance its textual expressiveness. The semantics are defined entirely by the Trellis hypertext model and the compositional rules imposed by parsing a program. We present the syntax only by

---

[5]These automatically firing "buttons" are just one of several interesting classes of events that appear in a new version of the Trellis hypertext model [Stot89a]. The new model has two times associated with each transition, the second always greater than the first. The first tells how much time must pass after a transition is enabled before it is fireable (selectable by a reader). The second tells when an unfired transition will fire automatically. In this timed framework, the original Trellis model can be thought of as having all transitions timed with (0 , ∞). The model in which SISO structures are used has, in addition, a timing of (0 , 0) on the transitions generated automatically for making single outputs.

example; the semantics of the "control structures" in Alpha were just presented in Figures 6 and 7.

The author of a hypertext document uses Alpha to specify in a structured manner a Petri net whose execution behavior represents his intentions, as well as to associate text and graphics elements with the Petri net components. A textual language approach avoids some of the problems with graphical construction, namely complexity and size, while still allowing the power of the Petri net-based representation. The current version of Alpha allows specification of sets and sequences of hypertext elements, as well as browsing cycles, alternative selections, and concurrency spawning.

A simple Alpha program is shown in Figure 8. In this example, several different forms of hypertext entity appear. In-line text is specified with quoted strings, and will appear as the contents of a window when browsed. Similarly, larger text or graphics elements can either be defined in the program (e.g., `TITLE_PANEL`) or included from external files (e.g., `engine_pic_1`) with the "extern" directive. Subnets, that is, places with a hypertext as value instead of simply text or graphics, can be defined either explicitly (e.g., `engine_components`) or externally with the "extern" directive (e.g., `directional_control`). When a subnet is defined, the initially visible windows are specified by a list of place names in the header. When such a subnet is invoked, actual parameters may be given to override this default startup marking. The Petri net document structure generated from this Alpha program is shown in Figure 9. This net has been optimized (as previously discussed) to remove the null-content places created during its composition from SISO structures.

4. DISCUSSION AND CONCLUSIONS

The Trellis model and methods have been represented as having programmable browsing semantics. Another well-known hypertext system, Apple's HyperCard, also has this feature. The main differences between our approach and that of HyperCard are important ones. First, the Trellis model separates link structure from definition language, making numerous languages for document class definition possible within one semantic framework. In HyperCard, in fact, there is no facility for link definition outside of HyperTalk programming. Secondly, HyperTalk is a Turing-complete language, so any analysis of HyperCard stacks can be as hard as general program analysis. The Trellis model, however, is based on Petri nets, which are more powerful than finite automata but not as powerful as Turing machines. We feel that this middle ground provides much of the browsing programmability of HyperCard while still retaining the ability to perform important reachability analyses on the state space of the document-defining automaton. These techniques have been previously explained [Stot89b].

A number of interesting questions about authoring-as-structured-programming need further investigation. A textual language approach avoids some of the problems with graphical construction, namely practical document size and complexity, while still allowing the power of a Petri net-based representation, but how far does the obvious analogy really go? Are the structures in Alpha sufficient for construction of a broad range of hypertexts? Perhaps some common situations will require a limited form of "goto," like the controlled loop exit in C (the "break" statement). In a browsing environment such as a hypertext encyclopedia, where the manner in which links are to be followed is largely unconstrained, a language must allow fairly free linking. But (here is the power of the approach) where browsing control is needed, a higher-level language must also allow easy expression of complex net behavior to implement the needed control. Though we have not designed any authoring languages with complicated control structures like those shown in Figures 1 and 4, it can certainly be done easily. A language-based approach is one way to define entire Trellis documents with higher-level browsing behavior at every node. For situations like this, in which numerous identical net components are needed, it avoids the tedious and error prone method of programming them on a node-by-node basis directly in the net.

Alpha specifications allow expression of only a subset of the class of general Petri nets. It remains to be shown what document forms (if any) are inherently excluded by Alpha, or by structured composition in general. Perhaps such forms are "expendable," in the sense that their important effects can be obtained with some other hypertext form that is composable. An interesting corollary (if one can be proven) that closely follows the structured authoring analogy is a demonstration that the subclass produced by composition of SISO structures can provide all useful hypertext document interactions (much like the proof that for every possible unstructured program there is a structured program that will realize the same computation).

Finally, the structured authoring approach, using hierarchy facilities and SISO structures like those of αTrellis and Alpha, favors document construction from the top down. Hypertext authoring methods that instead define the hypertext an entry at a time tend to be bottom-up. Bottom-up composition may feel more "natural" to an author, but composition of a hypertext that has a unified form and feel can be much more difficult. A top-down approach encourages production of hypertexts that are designed before assembly.

REFERENCES

[Hala88]   Frank G. Halasz. "Reflections on NoteCards: Seven issues for the next generation of hypermedia systems." *Communications of the ACM*, 31(7):836-852, July 1988.

[Moll86]   Michael K. Molloy. "A CAD tool for stochastic Petri nets." In *Proceedings of the ACM-IEEE Fall Joint Computer Conference*, pages 1082-1091, November 1986.

[Pete81]   James L. Peterson. *Petri Net Theory and the Modeling of Systems.* Prentice-Hall, Inc., 1981.

[Reis85]   Wolfgang Reisig. *Petri Nets: An Introduction.* Springer-Verlag, 1985.

[Stot88]   P. David Stotts and Richard Furuta. "Adding browsing semantics to the hypertext model." In *Proceedings of ACM Conference on Document Processing Systems* (December 5-9, 1988, Santa Fe, New Mexico), pages 43-50, ACM, New York, December 1988. An earlier version of this paper is available as University of Maryland Department of Computer Science and Institute for Advanced Computer Studies Technical Report CS-TR-2046 and UMIACS-TR-88-43.

[Stot89a]   P. David Stotts and Richard Furuta. *Timing Analysis of Synchronous Browsing in Petri-Net-Based Hypertext.* Technical Report CS-TR-2251 and UMIACS-TR-89-53, University of Maryland Department of Computer Science and Institute for Advanced Computer Studies, May 1989.

[Stot89b]   P. David Stotts and Richard Furuta. Petri net based hypertext: Document structure with browsing semantics. *ACM Transactions on Information Systems*, 1989. To appear.

[Stot89c]   P. David Stotts and Richard Furuta. "αTrellis: A system for writing and browsing Petri-net-based hypertext." In *Proceedings of the Tenth International Conference on Application and Theory of Petri Nets*, June 1989. Bonn, W. Germany.

[Shne87] Ben Shneiderman. "User interface design for the Hyperties electronic encyclopedia." In *"Proceedings of Hypertext' 87,"* pages 199-204, November 1987.

[Trig88] Randall H. Trigg. "Guided tours and tabletops: Tools for communicating in a hypertext environment." In *Proceedings of Conference on Computer-Supported Cooperative Work* (September 26-29, 1988, Portland, Oregon), pages 216-226, 1988.

[vanD88] Andries van Dam. "Hypertext '87 keynote address." *Communications of the ACM*, 31(7):887-895, July 1988.

Hypermedia Topologies and User Navigation

H. Van Dyke Parunak

Industrial Technology Institute
PO Box 1485
Ann Arbor, MI 48106
(313) 769-4049, van@iti.org

ABSTRACT

One of the major problems confronting users of large hypermedia systems is that of navigation: knowing where one is, where one wants to go, and how to get there from here. This paper contributes to this problem in three steps. First, it articulates a number of navigational strategies that people use in physical (geographical) navigation. Second, it correlates these with various graph topologies, showing how and why appropriately restricting the connectivity of a hyperbase can improve the ability of users to navigate. Third, it analyzes some common hypermedia navigational mechanisms in terms of navigational strategies and graph topology.

1. PROBLEM DEFINITION

Hypermedia is a set of nodes of information (the "hyperbase") and a mechanism for moving among them. One important criterion for classifying hypermedia is the topology of the links that join different nodes together. The degenerate case is the traditional book, in which the nodes of information are paragraphs, and the topology is simply a linear chain. Much of the power of computer-based hypermedia comes from its ability to manipulate more complex topologies, such as hierarchies, hypercubes, lattices, or even complete graphs.

As the complexity of the topology underlying a hypermedia system increases, users have more ways to move from one information node to another, and thus can potentially find shorter paths to desired information. This very richness quickly leads to the problem of users becoming "lost in hyperspace," reported as early as the ZOG work [Robe81].

2. COMMON NAVIGATIONAL STRATEGIES

Long before the advent of hypermedia, humans developed a number of navigational strategies to find their way around the world. This section articulates five of them, illustrating them from the domain of geographical navigation.

2.1. Identifier

The *Identifier Strategy* associates a unique identifier or description with each entity of interest, thus permitting the searcher to recognize the target. By itself, this strategy degenerates to exhaustive search (although, with the appropriate hardware, this search can be reasonably fast: consider using a helicopter to find a house with a fluorescent orange star painted on the roof). In the form of exhaustive search, it is applicable to any countable set of entities. More commonly, it is a component of other strategies.

2.2. Path

The *Path Strategy* gives the searcher a procedural description of how to get to the target: "Turn left at the first light and right at the second gas station, and it's the blue house [Identifier Strategy] on the right." The Path Strategy is useful in any countable space in which the number of links originating with any one node is typically much less than the total number of nodes. (If this is not the case, the task of finding the next step in a path is not significantly easier than going directly from the start to the target.)

Some topologies define a unique path between any two nodes. (We consider two paths the same if they contain the same links, even if one path traverses some of those links more often than does the other.) Other topologies permit multiple paths. One may conjecture that a small number of alternate routes is easier to use than either a single route or a large number of routes, but this is a matter for experimental investigation and is not pursued here.

2.3. Direction

Travelers apply the *Direction Strategy* when they follow directions such as "Go due north." Like the path strategy and unlike the identifier strategy, the direction strategy avoids exhaustive search. It differs from the path strategy in the framework that the traveler uses for guidance. In the path strategy, this framework is local to an individual node, and is stated in terms of the links originating at that node. In the direction strategy, the framework is global to the entire system, part of the matrix in which the nodes are embedded.

Directional frameworks can vary in their granularity. The coarsest defines one dimension (say, "north" vs. "south"), and cuts the search plane into two pieces. Finer systems include not only the four cardinal points (North, South, East, West), but intermediates (NE, NNE, ENE), and ultimately the full "degrees, minutes, seconds" of modern navigation.

The direction strategy as humans use it in geography depends on two characteristics of the embedding space: texture and comparability. *Texture* is the existence of some field or distinguished point relative to which directions can be established. *Comparability* is the existence of a relation (in this case, the direction relation) between any two points of the space. A sphere would naturally have no texture, but people on earth have used various features of our sphere to define direction: its axis of rotation (reflected in the direction of sunrise and the apparent stability of the pole star); its magnetic field; or the direction of flow of a prominent river (for example, the Nile in ancient Egypt). Comparability exists for geographic directions with the fine granularity of modern systems, but a primitive system that distinguishes only north from south cannot define a direction between two locations at the same latitude, and so lacks comparability. Thus we can distinguish three classes of systems from the perspective of directionality: those with no directionality, those with texture but not comparability, and those with both texture and comparability.

2.4. Distance

The *Distance Strategy* bounds search to a circle around the traveler's current location, which can be expressed in terms either of space or of time: "It's only a mile [ten minutes] from here." It is often used in connection with the direction strategy: "Go south for two kilometers." Like the path strategy, the distance strategy varies between topologies where a unique distance separates two points and those in which different paths provide different distances. Any space that supports the path strategy also supports the distance strategy, since distance can be defined along the path. Unique paths imply unique distance, but we will see an example of a space in which multiple paths exist but distances are still unique. Also like the path strategy, the distance strategy becomes degenerate in spaces in which one can move directly from any one point to any other.

2.5. Address

The *Address Strategy* refines the direction strategy by establishing an orthogonal set of coordinates: "Go to the corner of Huron and Division." For n dimensions with m divisions each, this approach reduces the search space from $O(m^n)$ to $O(m)$, since one can search each dimension independently.

3. MATCHING STRATEGIES WITH TOPOLOGIES

Our survey of navigational strategies has already suggested some restrictions on the kinds of spaces to which each can be applied. In this section, we develop a taxonomy of topologies for hypermedia, and identify the navigational strategies that can be used with each.

3.1. Definitions

The underlying model in which we couch our discussion of hypermedia topologies is graph theory.

For our limited purposes, a hyperbase H is an ordered pair $H = <N,L>$ where N is a finite set of information *nodes* and L is a set of directed *links* between pairs of nodes, defined in turn as ordered pairs $<m,n>$ of elements of N. Intuitively, a user can move directly from one node m to another n just when there is a link $<m,n> \in L$ between them, and the directionality of a link reflects the "normal" direction of traversal, which we assume is accessed differently by the user than the reverse direction. For example, one may be able to traverse a link in reverse only if one has first traversed it in the forward direction. Every hyperbase is thus trivially isomorphic to a finite directed graph $G = <V,U>$, by identifying the nodes N of H with the points V of G, and the links L of H with the arcs U of G.

For two nodes n,m, we write $P(n,m)$ (read "n is a parent of m") iff $<n,m> \in L$, and $A(n_1,n_m)$ ("n_1 is an ancestor of n_m") iff $\exists n_1,n_2,...,n_{m-1},n_m \in N:P(n_1,n_2)\&...\&P(n_{m-1},n_m)$. To these relations there correspond unary set-valued functions $P(m)$ (the set of all the parents of m) and $A(m)$ (the set of all the ancestors of m). We similarly define relations and functions C,D for children and descendants. For any set S, $Card(S)$ is the cardinality of S.

We assume that any hyperbase under discussion is *accessible*, which means $\exists m \in N:\forall n \in N-m:A(m,n)$.

Our definition of N as a set implies that all of its elements are distinguishable, and thus at a minimum the identifier strategy described above is applicable to any hyperbase.

3.2. Linear

The simplest topology is linear, in which each node has at most one child and one parent: $\forall n \in N:(Card(P(n)) \leq 1)\wedge(Card(C(n)) \leq 1)$ (Figure 1). If the inequalities are replaced with equalities, one has the special case of a ring. Otherwise, because of our accessibility assumption, exactly one node has no child and exactly one node has no parent, and the structure is a chain with these two nodes as its ends.

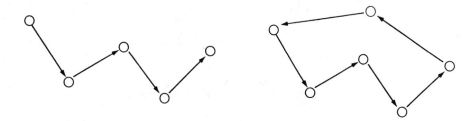

Figure 1: Linear (left) and Ring (right)

The non-ring linear topology supports all of the navigational strategies discussed in the last section, though they are hardly necessary, given the simplicity of the structure. The path strategy differs little from the ubiquitous identifier strategy, since in both cases one simply traverses the linear list of links. Accessibility and the limitation of one child and one parent per node imply that all links are head-to-tail, never head-to-head or tail-to-tail. Thus the structure defines a natural texture for directionality, and exhibits comparability as well. There is a unique distance between any two nodes, defined as the number of links between them, and a unique (though trivial) address for each.

In a ring topology, as in a sphere, there is no natural texture and thus no directionality, though one may be imposed by a distinguished entry point. Paths and thus distances are unique, as in the non-ring case.

3.3. Hierarchy

In a hierarchical topology, one node has no parents and the others have exactly one parent: $(\exists m \in N{:}Card(P(m)) = 0)\&(\forall n \in N{-}m{:}Card(P(n)) = 1)$ (Figure 2). This topology characterizes popular PC-based outline processors such as ThinkTank[TM] or PCOutline[TM].

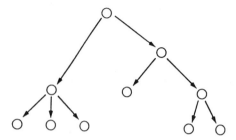

Figure 2: Hierarchy

The orphan element (the root of the hierarchy) is the node at which one enters the hyperbase. All links point away from the root, so any node is reachable from it. Furthermore, since a link once traversed can be followed in the reverse direction, one can go from any node back up (to the root if necessary), and then down to any other node. A unique path exists between any two nodes: from the current node, back up repeatedly to the unique parent of the current node until one reaches a node that is an ancestor of the target node, then along forward links to the target node. The existence of unique paths also implies unique distances between nodes, which are conveniently abstracted in terms of depths in the hierarchy of any two nodes and their nearest common ancestor. If the root is level 0, and two nodes at levels i and j have a nearest ancestor (least upper bound) at level k, then the distance between them is *(i-k)+(j-k)*. Hierarchies exhibit texture (toward or away from the root), but not comparability. The address strategy is not supported, though the unique path from the root to any node serves as a useful identifier of that node.

3.4. Hypercube/Hypertorus

The hypercube/hypertorus topology directly supports the address strategy for navigation, and is useful for domains that invite one to compare a number of items along a number of dimensions. An experimental implementation of this topology, SymEdit, is a useful tool for studying symmetrical patterns in literary documents, where one wishes to trace common themes through a number of different passages. More generally, many problems take the form of comparing a set of cases along a set of characteristics, and the hypercube organization is ideally suited to this task. Informally, the two-dimensional version of a hypercube-based hypertext may be thought of as a spreadsheet for text, in which each node is directly adjacent to four others, one on each side (Figure 3).

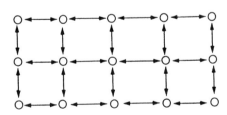
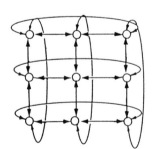

Figure 3: Hypercube (left) and Hypertorus (right)

More formally, define the union of two hyperbases $H_1 \cup H_2$ in the natural way as the hyperbase whose nodes are the union of the nodes of each of the original hyperbases and whose links are the union of the links of the originals. We do not require that the original sets of nodes be disjoint, or that the original sets of links be disjoint. A hyperbase with a m-dimensional hypercube topology is any that can be constructed as follows:

1. Initially, $H = <N, \emptyset>$. Determine m integer factors $F_1, ..., F_m$ such that $\prod_{i=1}^{m} F_i = Card(N)$. (Add dummy nodes to N if necessary to permit this factorization.)

2. For $i = 1$ to m

    a. Partition N into F_i sets $N_{i1}, ..., N_{iF_i}$, each with $Card(N)/F_i$ elements.

    b. For $j = 1$ to F_i

        i. Define a set L_{ij} of $Card(N_{ij})-1$ links among the members of N_{ij} such that $H_{ij} = <N_{ij}, L_{ij}>$ has a linear topology.

        ii. $H \leftarrow H \cup H_{ij}$.

As a result of this construction, each element has a unique address $<a_1 \in [1..F_1], a_2 \in [1..F_2], ..., a_m \in [1..F_m]>$, and the search to reach any node is on the order of $\sum_{i=1}^{m} F_i$ instead of $\prod_{i=1}^{m} F_i$, since each dimension may be searched separately.

Two interesting refinements of this topology are possible.

First, if the H_{ij} are constrained to be rings instead of linear, we construct a hypertorus instead of a hypercube.

Second, our informal picture of a two-dimensional hypercube as a spreadsheet implies that the network is isomorphic to a rectangular lattice (without crossing links). The formal construction does not enforce this constraint, which is not necessary for the address strategy for navigation, and so defines a *tangled* hypercube or hypertorus. The constraint of isomorphism to a rectangular lattice of the appropriate dimensionality can be added for domains in which natural orderings can be imposed on each dimension, yielding an *ordered* hypercube or hypertorus.

In general, a hypercube or hypertorus topology supports (nonunique) paths and distances. If the structure is ordered instead of tangled, paths are still nonunique, but distances (defined with a city block metric) are unique, and if the ordering further constrains all links in any hyperplane of the hypercube to be parallel (rather than opposing), a hypercube exhibits both texture and comparability. Without a distinguished point, a hypertorus (like a sphere) does not support either, even if it is ordered.

3.5. DAG

The constraint $\forall m \in N : A(m) \cap D(m) = \emptyset$ yields a DAG (Directed Acyclic Graph) topology (Figure 4).

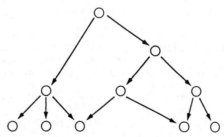

Figure 4: Directed Acyclic Graph

Most implementations have a single point of entry, forming a common ancestor of all nodes and yielding a semilattice. A DAG does not support the address strategy, but it does support nonunique paths and thus nonunique distances, and the absence of cycles together with accessibility defines texture (though not comparability).

3.6. Arbitrary

The least constrainted topology consists of any connected graph. If none of the constraints described above applies, the identifier, path, and distance strategies are the only ones available. Even the path strategy becomes useless as the graph approaches a complete graph, for then the navigational problem involved in selecting the next step along a path approaches the problem of going directly to the target node. So we may distinguish a partial arbitrary topology from a complete arbitrary topology, based on the degree of the nodes.

3.7. Summary

Figure 5 summarizes our conclusions about which topologies support which navigational strategies.

	ID:	Paths: Unique	Mult.	Direction: Text.	Comp.	Distance: Unique	Mult.	Address:
Linear	x	x		x	x	x		x
Ring	x	x				x		x
Hierarchical	x	x		x		x		
Hypercube (Ordered)	x		x	x	x	x		x
Hypercube (Tangled)	x		x				x	x
Hypertorus (Ordered)	x		x			x		x
Hypertorus (Tangled)	x		x				x	x
DAG	x		x	x		x		
Arbitrary (partial)	x		x				x	
Arbitrary (complete)	x							

Figure 5: Topologies and Strategies

4. NAVIGATIONAL AIDS IN HYPERMEDIA

Many navigational aids commonly implemented in hypermedia systems are effectively mechanisms for inducing a topology of reduced complexity on the hyperbase, and thus enlarging the set of navigational strategies that users can bring to bear. The aids that fit this characterization can be grouped into two classes: "beaten path" aids that help users find places they have already been, and typed links. Other aids, such as maps, do not induce a restricted topology, but are only useful under certain conditions that can be topologically characterized.

4.1. "Beaten Path" Mechanisms

"Beaten Path" navigational aids enable a user to return easily to places already visited, and include back-up stacks, path macros, and book marks.

A *back-up stack* keeps track of the nodes through which a user has moved, so that the steps can be retraced, bringing one back to the starting point. It induces a subspace with linear topology on the hyperbase, thus permitting application of the widest range of navigational strategies.

A generalization of the back-up stack is the *path macro*, which remembers a path and permits the user to move back and forth along it repeatedly, in essence building a subspace of more limited topology within which navigation is simpler. It records the most recent path of specified complexity (usually linear or hierarchical). In the case of a hierarchical path macro, when the user visits a node already in the macro along a different path, the older link to the node is removed from the macro and replaced with the newer one.

Book marks permit users to identify particular landmark nodes and jump directly to them from any point of the system. A book mark facility induces a one-level hierarchy whose root is the known entry point (for example, a pop-up window that lists marked locations). A home button that takes the user immediately to the entry point of the hyperbase is a degenerate example of a book mark.

4.2. Typed Links

If links are *classified* by different types, the topology induced by links of any one type may be much simpler than the overall topology of the entire system. For example, consider a one-level dictionary (a hierarchical topology) attached to a hierarchical hyperbase. The overall topology is a DAG, since one can access a single node of the dictionary from many different nodes of the main hyperbase. However, since each system is a hierarchy, and since the user distinguishes between accessing definitions and roaming about the main hyperbase, the distance strategy that ordinarily is not available in a DAG is still defined.

[Ande65] argues persuasively that while hierarchies are appealing because of their cognitive tractability, they do not capture the complexity of the real world. A parade example is the classification of four objects: a watermelon, an orange, a baseball, and a football. Different classificational structures emerge depending on whether we start with shape or origin (natural vs. artificial). In this case and many others, the world does not lend itself to hierarchical structuring, but people tend to think about it in terms of hierarchies anyway, even if they must be multiple hierarchies that are structurally inconsistent with one another.

The insight for hypermedia is that a hyperbase structured as a set of distinguishable hierarchies will offer navigational and other cognitive benefits that an equally complex system of undifferentiated links does not, even if the union of all the hierarchies is not itself hierarchical. The different classes of aggregation defined by [Garg88] are in effect classes of predefined hierarchies in a hyperbase.

The notion of combining simpler well-defined topologies to control the complexity of the larger system is anticipated in the context of menu systems in [Brow82].

4.3. Maps

A common feature of many hypermedia implementations is the use of maps, or graphical displays of nodes (often showing their titles, but with their contents hidden) and the links among them. An architype is the NoteCards Browser [Hala88]. [Conk87], among others, notes the difficulty of using maps productively for large systems, but the problem is not just one of size. Useful maps can be defined for extremely large systems of appropriately constrained topology. For example, NoteCards and Neptune support maps of subnetworks restricted by link attributes. The analogy of geographical systems suggests that either non-trivial paths and distances (as on an automobile touring map) or a fine-grained directional system (as on a marine navigational chart) permits a reasonable map, at least for portions of the system. The tangled web exhibited by Conklin has some nodes of very high degree, leading to locally degenerate paths and distances. It would be interesting to determine experimentally how navigational success varies as a function of the ratio $Card(N)/Card(L)$ for hyperbases of arbitrary topology.

5. CONCLUSION

The problem of navigation in hyperspace can be addressed by considering the navigational strategies that people apply in the physical world. The availability of these strategies in a hyperbase depends on the topology of the hyperbase. We have articulated a number of strategies, defined several topologies, identified the match between these two sets, and suggested how some common navigational aids can be understood in terms of a topological model.

REFERENCES

[Ande65]   Anderson, C., "A City is Not A Tree." *Architectural Forum* 122, 58ff.

[Brow87] Brown, J.W., "Controlling the Complexity of Menu Networks." *CACM* 25:7 (July), 412-418.

[Conk87] Conklin, J., "Hypertext: An Introduction and Survey." *IEEE Computer* 20:9 (September), 17-41.

[Garg88] Garg, P.K., "Abstraction Mechanisms in Hypertext." *CACM* 31:7 (July), 862-870.

[Hala88] Halasz, F.G., "Reflections on NoteCards: Seven Issues for the Next Generation of Hypermedia Systems." *CACM* 31:7 (July), 836-852.

[Robe81] Robertson,G., D.McCracken, and A.Newell, "The ZOG Approach to man-machine communications." *International Journal of Man-Machine Studies* 14, 461-488.

Design Issues for Multi-Document Hypertexts

Robert J. Glushko

Search Technology, Inc.
4725 Peachtree Corners Circle, Suite 200
Norcross, GA 30092

INTRODUCTION

Vannevar Bush conceived of hypertext as the "computer glue" that binds information from a wide variety of books, documents, communications, and other artifacts to enhance its accessibility and usefulness. However, most of the recent hyper-activity in research labs and in the marketplace falls short of Bush's vision. Most hypertext software is oriented toward hypertext as a new form of writing via incremental combination of bits and pieces of information. These hypertext programs typically provide little support for converting existing information from its more linear printed form. Where hypertexts have been created from existing text, they generally have been converted from a single encyclopedia ([Glus88], [Oren87]), a single reference document ([Fris88], [Perl88], [Raym88]), or a single system's documentation ([Egan89], [Walk88a]). Hypertexts that integrate the complete contents of more than one book or large document seem nonexistent, even though the expected benefits from such multi-document hypertexts were the original motivation for the concept.

In this paper I describe the design issues that have arisen in a project at Search Technology to build a multi-document hypertext whose major components are a 3000-page engineering encyclopedia and a 388-page standards manual:

* **Document selection** – Which documents should be included?

* **Extent of integration** – How tightly linked should the documents be?

* **Locus of integration** – Where in the documents should the links be?

* **Type of integration** – What kinds of links should there be within and between the documents?

DOCUMENT SELECTION

Selecting documents to incorporate in a hypertext is not a simple problem. The goal should not be to build a hypertext encyclopedia, a hypertext reference manual, or a hypertext version of system documentation. Instead, the goal should be to enhance the performance or enjoyment of people performing their jobs, using hypertext when it is appropriate to improve the access to and the usefulness of information. This view implies that the choice of documents to include in a hypertext should be dictated by a user and task analysis. Only when the intended users must combine information from more than one document to meet the information needs of the tasks they carry out is a multi-document hypertext called for.

For example, I use both a printed phone book and a printed software manual on my desk, and each would be more useful if I could browse and search them in hypertext form on my computer. Nevertheless, I need to strain to imagine a task for which I need hypertext connections between an electronic phone book and an electronic software manual. These documents seem too dissimilar in content, format, and intended purpose to justify or benefit from hypertext connections to each other.

So when should two documents be integrated in a multi-document hypertext? The motivation for combining more than one document in a hypertext is the conviction that each document adds value to the others, that the whole is greater than the sum of the parts. If two documents were written with the same purpose for the same audience with the same content, a user would only need one of them. Only when the documents differ in some significant way can they complement each other. However, to the extent that the documents differ, it must be true that from the perspective of the user of one document, at least some of the information in the other document is irrelevant some or all of the time. A final implication is that complementarity is not necessarily symmetric. A document can enhance the value of another without its use being enhanced in return.

After the task and user analysis has identified a document to include, it can be important to make similar (though certainly less thorough) evaluations about whether to include any of the documents that it cites. How well each cited document complements those already included is again the major consideration.

Case Study

These document selection issues can be explained more concretely using our current project as a case study. Our goal is to make it easy for designers to find and apply the information they need to build systems that are more consistent with the capabilities and limitations of the humans who operate those systems. Our initial project ([Glus88], [Glus89]) was to design an electronic version of the *Engineering Data Compendium* [Boff88], a 3000-page multi-volume engineering encyclopedia whose 1138 entries contain comprehensive information about human perception and performance. The *Compendium's* intended users are designers of systems with complex user interfaces who need detailed information about human perception and performance to make design tradeoffs but who typically have education and experience in another technical specialty [Linc88]. The *Compendium* entries are arranged in twelve major topic areas that roughly reflect a scientific taxonomy of human perception and performance; topic areas include vision, audition, other senses, perceptual organization, attention, and so on. In printed form, the *Compendium* is organized in three volumes that contain the entries and a fourth volume that contains a user's guide, index, glossary, and other aids for finding relevant entries.

The *Compendium* emphasizes the basic parametric data of human perception and performance, tabular summaries of data from research studies, predictive models, and perceptual and performance principles. For example, the *Compendium* takes 25 pages to relate the parametric details and predictive models for various phenomena of visual flicker. In contrast, the *Compendium* contains little explicit advice on the appropriate application of these basic data on visual flicker when designing visual displays. As a result, we sought documents that would complement the *Compendium's* comprehensive data with design guidelines in the context of specific applications.

Bill Cody [Cody89], Dan Sewell and others of us at Search Technology have been studying how designers identify, locate, and use information about human perception and performance to make design tradeoffs and meet system requirements. Among the documents used by designers is a 388-page military standard for human engineering design whose official title is *MIL-STD-1472-D, Human Engineering Design Criteria for Military Systems, Equipment, and Facilities* [DoD89]. *1472-D* is organized according to an equipment-oriented or task-oriented taxonomy, with sections for visual displays, audio displays, controls, control/display integration, anthropometry, and so on.

We chose to incorporate *1472-D* in our multi-document hypertext after in-depth analysis of several candidate documents and interviews with the users, editors, and authors of the *Compendium* and *1472-D* to determine the extent and nature of their overlap. *1472-D* is broader in coverage than the *Compendium*, contains more qualitative guidance on human engineering, and gives prominence to rules of thumb and expert opinion. *1472-D's* intended users are specification writers, designers looking for constraints or ideas for a particular design problem, or testers who use it as an evaluation checklist to verify compliance with the original specification. Taken together, this means that *1472-D* complements the *Compendium* more than vice versa. A designer may make more sense of quantitative information on perception and performance because of the context provided by *1472-D's* application guidelines, yet a user contractually required to follow *1472-D's* guidelines may not be interested in the *Compendium's* detailed scientific rationale for them.

1472-D poses a challenge for us with respect to the documents that it cites that we call the **tiering** problem. In the jargon of standards, the first **tier** is defined as the set of documents referred to by a given standards document. The second tier includes the set of documents cited by documents in the first tier, and so on. Standards documents are carefully modularized into many narrow documents to make them easier to maintain, but one standard may cite other standards and in effect treat them as if they were bundled into a single standard. That is, the first tier of references from the standard to other standards is often considered to be binding.

1472-D is explicit in its tiering requirement and lists 43 other standards documents that "form a part of this document to the extent specified herein (p. 3)." Therefore, if we choose not to include the cited sections of these standards in our multi-document hypertext, our system will be significantly less helpful for someone whose primary task involves using *1472-D*. At the same time, however, not including these documents cited by *1472-D* will have negligible impact on someone whose primary task in the multi-document hypertext involves using the *Compendium*.

The way in which documents complement each other in support of the intended users for their primary tasks should be the most important issue in selecting documents for multi-document hypertexts. But we did not discount more pragmatic considerations in choosing *1472-D*. The availability of computer-readable source files, the cooperation of its author, and its lack of copyright as a government document all contributed to our decision to use it.

EXTENT OF INTEGRATION: HOW TIGHTLY LINKED ARE THE DOCUMENTS?

While to some it may strain the definition of hypertext, it is obvious that a user may benefit from a multi-document hypertext in which each document contains links within it but no links to any other document; this is the situation I mentioned earlier with my hypothetical electronic phone book and software manual. Indeed, few or no links between documents may be a desirable goal of effective modular design in which document units are self-contained with minimal relationships to other units [Walk88b]. From a user's perspective at the user interface, it is easy to understand the extreme cases of zero integration and total integration.

Zero integration of two hypertext documents means that they appear totally separated and unrelated. The user selects a document to work with, but once this choice is made, no trace of the second document is ever seen as the user moves among different parts of the first document. Neither the entry points (like a Table of Contents or Index) nor the text units of the first document refer to parts of the second document. If the user conducts a search, the candidate list contains units from only one document. Once selected, a candidate text unit may contain cross-references to other parts of the same document, but not to the second document.

Total integration. At the other extreme, if two documents are totally integrated, the user has no separate view of each document. Instead, the user sees a collection of interconnected text units in which the idea of "belonging" to separate documents is not apparent. The user specifies some starting point in the text and sees no contextual boundaries that separate one document from another as different text units are viewed by traversing links between them. The starting point might be determined explicitly when the user starts to browse at some specified location (e.g., the "Home" card in *HyperCard*) or implicitly (e.g., by a query that generates a set of candidate text units), but in neither case is there a view that explicitly reflects the structure of separate documents. This extreme is the "seamless integration" of multiple documents expressed in visionary claims for hypertext like those of Ted Nelson's *Xanadu* system [Nels80].

There is a basic tradeoff here between the need for integration at entry points and the need for integration at the unit level. The more structure provided by the entry points, the more precisely the relevant text units can be located. For example, a Table of Contents that lists chapter headings and sub-headings will require the user to browse less within a chapter than one that lists only chapter titles. In contrast, a hypertext that contains an unstructured and coarse-grained entry point (like a "Home" card) will necessarily require complex links among units if readers are to find relevant information.

In between the extremes of zero integration and total integration is a wide range of choices about the extent of integration of multiple documents that appears in the hypertext user interface. Again, it is useful to begin by contrasting the clear endpoint cases before considering intermediate ones.

LOCUS OF INTEGRATION: WHERE ARE THE LINKS?

Integration solely in text units

Multiple documents have always been partly integrated solely by explicit interconnections of their component text units, with their entry points remaining totally separate. That is, documents may each have their own Table of Contents, but their component text units may contain cross-references to other documents. This is the model of integration of multiple documents used in most hypertext systems.

Integration solely in entry points

Multiple documents can be partly integrated solely by combining the entry points from which users generate a set of candidate text units for more detailed viewing. Conceptually, this is analogous to traditional bibliometric retrieval systems like *Dialog* or *Lexis,* in which different documents (or abstracts) are indexed together. A user query results in a list of candidates that satisfy the query. **The candidate text units are not themselves integrated in any way.**

A more sophisticated and user-oriented approach to integrating multiple documents solely by integrating their entry points would merge their Tables of Contents or the "back of the book" Indexes. It might be desirable to use the Table of Contents of the document with the broadest coverage as the "skeleton" into which the other documents are merged. A combined Table or Contents or Index might look like this:

```
1.0 Main topic A
        document 1, section 1.2
        document 2, section 2.4
 1.1 Topic B
        document 1, section 1.2.1
        document 3, sections 6.5-6.9
 1.2 Topic C
        document 1, section 1.2.2
        document 2, section 2.4.2
        1.2.1 Subtopic D
                document 1, section 1.2.2.1
                document 6, section 4
2.0 Main topic E
        document 4, section 3
        document 5, section 5.2.1
3.0 Main topic F
        ...
```

In this example, the multiple documents are integrated to the extent that any candidate list a user obtains from the merged entry points contains text units from more than one document. But as with bibliographic retrieval systems, none of the candidate units contains any explicit cross-references or links to other units.

Integration both in entry points and in text units

Now it should be easy to envision hybrid forms of multiple document integration in which the user interface combines documents both at their entry points and in their text units. This is the approach we have chosen in our combination of the *Compendium* and *1472-D* in a multi-document hypertext. At the entry points, we will augment the existing Tables of Contents and Indexes with several additional taxonomies that span the topics contained in the two books. These are being developed by Janet Lincoln, one of the editors of the *Compendium*. We are also developing a framework for deciding which links to create within and between the two documents that is described later in this paper.

HOW MUCH INTEGRATION OF MULTIPLE DOCUMENTS IS DESIRABLE?

Our own experience and that of other hypertext designers has shown that usability is enhanced by use of the explicit structure of documents, so we reject the *Xanadu* hypertext model in which multiple documents are integrated to the extent that their separate structures disappear. The task and document analysis we conducted to design the hypertext version of the *Compendium* led us to exploit the explicit structure of the *Compendium* in various hierarchical browsers for the Table of Contents, Index, and other access points, and to emphasize these structured entry points over context-free Boolean search techniques ([Glus88], [Glus89]). Similarly, our evaluation of other compact disc encyclopedias showed us convincingly that failing to use the explicit structure of documents and relying solely on full-text search can make it extremely difficult to find information in them.

The limited experimental literature on hypertext suggests that excessive integration through large numbers of links creates unusable "spaghetti documents" [Foss88]. Excessive linking causes serious problems of disorientation and cognitive overload for the user because it destroys most of the structural and contextual cues [Conk87]. Several researchers are working on new representations of hypertext link structures that may help to solve these problems ([Conk88], [Fein88], [Furn86]), but limiting the links in the first place seems like a more practical solution.

Our design team has chosen a moderate degree of multi-document integration in which users can readily see that documents maintain their separate identity but are enhanced by cross-references to information in other documents. The user selects one document as the primary focus of browsing or searching, but related information in other documents can be retrieved. The key difference is that choosing to view cross-referenced information from another document does not automatically switch the user's context to the second document.

Instead, in this middle range of integration the user has some control over the extent of contextual preservation or integration across different documents. Tom Coonan has been designing several alternative user interfaces that support this intermediate level of integration. The user can choose to display cross-referenced documents without changing context -- perhaps to view it in a pop-up window that temporarily overlays the current document. If the user chooses to change to the second document, he or she would then be prompted to decide how much of the current context should be carried along. For example, the "bookmarks" for the parts of the first document that the user has already viewed might be left behind or merged with the bookmarks for the second one.

I have presented the extreme positions on integration in this paper to make an intermediate approach seem reasonable at face value. However, the fact remains that the design question of **How tightly linked should the documents be?** is a legitimate research issue that has not yet been confronted seriously. Raymond and Tompa's [Raym88] innovative and thorough description of the cross-reference structure of the *Oxford English Dictionary* provides some foundations, however.

A FRAMEWORK FOR LINKING IN MULTI-DOCUMENT HYPERTEXTS

Much of the research in hypertext concerns the number and type of links among the units ([Conk87], [Hala88]), and we agree that link typing will enable great flexibility and power in hypertext representation. But from a practical standpoint, we have found it necessary to work at a coarser level of analysis and start with more basic questions about the kinds of links to create. First, we contrast **intra-document** links with **inter-document** links. Next, we contrast **explicit** links with **implicit** ones. Taken together, these two dimensions characterize four broad classes of links that I will now discuss in the order that we think they should be considered in the design of multi-document hypertexts.

Explicit intra-document links

Links of this class explicitly connect two parts of the same document, and include footnotes, "See also" cross-references, and pointers to figures, illustrations, or other non-textual components. These links are the easiest to identify when converting existing texts to hypertexts and they are probably the most usable and useful as well. Since good writers use these structural and rhetorical devices in predictable ways, it follows that a reader of the hypertext will find them predictable as well. People who have never heard the word "hypertext" know what footnotes are for and have reliable expectations about the likely number, length, relevance, and value of footnotes[1]. As a result, when printed documents are converted to electronic ones it is essential to exploit this sort of knowledge by capturing the explicit intra-document links first[2].

Implicit intra-document links

These links are those that are part of the logical structure of the document but which may be impossible to make explicit in the printed form because of limitations in the medium, the nature of the writing and production process, or publishing conventions. For example, every explicit "See also" link in a printed document implies a "Cited by" link in the opposite direction. Likewise, the first appearance of a Glossary item in the text can readily be linked to its definition in the "back of the book" Glossary in electronic form. We think that links of this type pose little risk of disorientation or cognitive overload because they follow naturally from the printed version of the document, so we consider them nearly as important as the explicit intra-document links.

Explicit inter-document links

Like the explicit links within a document, these links are easy to identify because they follow presentation conventions in the printed document and are often collected in reference or bibliography sections. Yet we think that they pose more challenges for the hypertext designer and reader than intra-document links, because it is much harder to predict the extent or usefulness of the information at the end of the link. An author may cite another document for many different reasons and the cited documents may add little value. To link or not to link hinges on the issue of complementarity that I discussed under the topic of document selection.

Implicit inter-document links

These are the links that might be closest to the vision of hypertext, namely links that are not explicit between related documents but that can be extracted by careful and creative analysis of the two texts and the relationship between them. But as George Landow

---

[1] Expectations about footnoting conventions may vary significantly for different readers and different kinds of documents. Practicing lawyers depend on the fact that law review articles typically contain hundreds of detailed footnotes to all the relevant cases, and are not surprised if the footnotes comprise 50% or more of the total text. Other disciplines might reject this footnoting style as excessively pedantic.

[2] We warn, however, against slavish mechanical translation of footnotes into hypertext links, because footnote structure and semantics can be complex. For example, a document may contain footnotes to other footnotes (or even to the footnotes of another document), or may use footnotes as an indirect addressing technique to refer to a section of text (so that cross-references can be specified prior to page layout). We doubt that the design and implementation contortions required to preserve exactly this granularity and complexity of hypertext structure are worth it. See footnote 1.

[Land87] noted, there is no consistent "rhetoric of hypertext" that makes it easy for a reader to understand what such links mean and what is likely to appear at the link destination. Doland [Dola89] has cautioned that creating links is an ideological act that may limit "interpretive diversity."

When we first began working in hypertext several years ago, we expected that it would soon be possible to extract these implicit links automatically with natural language processing or clever indexing techniques (see [Fox88]), but we have been disappointed so far and we are starting to conclude that implicit intra-document links are best identified by the hypertext reader. Mark Weaver came up with an analogy to used textbooks that helps to explain why. Weaver noted that if we created links based on our understanding of the document, some of the links won't fit with the understanding and context brought to the hypertext by another reader. Like a used textbook, some of the highlighting and margin notes may be useful to another student, but may be distracting or misleading at other times. We have decided in our current project to provide functions that make it easy for readers to create private links and notes rather than try to create many of them ourselves.

SUMMARY

Hypertexts that combine the complete contents of more than one book or large document come closer to the spirit of hypertext than hypertexts that are created from a single source or created incrementally from document bits and pieces. In designing such a multi-document hypertext, our team has identified several key design issues and devised analyses and practical rules of thumb for resolving them:

* Select documents to include based on a user and task analysis. The extent to which the documents complement each other for the intended users and tasks will determine the extent to which it makes sense to combine them with hypertext links.

* Exploit the user's experience with the printed document by appropriately transforming the Table of Contents, Index, and other entry points into electronic equivalents.

* Devise composite entry points like hybrid tables of contents or new taxonomies to provide an understandable perspective that spans the set of documents.

* Emphasize the links within each document before trying to support the explicit and implicit links between documents.

Our experience in this and previous projects confirms to us the attractiveness of the hypertext vision in enhancing the accessibility and usefulness of information, but also emphasizes the need for a disciplined approach to "hypertext engineering" [Glus88] that rests on task analysis, document analysis, and careful consideration of lessons from the technical writing and information retrieval disciplines.

ACKNOWLEDGMENTS

This work was primarily supported by the Designer's Associate project funded by the Air Force's Armstrong Aerospace Medical Research Laboratory at Wright-Patterson AFB, Ohio under contract AF #F33615-86-C-0542. Dr. Kenneth R. Boff is the program sponsor. My colleagues at Search Technology, especially Bill Cody, Tom Coonan, Dan Sewell, Mark Weaver, and Brad Wiederholt helped shape the ideas in this paper. Jonathan Grudin, Janet Lincoln, Gary Perlman, Pamela Samuelson, and Jan Walker also made important contributions.

REFERENCES

[Boff88]   Boff, K. R., and Lincoln, J. E. *Engineering Data Compendium: Human Perception and Performance.* AAMRL, Wright-Patterson AFB, OH., 1988.

[Cody88]   Cody, W. Designers as users: Design supports based on crew system design practices. *Proceedings of the 45th Annual Forum of the American Helicopter Society*, Boston, MA., 1989.

[Conk87]   Conklin, J. Hypertext: An introduction and survey. *Computer*, 20(9), 17-41. September 1987.

[Conk88]   Conklin, J., and Begeman, M. gBIS: A hypertext tool for exploratory policy discussion. *CSCW ' 88: Proceedings of the Conference on Computer-Supported Cooperative Work*, 140-152, 1988.

[DoD89]   Department of Defense. *MIL-STD-1472-D, Human Engineering Design Criteria for Military Systems, Equipment, and Facilities.* Washington, D.C., 1989.

[Dola89]   Doland, V. Hypermedia as an interpretive act. *Hypermedia*, 1(1), 6-19, Spring 1989.

[Egan89]   Egan, D., Remde, J., Landauer, T., Lochbaum, C., and Gomez, L. Behavioral evaluation and analysis of a hypertext browser. *Human factors in computing systems. CHI '89 Conference Proceedings*, ACM: New York, 205-210, 1989.

[Fein88]   Feiner, S. Seeing the forest for the trees: Hierarchical display of hypertext structure. *Proceedings of the ACM Conference on Office Information Systems*, 205-212, 1988.

[Foss88]   Foss, C. Effective browsing in hypertext systems. *User-oriented content-based text and image handling. Proceedings of the RIAO Conference*, March 21-24 1988, 83-98.

[Fox88]   Fox, E., Weaver, M., Chen, Q., and France, R. Implementing a distributed expert-based information retrieval system. *User-oriented content-based text and image handling. Proceedings of the RIAO Conference*, March 21-24 1988, 708-726.

[Fris88]   Frisse, M. Searching for information in a hypertext medical handbook. *Communications of the ACM*, 31(7), 880-886, July 1988.

[Furn86]   Furnas, G. Generalized fisheye views. *Human Factors in Computing Systems.* ACM: New York, 16-23, 1986.

[Glus88]   Glushko, R. J., Weaver, M. D., Coonan, T. A., and Lincoln, J. E. "Hypertext Engineering": Practical methods for creating a compact disc encyclopedia. *Proceedings of the ACM Conference on Document Processing Systems*, 11-20, 1988.

[Glus89]   Glushko, R. J. Transforming text into hypertext for a compact disc encyclopedia. *Human factors in computing systems. CHI '89 Conference Proceedings*, ACM: New York, 293-298, 1989.

[Hala88] Halasz, F. Reflections on NoteCards: Seven issues for the next generation of hypermedia systems. *Communications of the ACM*, 31(7), 836-852, July 1988.

[Land87] Landow, G. Relationally encoded links and the rhetoric of hypertext. *Hypertext '87 Papers*. Proceedings of a conference held at the University of North Carolina, Chapel Hill. November 13-15, 1987, 331-343.

[Linc88] Lincoln, J., and Boff, K. Making behavioral data useful for system design applications: Development of the *Engineering Data Compendium. Proceedings of the Human Factors Society 32nd Annual Meeting*, 1988.

[Nels80] Nelson, T. Replacing the printed word: A complete literary system. *Proceedings of IFIP Congress 1980*, North-Holland, 1013-1023, 1980.

[Oren87] Oren, T. The architecture of static hypertexts. *Hypertext '87 Papers*. Proceedings of a conference held at the University of North Carolina, Chapel Hill. November 13-15, 1987, 291-306.

[Perl88] Perlman, G., and Moorhead, A. Applying hypertext methods for effective utilization of standards. *Proceedings of COMPSTAN'88 Conference on Computer Standards*, IEEE, 55-59, 1988.

[Raym88] Raymond, D., and Tompa, F. Hypertext and the new Oxford English Dictionary. *Communications of the ACM*, 31(7), 871-879, July 1988.

[Walk88a] Walker, J. Supporting document development with *Concordia. IEEE Computer*, 21(1), 48-59, January 1988.

[Walk88b] Walker, J. The role of modularity in document authoring systems. *Proceedings of the ACM Conference on Document Processing Systems*, 117-124, 1988.

Asynchronous Design/Evaluation Methods for Hypertext Technology Development

Gary Perlman

Department of Computer and Information Science
The Ohio State University
2036 Neil Avenue
Columbus, OH 43210-1277
perlman@cis.ohio-state.edu

ABSTRACT

A process model used in the design and evaluation of hypertext systems is discussed. The model includes asynchronous processes of task analysis, document analysis, literature survey and systems evaluation, interpretation of data, designing and building systems, and collecting data. For each process, experiences with NaviText™ SAM, a hypertext interface to a reference source, are discussed. A variety of new methods for evaluation of experimental systems are presented along with several empirical results.

INTRODUCTION

The development of new hypertext systems is a candidate for some of the development techniques that have been successful in other dynamic fields. The iterative design and evaluation prototyping lifecycle used in user interface development and the experimental programming strategy used in artificial intelligence provide us with paradigms for exploring new possibilities for the online delivery of information. Figure 1 shows a data flow diagram of a process model of an asynchronous design and evaluation method I have used for developing systems, most recently hypertext systems. In this paper, I will illustrate this model of system development, discussing the model both in terms of my own work on the NaviText™ family of hypertext browsers ([Perl87], [Perl88], [Perl89b]), and in terms of other research. For each process in the model, there are issues in the methodology of developing a new technology that will also be addressed.

This document is based on a data flow diagram (see the primer below) that has been flattened out for presentation. The original document was built in the "Software Through Pictures" system [IDE86]. The numbered sections in this document are keyed to the activity numbers in the diagram. Being asynchronous, the actual order of activities may not match the order of the activity numbers.

This document will begin with a description of a data flow model of hypertext systems development research, including the processes and data (knowledge) stores. Then, experiences and results with NaviText™ SAM will be discussed in terms of the processes involved in its development. Ideally, the descriptions of the data flow elements would be popup notes, accessible during reading, but instead, some background on the data flow model must be covered. On a first reading, the rest of the introduction can be skimmed.

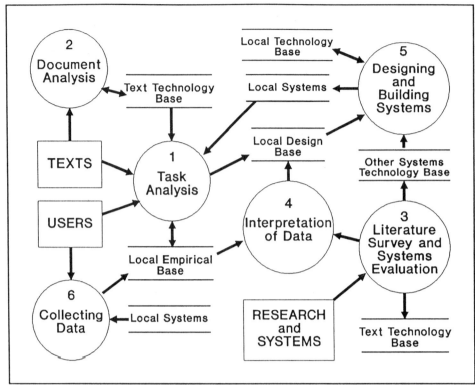

Figure 1. Data Flow Diagram of an Asynchronous Design/Evaluation Hypermedia System Development Process.

A Primer on Data Flow Diagrams

Data flow diagrams are used to model the flow and transformation of data in data processing systems. In data flow diagrams, boxes, bubbles, arcs, and bars are arranged graphically to model how a system works. <u>External entities</u> (shown as boxes) are sources or destinations of information, but are not modeled inside the system. <u>Processes</u> (shown as circles and often called bubbles) operate on data by transforming it or simply by routing it. <u>Data flows</u> (shown as arrows) represent data flowing through the system. <u>Data stores</u> (shown as bars) represent data structures or databases used in and controlled by the system. Data stores may appear more than once in the same diagram to simplify the flows and make the diagram easier to understand. All objects in data flow diagrams can be labeled with a name and sometimes a number. All objects (except externals) in data flow diagrams can be decomposed into sub-parts; processes can be decomposed into sub-diagrams, and stores and flows can be decomposed into component structure definitions. While data stores represent data structures at rest, data flows represent data structures in motion, to or from a process. Data flow diagrams do not represent flow of *control* through a system; any or all processes may be active at the same time, and the order of process activation is sometimes unpredictable. To *read* a data flow diagram, one focuses on the processes, one at a time, to understand their inputs and how they produce their outputs.

A Data Flow Model of Systems Development Research

Each of the processes, flows, and stores in Figure 1 represent an activity or result of hypertext research. The structure of the diagram is a reusable organizer for experimental hypertext development. Because of the iterative nature of system design, the flow of information in this system is non-linear, so Figure 1 will require a detailed explanation. First, the purpose, inputs, and outputs of processes will be described. Then, all the stores used by these processes will be described (in alphabetical order). After this introduction, a second pass through the processes will show how the model can help organize the asynchronous design evaluation process, as applied to NaviText™ systems. In the discussion, the following special fonts will be used to refer to *processes*, and data stores.

Process 1. *Task Analysis*.

PURPOSE: *Task Analysis* is used to determine the information processing needs of users. These needs depend on (1) the type of user, (2) the tasks being performed by the user, and to some degree, (3) the technology available to the user. Since the user changes over time, by gaining knowledge or becoming fatigued, another important factor is (4) time.

INPUT: The inputs to *task analysis* come from interaction with users and knowledge of their tasks, from the **Local Empirical Base** (e.g., usage data), from experiences with locally developed systems (**Local Systems**), and from task-specific analysis of documents (**Text Technology Base**).

OUTPUT: The outputs from task analysis can go into a **Local Empirical Base** or directly into a **Local Design Base**.

Process 2. *Document Analysis*.

PURPOSE: *Document analysis* is used to determine the information content, structure, and format of a (potential) hypertext. The importance of the analysis of logical vs. physical structure, identifying "natural" units of information, and the linking of this information has been discussed in detail in [Glus88] and [Glus89].

INPUT: The inputs to *document analysis* can be an analysis of particular texts, or a summary of understood text technology from a **Text Technology Base** (e.g., the uses of multiple hierarchical organizations or ways of representing multiple versions).

OUTPUT: The output of *document analysis* is an increased understanding of the structure of documents, stored in the **Text Technology Base**.

Process 3. *Literature Survey and Systems Evaluation*.

PURPOSE: *Literature survey and systems evaluation* builds on the lessons learned by other researchers. The article by [Conk87] not only surveyed many research and commercial hypertext systems, but also compared these systems along many dimensions. Such dimensions can be used to help organize the structure of design support bases.

INPUT: The inputs to *literature survey and systems evaluation* are (1) published research results and (2) local evaluations of existing systems.

OUTPUT: The outputs of *literature survey and systems evaluation* add to the **Text Technology Base** and to the knowledge of other systems (**Other Systems Technology Base**). Empirical results and experiences from external research and systems must also be considered by an evaluative process (*Interpretation of Data*).

Process 4. _Interpretation of Data._

PURPOSE: _Interpretation of data_ is used to filter data and experience from external and internal sources, with the goal of improving the quality of design knowledge. Classical issues of the evaluation of empirical research (measurement, sampling, data analysis and inference) all come into play.

INPUT: The inputs to _interpretation of data_ are the results of studies, either from research reports found from a _literature survey and systems evaluation_ or from internal studies in the **Local Empirical Base.** These include the results of controlled experiments, studies of usage, and reported phenomena. Particularly compelling for the iterative development of hypertext systems are _critical incidences_ of (usually problematic) usage, often gleaned from video protocols.

OUTPUT: The outputs from _interpretation of data_ go into a **Local Design Base,** a store of knowledge (design principles, guidelines, and rules) about how systems should be built.

Process 5. _Designing and Building Systems._

PURPOSE: _Designing and building systems_ generates artifacts that can serve a useful purpose and also be used to collect data to improve knowledge of hypertext systems technology. Each such artifact represents a _proof of concept_ of the design concepts in the **Local Design Base** and of the implementation tools and techniques in the **Local Technology Base.**

INPUT: The inputs to _designing and building systems_ include the **Local Design Base,** the tools and techniques for building systems from the **Local Technology Base,** and information from the **Other Systems Technology Base.**

OUTPUT: The outputs from _designing and building systems_ include working **Local Systems,** and new or updated tools and techniques for building systems (i.e., an improved **Local Technology Base**).

Process 6. _Collecting Data._

PURPOSE: _Collecting data_ is used to add to the **Local Empirical Base.** It involves the evaluation of **Local Systems,** either to improve those systems or to ultimately add to the **Local Design Base.**

INPUT: The inputs to _collecting data_ include input from users (e.g., via interviews or surveys), or from data collected from use of **Local Systems.**

OUTPUT: The outputs from _collecting data_ are stored in a **Local Empirical Base** from which _interpretation of data_ is possible.

Local Design Base. The Local Design Base contains the accumulated knowledge of how to design new systems by defining what functionality is needed (high-level) and how it is to be presented (lower-level). Typically, the Local Design Base is private to an organization, except that reports about design principles are may be published, some good examples of which are [Aksc88] and [Hala88]. [Smit86] provides a format for encapsulating user interface design ideas in a regular format. Such formats promote the effective use of design information. As an example of design information, in many systems, an important high-level design concept is the _bookmark_, which is used to keep track of interesting chunks of information (see

[Walk88]). In specific systems, bookmarks may be implemented in different ways. For example, in NaviText™ SAM, chunks of information can be marked by the user with numerical ratings or automatically marked by the system to indicate if a chunk has been seen before or gathered into a working set. As another example, SuperBook [Egan89] labels super-ordinate chunks with the number of subordinate chunks matching the most recent search key.

Local Empirical Base. The Local Empirical Base contains data collected from users during *task analysis* and about Local Systems while *collecting data*: results of surveys, usage logs, critical incidences of problems, etc. are included.

Local Systems. Local Systems are experimental, demonstration, or production quality systems developed or available locally. Each hypertext research site typically has one or more systems to which they apply ideas from their **Local Design Base** and their **Local Technology Base** and from which they can gather data for their **Local Empirical Base**.

Local Technology Base. The Local Technology Base contains the tools and techniques for the development of Local Systems. The tools typically include proprietary software libraries and the techniques include local software engineering practices. Modifiable source code is needed for a flexible research platform. The Local Technology Base may contain concepts from the Local Design Base that are implemented in software; this can make it difficult to see design decisions and how they were made, but simplifies development.

Other Systems Technology Base. The Other Systems Technology Base contains tools and techniques used in the development of non-Local Systems. Typically, the technology used in other systems must be inferred from published reports describing rationales for design or from careful examination of object code. For example, the NeXT (pre-release version 0.8) indexing software libraries, used in their hypertext help and reference library systems, are documented at the level of function prototypes, but some details (e.g., the list of built-in stopwords) can only be found in the object code of the library.

Text Technology Base. The Text Technology Base, contains knowledge of the structure of documents and how to represent them in an online form.

Application of the Process Model

The process model of asynchronous design and evaluation in Figure 1 has been used in the development of NaviText™ SAM ([Perl87], [Perl88], [Perl89b]) and in the development of the next generation based on experiences with NaviText™ SAM. The process model provides a framework in which the results of experimental systems development can be better understood. To illustrate this, the following sections will describe results (both hard data and informal observations) found with NaviText™ SAM and during the development of a more general NaviText™ system.

1. TASK ANALYSIS

Task demands vary widely, so it should not be surprising that a variety of hypertext models are needed to support a variety of tasks, just as a variety of database models are used to support various information needs. It probably does not make practical sense to argue about what is and what is not *real* hypertext, but we should be concerned about how system capabilities support (1) what kinds of users doing (2) what kinds of tasks over (3) what periods of use. Results about one type of system that supports a specific user in a task at a specific time should not be used to generalize to the design of systems to support other tasks and users.

One important task is the access of information in large reference documents in which the hypertext system is used as a browser. The most common case is that browsers are used to scan existing documents that have been re-engineered (see [Glus88]) to be in an online form. Examples of document browsers are SuperBook [Remd87], NaviText™ SAM [Perl88], and the Document Examiner [Walk88].

Task analysis was critical in the design of NaviText™ SAM. NaviText™ SAM is a hypertext interface to the [Smit86] collection of 944 guidelines for designing user interface software. The Smith & Mosier report has gone through several revisions during more than five years of development, and in [Mosi86], the results of a user survey provided quantitative information about the ways that the report was used. More so than trying to implement a particular model of hypertext, NaviText™ SAM was designed to support expert users in their information management tasks, the most detailed of which has been called the *checklist method* of using a reference source [Perl89b]. An overview of NaviText™ SAM is given in the section on *designing and building systems*. The checklist method is summarized below.

From the survey by [Mosi86] and from a survey sent to about 500 recipients of the [Smit86] guidelines, we determined that online access should support a variety of methods of *finding relevant user interface design information*, and should do so on a relatively *inexpensive hardware and software platform*. Our survey of potential users of NaviText™ SAM showed that most had access to PC's, and many fewer to Apple Macintosh and workstations. Additionally, the PC's to which potential users had access often did not have a hard disk and almost never used windowing software or a pointing device. Many machines were original PC's or XT's with limited processing power. Such hardware and software limitations placed considerable constraints on the sort of platform from which we could build a hypertext system that would satisfy the needs of many users. Still, a widely accessible platform avoids the irony of the often *cited* but seldom *seen* system.

The Checklist Method

The checklist method supported by NaviText™ SAM is a step-by-step method of applying reference source information to the design and evaluation of systems. In NaviText™ SAM, the design steps, based on [Smit84], include:

- finding relevant information by (1) browsing a dynamically expandable (fisheye view) table of contents, (2) hierarchically inherited keyword search (see *document analysis*), (3) following cross-references, (4) using a citation index, and (5) library-shelf search;
- prioritizing information by attaching ratings (numerical annotations) of relevance to a particular design task;
- defining design rules justified in terms of collections of source information.

The evaluation steps include:

- using relevant information as evaluation criteria for areas to which it was applied in design;
- rating conformance to the source design information by attaching ratings (numerical annotations of a new type) to the source design information;

- referring back to the full source information for important areas of design for which evaluated conformance was low.

Display 1 (top pane) shows a design/evaluation checklist used in decisions about NaviText™ SAM's response speed. The first column contains the guideline identifier. The next column (*) indicates that the guidelines have been read. The third column is the rated importance (of response time in NaviText™ SAM) of each guideline. The fourth column is the rated conformance to the guideline. These guidelines are sorted by identifier number, but they could be sorted by conformance and importance to highlight serious violations of critical guidelines. With long lists of guidelines, such sorting is essential. In NaviText™ SAM, the text of the guidelines can be accessed directly from the checklist, as shown in the bottom window of Display 1.

A checklist is not a great intellectual achievement, unless perhaps it is complete, but a generalizable method for managing checklists is an important concept for a design and evaluation tool that acknowledges human memory limitations.

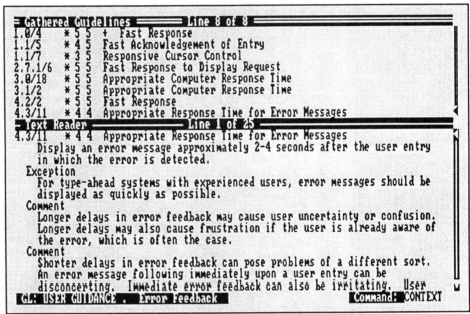

Display 1. A NaviText™ SAM design/evaluation checklist on response time.

Task Analysis with Friendly Users

In the continuing development of NaviText™ systems, we are working with standards documents like MIL-STD-1472 [DoD89]. With surprisingly little effort, we enlisted the help of what we call our *friendly users*, potential users of systems who are willing to put up with preliminary versions of systems because they are interested in the potential to help mold a system design. Via surveys and detailed personal interviews, we analyzed the tasks that system designers and evaluators have done with preceding versions of *1472*. While we had anticipated that such standards, being contractual obligations for multi-million dollar contracts, would be used extensively, we were surprised by the extent of the information demands made by such documents. During design and evaluation periods, our friendly users of 1472 spend anywhere from 10 to 30 hours per week with the document, using close variations of the checklist method, primarily with paper. In particular, we were impressed that checklists mapping system design to specific statements in 1472 were used to manage and later demonstrate conformance to the standard. Such non-linear associations between large documents resulted in the development of several essential new features for any hypertext system supporting standards use. There is a need for extremely flexible annotations, not only that can be attached to chunks of information, but that can be attached to paraphrases of parts of chunks of information. The rational chunking of information for one person (e.g., a document author) may not map well onto natural units for another person (see [Glus88]). There is a need for flexible viewing of documents, both in the amount and type of detail that is visible, and also to allow users to view documents in their original (paper, paged) form, so that they can communicate with colleagues who do not have access to an online version. One striking problem that we encountered was that our friendly users, although technically sophisticated, were poor at being able to appreciate the concepts of hypertext capabilities, as evidenced by their suggestions for the most obvious capabilities like following cross-references, long after such capabilities were explained to them. Evidently, the promise of hypertext is something that takes considerable explanation.

Cognitive Analysis

Underlying the utility of hypermedia systems is their ability to adapt to human cognitive limitations and capabilities. The transition from *browsing* to *keyword search* modes discussed in *collecting data* is analogous to the transition of novice to expert use of interactive systems in which menus and forms are supplanted by command languages or in which graphical interaction is replaced by function *quick* keys. Classic results on human memory limitations [Mill56] can be applied to the design of hierarchical and network browsers, and more recent work on spatial ability in hypermedia systems [Camp89] should underlie the design of systems.

2. DOCUMENT ANALYSIS

Although NaviText™ SAM has some annotation capabilities, those capabilities are mainly for annotations of existing *static* structures, not the definition of new *dynamic* structures. As such, the emphasis with NaviText™ systems has been on analyzing document structure and getting them online. Some of the lessons learned while representing the structure of documents may have applications to the design of authoring systems (see [Scha89]), but the main application we have found is in suggesting how to design documents to make them easier to get online and use effectively. In any case, reading is a more common activity than writing.

Getting the Information Online. The original document ([Smit86]) used with a NaviText™ system was obtained in online form from the authors. The base form was used to generate a well-human-engineered printed document, but it was not in a reasonable form for parsing the structure of the document because direct typesetting codes (e.g., point size 8, bold, etc.) were used instead of a structured markup language. Hand-editing and structural markup of the megabyte of text took about 30 hours. Although this was a lot of tedious work, it was minimal compared to the years of effort that went into the *content*. Other documents that we work with now require OCR (optical character recognition) and considerable cleanup, data conversions from one word processing format to another, parsing common formats like SGML or *troff*, and hand-entry.

Once a document is online, many formatting decisions must be made about which text can be filled and which must be displayed verbatim and about how to display figures that do not conveniently fit on the screen. The need to reformat and sometimes clip information is much like the adaptation of wide-screen movies to videotape; the *"window-boxing"* format, preferred by Siskel & Ebert on *At the Movies*, shows all the information but does not use the full screen. The more common method of scanning part of the image and panning can show more detail, and use the full screen, but sometimes with a loss of content. In any sort of media translation, a detailed knowledge of the content is critical, and decisions about difficult tradeoffs must be made.

<u>Structuring Information.</u> Even with a document online, it is still necessary to determine the structure of the document and how that structure will be represented in an online form. Like [Glus88], we have found it useful to be able to discuss document structuring with authors, and in the case of [Smit86], the logical structure of the document was discussed in detail in an introduction. The highly structured format of the document, both in the regular hierarchical structure of sections and subsections leading to guidelines, and in the structure of the guidelines themselves, was a major contributing factor to the selection of the report as a good candidate for a hypertext interface. Each of the six sections has a number, a title, an introduction, and subsections. Each subsection has a number, a title, an introduction, an optional example display, and guidelines. Each of the 944 guidelines has its own structure that made it attractive to offer dynamic view capabilities, like *"now you see examples, now you don't."* Each guideline has a number, a title, a statement of the guideline, and optional paragraphs containing comments, exceptions, examples, references to outside sources, and cross-references to other parts of the report. An example guideline is shown in Table 1. Work with [Smit86] exemplified that specific texts will suggest new capabilities that generalize to other systems.

In (re)structuring information, it is useful to consider the goals of users. Different tasks may be better supported by different chunking and structuring. A long-term benefit of hypertext might be to allow multiple structurings of the same content, adapting them to user goals. NaviText™ SAM allows users to create custom subsets of reusable parts of [Smit86].

<u>Removing Redundant Information.</u> A good reference document contains many aids to using the document effectively. Tables of contents (of different levels of detail), subject and author indexes, and structurally-based formatting all aid to the ease with which the information can be accessed. In the analysis of [Smit86], most such aids were determined to be redundant with information that could be derived dynamically. For example, [Smit86] contains tables of contents of three levels of detail: (1) one at the beginning of the report with the first two of three levels, (2) another with each section with the middle level, and (3) a 17-page reference table with 1021 entries at the back of the report. These tables are all redundant with the titles of the section, area, and guideline entries; any such table could be dynamically generated from an outliner and browsed with fisheye views [Furn86], so fixed tables of contents were avoided in NaviText™ SAM. There was considerable redundancy among guidelines (see the duplication of guideline titles in Display 1), because similar guidelines in different areas of the report were partially adapted to their context. They were left unchanged in NaviText™ SAM, but their presence suggests that authors of modern texts may want to adapt their writing to take advantage of hypertext capabilities.

A corollary of the ability of hypertext systems to remove redundant information is their ability to dynamically produce (or compute) additional information. In the guideline in Table 1, there is no context for the title, although this is provided as a running heading in the [Smit86] printed report. In NaviText™ SAM, context is available by a simple traversal up the spine of the hierarchy, and is bound to the

3.1.3/13 Letter Codes for Menu Selection

If menu selections are made by keyed codes, design each code to be the initial letter or letters of the displayed option label, rather than assigning arbitrary letter or number codes.

EXAMPLE

(Good) **m = Male**
           f = Female

(Bad) **1 = Male**
        2 = Female

EXCEPTION

Options might be numbered when a logical order or sequence is implied.

EXCEPTION

When menu selection is from a long list, the line numbers in the list might be an acceptable alternative to letter codes.

COMMENT

Several significant advantages can be cited for mnemonic letter codes. Letters are easier than numbers for touch-typists to key. It is easier to memorize meaningful names than numbers, and thus letter codes can facilitate a potential transition from menu selection to command language when those two dialogue types are used together. When menus have to be redesigned, which sometimes happens, lettered options can be reordered without changing codes, whereas numbered options might have to be changed and so confuse users who have already learned the previous numbering.

COMMENT

Interface designers should not create unnatural option labels just to ensure that the initial letter of each will be different. There must be some natural differences among option names, and special two- or three-letter codes can probably be devised as needed to emphasize those differences. In this regard, there is probably no harm in mixing single-letter codes with special multiletter codes in one menu.

REFERENCE

BB 1.3.6; MS 5.15.4.2.11; Palme, 1979; Shinar, Stern, Bubis, & Ingram, 1985.

SEE ALSO

4.0/13

Table 1. A sample guideline from [Smit86] with a variety of paragraph types.

context command. (The context is: Sequence Control, Dialogue Type - Menu Selection.) More compelling is the ability to let readers *look before they leap* and following a cross-reference. In Table 1, the SEE ALSO pointer to 4.0/13 in the printed form is optionally partially expanded to show the title of the text to which it points: *"Consistent Coding Conventions."* Similarly, references to outside sources can be partially expanded, automatically or interactively, as shown in NaviText™ SAM Display 2.

Reverse-Engineering Indexes. The [Smit86] report contains a hand-made subject index (but no author index). Rather than provide a special-purpose interface to the subject index, a decision was made early on to develop a keyword searching scheme that would replace the functions of an index. The logic is as follows: Instead of searching the index for terms that, once found, lead you to a location in the text (i.e., a page or paragraph number), keywords would be attached to the chunks of information. That way, a keyword search would lead to the same chunks of information as would an index search. The index entries (with **primary,** and secondary terms) in [Smit86] leading to the guidelines in Table 1 are shown below. The terms that are not redundant with those in the title are underlined. They are *index keywords* to be added to the title keywords.

<u>Coded</u> menu <u>options</u>, code <u>design</u>
<u>Keyed</u> <u>data</u> <u>entry</u>, menu selection
Menu <u>option</u> codes, code <u>design</u>
Menu selection, <u>keyed</u> <u>entry</u>

An index like [Smit86] is reverse-engineered, or *un-indexed,* as follows. All primary and secondary index terms in the index that lead to a chunk (page or chunk identifier) are added to the list of index keywords for that chunk, if they are not in the title of the chunk. Non-content words (i.e., traditional stopwords like: <u>and</u>, <u>of</u>, <u>the</u>) are filtered. Index keywords add richness to search without some of the false-alarm problems of full-text retrieval.

In a hierarchically structured system, in which matching a high-level chunk will also match all subordinates (using an inheritance mechanism), index keywords that appear in the index keywords or titles of superordinates can also be removed to conserve space. Such a scheme is used in NaviText™ SAM. An added benefit of the un-indexing is that it is not necessary to have multiple entries that ensure that searches for *"response time"* (indexed under <u>R</u>) and *"time to respond"* (indexed under <u>T</u>) will have the same result. Un-indexing is an effective process for aiding keyword search via the multiple access methods (e.g., synonymy) built into good indexes. When used as a replacement (as opposed to a complement) to indexes, it requires that users predict the terms in the index more so than when the index is present. Such term guessing can be aided by browsing. An implication of this approach is that keywords should be attached to chunks in the first place, and that search can be based on fields like *title*, *keywords*, and *text body*.

Although, there was no author citation index for the [Smit86] report, it was easy to generate one from the reference sections in the guidelines, automatically linking author names to guidelines citing them.

<u>The Book Metaphor</u>. Several systems have advocated a book metaphor so that the online version of information closely matches printed formats, even if there is no printed version. The rationale is that systems presenting online documents will be easier to learn and use if they closely match the way books look and work. For example, the Sun Help Viewer presents a paginated display that looks remarkably like a book page, and research has shown the system to be easy to learn [Camp89]. In other systems, like NaviText™ SAM, there are parallels between the original text and the hypertext presentation, but the mapping eluded some users if the mapping is not explained. NaviText™ SAM is like a book, but it attempts to make better use of information structure needed by *"power"* users:

- The <u>tables of contents</u> with varying amounts of detail are replaced by a dynamic outliner.
- The <u>index</u> is replaced by keywords attached to structures.
- <u>Cross-references</u> are made *dynamic* to allow *jumps* to related information.
- <u>References</u> to outside sources can be partially expanded or used as a <u>citation index</u>.
- <u>Running headings</u> on printed pages are replaced by context information.
- <u>Format</u> to reflect information type is made dynamic, e.g., information of generally low interest can be made invisible while other types of information can be highlighted.

With NaviText™ SAM we have found that an appropriate mental model must be provided to help users transfer their knowledge of how they use printed media.

<u>Multiple Versions</u>. In work with MIL-STD-1472 [DoD89], we have found it necessary to be able to represent multiple versions of documents. Military standards follow a predictable hierarchical format (there is a military standard for their format). When a standard is released, it may be updated by *notices*. For example, there were three notices to the predecessor of 1472D. Each notice contains new pages to be inserted, and pen and ink changes to be made by hand. There are no references to structures (i.e., paragraph numbers like 5.15.3.3.2) so it is a difficult task to determine where real changes occur. Additionally, there are

unpredictable changes in the layout of text, making line-by-line comparison impractical. We have found it useful to develop a revision control tool to represent changes at three parallel levels: (1) the printed page level, (2) the meaningful structure level, and (3) the word level. The last level is needed to highlight changes between successive versions.

<u>Multiple Documents</u>. Part of the vision of hypertext is that we will be able to move with ease from document to referenced document. In the [Smit86] report, there are 944 references from (coincidentally 944) guidelines to 173 outside sources. It would indeed be a tremendous achievement to get all these sources in an online form, but we have done some work to see what it would be like to get some. There are over 200 citations of an early version of [DoD89] from [Smit86], and these have been linked in a system. The two documents have had an incestuous relationship for years, and much of [DoD89] is copied *verbatim* from [Smit86]. Tracing for circular justification loops is not possible because in DoD standards, providing a reference source for a rule is not required. Based on a combination of *task analysis* and *document analysis*, we feel there is a need for <u>specific</u> functional support for each <u>specific</u> document type like [Smit86] and [DoD89], although there is considerable overlap of support needs among these and other reference documents. This suggests a need for customizability of the functionality of hypertext browsers, if they will be more than generally mediocre.

3. LITERATURE SURVEY AND SYSTEMS EVALUATION

A Hypertext Technology Assessment Project

[Conk87] compared many hypertext systems along 12 dimensions (i.e., features, capabilities of systems) and offered plausible classifications for different types of systems. [Hala88] discussed seven issues for the next generation of hypermedia systems. An evaluative survey of hypermedia functionality and its delivery form is one of the most common sources of design information, despite possible copyright and patent problems [Samu89]. One goal of our hypermedia technology assessment project is to find *all* dimensions on which systems can differ, and assess the practical utility of these differences for different types of users working on different types of tasks. For example, many systems have a capability for keyword searching. How important is it for there to be a full Boolean combination search capability? How does this depend on the type of users and the tasks they are working on? The particular implementations (including the user interface) and the methods of evaluation of such capabilities are critical; it is easy to set up a weak strawman using an *ad hoc* user interface to a limited, inefficient Boolean scheme, compare it to an interactive browsing system, and invalidly conclude that differences observed are meaningful. The field of software systems development is full of such comparisons of rotten apples to pale yellow oranges. Issues of comparisons among systems are discussed in more detail in the section on *interpretation of data*.

Another goal of the hypermedia assessment project is to develop a taxonomy of hypertext capabilities alongside those of more traditional information management technologies like information retrieval and databases. It should not matter if a system or a capability is *really* hypertext, only that it supports users in their tasks. For example, the GUIDE system added string search to present users with a marketable system even though it was outside their hypertext model [Brow87]. As another example, some hypertext researchers require that links (such as those to connect a software engineering design document with correlated code) must be independent of the source and destination to be considered *real* hypertext. Some links, like those to manage software project documents, may require *rich* links that include such essential information as the application to launch when traversing the link, but other applications may require little information in a link. With that in mind, our evaluations of a wide variety of systems focus on the effectiveness of functionality, to determine what tasks are possible with what capabilities. For example, there are many advantages to having information online, without using any hypertext concepts. An advantage of online access is full text search, but structured text allows people to use structure in search, in online display, and in preparing special purpose subdocuments. The following progression of capabilities shows that many benefits are obtained before we reach any functionality that any researcher would consider hypertext.

online	search, cut, and paste (by lines or proximity)
typed chunks	elision by type, simple formatting, level of detail, annotation
structures	views (e.g., hierarchical), formatting based on structure
hypertext	cut/paste/view by reference

As an example of an analysis of the wide possible range of functionality, consider the NaviText™ SAM *expand* function. The semantics of this function depend on the type of object being expanded and the workspace from where it being expanded. Different objects behave differently in different contexts. There are also options that control to where an object will be expanded: using stretch text, in the same window, or in another window. Such richness of functionality is not uncommon in object-oriented systems where each class of object has its own functionality. It is a challenge to understand such diversity of capability well enough to predict when it will be useful for a particular task.

4. INTERPRETATION OF DATA

The Method of Specific Advantages

Hypertext systems can be complex, with many functions and new user interfaces. Data collected on such systems must be analyzed with the assumption that it is difficult to control all conditions relevant to data collection. The effectiveness of hypertext capabilities should be demonstrated, but it can be difficult to separate the functionality from the systems that implement them. A capability may *out-perform* another only because of the choice of tasks, users, or because of artifacts of the implementation of the system in which the capability is implemented. Rather than criticize specific systems or researchers' evaluations of capabilities, I will present a method that can better quantify the performance advantages of capabilities within systems. The method also applies to the comparative evaluation of user interfaces and to systems in general. I will begin with an anecdote.

A student of mine wanted to show that graphical displays of networks were superior to tabular displays. He could have made some really bad tables and shown a gigantic superiority of graphical displays over tabular displays. Such bad tables would have been a *weak strawman*. For a *plausible strawman*, he needed to show that his tables had some intrinsic merit. To do this, he was careful to devise some tasks that would show *specific advantages* of tables over graphs, if the tables were well designed. His results showed task-specific advantages (faster responses to questions) of both graphics and tables; on some tasks tables were better than graphs, and in others, graphs were better than tables. This *cross-over interaction* is a critical aspect of argumentation in many empirical fields.

A *plausible strawman* for a condition provides data that shows a specific-advantage of the strawman over the condition. Mutually plausible strawmen provide specific advantages over each other. This allows for the possibility that both are mediocre, but it adds to the credibility that they are reasonable foils for each other. At the system level, some common plausible strawmen are existing (commercial) systems, their specific-advantage at least being notoriety. Another group includes print media, their specific-advantage being that they have been in use for a long, long time. At the feature level, there may be more than one way in a hypertext system to accomplish the same task. If a feature is never used, then perhaps it is useless or hard to use, but if feature A shows a specific-advantage (is used more, or is used more effectively, or is better liked) in one context, and B shows it in another, then more sound conclusions can be drawn about the merits of both features.

5. DESIGNING AND BUILDING SYSTEMS

An Overview of NaviText™ SAM

NaviText™ SAM provides PC-based support of the checklist method of design and evaluation with Smith and Mosier's [Smit86] *"Guidelines for Designing User Interface Software."* NaviText™ SAM was developed to create and explore a variety of hypermedia technologies in the context of solving specific information management problems. To evaluate new ideas in hypermedia, a research platform with control over source code is a *sine qua non*.

NaviText™ SAM Workspace Windows. There are eight workspace windows used by NaviText™ SAM. At any one time, at most three can tile the screen, the combinations of which were based on task analysis and feedback from users. The **Table of Contents** window is a dynamic outliner that shows all possible views of the main hierarchical structure of its document. The **References** window displays a list of references, with the facility to show detail about references and to gather (bookmark) chunks that cite a reference. The **Text Reader** is used for displaying larger blocks of text, such as section introductions and individual guidelines. The *view* of a guideline is determined by settings in the **Options** window, a data-entry form. The **Copy** window allows the comparison of any window contents with any other, and helps compensate for the size of the PC screen. Online expandable help is available in the **Help** window.

As potentially useful pieces of information are seen, they can be gathered into the **Gathered** set. This set can be scanned or searched, and details of the set can be expanded into the **Text Reader**. As texts are expanded, their identifiers (and linked titles) are placed in the **Expanded Text** window to allow backtracking and review. All NaviText™ SAM windows support a wide variety of operations: file interface, sorting, deleting and inserting text, and navigation using the standard arrow and paging keys. Examples are in Displays 1 and 2.

NaviText™ SAM Functions. The main functions in NaviText™ SAM are the dual *expand* and *conceal* operations that can be applied to sections, functional areas, guidelines, references, and other objects. The same objects can be *gathered* into the working set, on which several specialized functions are possible, most notably ratings by annotation, sorting on multiple keys, and report generation controlled by a hierarchy of display and format options. A hierarchical index keyword search with inheritance can also augment the gathered working set.

```
┌─Table of Contents────────────Line 7 of 19─┐
│Guidelines for Designing User Interface Software│
│ 1 DATA ENTRY                               │
│ 2 DATA DISPLAY                             │
│   2.0     General                          │
│   2.1     Text                             │
│     2.1/1          Conventional Text Display│▓
│     2.1/2    x     Printing Lengthy Text Displays│
│     2.1/3          Consistent Text Format  │
│   2.2     Data Forms                       │
│   2.3     Tables                           │▼
├─Text Reader──────────────────Line 8 of 12─┤
│ 2.1/2    x        Printing Lengthy Text Displays│
│ When a user must read lengthy textual material, consider providing that│
│ text in printed form rather than requiring the user to read it on-line.│
│ Comment                                    │
│   Reading lengthy text on an electronic display may be 20-30 percent│
│   slower than reading it from a printed copy.│
│ Reference                                  │
│   Gould Grischkowsky 1984                  │
│     Gould, J. D., and Grischkowsky, N. (1984). Doing the same work with│
│     hard copy and with cathode-ray tube (CRT) computer terminals. Human│
│     Factors, 26, 323-337.                  │
│   Muter Latremouille Treurniet Beam 1982   │
│ Alt-F1 for help  Alt-F10 to exit    Command: EXPAND│
└────────────────────────────────────────────┘
```

Display 2. A NaviText™ SAM fisheye view (top) with a guideline with an expanded reference (bottom pane).

A Hypertext Technology Base

NaviText™ SAM was developed as a special-purpose system, and as such, its applicability to other reference texts is limited (It has been applied to the UNIX® manual pages). The experiences with NaviText™ SAM have shown that there are generalizable capabilities in the system, and many of these have been extracted for use in the development of more general NaviText™ systems. Our current strategy is to use two complementary technologies in the development of hypertext browsers for large reference documents: (1) general information retrieval indexing and search engines, and (2) hierarchical outliners. The storage technology used in NaviText™ SAM includes: (1) dynamic memory allocation with caching of text for speed and garbage collection to free memory on small machines, (2) text compression to save disk space, and (3) version control. This technology has shown itself to be easily generalized. The NaviText™ SAM windowing software is also reusable. Some key developments for new documents have been necessary to support programmable operations and search of general annotations, particularly for group-shared annotations on documents. We plan to increase our use of established information management technologies to achieve efficient access to more document types.

6. COLLECTING DATA

Tasks and Performance Measures

In [Perl89a], I discuss methods for gathering data on user interfaces, many of which can be adapted to the empirical investigation of the utility of hypertext capabilities. With NaviText™ SAM, most data collection has been observational -- monitoring of usage patterns -- although there have been experiments in which users were placed through a series of tasks and observed over time. For gathering longitudinal data from most of the users of NaviText™ systems, we have methodological problems of controlling conditions and security problems, particularly for work using military standards. Like other empirical researchers ([Egan89], [Marc88], [Furn86], and [Camp89]), we have used a variety of tasks, collected a variety of measures, and compared them to performances of a variety of strawmen (see the section on *interpreting data*). On the task dimension, we have had users search for material relevant to specific topics, controlling the familiarity of the topics and the texts in use. Our measures have been frequency of use, task completion time, and discriminability (see below). We have used printed versions of texts and competing methods within systems for comparisons.

A Measure of Discriminability. In comparing access of information with NaviText™ SAM to the printed form, we were faced with a problem of retrieval evaluation (see [Salt83]). Research uses of large reference sources, such as one might go through in designing a user interface, are open-ended. For a particular design area, some information is clearly relevant while some is clearly irrelevant. In a resource like [Smit86], there are 944 guidelines, so it is no easy task to determine if all and only the relevant information has been found. In Display 1 there are eight guidelines on system response time, spanning four sections of the report. Because each guideline has been read and rated for relevance, we can be reasonably sure that they are relevant, but are these *all* the relevant ones? Any search-success measure must compensate for both retrieval errors: false alarms and misses. Signal detection theory [Coom70] may provide us with a fair method of evaluating the effectiveness of retrievals. There is a problem of deciding the truth of whether a piece of information is truly relevant, and this can only be overcome with expert ratings checked for inter-rater-reliability. Once a search task is set up, with ratings of relevance in hand, different access methods can be compared by their ability to discriminate among alternatives in the search space. This measure was developed and exercised to compare student prototype hypertext interfaces to [Smit86], and there is ongoing work on its refinement and validation.

Empirical Results from NaviText™ SAM

We have found that inexperienced users learning NaviText™ SAM needed help with the (lack of a) book metaphor. Without hard data on which to base our conclusion, we have concluded that it was extremely useful to tell users how to map their paper-based information finding skills to the NaviText™ SAM implementation of hypertext. A common new user comment was "I am not sure where to start" which was avoided with training on online reference documents.

Two phenomena are apparent in experienced users of NaviText™ SAM: (1) To become oriented with a new information space (particularly with its terminology), users explore the space with a fisheye view [Furn86] outliner and gradually migrate to a title and index keyword search strategy. This is related to a transition from recognition of menu options to recall of exact terms in a command language. (2) To avoid disorientation (see [Mant82]), users adopt a breadth-first-search (BFS) strategy of putting possibly interesting cross-references at the *end* of their browsing agenda, instead of following them as they are encountered (i.e., they avoid a depth-first-search (DFS) strategy).

The following time-line graphs show the sequence of actions taken by an experienced user of NaviText™ SAM. In the first task (Figure 2), the user is looking for user interface design guidelines for designing a window title bar. In the second task (Figure 3), the same user is looking for guidelines on the use of color in displays. The topics were chosen so that a topic familiar to the user would precede a less familiar topic to see how search strategy might be affected.

NaviText™ SAM has a built-in monitoring capability used for several purposes: creating macros, running demonstrations, and collecting usage data. Usage data can be analyzed to see what actions are being taken in which windows, and displayed in time-line graphs. The time-line graphs can be interpreted as follows. Across the horizontal dimension are actions taken by the user (not including help or navigation within and between windows). Along the vertical dimension are the windows in which the actions take place. The meaning of a command, like *expand*, depends on the window in which it takes place. For example, in an outliner, expansion means *"show detail"*, while in a text reader, it means *"follow a cross-reference."* Similarly, *"search"* in a window means to look for a combination of terms inside the window, while *"global search"* searches through the full information space. The type and position of the commands used in a search give good insights into the strategies being used. The action types, and their window-specific interpretations, are tabulated in Table 2.

Code Meaning

Code	Meaning
+	Gather (Set Bookmark)
	(in CONTENTS, it means to save guideline for review)
	(in READER, it means to put guideline on BFS agenda)
D	Delete (Unmark) * implies many
N	Next (Library Shelf Browsing Expansion)
P	Previous (Library Shelf Browsing Expansion)
R	Reorder (Using Multiple Sorting Keys)
S	Search
	(GLOBALly, it means hierarchical search with gathering)
U	Make Unique List (Remove Duplicates)
•	Expand
	(in CONTENTS, it means to show local detail)
	(in READER, it means to follow guideline cross-ref using DFS)
	(in GATHERED, it means to review guideline detail)

Table 2. Key for Interpreting Time-Line Graphs.

In the search for window-title guidelines (Figure 2), the user immediately begins with a keyword search (for window title) and after a few guidelines are gathered for later review, another keyword search (for display label) follows. This results in over 50 guidelines being gathered, and the user deletes many guidelines from the gathered set based on the titles, without expanding the detail of the guidelines. When pockets of interesting guidelines are found, a library-shelf search of adjacent guidelines is used. With little more expansion to full text, the list pruning is completed. Note that there was no use of the table of contents, designed to provide context to the user, nor the expanded set of guidelines, designed to provide a backtrackable trail (made unnecessary here because of the BFS strategy).

The second time-line graph (Figure 3) shows the sequence of actions taken by the same user in a subsequent search for information about the use of color in displays. This session is typical of one by an experienced NaviText™ SAM user who is marginally familiar with the coverage in the text of a topic; the table of contents is used for orientation in a new topic area, and a BFS strategy is used to avoid getting lost. Early actions involve the table of contents, which is being used as a fisheye view of the information space. As candidate information is encountered, it is gathered for later evaluation. After initial browsing of the table of contents, the gathered information is reviewed in more detail, and cross-references from useful chunks are gathered for later analysis to avoid getting lost

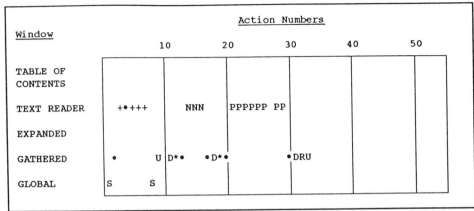

Figure 2. Time-line graph of a NaviText™ SAM search on <u>window titles</u>.

in hyperspace. The unusual expansion (following) of a cross-reference at action 17 is followed by gathering of the information and the expanded text (trail) is used to backtrack. A series of expansions from the gathered set are occasionally supplemented by further gathering of cross-references, which are added to the end of the gathered set for later consideration. After a series of decisions about the relevance of information in the gathered set, two global searches are attempted using terms seen in the body of the text (e.g., <u>spectr</u>, which abbreviates both spectrum and spectral).

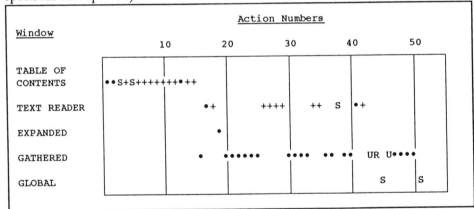

Figure 3. Time-line graph of a NaviText™ SAM search on <u>color displays</u>.

The NaviText™ SAM table of contents outliner and keyword index search are plausible strawmen for each other because the choice of which is used depends on the context. If one was always used first, then we would not know if the other was less useful, poorly implemented, was hard to use, or had some other deficiency.

SUMMARY

We need a framework to capture and organize information for the development of new hypermedia technology. The data flow diagram in Figure 1 is an attempt to reflect the asynchronous process of design and evaluation of hypermedia systems, a process more complex than an iterative design, implementation, and evaluation lifecycle. Many aspects of the diagram apply to systems more general than hypermedia systems; some apply to human-computer systems, some to any system.

Task analysis with friendly users and document analysis with specialized texts can produce ideas for new functionality in hypertext systems (e.g., dynamic views, checklist support). New techniques and demanding decisions are required to bring information online, and an appreciation of these would be useful to designers of documents targeted for print and online access. Hypertexts include structures of typed information chunks, but many benefits of accessibility come from being online, or having some structure. Users of full-featured hypertext systems need special training to take advantage all their capabilities. This training should help map mental models of how to use printed reference texts onto hypertext system functionality. A technology base of information management tools is a prerequisite for experimental development and evaluation of new hypertext technology.

A variety of usage data have been collected on NaviText™ SAM, a hypertext interface to a reference document ([Smit86]). Experienced users of NaviText™ SAM orient themselves in a novel information space using browsing strategies with a hierarchical outliner and by following cross-references. The same users choose the more direct keyword search to access information in familiar information spaces. It is necessary to have a technology base capable of supporting competing access methods (e.g., outliners and full-text search) to allow a fair comparison using the method of specific advantages. Experienced NaviText™ SAM avoid getting lost in hyperspace by using bookmarks to formulate a breadth-first-search rather than follow cross-references and effectively use a depth-first-search.

Current research is aimed at providing new methods to formulate queries and specify views (both online and for generated reports), and to evaluate their ability to help users find relevant information. A measure of discriminability, based on signal detection theory, is being validated as part of this effort.

ACKNOWLEDGEMENTS

Northern Lights Software's friendly users provided task analysis, document analysis, and usage data. Bob Glushko provided key conceptual advice. Sid Smith and Jane Mosier provided the first text for a NaviText™ system, and Tony Moorhead provided programming support. The following companies have donated software for the PC-based Hypertext Technology Assessment Project: askSam Systems, Brightbill-Roberts, Cognetics, Group L, Lotus Development, Northern Lights Software, Persoft, and over ten other packages are also being evaluated on loan. I would like to thank Stuart Bertsch and Phil Smith for their comments.

REFERENCES

[Aksc88] Akscyn, R. M., McCracken, D. L., & Yoder, E. A. (1988) "KMS: A Distributed Hypermedia System for Managing Knowledge in Organizations." **Communications of the ACM**, 31:7, 820-835.

[Brow87] Brown, P. J. (1987) "Turning Ideas Into Products: The GUIDE System." **Proceedings of Hypertext'87**. New York: ACM.

[Camp89] Campagnoni, F. R. & Ehrlich, K. (in press) "Information Retrieval Using a Hypertext-Based Help System." **ACM Transactions on Office Information Systems.**

[Conk87] Conklin, J. (1987) "Hypertext: An Introduction and Survey." Computer, 20:9, 17-41.

[Coom70] Coombs, C., Dawes, R., & Tversky, A. (1970) **Mathematical Psychology.** New York: Academic Press.

[DoD89] DoD (1989) MIL-STD-1472D: Human Engineering Design Criteria for Military Systems, Equipment and Facilities. Washington, DC: Department of Defense.

[Egan89] Egan, D. E., Remde, J. R., Landauer, T. K., Lochbaum, C. C. & Gomez, L. M. (1989) "Behavioral Evaluation and Analysis of a Hypertext Browser." **Proceedings of the CHI'89 ACM Conference on Human Factors in Computer Systems.** New York: ACM. 205-210.

[Furn86] Furnas, G. W. (1986) "Generalized Fisheye Views." **Proceedings of the CHI'86 ACM Conference on Human Factors in Computer Systems.** New York: ACM. 16-23.

[Glus88] Glushko, R. J. Weaver, M. D., Coonan, T. A. & Lincoln, J. E. (1988) "Hypertext Engineering: Practical Methods for creating a compact disc encyclopedia." **Proceedings of the ACM Conference on Document Processing Systems.** New York: ACM. 11-20.

[Glus89] Glushko, R. J. (1989) "Transforming Text into Hypertext for a Compact Disc Encyclopedia." **Proceedings of the CHI'89 ACM Conference on Human Factors in Computer Systems.** New York: ACM. 293-298.

[Hala88] Halasz, F. G. (1988) "Reflections on NoteCards: Seven Issues for the Next Generation of Hypermedia Systems." **Communications of the ACM, 31:7,** 836-852.

[IDE86] IDE (1986) Software Through Pictures™ Data Flow Editor (DFE) Manual. San Francisco: Interactive Development Environments.

[Marc88] Marchionini, G. & Shneiderman, B. (1988) "Finding Facts vs. Browsing Knowledge in Hypertext Systems." **Computer, 21:1,** 70-80.

[Mant82] Mantei, M. M. (1982) **A Study of Disorientation Behavior in ZOG.** PhD dissertation, University of Southern California.

[Mill56] Miller, G. (1956) "The Magical Number Sever Plus or Minus Two: Some Limits on Our Capacity for Processing Information." **Psychological Review, 63,** 81-97.

[Mosi86] Mosier, J. N. & Smith, S. L. (1986) "Application of Guidelines for Designing User Interface Software." **Behaviour and Information Technology, 5,** 39-46.

[Perl87]   Perlman, G. (1987) An Overview of SAM: A Hypertext Interface to Smith & Mosier's *'Guidelines for Designing User Interface Software.'* Wang Institute Tech. Report WI-TR-87-09.

[Perl88]   Perlman, G. & Moorhead, A. J. (1988) "Applying Hypertext Methods for the Effective Utilization of Standards." **Proceedings of the IEEE COMPSTAN'88 Conference on Computer Standards.**

[Perl89a]   Perlman, G. (1989a) "Evaluating How Your User Interfaces Are Used." **IEEE Software, 6:1,** January. 112-113.

[Perl89b]   Perlman, G. (1989b) "The Checklist Method for Applying Guidelines to Design and Evaluation." **Proceedings of INTERFACE 89.** Santa Monica, CA: Human Factors Society.

[Remd87]   Remde, J. R., Gomez, L. M., & Landauer, T. K. (1987) "SuperBook: An Automatic Tool for Information Exploration -- Hypertext?" **Proceedings of Hypertext'87.** New York: ACM. 175-188.

[Salt83]   Salton, G. & McGill, M. J. (1983) **Introduction to Modern Information Retrieval.** New York: McGraw-Hill.

[Samu89]   Samuelson, P. (1989) "Why the Look and Feel of Software User Interfaces Should Not be Protected by Copyright Law." **Communications of the ACM. 32:5,** 563-572.

[Scha89]   Schank, C. & Mamrak, S. A. (1989) "A Composition Environment to Support Scholarly Writing." Columbus, OH: Ohio State University, Department of Computer and Information Science. Technical report OSU-CISRC-6/89-TR27.

[Smit84]   Smith, S. L. & Mosier, J. N. (1984) "A Design Evaluation Checklist for User-System Interface Software." Report MTR-9480. Bedford, MA: MITRE Corporation.

[Smit86]   Smith, S. L. & Mosier, J. N. (1986) "Guidelines for Designing User Interface Software." Bedford, MA: MITRE Corporation.

[Walk88]   Walker, J. H. (1988) "Supporting Document Development with Concordia." **Computer, 21:1,** 48-59.

Towards a Design Language for Representing Hypermedia Cues

Shelley Evenson and John Rheinfrank

Exploratory Design Lab
Fitch RichardsonSmith

Wendie Wulff

Exploratory Design Lab
Fitch RichardsonSmith
Department of English
Carnegie Mellon University

Background

Hypermedia systems are no longer just interesting experimental software environments. They are common tools in the world of everyday work. People who do not program, but who are computer literate and who want to go beyond the capabilities of word processing, spreadsheet and presentation software packages now use systems like Apple's Hypercard, Owl's Guide, Silicon Beach's Supercard and Xerox's Notecards not only to communicate, but to perform tasks that involve creating and integrating knowledge. This raises some important issues for designers of hypermedia systems. One of the largest is how to represent which pieces of information are linked (or hyper) and which pieces aren't, within a given system or task domain. This, in turn, raises the issue of standards. Should representations of hyperness be consistent across systems and work domains, or should there be individual standards for representing hyperness within systems and work domains? The advantage of a standard is that it may assist users in discovering or labeling what is or isn't hyper across a wide variety of systems. The disadvantage is that a standard severely limits the opportunities for creating systems that are closely connected to the content of specific areas of work, work environments and work tools. Thus, the apparent choice is between adopting a rigid hypermedia cuing standard, or redesigning hypermedia cues for each application.

What is a design language?

One promising alternative is to create a set of tools that will encourage people (both interface designers and users) to directly shape (and reshape) hypermedia cues according to an evolving variety of needs, circumstances and subject matters. By creating such tools we would also be creating a shift in the conditions surrounding the use of the tools--we would, in effect, be creating a language that would enable people to design their own solutions. A design language, then, is a flexible collection of tools (elements), plus indications of the conditions determining their use (guidelines), that together allow people to use (and generate) expressions in response to situations.*

*Our work with design languages in graphic, product and user interface design has prompted us to apply design language theory to the representation of hyperness in multi-level documents. Our current work has focused on design languages for hypertext rather than hypermedia. In this paper we concentrate on the hyperness of words and related units of text. We expect that design language theory will be extensible to other forms of hypermedia and other aspects of hyper system design.

A brief characterization of written, printed, electronic and hyper texts

Oral to written to printed text -- words as referents
The unique breakthrough that written words brought to oral communication "was devised . . . when a coded system of visible marks was invented whereby a writer could determine the exact words that the reader would generate from the text." [7] The physical presence of the mechanically printed word on the page formalized the code even further by allowing readers, as recipients of acts of communication, to "feel the printed words . . . as visual units." [7] Furthermore, "print situates words in space more relentlessly than writing" and, by implication, even more relentlessly than speech. [7] Printed words transmit ideas in fixed form, with "form" referring simultaneously to visual representation, meaning and sequence, and "fixed" to the fact that no aspect of form can be changed after the type has been printed on the page.*

Printed text -- words as representations
A printed word is also a particular combination of symbols chosen from a larger, finite and common set of symbols. (In the English language, the set consists of the 26 characters of the alphabet, plus various punctuation marks. In oriental languages, the set consists of single and multiple brush strokes.) Typographers are concerned with the shape and identity of individual symbols, the grouping of symbols into words, the organization of words on the page and even the semantic properties that a particular symbolic style (typeface or font) communicates to the reader. Typographers expect that as long as a word is legible, and as long as the meaning associated with the word is known by the reader, the word will "work." For typographers, and for most people who have visual sensitivity or training, a printed word "is" more than it's associated meaning (the referent of the word). It is also a collection of symbols (a representation). For example, a casual reader who encountered the word "cat" might think immediately of an actual cat, while a person trained to see visually might consider the letterforms C A T, their relationship to each other, their position on the page, etc. Thus, printing creates a common set of representations in the same way that words provide a common set of referents.

Electronic (but not hyper) text -- words as changeable objects
Electronic text adds another dimension to the perception of words: objecthood. Electronic words are no longer simply fixed forms with fixed referents and representations, they suddenly appear as objects that can be manipulated. Electronic words can be selected, replaced, respelled, displayed in different fonts, etc. almost instantaneously. Electronic words temporarily become objects that everyone can transform in a way that was, in the past, generally reserved for typographers or graphic designers. Computer systems offer people numerous possibilities for the construction, positioning and display of words, all of which have the potential to enhance or detract from the way the word "works." Unfortunately, most electronic systems do not give people any indication of this potential for change (or how to use it) beyond what is expressed by the position of the cursor. In addition, the appearance of text displayed on the screen is also frequently misleading. Electronic text looks like print and therefore gives the impression of being limited by the same constraints as print. The result is that people are unable to take advantage of electronic text's full potential. There are plenty of references to "fontitis" attesting to people's misuse of the opportunities for change presented by electronic text. [8]**

---

*We recognize the role of underlining and annotation in people's participatory interactions with printed texts, but these are superimpositions on rather than changes to the original communication. An annotated document is different from the original, but one can still make the claim that the original document exists, unchanged, underneath the handwritten marks.

**Some graphic design software applications do suggest that text can be seen and used as an object for manipulation, but this is because they are object-based, rather than text-based applications.

printed hypertext [2]

Hypertext -- words with lives of their own
Footnotes and figure or reference notes in printed documents are, perhaps, the oldest forms of hypertext. Good examples of directed verbal cues are the expressions *see, for example* and the use of numbers (like *Figure 7*) in dictionaries and reference books. These cues all point the reader in other directions or give the reader more context for interpretation.*

Naturally, hypertext in the printed world suffers from the constraints of print. It is limited to a single visual representation, it is static and it is sequential. Printed words, as units of information, have no inherent ability to actively lead the reader elsewhere. They do, however, point to where the reader can go next. Thus, in printed text, the responsibility for executing hyperness belongs to the reader.

On the other hand, hypertext in electronic documents is characterized by flexibility of form--by the potential for multiple, non-sequential, dynamic referents, representations, manipulations and actions. Electronic hypertext differs most from the printed variety by positioning words as actors with lives of their own. Words in electronic hypertext have the potential to be coupled to actions. In this sense, the job of pointing to hyperness is assumed by the system and delivered according to direction from the user.**

*The use of this kind of linking in printed reference books could explain why so many of them have been selected for translation into electronic hypermedia documents. [3]

**We anticipate that words within electronic hypertext systems will eventually be able to change by themselves. People will be able to instruct words to function as autonomous agents. In these cases, words--as actors--will automatically deliver underlying content and transport people to new locations within an information space.

The problem: Cues for words with lives of their own

Can words with lives of their own express the nature of that life?
How will people who interact with electronic hypertext know:
1) Which words have the potential to be changed--are merely electronic
(already a magical thing to new users)?
2) Which words have lives of their own--are pointers to other information or automatic
doors to other places (super magic)?
3) Where active words may lead them?
Finally, what tools can help systems designers make these distinctions clear to users?
And, can the same tools be adopted by users to create distinctions of their own?

Current solutions

Font design
As a common practice, most systems have used bold, italic or underlined text to indicate a
word is that is hyper. The user is informed of the convention at the beginning of a
document and is usually expected to remember it throughout the document. The problem
with this approach is that bold type and italic type have historically been used to indicate
something else. [4] Typographers have generally used bold type to indicate a new section
or thought, or to emphasize the title of a document. Italic type has been used as a
similar, but less intrusive form of highlighting. Underlining is an odd convention to use
in an electronic medium, because it is carried over from the hand-written system.
Underlining was developed as a way to change the form of text that had already been
written. Bold, italic and underlining have rarely meant "word with a life of it's own."
And, in most of these cases, it may not only be difficult for users to remember a new
application of an old convention, but it may also be difficult for the designers themselves.

Of all the typestyles commonly available in electronic systems, shadowed or outlined
type would seem the most logical choice for cuing active words. These styles could take
advantage of the semantic properties of shadowing by giving the reader a sense that there
was something "behind" the chosen word. However, most typographers would suggest
that using these typestyles in conjunction with plain text would disrupt the flow of text
on the page (or screen) and interfere with readability.

Perhaps typographers could design an entirely new set of characters--one which would
clearly signal hyperness, but which wouldn't detract from readability. Or perhaps they
could design a hyper variation (or style) for standard fonts, in much the same way that
italic fonts were designed from the standard versions.

shadowed type cuing an active word

Punctuation marks

Punctuation marks are standard symbols that allow users of language to clarify the meaning of words or groups of words. When used for a single word, a punctuation mark often seems to enhance the intent of the author. Again, because of past history, all of the current marks should probably be limited to their current standard use in electronic hypertext. But this does not rule out the use of punctuation-like marks.

Marks with some potential may be the asterisk or sub and superscript text, both of which are sometimes used to reference footnotes or to indicate omissions. We also have some marks that stand for words (&,$)--maybe we could design a new mark that represents hyperness? Intermedia uses a marker icon as a cue. In the Intermedia system these cues are anchors that can lead to one or more links.[9]

New!

NO.

&

Organizing text on the screen

Users have learned to accommodate some degree of variability in the organization of paragraphs on the printed page. Depending on the degree of variability, users are still able to understand that the underlying organizational message is new paragraph. One common practice in book design is to use indentation for the first word of the second and each succeeding paragraph. Another approach is to leave one line space between paragraphs. Many people have experimented with indenting paragraphs and organizing them in different positions on the page with varying degrees of success. e.e. cummings has been successful in using non-standard arrangements of text to add unexpected, multiple dimensions to language.

There may be some new way of organizing the text on the screen to indicate hyperness. Early work has already been done along these lines. [1,6,9]

Sally and Jane went on a
field trip to Anderson's farm.
The first animal they saw was a
cow
and Sally said, "I know what

Sally and Jane went on a
field trip to Anderson's farm.
The first animal they saw was a
cow — other farm animals
and Sally said, "I know what

Sally and Jane went on a
field trip to Anderson's farm.
The first animal they saw was a
and Sally said, "I know what

organizing text on the screen: the transition from a non-activated to an activated word

Future directions

All of the existing electronic hypertext cuing solutions--giving more meaning to the visible marks we already know as the alphabet, adding a new kind of mark to the existing set, or capitalizing on the spatial organization of text on the screen--have some potential for addressing the cuing problems that words with lives of their own present for readers and authors of electronic hypertext systems. But, none of these approaches--even with the extensions we have indicated--seems likely to satisfy the reader's need to comprehend or the author's need to communicate the nature of hyperness.

A new underlying structure
The earliest forms of representational language used the shapes of objects in the world as structural models to create pictures. When ideas became too complex to express through pictures alone, determinative signs were introduced to further characterize and define the original signs. A determinative sign was traditionally used after a picture and referred to the same object as the original picture. To illustrate: a picture of an egg followed by a name-sign might show that the person being referred to was a woman. This innovation reinforced the power of the existing sign-set and enriched the communicative function of the language.

We may once again have reached a point in the development of communication media where our sign-set limits our ability to express ideas and relations. Our current set of representational signs (the alphabet) uses relatively linear oral and printed communication as it's structural model. This model constrains our ability to extend existing signs into multi-dimensional communication spaces. In order to realize the full potential of these new frameworks, we need richer underlying structures--and associated sign-sets--that go beyond what has been provided by orality, writing and printing.

There are non-linguistic sets of signs which have drawn on other forms of communication for their structural models. Musical notation is one example. Dance notation is another. These and other sets of visualization/verbalization practices might provide starting points for developing an underlying structure and a set of signs for hypermedia systems. "The idea of genius behind the great invention of writing was an intuitive grasp of the principle that graphic signs have no limitations for the purposes of human communication other than those which derive causally from their primary parameters as visible marks . . . graphic communication is free to draw upon other modes of communication as structural models." [5] The same can be said of hypermedia systems design.

Towards an action-based sign-set

We are proposing that a new graphic sign-set for the representation of hypermedia cues be developed from a new underlying structure--a structure based on the set of potential actions within hypermedia systems. So far, the set of potential actions we have identified (presented here from the designer's point of view) includes:

1. Beginning--the setting of a gestalt expectation about what follows;

2. Priming--the creation of a pattern of interpretation and the awareness of the paradigmatic frame;

3. Orienting--the provision of landmarks, benchmarks and other place-finding and place-remembering devices;

4. Navigating--the provision of maps, map-building tools and other place-describing conventions;

5. Linking--the identification and definition of content relationships, including a taxonomy of relations;

6. Framing--the ability to group a cluster (or order pieces) of content within a supporting infrastructure;

7. Contextualizing--the exposition of the embedding circumstances or situations that produce the conditions for determining meaning;

8. Reflecting--the provision of metalinguistic devices that can be used to build evocative extensions of domain and reach;

9. Annotating--the marking of text with meaningful, complementary content;

10. Speciating--the means for the social construction of genres of exchange;

11. Skilling--developing the ability or capacity to process text concurrent with the actual processing of the text; and

12. Acculturating--the emergence of new forms of literacy, particularly in the use of integrated multi-media.

Scenario one--a sign set based on action

We have envisioned a scenario showing what a sign-set based on action might be like. In this first hypothetical hypertext system, we have limited ourselves to the action of linking. Within this space, we have identified the sub-actions of both adding and reading: footnotes, definitions, expansions, revisions, related topics and new tree branches. We designed two sets of cues (iconic and symbolic) that someone could place in the text to indicate: 1) that there was a link associated with a word and 2) what type of sub-action would be possible. Then, someone viewing the cues would know that there was a link and, if he or she knew the referents of the icons or symbols, he or she could interpret the potential action. Some basic rules for the use and interpretation of the cues would also be helpful, such as: "The cue always appears after the word it is associated with," or "If there is more than one cue, they should appear in an order that reflects the order of the links."

	iconic	symbolic	
footnote			Sally and Jane went on a field trip. The first animal they saw was a cow and Sally said, "I know...
definition			
expansion			*iconic in use*
revision			Sally and Jane went on a field trip. The first animal they saw was a cow and Sally said, "I know...
relation			
new branch			*symbolic in use*
	iconic	*symbolic*	

This approach could be helpful in the acts of composing and consuming hypertext, but it is limited. The designers of action-based sign-sets must think of all the types of actions that could take place in the system and then provide the appropriate cues.

Towards a design language for hypermedia cues
We are also proposing that a new action-based sign-set complement the existing alphabetic sign-set in much the same way that determinative signs worked with pictures-- by adding a set of elements and guidelines for their application.

Scenario two--action-based sign-sets and design language
Rather than require designers to create iconic or symbolic cues based on individual actions, why not provide both designers and users with sets of representational elements and guidelines for combining them in order to create cues? We have envisioned another scenario showing an example of a sign-set based on action, and then generated and used from a design language perspective.

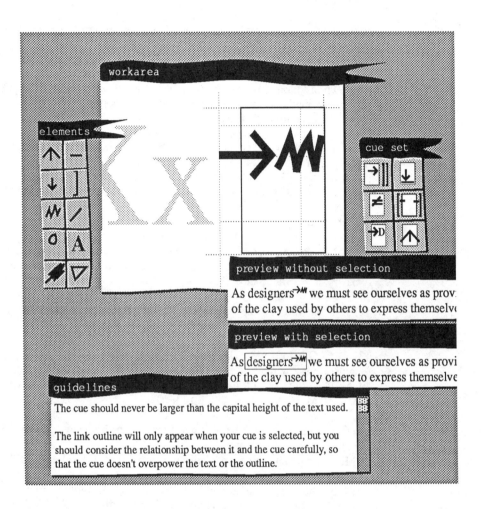

sketch of a tool for creating cues from elements and guidelines

Conclusion

All of the above is but a brief outline of how design languages might be applied to hypermedia systems. Innovations in hypermedia design languages, if developed further, may well help close the gap between hypermedia designers and users. Bridging this gap is especially important when people use systems to create (or design) knowledge within their own task domains. The Intermedia system developed by IRIS at Brown University has already made progress in this direction. [9] For electronic text, hypertext and hypermedia, continued growth in our capacities for composition and comprehension will hinge on what the design community provides as conceptual raw material for mediation between composer and consumer. The opportunities for participation presented by that raw material will be as important as the content. As designers, we must see ourselves as providers of the "clay" used by others to express themselves and thereby socially construct understanding, as well as notions of creativity and potentials for innovation.

References

[1] R. M. Akscyn, D. L. McCracken and E. A. Yoder. "KMS: A Distributed Hypermedia System for Managing Knowledge in Organizations." Communications of the ACM, V.31, N. 7, 1987. pp 820-835.

[2] J. Blumenthal. The Art of the Printed Book 1455-1955. Pierpont Morgan, New York, 1984.

[3] R.J. Glushko, M. D. Weaver, T. A. Coonan and J. E. Lincoln. "Hypertext Engineering: Practical Methods for Creating a Compact Disk Encyclopedia." Proceedings of ACM Conference on Document Processing Systems (December 5-9, 1988, Santa Fe, NM). ACM, New York, 1988. pp.11-20.

[4] F. W. Goudy. The Alphabet and Elements of Lettering. Dover, New York, 1962.

[5] R. Harris. The Origin of Writing. Open Court, La Salle, IL, 1986.

[6] J. Nannard, M. Nannard and H. Richey. "Conceptual Documents: A Mechanism for Specifying Active Views in Hypertext." Proceedings of ACM Conference on Document Processing Systems (December 5-9, 1988, Santa Fe, NM). ACM, New York, 1988. pp.37-42.

[7] W. J. Ong. Orality and Literacy. Methuen, London, 1982.

[8] A. van Dam. "Hypertext 87 Keynote Address." Communications of the ACM. V.31, N. 7, 1987. pp 887-895.

[9] Nicole Yankelovich, Karen E.Smith,L. Nancy Garrett and Norman Meyrowitz. "Issues in Designing a Hypermedia Document System." Multimedia in Education. Apple Educational Advisory Council: Learning Tomorrow, Spring 1987. pp.35-87.

We would like to thank Stu Card, Xerox Parc, and all of edl for valuable contributions to this work.

Facilitating the Development of Representations in Hypertext with IDE

Daniel S. Jordan
Daniel M. Russell
Anne-Marie S. Jensen
Russell A. Rogers

System Sciences Laboratory
Xerox Palo Alto Research Center
3333 Coyote Hill Road
Palo Alto, CA 94304

ABSTRACT

Hypertext systems are used for a variety of representational tasks, many that involve fairly formalized structures. Because hypertext systems are generally intended for developing informal (unstructured data) and semi-formal (semantic networks) structures, developing more formal structures can be difficult. Regular patterns in structures must often be recreated from primitive elements (individual nodes and links) resulting in a high overhead cost. In this paper we describe the Instructional Design Environment, or IDE, a hypertext system application that facilitates the rapid and accurate creation of regular network patterns in hypertext. IDE focuses on the task of instructional design, but its facilities are general and useful to many representation tasks. IDE features *structure accelerators* that provide simple menu interfaces to (1) define network structures out of patterns of typed node and link connections, (2) create new node types that contain structured content, and (3) tailor the interface for creating cards, links and structures to focus attention during different stages of the representation task. These mechanisms allow the user to tailor the hypertext environment to better meet his or her representational needs. We also report on the field use of IDE by instructional designers.

1. INTRODUCTION

Hypertext authoring systems are generally intended to help users organize information for the writing task. Hypertext systems are also used in tasks for organizing information into representations more formal than those used in writing, such as analyzing policy decision-making [Mars87], capturing early design decisions [Conk87b], and computer-aided design [Deli87]. The advantage of using hypertext for these and similar tasks over, for example, relational database systems, is the enormous flexibility offered the user in representing structures. The basic node-and-link construct of hypertext is powerful enough to incorporate structures ranging from the formal (e.g., relational tables) to semi-formal (semantic networks) to informal (unstructured data), in a single environment. One disadvantage of building these structures in hypertext is the high cost, or "cognitive overhead" [Conk87a], the user pays in performing tasks such as creating, naming and organizing links and nodes. This cost becomes particularly acute when building more formal structures with regular and recurring patterns. Repeatedly performing the same sequence of operations becomes extremely tedious. The result is either: (1) that hypertext will not be used for the task, even though it has the representational power, or, worse, (2) that hypertext *will* be used, but will discourage the user from properly building structures, causing improper or "sloppy" structures to be built instead.

In this paper we describe three mechanisms that accelerate the task of building accurate representations in hypertext. *Template cards* allow users to specify the contents of cards in advance based on type. *Autolinks* and the *Structure Library* allow users to define network structure "types" out of card and link types. *Modes* allow users to tailor the interface for creating cards, links and structures. We have implemented these mechanisms in the Instructional Design Environment, or IDE. Our project focuses on the representation tasks found in instructional design, but the mechanisms of IDE are general and would benefit any representation task.

In the next section we describe the instructional design process. In Section 3 we introduce the IDE system, and in Section 4 describe the NoteCards hypertext system, on which IDE is built. Sections 5 through 8 introduce and describe the three structure accelerators in IDE. Section 9 discusses sharing representations built in IDE. In Section 10 we give an example of IDE in field use, and in Section 11 draw conclusions about the system.

2. THE PROCESS OF INSTRUCTIONAL DESIGN

The process of instructional design is typical in its representational requirements. The task often involves the management of large amounts of complex information. Typically, the process of instructional design extends from analysis of the domain knowledge to be taught, to the development and delivery of the instructional materials. The instructional designer decides what to cover in a course, and how to organize, present and, finally, produce the course materials. Determining the course content involves a "front-end" analysis of the domain and requires significant research and careful analysis of both the domain knowledge and applicable instructional principles. The instructional designer determines the instructional goals of the course, collects and analyzes knowledge about the domain to be taught, and then structures that knowledge according to the instructional goals. At the end of this process the designer produces instructional deliverables organized into a lesson sequence consisting of presentations, exercises, tests, and other material designed to achieve the instructional goals. Instructional deliverables are often multi-media based.

These tasks make instructional design an exercise in creating, developing and coordinating knowledge representations.

3. THE INSTRUCTIONAL DESIGN ENVIRONMENT

IDE is a hypertext-based multi-media environment that facilitates the task of building representations in the instructional design process, from conception of instructional ideas and objectives to delivery of actual instruction. IDE emphasizes the "front-end" analysis portion of instructional design, where domain knowledge is analyzed and structured into semantic networks with specific patterns. This crucial step of the design process is what we believe largely determines the effectiveness of the delivered instruction.

IDE promotes effective performance of this representation task with *structure accelerators* that greatly reduce the overhead costs incurred in creating groups of nodes and links. These accelerators enable the designer to quickly capture and reuse regularites in structures as they emerge, within an environment that continues to support informal structuring. In this way, IDE encourages the development of complex network representations that may better capture the structure of the knowledge being analyzed. Our hope is that this will improve the effectiveness and quality of the final instructional material.

IDE is built on NoteCards, an extensible, full-featured hypertext system [Hala87b]. IDE extensively tailors and extends the NoteCards system through NoteCards powerful programmer's interface [Trig87], and passes much of this tailorability onto the instructional designer through simple menu interfaces. Because of its tailorability, IDE can support many different methods of instructional design, such as Mager's model

[Mage62] and Gagne's learning hierarchy [Gagn70], giving instructional designers tremendous flexibility in pursuing their methodology of choice.

IDE is a large system containing many features. We present only some of these features in this paper; others have been described elsewhere [Russ89].

4. OVERVIEW OF NOTECARDS

NoteCards [Hala87b] is designed to help people record, manipulate and structure information. NoteCards provides facilities to create, organize and manage a semantic network of typed nodes as *notecards* connected by typed *links*. A notecard is the electronic version of the paper notecard, and contains text, sketches, graphs or other editable substances. Links connecting notecards are typed and unidirectional. The database of notecard substances and link connections are stored in a *notefile*. Figure 1 displays several notecards from a user's notefile. The large notecard at the top of the figure is a *Browser* card that contains a pictorial graph of a network of notecards. In browsers and other cards, linked notecards are represented by link icons (which appear as boxed text). Selecting the link icon with the mouse traverses the link, and displays the destination notecard. In browsers, links between cards are represented by lines drawn between their two respective icons. Browsers provide a very useful means of viewing the structure of a network.

Extensibility in NoteCards

NoteCards provides a powerful programmer's interface of over 150 functions for extending and tailoring the basic NoteCards environment. Any operation available in the user interface is available in the programmer's interface. NoteCards also supports a card *types mechanism* that features an inheritance hierarchy for creating new card types by specializing existing card types. IDE makes extensive use of both the programmer's interface functions and the types mechanism, building on top of NoteCards.

5. FACILIATING THE REPRESENTATION TASK IN IDE

A primary goal of IDE is to facilitate rapid and accurate development of complex networks. Toward this goal IDE supports *structure accelerators* that speed up user interactions while guiding structural development. In the next three sections we describe three structure accelerators: (1) Template cards, (2) Autolinks and the Structure Library, and (3) Modes.

6. CREATING STRUCTURED CONTENT

An advantage of using hypertext for representating semantic networks is that nodes may be typed and, as cards, may contain arbitrary amounts of information. In many cases, however, the user may wish to start from other than blank typed cards, and include previously structured content in cards used for similar purposes. IDE allows users to specify in advance the contents of cards with *Template cards*.

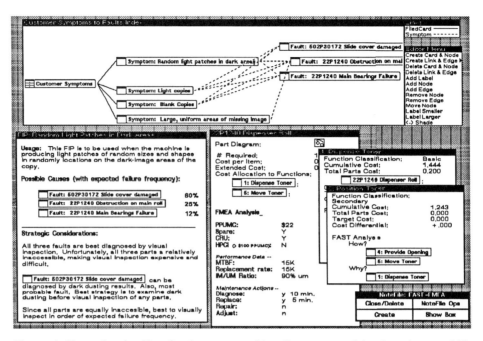

Figure 1. Example of a NoteCards screen, with a Browser card (top) and several Text cards, with embedded link icons.

Template cards

Template cards allow users to define new text-based card types by editing a "master template" card for each type. New instances of a template card type are created with the properties and text of the master template, and may include graphics, links to other cards, and other items. Template cards specialize *Text* cards by using the Notecards types mechanism. In the types mechanism, each card type inherits its properties, substance and functionality from its parent in a card type hierarchy. The types mechanism allows the programmer to tailor the environment by adding useful card types, and IDE's Template cards passes this tailorability onto the non-programming user with simple menu interfaces.

IDE supports a library of about 20 default template types, including Component, Concept and Skill cards. These templates all contain fields that appear in the text with blank values that are to be filled in by the user. For example, a Component card, shown in Figure 2, contains fields for a machine component's name, part number, possible failure modes, and other properties. A field might be filled in with a link to another card, graphics, or just plain text. The right side of Figure 2 shows an example of how the fields of a Component card might be completed. Here the instructional designer analyzed the Developer Housing unit of a large copier according to the fields given in the template, as part of a task analysis for creating instruction on copier repair. Template cards also provide a menu interface for editing a card type's bitmap identifier that appears on the left of link icons (see Figure 2). This identifier enables quick interpretation of link icons of cards of many different template types.

Instructional designers have found Template cards particularly useful since their task involves recording textual information with a standard format. Template cards accelerate the creation of networks by allowing the user to specify in advance text common across cards, removing the need for redundant retyping and reformatting.

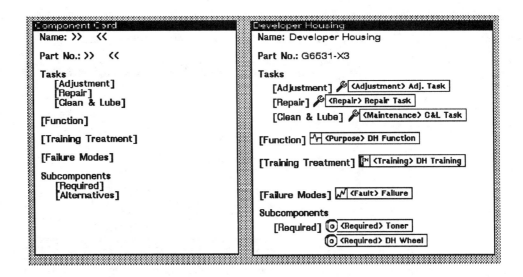

Figure 2. Two Component cards, one with original empty fields (left) and one filled in (right).

7. GUIDING AND ACCELERATING NETWORK DEVELOPMENT WITH AUTOMATIC LINKING

Much of the time spent in creating networks is spent creating links between cards. In this section we describe two structure accelerators, *Autolinks* and the *Structure Library*, that automate steps in the linking process.

Autolinks

When creating a new link to a new card, if the structure of the network being created is already known, the types for the new link and card can be determined from the type of the source card. Autolinks capitalize on this fact and allow users to specify in advance (1) the type of the link, and (2) the type of the destination card in a link connection, eliminating the need to specify these parameters at link creation time. For example, in a task analysis of copier components, the designer may know in advance that each component will have a failure mode and several repair tasks associated with it. Figure 3 illustrates how different copier components for this analysis would produce identical types of link connections. Autolinks allow each link connection to be created with one mouse click by specifying in advance the parameters of the connection.

Autolinks reside as buttons in the text of the source card of the link connection. Autolink buttons are delineated from text by square brackets ([ ]). Selecting the autolink button creates a new link of the specified type to a new card of the specified type, placing the new link icon next to the autolink button. The Component card in Figure 2 contains seven autolink buttons, including one for each of the link connections displayed in Figure 3.

Rapid extension of networks to any level of depth

Autolinks feature a "creation depth" parameter for automatic creation of additional levels of a network. This feature is very powerful when used with template cards. If an autolink links to a template card that also contains autolinks, these second-level autolinks will also be activated when the top-level autolink's creation-depth parameter is greater than 1. Thus, the user can recursively "grow" an entire network of cards and links with a single mouse click. (This network will necessarily be a hierarchy, since autolinks currently cannot cross-reference each other.) Figure 4 shows several master templates with imbedded autolinks and the 4-level structure they would create by selecting an autolink button that was set to create a new EO ("Enabling Objective") card.

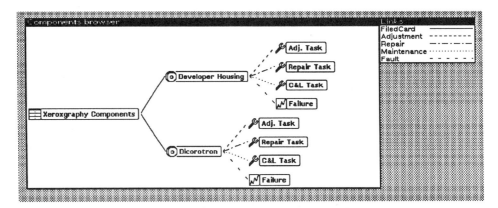

Figure 3. A Browser card displaying similar fault/task substructures containing Component cards ("Developer Housing", "Dicorotron"), Fault cards ("Failure") and Task cards.

In addition to the link type, card type and creation depth, other editable autolink parameters are the title of the destination card and the location of the new link icon in the source card's text. The user may also specify that autolinks be "one-shot" buttons that are deleted from the text after the new link is created.

Distributed vs. Centralized Structure Definitions: Autolinks and the Structure Library

When autolinks are placed in master templates, they together *implicitly* define a structure since the structure information is *locally distributed* across the autolinks and templates. Activating an autolink creates a structure that grows locally at each level. Sometimes, however, the user may wish to create structures that cannot be implicitly defined by autolinks and templates, such as when the local linking of a card's type depends on its position in a larger network. In this case, a network's structure needs to be specified *globally*, and its local node and link relations *explicitly* defined. The Structure Library in IDE allows users to explicitly define structures by creating a "master structure type" from an existing structure instance composed of interconnected cards and links. A master structure contains only information about the types of cards and links, and their interconnectivity, found in the structure. New structure instances created from a master consist of new card and link instances of the types occurring in the master. Users can link to new structures as they do to new cards.

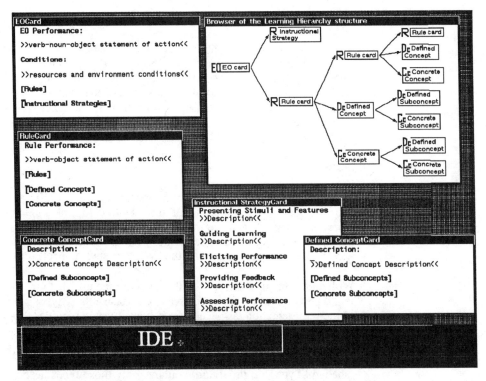

Figure 4. Master templates with embedded autolinks (left and bottom cards), and a browser displaying a structure "grown" from clicking on a single autolink.

Guiding structural development of networks

Autolinks, the Structure Library and Template cards together direct the rapid development of semantic networks according to predefined yet tailorable specifications. Template cards containing autolinks set to link to other template cards or to library structures direct the user to create link connections that will produce a network structure of a guaranteed form. Because autolinks and the library structures are an *optional* alternative to creating link connections, this structural form is encouraged but not imposed.

Gains in speed and effort of building networks

Great gains in the speed of building networks are achieved with autolinks and the structure library. The usual 5-mouse click operation of selecting (1) the new link operation, (2) the new link location in the text, (3) the new link type, (4) that a new destination card be created, and, finally, (5) the destination card type, reduces to a single mouse click with an autolink. The savings in mouse clicks becomes approximately exponential with the number of levels created. The structure in Figure 4, for example, which was created with one mouse click with autolinks, would require 5 x 13 = 65 mouse clicks to create without autolinks.

Significant gains in the cognitive effort to build networks are also achieved. Because a network's patterns are stored in the autolinks, templates and structure libraries, the need to remember specific node-and-link patterns as one builds a network is virtually eliminated. Only deviations from these patterns at creation time need be noted. The result is a great reduction in cognitive overhead. Users of IDE have reported a tremendous savings in the cognitive effort expended in building networks.

8. FOCUSING THE USER'S ATTENTION ON THE IMMEDIATE TASK

A byproduct of having the ability to easily define new template card and structure types is that the library of these types quickly becomes large and unwieldly. Searching menus for types relevant to the immediate task can be difficult. For example, the 20 default IDE template card types apply to different stages of the instructional design process, and the designer would only want to use a few of them at one time. To eliminate the problem of searching through a large "types library", and to simultaneously help focus the user's attention to the current task, IDE provides *Modes*.

Modes

Modes help the user to concentrate on developing specific portions of a network by allowing users to tailor menus that interface to card, link and structure types. Only those types currently relevant are made salient. With Modes, IDE extends the philosophy of adaptability in NoteCards (see [Trig87]), by providing interfaces for users to change the way in which *they* interface with the hypertext environment.

With modes the user can specify the layout of menus used for selecting (1) card types, (2) link types, and (3) library structures to emphasize those types relevant to the current stage of the representation task. The user can easily switch modes. For example, during a task analysis the instructional designer may only use Component and Function cards, and during instructional sequencing use Script and Course cards. Figure 5 shows an example of IDE in Task Analysis mode. The menu for creating new cards (the pop-up menu labelled "Type?" in the figure) contains only those types needed in this mode. All other types are accessible under the "Other" submenu. Thus, the user is not distracted by card types irrelevant to the immediate task analysis.

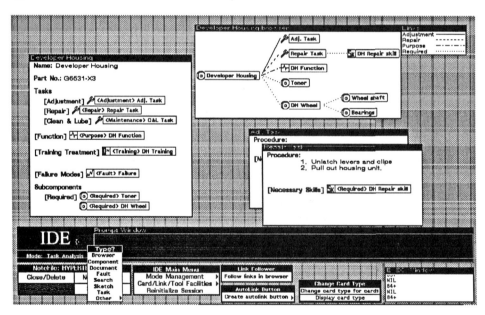

Figure 5. Example of an IDE screen in Task Analysis mode.

If a Browser card is created in a particular mode (such as the "Task Analysis" browser in Figure 5), only those link types in that mode are visible. Browsers used with modes are similar to the "webs" found in Intermedia [Garr86, Yank85].

The IDE Library contains four default modes that reflect generic stages we have identified in instructional design: Data Collection, Task Analysis/Structuring Knowledge (TASK), Sequencing and Delivery. These modes and their corresponding stages in the instructional design process are described in more detail in [Russ89].

---

9. STORING AND SHARING DEFINITIONS OF STRUCTURE ACCELERATORS

Definitions for template cards, autolinks, library structures and modes are all stored in a special notefile called a *definitions notefile*. Definitions notefiles provide a clean, modular distinction between the parameters that specify how the environment is to be tailored, and the code that implements the tailorization. Definitions notefiles promote both sharability and collaboration. By passing around these notefiles users may easily share definitions. Definitions notefiles may be merged together, allowing collaboration between and integration of representational paradigms. For example, exchanging definition notefiles has made collaboration easy between our groups in California and in New York state. Sharing definition notefiles facilitates group efficiency by (1) elminating the redundancy of redefining structure accelerators, and (2) avoiding the costly duplication of problems encountered by previous designers.

It is solely the information in these definition notefiles that tailors the hypertext environment to the specific representation task. In fact, the "instructional design" part of IDE resides in the definition notefiles defined by us and our users. Thus, the IDE mechanisms described in this paper, because their parameter values are stored separately, are truly general to all hypertext-based tasks.

10. CREATING INSTRUCTION IN HYPERTEXT: IDE IN USE

IDE is currently in use at a number of sites both inside and outside of Xerox. We have been closely monitoring our users to obtain feedback on existing tools and to identify needs for new ones. IDE is being used for instructional design in a number of domains, including stastistics, copier repair and foreign language instruction [Schw89]. In this section we present a case of IDE in use.

A Case Study: Creating instruction for complex machinery

One instructional designer is using IDE to develop instructional material for the repair of printing systems. This user is performing a functional analysis of both copier and laser printer components in order to explain the relationship between familiar copier components and components in the new laser printing systems. Figure 6 shows a browser this user created that contains a network description of the possible different charging systems used in copiers and printers. This structure emphasizes that different components can be used to perform the same function of laying a uniform charge on a photoreceptive belt. This fact is articulated by connecting Component cards to the same Function card. In Figure 6, the "Scorotron" Component card is linked to Component and Function cards representing its subcomponent ("Coronode") and function ("Charge the belt"), respectively. Its Function card is linked to a Concept card ("Opposites attract") that represents a concept needed for a proper understanding of the Scorotron's function.

This designer created these cards and their structure in a "Task Analysis" mode. This mode contains the Component, Function and Concept card types, and Purpose, Required and Concept link types, among others. Autolinks residing in the Component cards were used to create new Purpose links to Function cards, and new Subcomponent links to other Component cards (see the browser in Figure 6). Autolinks in the Function cards created Concept links to Concept cards. During the task analysis, this designer rapidly created networks with this card-and-link pattern by activating an autolink that linked to a Component card with a creation depth of 4. This reduced to a single mouse click the task of generating the substructure that represents a task analysis for each component.

The autolinks and template cards encouraged this user to develop a task analysis structure of this general form. By using these templates, this user avoided needing to make additional decisions about how to develop the structure. It is worth emphasizing, however, that templates and their autolink buttons only *suggest* structural forms, and that it is up to the user to realize at creation time that, for example, the Function cards to which the Dicorotron and Scorotron cards in Figure 6 link should be the same Function card and not two different ones.

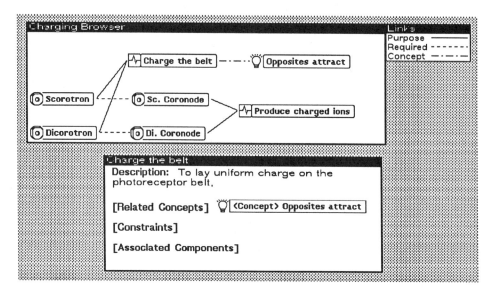

Figure 6. A Browser card (top) and Function card (bottom) created by an IDE user for representing the charging components and their function.

11. CONCLUSIONS

Using hypertext for representation tasks that involve formalized structures can be difficult. IDE is a hypertext system application that facilitates rapid and accurate development of formal structures with the use of structure accelerators. IDE benefits the user by *encouraging* the creation of regular network patterns, and, therefore, *promoting* effective performance in the analysis of domain knowledge. The usefulness of IDE is not limited to instructional design. Template cards, Autolinks, the Structure Library and Modes would benefit design tasks other than those involving instruction, as well as other representational tasks not involving design. Other applications of hypertext systems for instruction such as Intermedia and BALSA [Yank85] have also extended their applicability to other domains to various degrees.

Tailorability, Flexibility and IDE

IDE addresses a number of hypertext issues, two of which we briefly discuss here. Tailorability is an important issue for hypertext systems [Hala87a, Trig87]. IDE extends the tailorability of NoteCards by allowing the user to (1) create, modify or delete types defining cards and structures, and (2) modify the menu interface of the hypertext environment to suit his or her needs.

Flexibility to represent information is also an important feature of hypertext [Trig87]. Within the domain of instructional design, IDE gives the user great flexibility to implement the design model of his or her choice. Using Template cards the instructional designer can define fields or other formatted contents for cards to hold information in a form consistent with the design model. Autolinks and the Structure Library can be used to define structures that reflect the representational specifications of the model. Modes can be used to represent the individual stages of the instructional design process recognized by the model.

In conclusion, IDE and its structure accelerators described in this paper address several critical needs for building representations in hypertext, as well as several important general hypertext issues.

ACKNOWLEDGEMENTS

We would like to thank Richard Burton for his comments on an earlier draft of this paper, and more importantly for his past guidance of the IDE project. We are grateful to Robby Robinson, Bob DeRoller, Phil Ondocin and Ken Hansen of Xerox Corporation and Joe Psotka of the Army Research Institute for their support of IDE. We thank Jonathan Cohen for his contributions to the system, and the NoteCards group (Randy Trigg, Peggy Irish and Randy Gobbel) for their aid, advice and bug fixes.

REFERENCES

[Conk87a] Conklin, J. Hypertext: An Introduction and Survey. *Computer*, 20, 9, 17-41. Chapel Hill, NC. 1987.

[Conk87b] Conklin, J. and Begeman, M.L. gIBIS: A Hypertext Tool for Team Design Deliberation. *Hypertext '87 Papers*, 247-251. Chapel Hill, NC. 1987.

[Deli86] Delisle, N. and Schwartz, M. Neptune: A Hypertext System for CAD Applications. *Proceedings of ACM SIBMOD International Conference on the Management of Data* (pp. 132-143). Washington, D.C. 1986.

[Gagn70] Gagne, R. *The Conditions of Learning*. New York: Holt, Rinehart and Winston. 1970.

[Garr86] Garrett, L.N., Smith, L, and Meyrowitz, N. Intermedia: Issues, Strategies, and Tactics in the Design of a Hypermedia Document System. *Computer-Supported Cooperative Work (CSCW '86) Proceedings*, (pp. 163-174). Austin, TX. 1986.

[Hala87a] Halasz, F.G. Reflections on NoteCards: Seven Issues for the Next Generation of Hypermedia Systems. *Hypertext '87 Papers*, 345-365. Chapel Hill, NC. 1987.

[Hala87b] Halasz, F.G., Moran, T.M., Trigg, R.H. Notecards in a Nutshell. *Proceedings of the ACM CHI+GI Conference* (pp. 45-52). Toronto. 1987.

[Mage62] Mager, R. *Preparing Instructional Objectives*. Palo Alto, CA: Fearon. 1962.

[Mars87] Marshall, C.C. Exploring Representation Problems Using Hypertext. *Hypertext '87 Papers*, 253-268. Chapel Hill, NC. 1987

[Russ87] Russell, D.M., Moran, T.P., & Jordan, D.S. The Instructional Design Environment. In *Intelligent Tutoring Systems: Lessons Learned*. J. Psotka, L.D. Massey, & S.A. Mutter (Eds). Lawrence Erlbaum Associates, Inc. Hillsdale, NJ. 1987.

[Russ89] Russell, D.M., Burton, R.R., Jordan, D.S., Jensen, A., Rogers, R.A., Cohen, J.C. *Creating Instruction with IDE: Tools for Instructional Designers*. Xerox Palo Alto Research Center Report (System Sciences Laboratory) P88-00076. Palo Alto, CA. 1989.

[Schw89] Schwartz, M. & Russell, D.M. FL-IDE: Hypertext for Structuring a Conceptual Design for Computer-assisted Language Learning. *Instructional Science*, 18, 5-26. 1989.

[Trig87] Trigg, R.H., Moran, T.P., Halasz, F.G. Adaptability and Tailorability in NoteCards. *Proceedings of INTERACT '87*. Stuttgart, West Germany. 1987.

[Yank85] Yankelovich, N., Meyrowitz, N., van Dam, A. Reading and Writing the Electronic Book. *Computer*, 18(10). 1985.

JANUS: Integrating Hypertext with a Knowledge-based Design Environment

Gerhard Fischer
Raymond McCall

University of Colorado, Boulder
Boulder, Colorado 80309

Anders Morch

Intelligent Interfaces Group
NYNEX Science and Technology
White Plains, NY 10604

ABSTRACT

Hypertext systems and other complex information stores offer little or no guidance in helping users find information useful for activities they are currently engaged in. Most users are not interested in exploring hypertext information spaces *per se* but rather in obtaining information to solve problems or accomplish tasks. As a step towards this we have developed the JANUS design environment. JANUS allows designers to construct artifacts in the domain of architectural design and at the same time to be informed about principles of design and the reasoning underlying them. This process integrates two design activities: construction and argumentation. Construction is supported by a knowledge-based graphical design environment and argumentation is supported by a hypertext system. Our empirical evaluations of JANUS and its predecessors has shown that integrated support for construction and argumentation is necessary for full support of design.

KEYWORDS

Hypertext, knowledge-based systems, construction, argumentation, informed design, human problem-domain communication, construction kits, design environments, issue-based information systems (IBIS), procedural hierarchy of issues (PHI) methodology.

INTRODUCTION

We have worked for a number of years on the development of computer systems, including hypertext systems, to support designers in a wide range of fields, including architecture and software design. Hypertext systems and other complex information stores generally offer little or no help to designers in finding information useful for activities they are currently engaged in. This is a major deficiency, because designers are not interested in exploring hypertext information spaces *per se* but rather in obtaining information to solve problems or accomplish tasks they are dealing with. As a step towards correcting this deficiency we have developed the JANUS design environment. JANUS allows architectural designers to graphically construct artifacts by direct manipulation and at the same time to receive information useful to what they are doing from hypertext activated by knowledge-based agents. The information they receive concerns principles of design and the reasoning underlying them. This work has implications for a number of issues in hypertext research, including what types of links there should be, what style of user interface should be used, the "lost in hyperspace" problem, retrieval of information without browsing [Aksc88], as well as integration of hypermedia with AI technology [Hala88].

The Information Problem in Design

Designers in a wide range of fields--including architectural, industrial, engineering and software design--need better access to information. They seldom have in their heads all the knowledge needed for good design. Even expert designers can no longer master all the relevant knowledge, especially in technologically oriented design, where growth and change of the knowledge base are incessant. Designers typically cannot keep up with developments in their own fields much less in other fields of potential relevance.

While the quantity and complexity of design information continually increases, designers' abilities to locate and manage useful information does not. The large and growing discrepancy between the rates of information generation and use puts a limit on progress in design. Overcoming this limit is a central challenge for creators of design information systems and thus an important topic for hypertext research.

Conventional information systems offer little hope of providing designers with adequate access to information. Retrieval in such systems is based on content search, which typically means keyword and free-text search. This approach only becomes useful if designers know three things that they very often do not know:

  1) that they need information, i.e., that their knowledge is inadequate for certain

     tasks,

  2) that the needed information is likely to exist and be in the information

     system, and

  3) how to retrieve it, e.g., what keywords to use.

Conventional retrieval also has problems in effectiveness and efficiency. Its effectiveness is limited by a seemingly unavoidable tradeoff between the two standard measures of effectiveness: precision and recall. The former denotes the fraction of retrieved items which are relevant; the latter, the fraction of relevant items in the information base which are retrieved. No conventional approach can come close to finding all those items and only those which are relevant. Typically, users must wade through large amounts of retrieved items to find small amounts which are useful. The inefficiency of conventional retrieval is problematic for designers because of both the effort and the time involved. These interfere with design by creating distractions and interruptions.

JANUS substantially reduces these problems for design by integrating a knowledge-based system with an issue-based hypertext system. In this paper we describe JANUS using examples of its application to the domain of kitchen design. We begin by explaining the two independent lines of research which led to the creation of JANUS. The genealogy of JANUS is shown in Figure 1.

One line of research pursued the development of issue-based hypertext to support the design activity of argumentation; the other pursued the development of knowledge-based design environments to support the design activity of construction. Argumentation is the activity of reasoning about a design problem and its solution. It is predominantly verbal but can be partly graphic. Construction is the activity of creating the solution's form. In many design fields, such as architecture and industrial design, construction is a graphic activity and is traditionally done by drawing.

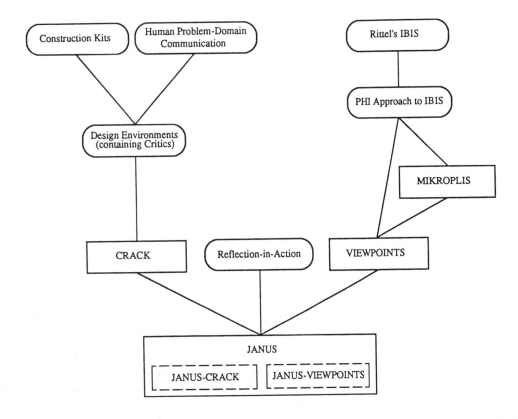

FIGURE 1. Conceptual frameworks (in ovals) and system-building efforts (in rectangles) leading to JANUS.

ISSUE-BASED HYPERTEXT SUPPORTING ARGUMENTATION

IBIS and PHI

Research aimed at developing systems supporting designers' argumentation activities was originated by Rittel [Ritt72]. His aim in doing so was to improve design by improving the reasoning on which it is based. This work ultimately inspired the development of hypertext systems such as gIBIS [Conk87][Conk88] and the ones described in this article.

The central concept behind Rittel's work was that of Issue-Based Information Systems (IBIS) [Kunz70]. In an IBIS, information is organized around the discussion of questions, referred to as *issues*. The method of discussion is deliberation, i.e., considering arguments for and against various proposed answers to the issues. The issues in an IBIS are connected to each other by a variety of relationships such as *is more general than*, *leads to*, and *is similar to*.

The Procedural Hierarchy of Issues (PHI) approach [McCa87] extends IBIS by broadening the scope of the concept *issue* and by altering the structure relating issues, answers and arguments. In Rittel's IBIS, an issue is a design question which can be deliberated. In PHI, an issue is *any* design question, whether deliberated or not. PHI replaces the various inter-issue relationships in Rittel's IBIS with *serves* relationships, defined as follows:

> Issue A serves issue B if the answers to A influence what answers are given to B, i.e., if the answering of B depends in some way on the answering of A.

The main serve relationship in PHI is the *subissue of* relationship, defined as follows:

> Issue A is a subissue of issue B if A serves B and B is raised before A.

Unlike the original IBIS, PHI does not rely on deliberation alone for resolving issues. A second crucial process is the recursive decomposition of issues into subissues. This characteristically results in a tree-like structure of an issue with subissues, such as that shown in Figure 2. PHI also allows hierarchies of answers with subanswers and arguments with subarguments.

ISSUE 101:
What should the arrangement of the various components of the kitchen be?
    SUBISSUES:
    102: What are the various components of the kitchen that need to be arranged?
    103: What should the locations of these various components be?
        SUBISSUES:
      104: What should the locations of the various architectural features be?
        SUBISSUES:
      105: What are the various architectural features?
      106: What should the location of the walls be?
      107: What should the location of the doors be?
      108: What should the location of the windows be?
      109: What should the location of the plumbing be?
    110: What should the location of the equipment area be?
        SUBISSUES:
      111: What is the longest usable wall length?
    112: What should the location of the eating area be?
    113: What should the circulation pattern be?
    114: What should the locations of the various components of the equipment area be?
        SUBISSUES:
      115: What are the components of the equipment area that need to be arranged?
      116: What should the location of the cleanup center be?
      117: What should the location of the cooking center be?
      130: What should the location of the storage center be?
      118: What should the location of the preparation center be?
      119: What should the locations of the various components of the cleanup center be?
      123: What should the locations of the various components of the cooking center be?
      127: What should the locations of the various components of.the storage center be?
      131: What should the locations of the various components of the preparation center be?

FIGURE 2. A Hierarchy of issues with subissues. This hierarchy was created with the MIKROPLIS hypertext system. The numbering of issues is by the order in which they were proposed.

An advantage of PHI over the original IBIS is that it more completely and accurately models the task structure of the design process and the information useful for tasks. According to the theory on which PHI is based, every task in a design project can be modeled as an attempt to resolve an issue [McCa86]. The information useful for design tasks can then be found by following the links connecting issues to their deliberative discussions--i.e., answers, subanswers, arguments and subarguments--and to the issues which serve them.

The above-mentioned problems of information retrieval can be overcome for some but not all design tasks by structuring hyperdocuments according to the principles of PHI. The link structure of a PHI hyperdocument allows designers to retrieve information useful for current tasks effectively and efficiently by means of navigation. The link labels in screen displays also tell designers

> 1) of the existence of information useful for current design tasks,
>
> 2) the basic nature of this information and
>
> 3) how to retrieve it (by clicking on it).

PHI Hypertext

We have developed two stand-alone PHI hypertext systems. One is MIKROPLIS [McCa83]; the other is VIEWPOINTS [Fisc89]. MIKROPLIS is a text-only system which superficially resembles an outline processor but can handle graphs with thousands of nodes. At the nodes are texts of essentially arbitrary length. The contents of clusters of linked nodes are displayed in outline format (shown in Figure 2). Retrieval is by navigation and/or use of an English-like applicative query language providing both structure search and content search [Hala88]. This allows retrieval of complex substructures of the hypertext network using numeric identifiers, indexed terms or substrings in combination with descriptions of network structure. VIEWPOINTS is implemented in HyperCard on the Macintosh. It has fewer retrieval capabilities than MIKROPLIS but can store graphics as well as texts at nodes. A screen image from VIEWPOINTS is shown in Figure 3.

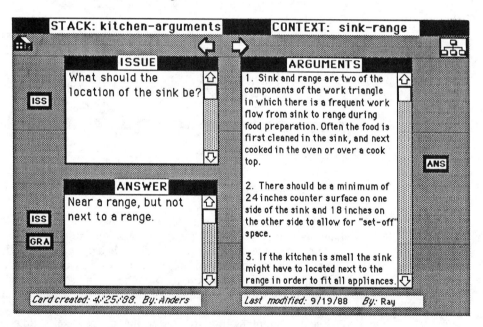

FIGURE 3. A screen image from the VIEWPOINTS hypertext system.

KNOWLEDGE-BASED DESIGN ENVIRONMENTS SUPPORTING CONSTRUCTION

Human Problem-Domain Communication

To shape the computer into a truly usable and useful tool, users must be able to work directly on their problems and tasks. The goal of human problem-domain communication [Fisc88a] is to eliminate computer-specific programming languages and instead to build layers of abstractions with which domain specialists--such as kitchen designers--can feel comfortable. Human problem-domain communication provides a new level of quality in human-computer communication because the important abstract operations and objects in a given area are built directly into the computing environment. The user can therefore operate with personally meaningful abstractions which reduce the transformation distance between problem-oriented and system-oriented descriptions.

CRACK (Critiquing Approach to Cooperative Kitchen Design) [Fisc88b] is a knowledge-based design environment which represents a step toward human problem-domain communication in architectural design. A screen image of CRACK is shown in Figure 4.

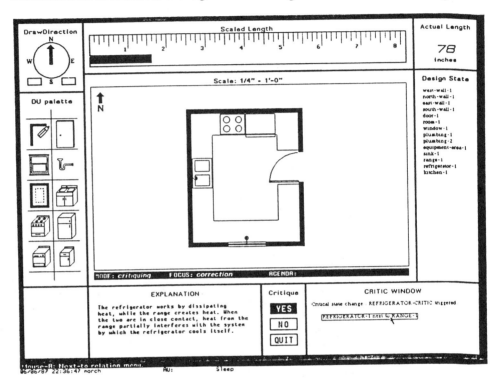

FIGURE 4. A Screen image from CRACK.

Construction Kits

Construction kits are system components that represent steps toward human problem-domain communication by providing a set of building blocks that model a problem domain. The building blocks in CRACK, called design units (DUs), define a design space (the set of all possible designs that can be created by combining them using the "language of kitchen design") and a design vocabulary (represented by the "Palette", on the left in Figure 4). Construction kits are domain-specific programming languages that help users to formulate solutions to complex problems and that allow them to create complex artifacts without having to master the many details inherent in general purpose programming languages. They eliminate a number of prerequisite skills, thus allowing users much more time to practice and work in their actual areas of interest and expertise.

Beyond Construction Kits: Critics and Design Environments

Human problem-domain communication and construction kits are necessary but not sufficient for good design. Upon evaluating prototypical construction kits we found that they do not by themselves assist the user in constructing interesting and useful artifacts in the application domain. To do this they would need knowledge for distinguishing "good" designs from "bad" designs together with explanations which justify this knowledge. Kitchen design, for example, involves more than selecting appliances from a palette; it involves knowing how to combine these simple building blocks into functional kitchens. Knowledge about kitchen design includes design principles based on building codes, safety standards, functional preferences and other considerations.

Design environments, such as CRACK, combine construction kits with critics. Critics use knowledge of design principles to detect and critique partial solutions constructed by the designer. Critics in CRACK are state-driven condition-action rules which are triggered when non-satisficing partial solutions are detected. The critics display criticism (such as, "Refrigerator next to range") in the "Critic Window" (lower right corner in Figure 4). If designers want more information, they can make requests for explanations (lower left corner in Figure 4) and suggestions by clicking with the mouse on the text of the criticism. The critics create the text displays dynamically and in the proper context as users are constructing the design.

LIMITATIONS OF THE TWO TYPES OF SYSTEMS

The above-described systems have been tested in use long enough for their basic capabilities and limitations to become apparent. MIKROPLIS and VIEWPOINTS have been used to create issue-bases for a variety of problem domains, including software, architectural and urban design as well as environmental and health care policy making. CRACK has been tested in use by both student and professional designers.

A clear lesson which has emerged from the use of MIKROPLIS and VIEWPOINTS is that PHI hypertext alone cannot fully realize the goal of informing designers while they design.

PHI hypertext works as long as designers are actually working on resolving issues with the hypertext system. While working in this predominantly verbal mode, the designer is automatically shown the information known to be relevant to the issue being worked on. Unfortunately, there is a crucial type of design activity which cannot effectively be handled in PHI hypertext: construction.

Our students consistently proved unable to do construction within PHI itself. But, once they left PHI hypertext to work on construction, the hypertext exhibited the characteristic weakness of conventional retrieval systems--i.e., designers got information from it only if they knew to ask for such information and knew how to ask correctly. The PHI link structure could no longer automatically alert them to the existence of information useful for current tasks. Thus, during construction PHI hypertext failed to achieve its goal of adequately informing designers.

The inability to do construction in PHI even occurred when students did PHI without use of computers, thus it is not an artifact of the hypertext implementations. This result was surprising at first, since video-taped protocols revealed hand-drawn construction to involve continual deliberation and decomposition of issues. The explanation for this apparent paradox is that PHI's argumentation is *about* construction, *not the same as* construction. Construction and argumentation are distinct modes of design. Both are required for good design, but they cannot be done simultaneously. This conclusion nicely fits Schoen's theory of design as reflection-in-action [Schoe83], with his concepts of reflection and action corresponding, respectively, to argumentation and construction.

Tests of CRACK revealed that it also did not go far enough toward achieving its goal, i.e., the goal of informing its users about construction. CRACK's rules for kitchen design were not intended to be inflexible commandments, but rather rules of thumb to which exceptions can and should be made. While users were in principle free to ignore CRACK's criticism, in practice they had difficulty judging when and how to do so. CRACK's brief "explanations" failed to reveal the complex argumentative background-- including assumptions, conditions and controversies--behind its critiques. Without this background it was difficult for users to make the intelligent exceptions characteristic of good design.

Evaluations of these systems together with studies of designers by ourselves and others show that integrated support for construction and argumentation is essential for full support of design. Schoen's theory of reflection-in-action states that constant alternation between action and reflection, i.e., between construction and argumentation, is the hallmark of good design. The shift to argumentation occurs when designers need to evaluate what has been constructed, are stuck in problematic situations or need to think about what to do next. The critiques given by CRACK allow this but in far too limited a way. Some way is needed of coupling systems like CRACK and VIEWPOINTS to overcome their deficiencies. JANUS provides such a coupling.

JANUS: AN INTEGRATED DESIGN ENVIRONMENT

The JANUS Concept

JANUS' concept for integrating CRACK and VIEWPOINTS derived from the observation that CRACK's criticism is really a limited type of argumentation and can be mapped directly into PHI form. In particular, the construction actions can be seen as attempts to resolve issues. For example, when a designer is positioning the refrigerator in the kitchen the issue being resolved is "Where should the refrigerator be located?"--or some paraphrase of this. Criticism which appears in CRACK's "Critic Window" (lower right in Figure 4) corresponds to a general answer to the construction issue. For example, "REFRIGERATOR-1 next to RANGE-1" (in Figure 4) corresponds to the answer, "Do not put the refrigerator next to the range." Finally, what appears in CRACK's "Explanation" window (lower left in Figure 4) is an argument for this answer.

The fact that CRACK's criticism can be put in PHI form shows that its knowledge-based critiquing mechanism actually connects construction with argumentation--albeit very limited argumentation. This means that CRACK and VIEWPOINTS could be coupled by using CRACK's critics to provide the designer with immediate entry into the exact place in the hypertext network where the argumentation relevant to the current construction task lies. This would solve two problems: it would greatly enrich the argumentative information provided by critics and it would allow PHI hypertext to be used during construction. Such a combined system could provide argumentative information for construction effectively, efficiently and without designers' having to

1) realize they need information,

2) suspect that needed information is in the system or

3) know how to retrieve it.

JANUS is the integration of the two systems, CRACK and VIEWPOINTS, in a common computing environment: the Symbolics Genera Software Environment. JANUS is named for the Roman god who had two faces looking in opposite directions and who symbolized a variety of dualities, such as beginning and ending, rise and fall, entry and exit. In the JANUS design environment the two faces correspond to construction and argumentation--and to the coupled software systems JANUS-CRACK and JANUS-VIEWPOINTS.

JANUS-CRACK: Janus' Construction Component

JANUS-CRACK supports the construction of an artifact either "from scratch" or by modifying an already constructed artifact. To construct "from scratch," the designer chooses building blocks from a design units "Palette" (upper left in Figure 5) and positions them in the "Work Area" (upper right in Figure 5). Protocol studies have shown that designers use design units at different levels of abstraction in the same project [Akin78][Fisc88b]. Therefore, JANUS-CRACK allows the designer to select different palettes each of which contains design units at a different level of abstraction. In the current version of JANUS-CRACK there are two such palettes, one containing specific appliances (shown in Figure 5) and one containing the more abstract design units of "work centers," such as cleanup center, cooking center and storage center.

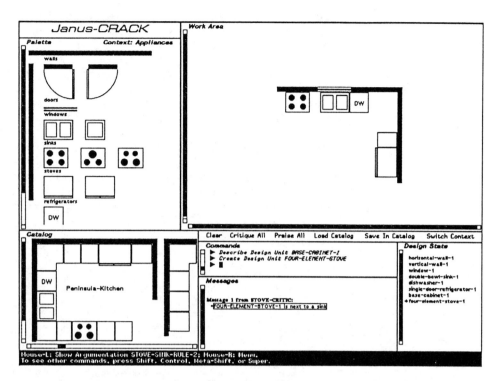

FIGURE 5. A screen image from JANUS-CRACK.

To construct by modifying an existing artifact, the designer uses the "Catalog" (lower left in Figure 5), which contains many previously designed kitchens. The designer can browse through this catalog of examples until an interesting design is found. This design can then be selected and brought into the "Work Area," where it can be modified to the designer's liking. In this way the designer can avoid many of the difficulties of starting "from scratch."

There are currently two types of examples in the catalog: "good" designs and "bad" designs. The former satisfy all the rules of kitchen design and will receive no negative criticism from the system's critics. People who want to design without knowing the underlying principles might want to select one of these, since minor modifications of these will be probably result in little or no negative criticism from the critics.

The "bad" designs in the catalog are there to support learning about principles of design-- in this case principles of kitchen design. By bringing these into the "Work Area" the user can subject them to critiques by the system--either by repositioning design units in the selected example or by activating the "critique all" command, which fires all critics. This will show what principles of kitchen design are incorporated into the system. It will also provide the user with entry into the hypertext system where the larger argumentative background of the principles can be explored by navigation.

The "good" designs in the catalog can also be used to learn design principles and explore their argumentative background. This can be done by bringing them into the "Work Area" then using the "praise all" command. This command causes the system to display all of the rules which the selected example satisfies. This positive criticism also provides entry points into the hypertext argumentation.

JANUS-VIEWPOINTS: Janus' Argumentation Component

The PHI hypertext component of JANUS is implemented using Symbolics' Concordia and Document Examiner software. Concordia is a hypertext editor [Walk88] which we used to create the issue base. The Document Examiner [Walk87] provides functionality for on-line presentation and browsing of the issue base by users. To use this software for PHI we had to map the documentation structure of the Document Examiner--including sections, subsections, subsubsections and fragments--into the argumentative structure of PHI--including issues, subissues, answers, subanswers, arguments and subarguments. Concordia allowed us to do this and to display argumentation in the same sort of outline format used in MIKROPLIS. Document Examiner allows users to navigate in the issue base by using the mouse in several different types of displays.

Many displays in JANUS-VIEWPOINTS are composites of related texts representing "argumentative contexts." The "answer" context (in the main "Viewer" pane in Figure 6) contains an answer and its arguments. The "issue" context (in the "Outline" pane, upper right in Figure 6) contains an issue with its answers and their arguments.

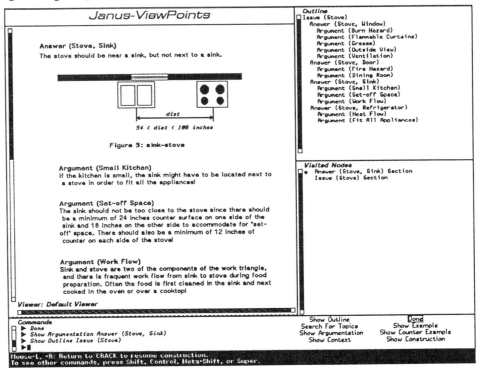

FIGURE 6. A screen image from JANUS-VIEWPOINTS.

When users enter JANUS-VIEWPOINTS from JANUS-CRACK they are brought into a section of the PHI issue base determined by and relevant to their current construction situation. They do not have to hunt for relevant information. Their point of entry into the hypertext network will contain relevant information. But since the argumentation on an issue can be large and complex, they can use the initial display of relevant information as the starting place for a navigational journey through the issue base. Each traversal of a PHI link will take them to additional relevant information which argues the current construction issue in more detail. Thus the chances of becoming "lost in hyperspace" are reduced. Upon completion of the examination of the relevant argumentation the designer can return to construction and complete the current task.

Critics as Hypertext Activation Agents

JANUS' knowledge-based critics serve as the mechanism linking construction to argumentation. As is the case with CRACK, the critics in JANUS have knowledge about how design units should and should not be arranged. They "watch over the shoulders" of designers doing construction and critique their work, displaying the criticism in the "Messages" pane (center bottom in Figure 5) if design principles are violated. In doing so they also identify the argumentative context in JANUS-VIEWPOINTS which is appropriate to the current construction situation.

For example, when a designer is positioning a stove in the "Work Area" as in Figure 5, the stove critic fires and detects that the stove is too near the sink. It therefore displays the appropriate criticism in the "Messages" pane--as is also shown in Figure 5. To see the argumentation surrounding this rule the designer has only to click on the text of this criticism with the mouse. The argumentative context shown in Figure 6 is then displayed.

Evaluation of JANUS.

We have evaluated JANUS with subjects ranging from neophyte to expert designers and from neophyte to expert computer users. We found that no user group had any significant overall advantage in using the system. Design students were more familiar with the general application domain but learned to use the system without much difficulty after some initial practice. Computer science students were able to understand the critics and learned from them to create reasonable kitchen designs. Users uncertain about criticism from the system or interested in more background information about design principles entered the hypertext system by clicking on the criticism. No users got "lost" in the hyperdocument; none failed to complete the construction task.

CONCLUSIONS AND FUTURE WORK

Conclusions

JANUS represents not merely a system building effort but a theoretical framework for application of hypertext to design. Our preliminary evaluation of the JANUS system has demonstrated that hypertext can be used in conjunction with knowledge-based design environments to inform designers effectively, efficiently and without their having to know

> 1) that they need information, i.e., that their knowledge is inadequate for certain design tasks,
>
> 2) that the needed information exists and is in the system, or
>
> 3) how to retrieve it.

PHI hypertext systems like VIEWPOINTS and design environments like CRACK individually help to improve design, but they have significant limitations. Integrating them in a system like JANUS overcomes many of these limitations. PHI's task-oriented links make navigation effective in locating information for design tasks once the verbal representations of these tasks as issues have been located. Construction kits support human problem-domain communication; adding intelligent critics to create design environments promotes better construction. When PHI hypertext and design environments are combined as in JANUS, the critics alert the designer to the existence of information relevant to current construction tasks and provide immediate and effortless entry into the exact location in the hypertext network where the useful information lies.

Future Work

In the course of developing JANUS we have found a variety of topics for future research. Roughly speaking, these can be categorized into issue dealing with 1) the construction system (JANUS-CRACK), 2) the argumentation system (JANUS-VIEWPOINTS) and 3) the connections between these two.

Within the construction system alone there are many issues which need further exploration. .One is that of what would be needed if the construction task were scaled up-- e.g., from a kitchen to a house to an apartment building to a cluster of apartment buildings. It seems that the current flat structures of the palette, the catalog and the construction state (in the "Work Area") would be inadequate. What then should these structures be? How should their information be managed? Should hypertext be used? If so, how should this construction hypertext system relate to the argumentation hypertext system?

Within the argumentation system there is a pressing need for authoring to be integrated with browsing. Allowing *ad hoc* authoring during browsing would enable the designer to annotate the issue base, record decisions on issues and generally personalize the argumentation. This in turn would create the need for certain basic kinds of inference mechanisms. For example, if the designer has rejected the answer "dining area" to the issue "What functional areas should the kitchen contain?" then the system should probably not display any issues, answers or arguments which presuppose or assume that the kitchen has an eating area.

Construction and argumentation might usefully be connected in a number of additional ways. Catalog examples could be used to illustrate argumentation, and argumentation could be used to help in selecting examples from the catalog. Argumentation could be used to help designers select items from the palette--or even to select palettes. Designers might want to see the relevant argumentation *before* they place items in the work area. Subissue structures might be used to suggest the nature and order of construction tasks.

Finally, while kitchen design has been a useful starting point, the real significance of the JANUS approach lies in its applicability to a wide range of problem domains. We therefore plan to test it in several other domains, including software design.

ACKNOWLEDGEMENTS

We would like to thank our colleagues and students who helped us critically evaluate the usefulness of the systems described in this paper. The research was supported in part by Grant No. MDA903-86-C0143 from the Army Research Institute and by grants from NYNEX Corporation and Software Research Associates (SRA).

REFERENCES

[Akin78]   Akin, O. "How Do Architects Design?" in **Artificial Intelligence and Pattern Recognition in Computer-Aided Design**, J. Latombe (ed.), North-Holland, New York, 1978.

[Aksc88]   Akscyn, R.; McCracken, D.; and Yoder, E. "KMS: A Distributed Hypermedia System for Managing Knowledge in Organizations," **Communications of the ACM**, Vol. 31, No. 7, July, 1988, pp. 820-835.

[Conk87]   Conklin, J.; Begeman, M., "gIBIS: A Hypertext Tool for Design Deliberation," **Hypertext'87 Papers**, University of North Carolina, Chapel Hill, NC, November 1987, pp., 1987, pp. 247-251.

[Conk88]   Conklin, J.; Begeman, M., "gIBIS: A Hypertext Tool for Exploratory Policy Discussion," **Proceedings of the 1988 Conference on Computer-Supported Cooperative Work**, Association for Computing Machinery, 1988, pp. 140-152.

[Fisc88a]   Fischer, G.; Lemke, A. "Construction Kits and Design Environments: Steps Toward Human Problem-Domain Communication," **Human-Computer Interaction**, Vol. 3, No. 3, 1988, pp. 179-222.

[Fisc88b]   Fischer, G.; Morch, A. "CRACK: A Critiquing Approach to Cooperative Kitchen Design," **Proceedings of the International Conference on Intelligent Tutoring Systems**, ACM, New York, June 1988, pp. 176-185.

[Fisc89]   Fischer, G.; McCall, R., Morch, A. "Design Environments for Constructive and Argumentative Design," in **Proceedings of the ACM Conference on Human Factors in Computing Systems (CHI'89)**, May 1989, pp. 269-275.

[Hala88]   Halasz, F. "Reflections on Notecards: Seven Issues for the Next Generation of Hypermedia Systems," **Communications of the ACM**, July, 1988, pp. 836-852.

[Kunz70]   Kunz, W.; Rittel, H. "Issues as Elements of Information Systems," **Working Paper 131**, Institut fuer Grundlagen der Planung, Stuttgart, 1970.

[McCa83]   McCall, R; Schaab, B.; and Schuler, W. "Information Station for the Problem Solver: System Concepts," in **The Application of Mini- and Micro-Computers in Information, Documentation and Libraries**, C. Keren and L. Perlmutter (eds.), Elsevier Science Publishers B.V., North-Holland, 1983, pp. 245-251.

[McCa86]   McCall, R. "Issue-Serve Systems: A Descriptive Theory of Design," **Design Methods and Theories**, Vol. 20, No. 3, 1986, pp. 443-458.

[McCa87]   McCall, R. "PHIBIS: Procedurally Hierarchical Issue-Based Information Systems," **Proceedings of the Conference on Architecture at the International Congress on Planning and Design Theory**, American Society of Mechanical Engineers, New York, 1987, pp. 17-22.

[Ritt72]   Rittel, H., "On the Planning Crisis: Systems Analysis of the 'First and Second Generations,'" **Bedriftsokonomen**, No. 8, 1972, pp. 390-396.

[Schoe83]   Schoen, Donald **The Reflective Practitioner**, Basic Books, New York, 1983.

[Walk87]   Walker, J. "Document Examiner: Delivery Interface for Hypertext Documents," **Hypertext'87 Papers**, University of North Carolina, Chapel Hill, NC, November 1987, pp. 307-323.

[Walk88]   Walker, J. "Supporting Document Examiner with Concordia," **IEEE Computer** January 1988, pp. 48-59.

Towards An Integrated Maintenance Advisor[1]

Phil Hayes and Jeff Pepper

Carnegie Group, Inc.
5 PPG Place
Pittsburgh, PA 15222

1. THE PROBLEM

Large, complex systems such as telephone switches or aircraft have associated documentation sets that frequently extend to several tens of thousands of pages. When a failure occurs, locating relevant sections of the documentation to determine appropriate corrective action can be time-consuming. The problem is compounded because documentation changes frequently to accommodate engineering changes, product updates, and newly identified problems and solutions. Boeing, for instance, issues a full set of revised documentation every 90 days.

Putting the documentation on-line can ameliorate these problems, both in terms of speeding the distribution of updates and in terms of locating relevant sections of the manual by keyword search. Information retrieval can be further enhanced by using a hypertext representation for the documentation. This provides the potential for much easier browsability and location of relevant sections through cross-reference links between different components of the documentation. However, this approach also has its problems. Keyword search is notoriously inaccurate [Blai85] and will often fail to locate the appropriate sections. Keyword search needs to trade off recall (the proportion of appropriate references found) against precision (the proportion of references that are relevant). As Figure 1 shows, typical results as represented by the Medlars Information Retrieval System [Salt89] do not allow both measures to rise much above 50% simultaneously (point B), though one can be traded off against the other (points A and C). Moreover, appropriate cross-referential links in a hypertext require a very large human indexing effort and are hard to maintain in the face of documentation changes.

Fortunately, recent advances in automatic content-based text processing can in many cases resolve these problems with on-line/hypertext documentation. It is now possible to search and index documents on the basis of the concepts they contain, rather than just on the basis of keywords. Such an approach can dramatically raise both recall and precision simultaneously. As shown in Figure 1, these techniques resulted in average recall of 94% and average precision of 84% (point D) across the 674 distinct categories handled by the CONSTRUE news story categorization system [Haye88,TB89] built by Carnegie Group. These conceptually-based text processing techniques can be used both to locate relevant sections of the documentation and to automatically generate the cross-referential links necessary for a useful hypertext representation.

---

[1]Many of the ideas in this document have been developed in the context of ongoing discussions with other Carnegie Group personnel, particularly **Gary Kahn**, and also including **Phil Hainline**, **Peggy Andersen**, and **Dick Herman**.

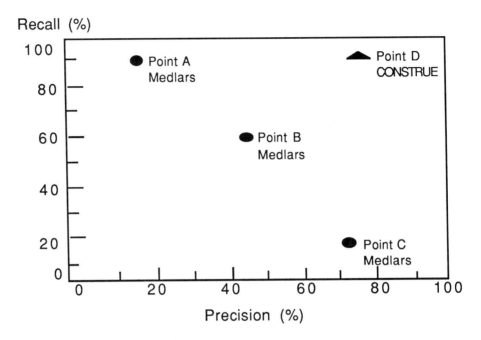

Figure 1: Recall and Precision figures for the Medlars Keyword-Based Information Retrieval System and for the CONSTRUE News Story Categorization System

A radically different approach to diagnostic support has recently emerged with expert diagnostic systems, such as the Carnegie Group TestBench ^{TM} product [Kahn87]. Such systems encode expert diagnostic knowledge and provide troubleshooting advice to the technician trying to fix the problem. This advice is generated by a general purpose "inference engine" which uses an application-specific knowledge base containing troubleshooting information about the system under maintenance. The diagnostic expert system typically interacts with the user in an advisory mode, suggesting tests and repairs and freeing the user from the need to navigate voluminous documentation.

Expert diagnostic systems are highly effective with relatively small, focused applications (i.e., where the knowledge base contains up to several thousand rules or objects). However, because the construction and maintenance of knowledge bases is still a labor-intensive process, this approach can be inappropriate when applied to very large, complex systems such as telephone switches or aircraft where the number of faults and other knowledge base objects may run into the hundreds of thousands. Moreover, even if extremely large diagnostic systems could be constructed, the uniform interpretive mechanisms they employ would represent overkill in many simple situations and would lack the appropriate generic process information to deal effectively with novel problems. In both kinds of situations, it may be more effective to augment the advisory function of a diagnostic expert system with an "expert librarian" function that would assist the technician in accessing relevant sections of the written documentation.

This paper outlines a framework for supporting fault diagnosis in complex systems that addresses all the problems outlined above by combining the best features of the solutions discussed. It is based on a conceptually-indexed hypertext representation of written documentation along with tightly integrated diagnostic subsystems. We have termed this approach the Integrated Maintenance Advisor, or IMAD, since it integrates several technologies and provides the user with both troubleshooting and browsing advice.

The IMAD approach has the following advantages:

- hypertext provides an easily browsable representation for written documentation;

- conceptual indexing allows relevant sections of the documentation to be located quickly and accurately;

- tight integration of diagnostic expert subsystems allows the user to switch seamlessly between browsing and following the instructions of a diagnostic expert system in situations where he needs that additional level of support.

Problem diagnosis is far from the only kind of situation where people need assistance in accessing large sets of documentation. Similar needs arise in the design process. Aircraft manufacturers, for instance, maintain very large sets of documentation on standards for the manufacturing process. Creating a specific manufacturing process plan is largely a matter of finding, modifying, and combining information that already exists. A subset of IMAD, providing the librarian functions but not the diagnostic advisor, may also be appropriate for those areas.

The remainder of this paper focuses on fault diagnosis applications, presenting first a general framework for such applications and then an example of that framework for a specific application.

2. THE FRAMEWORK

This section describes the IMAD approach to supporting fault diagnosis for complex systems along the lines outlined above. It represents a design in progress and has not yet been implemented. It is presented in terms of the following components:

- An *Expert Librarian* providing

    - hypertext representation of written maintenance documentation

    - hierarchical representation of the system covered by the documentation

    - conceptually-based indexing for the hypertext

- An *Expert Diagnostic Advisor* providing diagnostic subsystems

- *Integration* between the Expert Diagnostic Advisor and documentation hypertext in the Expert Librarian

These are discussed in sequence.

2.1. Hypertext of Written Documentation

The foundation of IMAD is a hypertext representation of existing written maintenance documentation of the complex system under consideration. We assume that this documentation is in page-oriented form. Each page is converted into a node in the hypertext. Navigation through the hypertext is possible through forward and backward page-turning and through a hierarchical table of contents. If the documentation is available in on-line format, presumably written in some mark-up language, then the formatted version of that is used for the hypertext nodes, while the mark-ups are used to generate the hierarchical table of contents. If the documentation is available only in hard-copy form, currently a very common situation, then a scanned image of the pages is used in the hypertext nodes for presentation to the user, and the table of contents is generated from an

ASCII version of the text of the document, obtained through OCR techniques from the page images.

With this much of IMAD, a technician has approximately the same degree of assistance as he would get from written documentation. As a practical matter, it is important to provide this base level of functionality in a very solid way, so that users do not feel that they have lost desirable features of the hard-copy documentation.

2.2. Hierarchical Representation of System under Maintenance

For the purposes of both the conceptually-based indexing of the documentation hypertext and the construction of expert diagnostic subsystems, some form of abstract representation of the system under maintenance is needed. We assume at minimum that we have a hierarchical breakdown of the system in terms of components and subcomponents. Each component in the component hierarchy is labeled with the words and phrases that can be used to describe it both specifically (spar 7 (in the left wing), a ft76-903 fastener) and generically (the spar, the bolt). The generic descriptions may be supplemented by information about the type of component (fastener, electrical, electronic, hydraulic subsystem, etc.).

2.3. Conceptually-Based Indexing

Using the hierarchical system breakdown, the associated component descriptions, and more general knowledge about how things are expressed in maintenance documentation (such as the concepts of replacement, installation, connection, etc.), IMAD automatically constructs conceptually-based indexing to facilitate access to and navigation around the documentation hypertext.

This access and navigation is mediated through a graphical display of the component tree. By clicking on any component in the tree, the user is presented with a *precis*, an automatically generated index frame summarizing all references to the component throughout the hypertext. These references will often be extensive and so will be grouped according to type of reference, including repair procedures, structural description, usage restrictions, and so on. Selecting an entry from the precis gives the user the corresponding documentation page, which may in turn provide links to other pages in typical hypertext fashion. The user may choose to see only the entries for the component as a whole or also include references to any of its subcomponents.

Categorizing references by type in this way is a significant extension to the undifferentiated reference more usually found in hypertexts. When there are dozens or hundreds of references, it could make the difference between finding or not finding the desired information. The construction of categorized indexes is also an area where conceptually-based automatic methods offer particularly significant advantages. Not only do such indexes require a great deal of effort to construct and maintain manually, but it also may be feasible to make the automatic recognition of the various kinds of reference largely domain-independent. This is based on the assumption that the kind of language used in, for instance, a structural description has many similarities across different domains.

The user may also gain selective access to the component tree from the documentation. Specifically, by clicking on any mention of a component in the text, the user can obtain a view of the component tree with the component the user clicked on centered and highlighted. The user is then free to move to the precis for that or for any other component in the usual way.

The techniques used to build the precis frames and to find the references to components in the text are based on the text categorization techniques that Carnegie Group has developed in the context of news story categorization [Haye88] and is now offering in generalized packaged form as the Text Categorization Shell [TB89]. These techniques allow the appropriate references to be found and index entries made on a conceptual basis, rather than based on the occurrence of specific key words and phrases. This insensitivity to the way that potential references are phrased makes it possible to generate almost all the appropriate references automatically (high recall) while minimizing the number of irrelevant references and index entries (high precision).

2.4. Expert Diagnostic Advisor

The Expert Diagnostic Advisor component of IMAD is provided by Carnegie Group's TestBench product [Kahn87]. TestBench presents the user with a decision tree of tests leading to an eventual diagnosis and repair recommendation. This decision tree is generated automatically from an underlying knowledge base of faults, tests, and repair procedures, and its structure can be modified dynamically at runtime by exception rules provided by domain experts. As with any knowledge based system, the task of building a knowledge base is labor-intensive, and generally such applications are not built for entire systems of the complexity of an airplane or telephone switch. The IMAD approach, therefore, is to develop a set of focused diagnostic applications, each of which addresses a subsystem of the overall system. Such subsystems would typically be chosen on the basis of the difficulty of the diagnosis and the difference in skill level between expert troubleshooters and "typical" troubleshooters. Each focused diagnostic application will have its own knowledge base, but will refer to components from the overall system structure tree in a uniform manner.

In some cases, it will be possible to reduce significantly the amount of knowledge engineering effort required to produce the expert diagnostic subsystems by automated processing of the written maintenance documentation. In particular, when the written documentation contains troubleshooting procedures where tests and actions are identified in a stylized way, it will be possible to construct an initial knowledge base automatically. This automated text processing would be in addition to the regular documentation processing for references and index entries, but would use similar, conceptually-based techniques.

2.5. Integration between Expert Diagnostic Advisor and Expert Librarian

The Expert Diagnostic Advisor operates by presenting a series of tests to the user. Which test is presented at a given time is determined from the results of previous tests and the knowledge base of faults. This format is naturally compatible with a hypertext -- the different outcomes of the tests correspond to links in a hypertext and can be presented to the user in a similar way.

Transitions from the Expert Librarian to the Expert Diagnostic Advisor are also relatively straightforward. For each component or subsystem reference in the documentation, the user may ask for diagnostic assistance in a similar way to asking for the location of the component in the component hierarchy. If the component is located in a subsystem which is covered by a diagnostic knowledge base, the user will be presented with a list of known faults in that component. On selecting one of the faults, he will enter the Expert Diagnostic Advisor at the appropriate point in the diagnosis. This greatly facilitates diagnosis, since the diagnostic expert system can shortcut much of the diagnosis if the fault and faulty component can be identified by the technician in advance. It is a lot easier, for instance, to diagnose a problem in a faulty radar mount than to diagnose the same problem starting from the point where one only knows that the radar is not tracking properly.

There are also reverse connections from the Expert Diagnostic Advisor to the Expert Librarian. In particular, any component referenced in the diagnostic expert system can be treated in the same way as in the documentation, as an index into the component hierarchy. Moreover, instructions for repair procedures or performing diagnostic tests are linked to the points in the documentation that give instructions on performing these procedures. It should be possible to generate both kinds of linking automatically by the same kind of conceptually-based text search as used for the indexing of the documentation hypertext. If the user follows such a link from the diagnostic subsystem to the documentation without completing a diagnosis, the current state of the diagnostic session is preserved, and the user may return to it later after browsing as much as desired.

3. DEVELOPMENT SCENARIO

This section describes how an IMAD might be created for a large, complex system. Figure 2 illustrates this process.

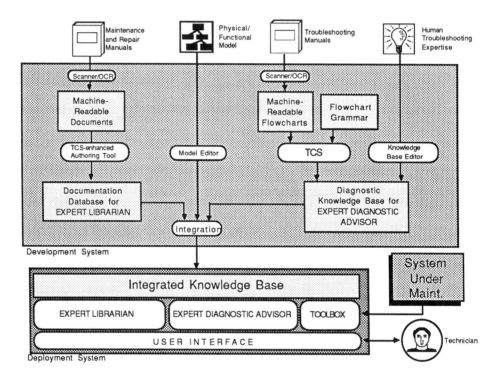

Figure 2: IMAD Development and Deployment Process

In the scenario given here, the system under maintenance is a HAWK missile system, widely used by the U.S. Army and other NATO countries. The HAWK is a very complex weapons system [Kelle89], but its degree of complexity is typical of the kind of systems where we feel IMAD would apply.

First, the developer defines a physical and/or functional model of the HAWK. This is a simple hierarchical structure, where the HAWK is defined in terms of its major systems (high-power illuminating radar, command-and-control computers, etc.), subsystems, and so on down to the component level, the field-repairable-unit level, or whatever level of detail is desired. This model is built using a graphical editor.

Once the structure of the model is defined, the developer goes back through and annotates it with all terms that are used to describe the components, subsystems and systems of the HAWK, as well as its tests and repairs. This is the second step: the creation of a standard dictionary of terms which will be used to ensure that the two major components of the IMAD, the Expert Librarian and the Expert Diagnostic Advisor, can be merged seamlessly.

The last step in model-building is to mark which portions of the model are (or will be) covered by diagnostic expert systems. This is necessary for supporting the final merging of hypertext with diagnostics, and can also be used to graphically illustrate which portions of the overall HAWK system are covered by expert system advisors and which are only covered by hypertext and other structured documents.

Once the model has been created and annotated, the documentation hypertext is created. This hypertext contains the bulk of the maintenance and repair manuals for the HAWK, including graphical material (schematics, diagrams) as well as test and repair instructions. The construction of this hypertext is semi-automated, and is done using a conceptually-based text processor based on the TCS (Text Categorization Shell) technology.

Certain other documents have a high degree of underlying structure, and these documents can undergo further processing. In the case of the HAWK, there are hundreds of pages of troubleshooting manuals in flowchart form. These manuals are converted into two different forms. First, they are converted into hypertext the same way as other manuals. However, they are also processed by another conceptually-based text processor which extracts the underlying meaning of the text and converts the flowcharts directly into knowledge base structures that can be used by the Expert Diagnostic Advisor. In essence, this is the automated creation of a diagnostic knowledge base.

Next, there is human troubleshooting expertise that needs to be captured using traditional, labor-intensive knowledge engineering. This expertise is captured using a graphical knowledge base editor, such as the TestBuilder editor [Kahn87] provided with TestBench. The diagnostic knowledge base that results from this is linked with the other diagnostic knowledge base that was automatically created from flowcharts.

Finally, the two different types of knowledge are merged. Using the physical/functional model as a guide, the documentation hypertext is linked with the diagnostic knowledge base. For each fault that is described in the diagnostic knowledge base, a reference to that fault is inserted into the documentation hypertext at the frame where the faulty part or subsystem is described. This permits easy switching from browsing mode to diagnostic advisor mode at runtime.

The entire merged IMAD is now ready to be used.

4. DEPLOYMENT SCENARIO

This section describes how the IMAD created for the HAWK missile system in the previous section might be used at runtime. Since IMAD has not been fully implemented yet, we will confine our discussion to general issues of functionality and navigation, and not attempt to describe a specific user interface.

Essentially, the runtime IMAD behaves as a "smart book", relying on the book paradigm as its primary model. The user can browse on-line documents in much the same way as browsing a book, with the usual hypertext navigation commands available. There may be a number of books available, and each one can be browsed page-by-page or indexed by chapter and section.

The runtime IMAD can also be used in other ways, however. Since there is a physical/functional model of the HAWK, the user can switch to that model and browse the model; i.e., move upward into nodes that represent larger systems or downward into nodes that represent finer levels of detail. Since at this point the user is no longer browsing any particular book, the runtime IMAD displays a precis of information for whatever node the user has selected. This precis is a condensed list of all information available about that node, organized by category (for example, all inventory and parts information for the node, all information on how to test that node, all repair instructions for the node, all schematics, all known faults, and so on). The user can scroll individual sections of the precis, select individual items, and follow links from them into the relevant point in the documentation hypertext.

The runtime IMAD can also be used as a diagnostic advisor. Whenever the system is displaying information about some part of the HAWK, it also shows a list of all faults in that part that are covered by one or more diagnostic expert systems. The user can simply select one of those faults, and IMAD switches to diagnostic advisor mode. The user can switch back and forth at will between the diagnostic advisor and the more traditional browsing mode, depending on whether the user wants to receive troubleshooting advice or peruse the on-line documentation.

When a repair is performed, regardless of whether it was recommended by the diagnostic advisor or selected directly by the user, the runtime IMAD offers the means to hook into other field-service support applications, such as inventory updates and work order closing software. This integration with traditional applications is offered throughout IMAD, providing a powerful, flexible "maintenance support environment" for the user.

5. SUMMARY

This paper has presented a framework for supporting fault diagnosis in complex systems. The framework is based on a marriage of diagnostic expert systems with a hypertext representation of written documentation, supplemented by conceptually-based text processing techniques. This fusion of technologies provides significant advantages over existing approaches. In particular:

• Use of a hypertext representation for documentation without the other two technologies will result in a system where the documentation is easier to browse than hard-copy documentation, but where ease of location of relevant information will be little improved. Moreover, such a system lacks the expert assistance possible through diagnostic expert systems.

• Use of diagnostic expert systems without a full representation of the documentation cannot serve the needs of complex systems because of practical limitations to current diagnostic technology. Moreover, such a system does not allow a technician to browse for greater understanding or insight into the system being maintained.

• A system which merged a documentation hypertext with diagnostic expert systems without use of conceptually-based text processing techniques would face major problems in the construction and maintenance of the necessary documentation indexing and of the cross-linking between the documentation and diagnostic subsystems. Both kinds of links are essential to proper functioning of the arrangement and to be practical, they must be constructed automatically. Only by using conceptually-based techniques, rather than keyword-based techniques, can such automatic construction be made accurate enough.

The framework presented thus combines the advantages of all the component technologies to achieve an effect that could not be achieved by any of them alone. We believe that this approach will yield major benefits in supporting fault diagnosis for complex systems.

REFERENCES

[Blai85] Blair, D. C., and Maron, M. E. "An Evaluation of Retrieval Effectiveness for a Full-Text Document-Retrieval System". *Comm. ACM 28*, 3 (March 1985), pp. 289-299.

[TB89] *Text Categorization Shell: Technical Brief.* Carnegie Group, Inc., Pittsburgh, 1989.

[Haye88] Hayes, P. J., Knecht, L. E., and Cellio, M. J. A News Story Categorization System. *Proc. 2nd Conf. on Applied Natural Language Processing,* Assoc. for Computational Linguistics, Austin, Texas, February, 1988, pp. 9-17.

[Kahn87] Kahn, G., A. Kepner, J. Pepper. TEST, a Model-Driven Application Shell. *Proceedings of the Sixth National Conference of the American Association for Artificial Intelligence,* 1987.

[Kahn87] Kahn, G. S. From Application Shell to Knowledge Acquisition System. *Proc. Tenth Int. Jt. Conf. on Artificial Intelligence,* August, 1987.

[Kelle89] Keller, Brian C., Thomas R. Knutilla. "Building a Diagnostic Expert System". *Ordnance* (May 1989), pp. 44 - 45.

[Salt89] Salton, G. "Another Look at Automatic Text Retrieval Systems". *Comm. ACM 29*, 7 (July 1986), pp. 648-656.

Distributed Hypertext for Collaborative Research: The Virtual Notebook System

Frank M. Shipman, III, R. Jesse Chaney, and G. Anthony Gorry

Baylor College of Medicine, Houston, Texas

INTRODUCTION

We are developing the Virtual Notebook System (VNS) to facilitate information acquisition, sharing and management in collaborative work. Our main concern is enhancing the productivity of scientific groups engaged in basic and clinical research in an acaademic medical center. As the name implies, the VNS is an electronic analog to the scientist's notebook, and it functions as the repository of data, hypotheses and notes, patient information and the like. But unlike the traditional notebook, the VNS is expressly designed to enhance information sharing among the members of scientific teams. A hypertext program we have developed is the foundation for this sharing, and it enables us to integrate into the VNS a variety of computer-based information resources that are so important in biomedicine.

Our principal goals were to support collaborative work and facilitate the distribution of the VNS in a heterogeneous computing environment. Early prototypes of the Virtual Notebook System used Xerox's NoteCards and later Knowledge System's KMS. [Gorr88] But these hypertext systems lacked features we needed. NoteCards did not allow groups concurrent access to the hypertext network and so made collaborative uses of the system difficult. KMS provided concurrent access, but could not easily incorporate external information resources and applications. Further, neither system ran on a number of the platforms that are already in place at Baylor. While other hypertext systems were discussed in the literature, some with quite appealing functionality, we found all ultimately lacking for our application. [Conk87] In some cases, the systems were simply not available in a supported form; in others, foreign applications could not be integrated with the hypertext; and for some, highly-specialized hardware or operating systems were required. Therefore, we somewhat reluctantly undertook the development of our own hypertext system for the VNS.

The result of our effort which is described here is a hypertext system implemented in the Sybase relational database. The hypertext is intimately connected to a number of the features of the VNS. We have maintained a clear distinction between the user interface, written in the X Window System and the data access mechanism for the hypertext. This has helped us integrate information resources into the VNS. While our main goal has been to support biomedical research, we believe that the information acquisition and management tools we built for researchers will prove valuable in other settings. Certainly the technologic infrastructure we are developing - the communications architecture and the linkages to information resources and other institutions - will serve purposes at Baylor in addition to those of research. Administrative and managerial duties require similar task coordination and integration.

HYPERTEXT FOR THE VIRTUAL NOTEBOOK

The design of the VNS envisions a number of work group servers (WGSs) connected through a network. A WGS would provide local information storage and management by maintaining the group's hypertext in a relational database on the group's server. Through a special Gatekeeper computer, users of a given WGS could share information with other groups and access information stored on other servers. The integration of the Gatekeeper and the WGSs is an important function of the VNS.

The VNS is to serve as a notebook, so the basic unit in the hypertext is a page which is generally the size of a sheet of paper, but which the user can can resize within the limits of the screen. A user may create pages that allow no subsequent modification of their contents - for example for a researcher's notebook, or pages.that can be modified at any time.

A page contains a number of information objects: text (research notes, electronic mail) or images (graphs, pictures). The user can create text objects with an EMACS-like editor or make use of the X Window System's selection service to transfer text from other windows. Our snapshot tool permits a user to sweep out any portion of the screen with the mouse cursor and place the resulting image on a notebook page. And as discussed below, the user can create information objects in sessions with information resources (such as the library) using our paste facility to move information from the resource directly onto a notebook page. Figure 1 shows a notebook page with text and image objects and other pages collapsed to iconic form.

The user can also "copy" objects from existing pages. When objects are copied from pages only a reference to the object is retained in the page; the object itself occurs only once in the database and is shared among pages. Indeed, much of the support for collaboration in the Virtual Notebook is based on the sharing of objects through our distributed hypertext system. The information objects which comprise a page may in fact be distributed among several work groups' fileservers.

A user can create a new page at any time, adding and editing text, sweeping out images off the screen, or copying objects from existing pages. After the layout and content of a new page are to the user's liking, the page composition (information objects on the page, their location and size), page creator, the page's title, and time of page creation are stored in the relational database.

A VNS mail tool permits the user to mail and receive pages of a notebook. As not all scientists will have access to the VNS, we encode the pages for mailing in PostScript. This allows the page to be displayed or printed on standard PostScript devices. A VNS user may send a hypertext page to anyone who has an electronic mail address and the ability to view or print PostScript.

Pages may contain links, references to other pages in the hypertext web. A web of pages connected by links is referred to as a notebook. A user may work with many notebooks, some of which may be shared by members of his immediate work group or by other users of the VNS while some notebooks may be private. In creating a new link on a page, the user simply positions the link in the "source" page and then clicks the mouse in the "destination" page. Information for the new link is stored immediately in the database and the new link appears in the source page..

A link on a page may point to any other page, so a single notebook may share pages with other notebooks. A link appears as a small icon on a page and allows rapid movement from one page to another. When a user moves the mouse cursor over a link a small window pops open providing information about the link and the page to which the link points: link title, link owner, destination page title, and page owner. Moving the cursor out of the link closes the information window. This provides users with a way to "preview" the page which the link references. Clicking the left mouse button while in a link causes the linked page to appear in a new window.

Links belong to the owner(s) of a notebook and although they appear to be on the page, they are, in fact, stored separately from the page. Two users might share a page, seeing the same information objects on it, but view different links. This is because the page is assembled dynamically for a given user. From the page composition and link information (creator, types of links, and positions on the page), all of which are retrieved from the relational database, the hypertext application assembles a page on demand and overlays it with the appropriate links. Help pages may have links from every user in the system, though each user wants to see only his personal annotations. Figure 1 shows several open pages with various information objects and a links.

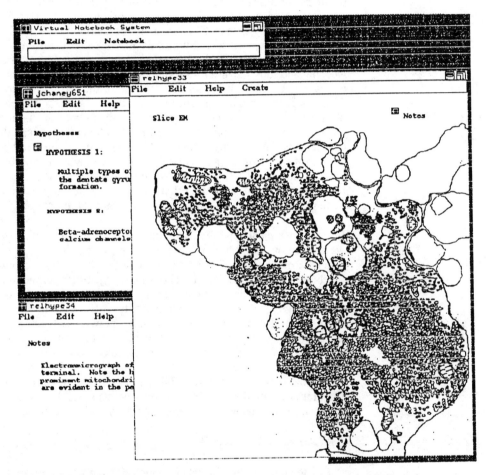

Figure 1. - Portions of Notebook Pages

A first time user of the Virtual Notebook System is given a notebook with his home page containing a link to his so-called scrapbook. The Scrapbook is, as its name implies, a temporary repository for new objects that the user has not had a chance to organize. It is particularly useful in capturing information during interactions with information resources. New pages of the scrapbook are created as needed and each may contain many text or image objects. Each user's home page contains a link to the most recently created page of that user's Scrapbook. The pages of the Scrapbook are automatically linked together in a linear matter from the most recently created page to the oldest page. New objects pasted into the Scrapbook are always put on the most recently created page.

NAVIGATION

Using hypertext to support large workgroups provides some problems that have not been addressed satisfactorily by previous hypertext systems. With a group of eight to ten people all sharing a one or more notebook and probably maintaining individual notebooks as well, the problem of finding information is apt to be acute. The typical hypertext method of navigation, namely following embedded icons, is not satisfactory. [Hala88]

We provide a "filtering" mechanism for pages, objects, and links to support directed navigation by the user. Malone uses the concept of filtering in describing his Information Lens system, "Even though the term [filtering] has a literal connotation of leaving things out, we use it here in a more general sense that includes selecting things out of a larger set of possibilities." [Malo87] Such filtering in the Lens systems is analogous to the information scanning, sorting, and disseminating that is so important in biomedical groups. In the hypertext, filtering involves searching a set of objects or pages to find those that meet a defined condition. Each of the items (information objects, links, pages, notebooks, and users) in the VNS may possess a number of attributes that are used for indexing and subsequent retrieval of the objects. Certain attributes are added.by default and others may be added by users. An example of the former are time stamp, the identity of the creator, and certain type-specific information such as the sender of mail pasted as an object on a page. The user may additionally index objects under selected terms of a common work group vocabulary. With this indexing, users can then find particular kinds of objects in the hypertext with direct calls on the data base rather than through browsing through the hypertext. (For example, find the images created by Joe in the last month.) The substance of the data and the structure of the hypertext network may be used as part of the description for filters. Filtering will be especially helpful in work groups where often members will be looking for information they did not organize.

Besides the typical hypertext browsing mechanism and the directed navigation of filtering, we have provided a hierarchical browser for the hypertext. The hierarchical browser provides an outline of page titles for a notebook. The browser initially shows the notebook's home page title. By choosing a page title with the mouse, another level in the outline appears. This level contains the titles of the destination pages of the links in the chosen page. The user also has the ability to bring up the actual page of the notebook from within the browser. The hierarchical browser is similar is function to the Browser Card in the NoteCards system, except that the detail (or depth) of the browser is interactively controlled. The browser also allows the user to search for page titles and to mark pages for easy access later. The hierarchical browser allows a variation on the traditional hypertext browsing ability in that the browser allows following links without the cluttering of the screen with the whole pages. This is useful for traversing large networks where the user has some familiarity with page content.

DATABASE MANAGER

All of the data in the Virtual Notebook System are stored in a relational database on a WGS. When a page from the notebook is to be displayed, the hypertext program retrieves all the information objects and links and creates a window in which it displays the page. When a page contains references to information objects not stored on the WGS, the Gatekeeper resolves these references through a mapping it maintains of object names and WGSs. The Gatekeeper can then retrieve the non-local objects for use in the hypertext display, and hypertext application running on one WGS may incorporate information objects from others. We plan to make extensive use of the ability of a Sybase dataserver to make remote procedure calls to other Sybase dataservers on different machines. This will allow us to have a dataserver to assume this Gatekeeper function.

Though users of VNS may share data across several machines, most of their work will be done on their local work group machine. This arrangement distributes the processing load and disk utilization in accordance with the group activities. Within the constraints imposed by Sybase, each work group may choose its computer hardware based upon projected computing power, disk requirements, availability of other software, and cost. The decentralization of the hypertext also provides a greater degree of fault tolerance. Machines may be off-line and not prevent everyone from using VNS. The power supplied by using a distributed relational database makes many other issues for a hypertext system easier to solve. We rely heavily on the Structured Query Language (SQL) calls for its searching power and flexibility. Other programs have easily been developed which make use of these database calls. Problems which would otherwise come up with concurrent access are solved more easily by the dataserver's maintenance of data consistency. Locking mechanisms are provided by the dataserver. Access control, data security, can be implemented at the database level, in addition to the operating system level. The

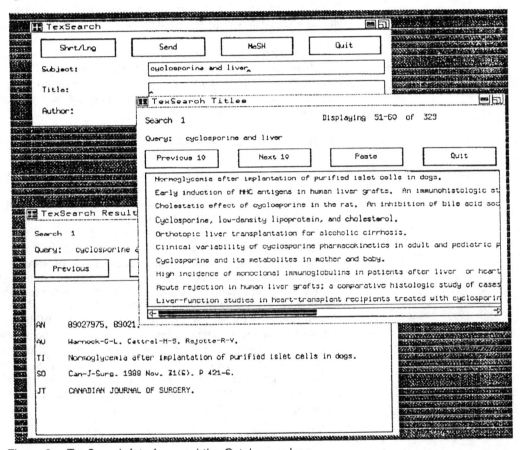

Figure 2. - TexSearch Interface and the Gatekeeper Icon

INFORMATION RESOURCES

With the Gatekeeper, we try to provide a seamless interface between the Virtual Notebook System and information resources distributed across hardware and software platforms. The Gatekeeper embodies X Window System interfaces to a variety of important resources including standard UNIX resources like electronic mail, the C shell, and USENET bulletin boards and other more specialized facilities for bibliographic information, genetic sequencing information, clinical data bases and others. In interacting with these resources, a scientist can move information into the notebook. With one button click, information from the resource is pasted to the user's Scrapbook.

An example of this facility is our interface to Medline, an important database of bibliographic and abstract information on articles from medical journals. Medline is distributed by the National Library of Medicine. The version that we use is the TexSearch database, maintained at the M. D. Anderson Cancer Research Center in the Texas Medical

Center. The interface provided within the VNS masks the required network interconnection. Our interface, which is similar to the Grateful Med interface developed by the National Library of Medicine, is shown in Figure 2.

Similar interfaces exist for the Methodist Hospital Information System (HIS), a very important resource for our clinical faculty and for EuGene, a program for nucleic acid and protein analyses developed at Baylor's Molecular Biology Information Resource. We are adding interfaces to other information resources.

We are developing a scanner interface to allow the introduction of printed materials and images directly into the notebook for annotation. Currently Baylor is developing the Baylor Departmental Information System (DIS) and when completed this database of grant and personnel data will be available through a VNS interface.

Our integration of these diverse information resources through a hypertext system, to our knowledge, is unique. We feel that the hypertext paradigm is the most appropriate for this task, because of the ability to contain and organize information in many different forms. Currently the system only supports image and text data, but future versions could contain audio, video, and animation as well.

WINDOW SYSTEM

Our program development has been done in the X Window System. The hypertext program runs as a client to an X server. The X server and the VNS may be running on different computers connected by our network. By exploiting the client/server model of X we are able to distribute computing power and load.

One of the most important reasons we have developed in X is its potential to become a *de facto* standard for many hardware manufacturers and software developers. We currently can run our hypertext on several types of hardware, Sun Microsystems, Masscomp, Macintoshes, Unix-based PCs and NCD X terminals, although the performance varies across these platforms. X servers are being developed which will allow us to run the Virtual Notebook on MS DOS compatible computers. With the further development and stabilization of the X Window System, scientists will be able to use existing hardware and software, in which they may have great deal invested, and exploit the functions of the VNS. An X server running on a PC, a Macintosh, or an X Terminal does have some limitations, however, we feel that a typical user could be well served by such and as requirements rise, a more powerful workstation can be obtained without loss or change of function.

FUTURE DEVELOPMENT

The Virtual Notebook System is intended to support work groups in the biomedical setting. The need to integrate the system into a heterogeneous environment has dictated a number of the design features. The system has been organized in a manner to facilitate the gradual progression of the VNS towards a general purpose system. Much thought has gone into the initial architecture to allow future work in the areas of document preparation, versioning, and the addition of dynamic objects and links. We believe that through separating the data and the interface and by using a distributed relational database to store the data, we will be in a strong position to address these more general and advanced issues after the initial implementation is complete.

REFERENCES

[Gorr88]   Gorry, G.A., et al., "A Virtual Notebook for Biomedical Work Groups," *Bulletin of the Medical Library Association*, Vol. 76, No. 3 (July 1988), pp. 256-267

[Conk87]   Conklin, E.J., "Hypertext: An Introduction and Survey'" *Computer*, Vol. 20, No. 9, (Sept. 1987), pp. 17-41

[Hala88]   Halasz, F.G., "Reflections on NoteCards: Seven Issues for the Next Generation of Hypermedia Systems," *Communications of the ACM*, Vol. 31, No. 7, (July 1988), p. 836-852

[Malo87]   Malone, T.W., et al., "Intelligent Information Sharing Systems," *Communications of the ACM*, Vol. 30, No. 5, (May 1987), pp. 390-402

ACKNOWLEDGMENT

The work reported here was supported in part by Grant LM040905-01 from the National Library of Medicine. We wish to acknowledge the work of Stan Barber, Andrew Burger, Norman Furlong, Kevin Long, and Eric Taylor. Several of the applications discussed in this paper are the result of their work.

Sun's Link Service:
A Protocol for Open Linking

Amy Pearl

Sun Microsystems
2550 Garcia Avenue
Mountain View, CA 94043

ABSTRACT

Sun's Link Service, a product shipped with Sun's programming in the large software development environment, the Network Software Environment, allows users to make and maintain explicit and persistent bidirectional relationships between autonomous frontend applications. The Link Service defines a protocol for an extensible and loosely coupled, or *open*, hypertext system. An interesting instance of this is the ability to link to objects in *closed* hypertext systems if they integrate with the Link Service. The Link Service addresses link maintenance and automated versioning. Link endpoints, or nodes, are defined by the integrating applications, and are not restricted to points, whole documents, or *cards*.

INTRODUCTION

The majority of the current generation hypertext systems are monolithic: they manage the storage of data as well as linking information. They are designed to be *turnkey*, or complete, authoring tools, supporting some range of media and offering users the ability to make connections between nodes in the system. The author edits data, of whatever media, in the hypertext system, and organizes the data into nodes, using the system's hypertext user interface. The system provides all available editors for manipulating the data as well as mechanisms for manipulating the links. The node data representation in these hypertext systems is structured and proprietary. All these frontend applications are closely coupled with the underlying hypertext substrate. As a result, these systems are *closed* because authors are dependent on the node editing capabilities that the hypertext system provides. If the system does not provide the particular media type editor that the user requires, only the hypertext system developers can make that functionality available. [Aksc87] [Camp87] [Engl84] [Trig86] Some other problems that result from such closed systems are the inability to link to pre-existing objects, and the inability to access the objects in the hypertext from outside the hypertext system.

Sun's Link Service assumes a layering of editing functions, where the management of data and the management of links is loosely coupled. The link and node data are stored separately. Editing and storing of objects is managed by independent editing applications, which also provide a portion of the frontend operations for operating on links. The Link Service stores only *representations* of the nodes, rather than the nodes themselves. This permits the nodes to be represented in any data format, and any existing application to be added as a front end. The majority of the linking functionality, including storage of the link information, is provided by a separate, shared backend. The Link Service provides both this backend as well as a library for the applications that defines a protocol for integrating with the Link Service. In such an *open* hypertext system, independent applications can integrate linking mechanisms into their standard functionality, and become part of an extensible, loosely coupled, frontend interface to the hypertext system (see figure 1). Incorporating existing editors aids users, since they don't have to adapt to new editors, and the range of media available is independent of that explicitly provided by the Link Service. One interesting feature is that the frontend application the user may wish to have incorporated with this service may be another, presumably closed, hypertext system. For example, if a closed hypertext system such as KMS were integrated with the Link Service, users could make links between any KMS object and any object managed by another application integrated with the Link Service.

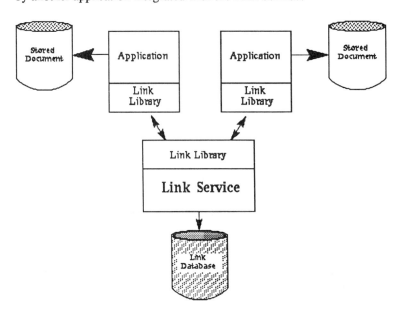

Figure 1. An Architecture for Open Hypertext

The Link Service is a product shipped with Sun's programming in the large software development environment, the Network Software Environment, NSE. We would like to see integration with the Link Service become a standard part of each application running on Sun workstations. In this paper I describe some of the issues involved in open hypertext, the features and implementation of our system, and, finally, some future goals.

ISSUES IN OPEN HYPERTEXT

An open hypertext system emphasizes autonomy and extensibility. This frees the frontends from the constraints of homogeneity, which is useful when considering application-specific details. In the case of editing objects, application-specific refers to such things as how to create and manipulate the application's objects. In the case of manipulating links the definition of a node, or linkable object, is application-specific. The primary cost of this flexibility is a potential loss of consistency, notably in application controlled areas such as the user interface and versioning. The Link Service specifies only the linking behavior for the frontend applications. Because our layers separate control of object and link data management, the Link Service has limited control over versioning, and has no control over the user interface for editing objects, the applications' portion of the user interface for handling links (link indication and object selection), concurrent multi-user features, data integration, or other interactions between frontend applications. Maintaining link consistency between a set of changing documents not under central management is also a difficult issue in open hypertext. In this section, I describe these issues, and how the Link Service addresses them. I also describe a particular

problem that face applications whose data has no structure, like flat ASCII text editors, and some of the issues in the SunOS environment, which is multi-tasking and distributed.

Linkable objects

Since most linking systems consider the data objects to be part of the information that they manage, they must go to some lengths constraining what comprises a linkable object, or *node*. For simplicity, many of these systems require that one or both ends be a whole unit, like a card, or document [Conk87]. The Link Service has no control over the objects, and therefore the definitions and granularity of nodes are left to the applications themselves. Nodes may be whole documents, spans of text, points (either insertion or geometric), whatever the managing application can uniquely identify and reconstitute from that unique identity. The Link Service requires that applications mark their objects that have links with a link indicator, such as an icon, or glyph. For consistency, we provide a particular bitmap (see figure 4).

User interface

One of the design goals for the Link Service was to have minimal impact on the look and feel of the integrating applications. Our goal was to be minimally intrusive both for application integrators as well as for application *users* who may be unconcerned with linking. We accomplished this by segregating the user interface for *linking* as much as possible from the application's pre-existing user interface for editing. Thus, the application integrator has minimal work to do to their user interface to integrate with the Link Service. And users who previously used the application see minimal change to its user interface. The majority of the linking interface is contained in the separate linking command panel, that, like the applications, resides on the desktop. This appears the same across applications (see figure 2). Only two aspects of the user interface for linking affects these applications, and here is where inconsistencies can arise:

- they must provide some mechanism for selecting or indicating their objects when the user wants to do link operations on them

- they must provide some visual indication (such as an icon or glyph) for their objects that have links.

Notably, several of the applications that have already integrated with the Link Service have different *selection* paradigms. Preserving the user interface of existing CASE applications effectively eliminates general interface consistency among these applications. The implementation of the functions for editing the data are left to the application, and the linking interface doesn't affect these operations at all.

Another user interface issue raised by applications integrating with the Link Service is the distribution of function. Because the Link Service and the applications are separate processes, decisions must be made about which of them is responsible for exception handling or dialogues with the user. In general, these issues are not faced by closed hypertext, as the system is designed as an integrated application. The Link Service can only achieve some of this consistency of user interface if user interface standards, such as OpenLook [Hoeb89], are applied to all the applications.

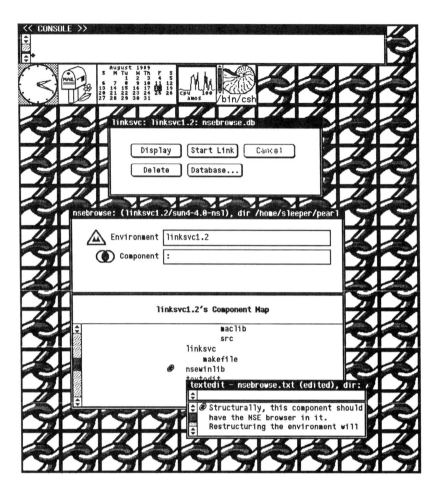

Figure 2. The NSE browser, *textedit*, and the Link Service Command Panel

Link maintenance

When one end of a link is deleted (e.g. a file containing the reference to the end of the link is deleted), the link becomes invalid. In an open hypertext system, it is difficult for the system managing the links, and consequently the application managing the node at the other end of the link, to know that the link is no longer valid. In the Link Service there are two mechanisms for discovering dangling links: implicit and explicit. The implicit discovery occurs when a user attempts to follow from the valid end of the link to the invalid node. The Link Service informs the user that the link is no longer valid and suggests deletion of the link. However, if both ends of the link become invalid before a user attempts to traverse the link, the invalid link cannot be discovered in this way. The Link Service provides an explicit link garbage collection mechanism, called *Confirm All* that goes through and checks whether each object in each link is still valid by querying that object's managing application. A closed hypertext system can more easily detect such changes that disturb link consistency. It is possible to do so in an open hypertext system, but imposes additional burdens on the frontend applications.

Versioning support

Versioning in hypertext is generally a complex issue [Hala87]. Versioning of nodes may or may not be independent of specific versions of links to those nodes. While the Link Service leaves the issue of versioning of the data objects to the individual applications, it still must handle versioning of the *sets* of links, as Intermedia [Meyr86] does. Unfortunately, the consistency of a versioned hypertext body cannot be guaranteed if the nodes are not versioned along with the links between them. Since the Link Service is unable to enforce any connection between the versioning of the data objects and the link objects, it cannot guarantee the consistency of the hypertext *corpus*. In a separate but related issue, users may want a link to connect to a specific version of a node. Applications *can* embed version information in the key for the object that they store with the link database. Targeting the right granularity of versioning for a hypertext system is a difficult issue, whether the system is open or closed. PIE supports versioning for both a set of links as well as the data objects [Gold87]. Controlling versioning policies, and maintaining consistency, is possible, and easier in such a closed hypertext system, though still not trivial.

Handling structureless documents

Applications that integrate with the Link Service store in the link database unique keys for their objects. This is easy for applications that maintain unique internal identifiers for their internal objects. Unfortunately, text editors and other applications that operate on unstructured documents, such as ASCII text files, assume little, if any, structure or semantics about these files. In the current implementation of our link-aware text editors, we use an admittedly too simple method for constructing the key. We assume that the object eligible for linking is a single full line of text. The key is the composition of the text file name and the contents of the line of text. When the editor subsequently has to display this object, it loads the file named in the key, and searches for the first line in the file that matches the line of text in the key. In Intermedia [Evet87] links are defined by position and extent, along with a timestamp, which are tracked as the document changes. This allows the linking of *arbitrary spans* of text. One problem with this method is the overhead of computing a link position after the file has been heavily edited. An additional problem in the non-object model world of Unix is that there is no protection of the file from modification by non-link integrated applications, which can disturb any accounting.

Issues in the distributed workstation world

A Sun workstation environment is multi-tasking and file systems on remote file servers may be transparently available to users. Several issues arise in this kind of an environment, not all of which are particular to open hypertext systems:

> *Remote nodes* Because a user has access to remote file systems, links may be made between nodes that reside on different machines. There must be some addressing mechanism for the Link Service to locate the object on the network using information stored in the link. When, if ever, should it be apparent to a user that linked objects reside remotely? Following a link may be costly, especially if the destination node resides remotely. It may be desirable to indicate, or allow queries about, the *cost* of following a link. Hyperties [Shne86] allows users to preview nodes. It may be a good idea to allow users to at least preview the cost of following a link, if that cost may be high.

> *Link server location* When users interact with the Link Service, where on the network should that process be located? Should there be one link server for each user, one for each physical or logical machine, or one for each notion of a 'working environment'? Must these servers communicate with each other?

> *Application invocation* This issue is of particular concern in an open hypertext system, where the application frontends are separate processes from the hypertext server. At any time, many separate application frontends may or may not be executing. The user can follow a link to a node managed by an application that is not currently running. Should the link server invoke that application, and if so, by what mechanism? And, in a networked environment, on what machine?

IMPLEMENTATION

Whenever practical, it is good design practice to create systems that are extensible by published protocols. There is a tension between support for heterogeneity that is a goal of such open systems and the notion of integration, one of our major design goals, which is aided by homogeneity. An open system implies that the system can be extended to mediate different heterogeneous implementations; integration implies much greater cooperation and conformity. The Link Service modulates this tension by defining as simple and unrestrictive a protocol as possible. In this way we preserve the autonomy of individual tools, yet provide some measure of integration. Integrating with the Link Service requires minor modification of the applications. They implement a simple protocol, described below, requiring little change of them. The Link Service includes the protocol specification, a link *server* program, a library for integrating new applications, and utilities for managing the link databases. An integrated, link-aware, simple flat text editor (Sun's *textedit*) accompanies the Link Service. This section describes briefly what the end user actually sees, and the underlying architecture and protocol implementation.

What the User Sees

To start the Link Service, the user invokes it, resulting in the appearance of a main command panel.

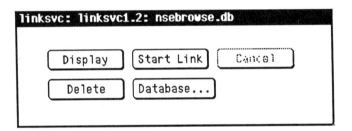

Figure 3. The Link Service Command Panel

Users explicitly invoke the integrated applications whose objects they want to view. In order to make a link, the user selects an object in one application, presses the *Start Link* button (which then changes to *End Link*) in the command panel to indicate the start of a link, selects the second object in an application, and presses *End Link* button to indicate the end of the link. The linked objects now have link indicators marking them.

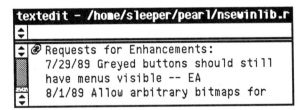

Figure 4. Link indicators in *textedit*

Subsequently, users can select either object, press the *Display* button in the command panel to indicate that they want to follow the link. Linkable objects can have multiple objects to which they are linked, as well as be the destination of multiple links. If there is only one link for the selected object, the object on the other end of the link is displayed by the application that manages it. If there is more than one link emanating from that object, the Link Service provides a dialogue box that lists the objects that can be displayed. The user selects one of the objects, and the application of the object at the other end displays the object.

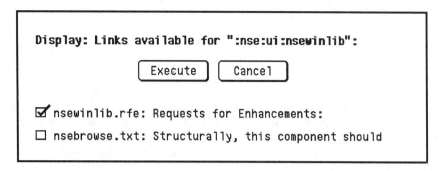

Figure 5. The Display Dialog Box

Since the Link Service is shipped as part of the NSE, its versioning facility supports the NSE's versioning paradigm. The NSE handles versioning for integrating between private and public workspaces. Versioning of NSE objects, such as link databases, follows a copy-modify merge paradigm [Adam89]. The merging mechanism for link databases is called *linkdb_resolve*. When a developer has completed some significant phase of development and testing, and wants to merge changes of a link database into a public workspace, they ask the NSE to merge the database back to the public workspace. The NSE automatically detects whether some other user has made changes in the public workspace since the user acquired the database into their private workspace. If so, the NSE invokes *linkdb_resolve*, which presents a window-based merging tool. Users may compare the version of the objects in the link database in their private workspace to those in the public one. In the merging subwindow, *linkdb_resolve* presents a best-guess merge of those link objects that appear to be able to coexist between the two workspaces. After running *linkdb_resolve*, users must run the explicit link maintenance function to detect any dangling links before again attempting to copy back their link database to the public workspace.

The protocol

The Link Service design separates the link data from the object data. The object data is managed by the individual application frontends. In order to make links between objects managed by different applications, these applications communicate using the Link Service. The Link Service command panel is part of a separate server process that runs on the user's machine. This process mediates communication between the integrated, link-aware applications. The Link Service provides a link library that applications include in order to communicate with the link server. This library is also part of the link server process. The applications communicate with the central link server process, which controls access to the link database (see figure 1).

This communication implements the Link Service protocol. The manager of the object *data* provides an interface for a user to create and modify those objects, and provides the application-specific functions to do what the user asks (e.g. edit text or graphics). Similarly, the Link Service provides the interface for the user to create and modify the *links* between the data objects, and provides the functionality for these requests. The link server manages access to a link database which stores the *link* data. When an application begins to execute, it registers with the Link Service, announcing its availability for displaying links, and telling the service what class of object, or data representation, it handles. Later it provides keys for its objects, and includes this class with those keys. This enables the link server to identify what registered application can handle requests about each object. The application also registers a set of functions that the Link Service can call in order to communicate with that application. The Link Service sends three kinds of messages to the applications. These messages ask the application to:

- provide an application specific key (ASK) for the applications's currently selected object

- display the existence of an object with a specific ASK.

- validate the existence of an object with a specific ASK.

The Link Service also relays state changes to registered applications, e.g. if a link has been made to one of the application's objects. Link Service links are pairs of pointers to the linked objects. These connections are stored in link databases, named by the user, which leaves the applications' object storage undisturbed.

Integrated standalone applications

At present, we have integrated four Sun applications with the Link Service. They are: *textedit*, Sun's window-based simple text editor; *vi*, Unix's terminal-based simple text editor; the NSE browser; and *SunTraq*, Sun's project scheduling tool. Outside of Sun, third party vendors have integrated products such as document processing packages and CASE frontend tools such as structured analysis and design tools. All of these applications are window based, are event driven, and have some notion of selection within the application. They all existed before the Link Service, and were not originally developed with the Link Service in mind.

The primary issues that arise when integrating applications are: what is an identifiably linkable object in the application's object space, how can the application represent that object by a unique identifier, and how does the user select or identify the object on which they want to perform link operations? Intermedia [Meyr86] faced similar problems, but developed customized frontend applications (InterText, InterDraw, InterPix, InterSpect, and InterVal) themselves. This gave them greater control over their design, implementation, integration and consistency.

EXTENSIONS

The Link Service today is an initial attempt at a protocol that encourages independent applications to communicate about their objects in a fairly restrictive way. It has provided us with valuable feedback from application integrators about changes and improvements they would like to see. In this section I discuss the need to generalize the programmatic interface; the move at Sun toward a more consistent look and feel in all applications, and how that impacts our hypertext interface; and expanding the types of links that can be permitted between objects.

In the current implementation, the messages that applications are expected to support are few (display or verify this object), and specified by the protocol. We would like to permit applications to extend the set of possible messages arbitrarily. We expect the set of messages to expand to at least support notification and data transfer. This means that applications can agree on their own protocols for increased application integration.

As discussed earlier, imposing little control over the applications permits an inconsistent user interface across application frontends. However, Sun is currently addressing the general issue of a consistent look and feel among all applications that run on Sun workstations. OpenLook is the specification for such a consistent application user interface [Hoeb89]. OpenLook currently makes recommendations for selection (solving the above inconsistency), as well as for cut, paste, and property sheets, but not for other hypertext-specific user interface, such as link indication. Once applications' user interfaces become more consistent with each other, by conforming to the OpenLook guidelines, we will be able to embed more of the linking user interface into the applications.

Currently, Link Service links are untyped, have no attributes, and no directionality. Types and attributes allow contextual behavior in link operations, and variation in the kind of relationship between endpoints. Types and attributes have been discussed in the hypertext literature [Trig83] [Conk87]. It is difficult to ascertain *a priori* the set of link types that integration programmers and end users will require. We prefer to allow the dynamic creation of types, rather than having a pre-defined fixed set, with a fixed set of associated semantics.

An example of the kind of hypertext application that the Link Service can enable is a frontend authoring application that, like Notecards or Hypercard, uses the card metaphor. The frontend would manage the cards, or the linkable objects they contained, and would register the unique identifiers for endpoints of links with the Link Service. All the customizing of display would be managed by the card authoring application. Another example of a hypertext-based application that could be developed using the Link Service as a platform is a tool to document the relationship between objects that are part of a software development cycle. This is, for example, one of the goals of DynamicDesign, from Tektronix [Bige87]. It should be possible to identify, using the software developer's existing applications, what requirements have not yet been fulfilled, or what bug reports have been satisfied by the current product. With an application that connects the relevant software development objects using the Link Service, the user could query the application about the state of these relationships.

CONCLUSION

With an open protocol, the power of each element of a system expands as it interoperates with others. Open linking can make the power of hypertext available to the world of software. We hope to see linking, and attendant hypertext capabilities, as much a standard part of the computer desktop as the cutting and pasting of text are today.

ACKNOWLEDGMENTS

For their contributions to the design of Link Service 1.0, I would like to acknowledge Dan Walsh, Russel Sandberg, Dave Goldberg, Evan Adams, Azad Bolour, Masahiro Honda, Scott Ritchie, and Tom Lyon. Sami Shaio and Judith Parkes were major contributors to our thinking about linking to unstructured documents. Azad Bolour provided the interface for *dbm*, a Unix database; Thomas Maslen integrated *textedit*, our first application, and provided a link database interface for the NSE's merge program.

My thanks to Dennis Abbe, who said of the design "this sounds a lot like hypertext," and handed me articles on Notecards. And my thanks to Carolyn Foss, Dwight Hare, Sami Shaio, and Nancy Yavne for reviewing this paper.

REFERENCES

[Adam89]   E. Adams, M. Honda and T. Miller. "Object Management in a CASE Environment", Proceedings of the 11th International Conference on Software Engineering, May 15-18, 1989, Pittsburgh, pp. 154-163.

[Aksc87]   R. Akscyn, D. L. McCracken, and E. Yoder. "KMS: A Distributed Hypermedia System for Sharing Knowledge in Organizations." *Hypertext '87 Papers*, Chapel Hill, NC, November 13-15, 1987.

[Bige88]   J. Bigelow. Hypertext and CASE, IEEE Software,V5 N2, March, 1988.

[Bige87]   J. Bigelow and V. Riley. Manipulating Source Code in DynamicDesign, *Hypertext '87 Papers*, Chapel Hill, NC, November 13-15, 1987.

[Camp87]   B. Campbell and J. M. Goodman. "HAM: A General-Purpose Hypertext Abstract Machine," *Hypertext '87 Papers*, Chapel Hill, NC, November 13-15, 1987.

[Conk87]   J. Conklin. "Hypertext: An Introduction and Survey," IEEE Computer, September, 1987, pp. 17-41.

[Engl84]   D. C. Englebart. "Collaboration Support Provisions in AUGMENT," Proceedings of the AFIPS Office Automation Conference, Los Angeles, California, February 20-22, 1984, pp. 51-58.

[Evet87]   C. Evett. "Tracking the End-Points of Persistent Links in Text Documents," *Hypertext '87 Position Paper*, Chapel Hill, NC, November 13- 15, 1987.

[Gold87]   I. Goldstein and D. Bobrow. A layered approach to software design., In D. Barstow, H. Shrobe, and E. Sandewall (Eds.) *Interactive Programming Environments*. McGraw-Hill: 1987, pp. 387-413.

[Hala87]   F. G. Halasz. "Reflections on NoteCards: Seven Issues for the Next Generation of Hypermedia Systems," *Hypertext '87 Papers*, Chapel Hill, NC, November 13-15, 1987.

[Hoeb89]   T. Hoeber. The OPEN LOOK Graphical User Interface Style Guide, Sun Microsystems, May 1989

[Meyr86]   N. Meyrowitz, et. al. *Intermedia: The Architecture and Construction of an Object-Oriented Hypermedia System and Applications Framework*, Proceedings of OOPSLA '86, Portland, OR, September, 1986.

[Shne86]   B. Shneiderman and J. Morariu. "The Interactive Encyclopedia System (TIES)," Department of Computer Science, University of Maryland, College Park, MD 20742, June 1986.

[Trig83]   R. H. Trigg. *A Network-based Approach to Text Handling for the Online Scientific Community*, Ph.D.. Thesis, University of Maryland, 1983.

[Trig86]   R. H. Trigg, L. Suchman, and F. G. Halasz. "Supporting Colaboration in NoteCards." *Computer-Supported Cooperative Work (CSCW '86) Proceedings*, Austin, TX, December 3-5, 1986.

A Visual Representation for Knowledge Structures

Michael Travers

MIT Media Lab
Massachusetts Institute of Technology
20 Ames St
Cambridge MA 02139
mt@media-lab.media.mit.edu

ABSTRACT

Knowledge-based systems often represent their knowledge as a network of interrelated units. Such networks are commonly presented to the user as a diagram of nodes connected by lines. These diagrams have provided a powerful visual metaphor for knowledge representation. However, their complexity can easily become unmanageable as the knowledge base (KB) grows.

This paper describes an alternate visual representation for navigating knowledge structures, based on a virtual museum metaphor. This representation uses nested boxes rather than linked nodes to represent relations. The intricate structure of the knowledge base is conveyed by a combination of position, size, color, and font cues. MUE (Museum Unit Editor) was implemented using this representation to provide a graphic front end for the Cyc knowledge base.

INTRODUCTION

Cyc and Knowledge Representation

The Cyc project [Lena88] is an effort to build a very large knowledge base that encompasses a broad range of common-sense knowledge. The knowledge base consists of a network of interrelated *units* (frames), each of which corresponds to a thing to be represented. These can be physical objects, abstract concepts, classes, or anything else of interest. Cyc presently consists of about a hundred thousand units; it is projected to have several million when it is completed[1].

---

[1]Some details of Cyc have been simplified in this paper. For a fuller presentation, see [Lena88].

Units contain *slots* that represent properties of the unit. Slots are themselves units; by convention, their names begin with a lowercase letter. Slots have values which are usually lists of other units. Within text or programs units are designated by a prefix of "#%". This prefix may be omitted if there is no question of ambiguity. A typical unit presented as text looks like this:

```
#%People:
#%english: ("The class of all human beings")
#%specs: (#%Workers #%MalePeople #%FemalePeople
    #%USCitizens ...)
#%genls: (#%Mammals #%IntelligentEntities)
#%allElements: (#%MikeTravers #%DougLenat
    #%BobDobbs ...)
#%canHaveSlots: (#%citizenship #%languagesSpoken
    #%countryOfOrigin...)
...
```

Figure1. Textual representation of a Cyc unit.

This unit represents the class of all people, and its slots specify that it has specializations (subsets) such as #%Workers and #%MalePeople, generalizations (supersets) #%Mammals and IntelligentEntities, and elements that include all the individual people that Cyc has reason to know about. The #%english slot contains human-readable documentation. #%canHaveSlots is an example of a slightly more complex slot. It specifies that elements of the class #%People are allowed to have the properties (slots) of citizenship and languages spoken.

MUE, a Navigation Tool for Cyc

Although Cyc is primarily a knowledge base for use by AI programs, the knowledge it contains can and must be accessible directly by humans during Cyc's developmental stage. It thus becomes necessary to treat Cyc as a knowledge exploration environment. The notion of a knowledge environment based on detailed representation was an important precursor to the development of Cyc [Lena84].

A large, densely interconnected structure like Cyc poses formidable navigation problems. When the MUE effort began, the Cyc user interface consisted of a textual browser/editor, and a node-and-line graphical display that was becoming impossibly tangled as the knowledge base grew. MUE began as an effort to design a new graphic browsing interface that exploited the spatial navigation skills of the user by mapping the KB into a simulated physical space.

The original plan for a spatial interface was to use virtual environment technology such as head-mounted displays [Fole87] to present the knowledge base as a museum. The Cyc museum was to have used floors, sections, corridors, exhibits, alcoves, display cases, and other architectural metaphors to effectively spatialize the highly abstract structure of Cyc. This plan was inspired by the museum's traditional role as a place to present broad areas of knowledge; and by theories of architectural space that utilized overlapping hierarchical structures similar to those of Cyc [Alex64].

Creating a virtual space to represent Cyc is not straightforward. Because Cyc is so densely interconnected, it does not map easily into a geometric space. The museum would have to have spacewarps or wormholes to connect related units that might be far removed in the museum space. While Cyc's structures are similar to certain architectural formalisms, in practice they are far too deep, bushy, and tangled to map directly into a navigable architectural space. Cyc's structures are also rather fluid, in that new intermediate levels are constantly being created. Thus a fixed mapping of units to architectural features seemed impossible to implement.

The solution was to use a uniform metaphor of rooms. Rather than assign some units to larger levels of architecture, every unit representation in the museum space was simply a room. Every unit could appear both as its own room or as an object inside another room. The museum traveller could "jump in" to any visible unit and find herself warped to an entire room that represented that unit. Within a room, objects would appear at fixed places. Certain sets of units that did have a ready mapping into two- or three-dimensional space (*i.e.*, geographic information) could be browsed via ordinary spatial operations.

With this metaphor, in a certain sense, everything is inside of everything else! When you enter a unit, it becomes outermost, and the things that are connected to it become included in it, including the room you just left. For instance, if you enter the Serengeti room, inside it will be areas devoted to inhabitants of the region such as the Masai tribe, gazelles, and tourists. But if you enter the Masai unit, inside there will be an area labelled locales that will include the Serengeti and other places frequented by the nomadic Masai.

The full-scale virtual environment has yet to be implemented. However, the notion of representing a unit as a room and related units as being inside that room was used to create a less ambitious two-dimensional browser. The implemented version does not try very hard to preserve the properties of physical space. Instead, the notion of warping has become the primary navigational technique.

A MUE display is a set of nested boxes, each box representing a unit. For example, the #%Person unit above would be drawn as the set of boxes below.

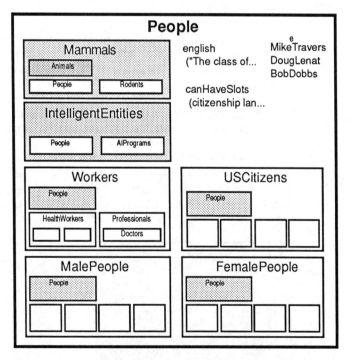

Figure 2. A MUE Display.

Each internal box is recursively subdivided and elaborated as space permits. In practice, a 1024 x 1024 screen permits from three to six levels of recursion (more than can be shown here). The details of the layout algorithms are explained below.

Hypertexts and Semantic Networks

Hypertext and KB-networks share some superficial similarities: they are structured as graphs, and they claim to represent, present, or even constitute "knowledge". But these similarities are rarely acknowledged to be as important as the differences in purposes and styles assumed by the two projects. In fact, their is some low-level hostility between the two groups: Hypertext people believe that the AI project of formal representation is unnecessary, while AI people feel that the hypertext goal of putting text online is unwarranted interference with their more ambitious goal of putting knowledge online in a form that can be used by programs as well as people.

The nature of representation in these two similar yet disparate schemes is a complex philosophical issue that cannot be treated here. For our purposes, it will suffice to simply think of knowledge representation languages as simply a new form of text, albeit a highly dynamic form that can rearrange and represent itself in novel ways. This view will allow us to make use of the highly developed formal methods of AI without having to accept its concomitant semantic theories.

DISPLAY LAYOUT IN MUE

This section explains how various visual elements of the MUE display are related to the Cyc structures they represent.

Units are Boxes

Units are represented on the screen by nested rectangular boxes. The unit's name appears at the top of the box, unless the box is smaller than a fixed size. or the name is too large. In those cases, moving the mouse over the box will cause the full name to appear.

Every MUE unit display is recursively detailed. That is, the neighbors of every unit box are displayed within it up to the limits of screen space.

Relationships are indicated by inclusion

MUE's basic display technique is to show relationships by recursive inclusion. If, for instance, #%BlueCollarWorker is a #%spec of #%Worker and has three specs of its own, than this might appear as:

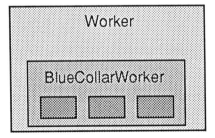

Figure 3. Use of inclusion and color to indicate recursion depth of a relationship.

Color is used to indicate type and nesting depth of relationships

In the MUE display, color is used in two ways: hue is used to indicate the type of relation (*i.e.*, blue indicates #%specs relations) and saturation is used to indicate the depth of the relationship from the current outermost unit. For instance, in the above display of Workers, the blue color becomes more saturated as you go inwards from more general to more specialized units.

Graph structure is made evident through recursive nesting

The Cyc KB as a whole is an unrestricted labelled graph, but certain of its slots are defined so as to form subgraphs that take the form of trees or directed acyclic graphs (DAGs or tangled hierarchies). #%specs and its inverse #%genls are the most important of these, but there are others, such as #%parts and #%partOf. Slots fall into a tangled hierarchy of their own as specified by the #%specSlot and #%superSlot relations. MUE uses these subgraphs as a navigational skeleton.

For MUE's purposes, relations are divided up into classes, based on the information encoded about them in Cyc. The two classes most relevant to the structure of screen layouts are restrictions and loosenings. For example, #%specs is a restriction while #%genls is a loosening. In general, if a slot is a loosening its inverse will be a restriction.

Each unit display is divided up into four or fewer sections: restrictions (usually the bottom half of the box), loosenings (the upper left quadrant), misc slots, and elements (which together occupy the upper right quadrant). See Figure 2.

NAVIGATION IN MUE

The previous section dealt with MUE displays as static visual constructs. This section explores how these elements are used dynamically during the process of navigation through knowledge structures.

The outermost box is the focus unit

The user is considered to be in a particular unit or room. This unit is represented by a box the size of the screen and is referred to here as the *focus*. MUE tries to display units that are in the neighborhood of the focus, as defined by distance along a given set of relationships. It does this simply by recursively elaborating the unit display boxes until they become too small to include any more detail.

Navigation in Cyc is done by mousing on an inner unit display box, which will expand to the size of the full screen and become the focus of the next display.

Movement is via re-rooting

Mousing on a unit display will cause that unit to become the focus of a new display. This shifts the positions and sizes of all of the unit displays present. In the box representation, this can be thought of as turning a display inside-out, since the moused-upon inner box will become the outermost box of the new display, while the former outermost box will become an inner, smaller one. This process may also be thought of as re-rooting a tree by turning an arbitrary node into the root of a new tree:

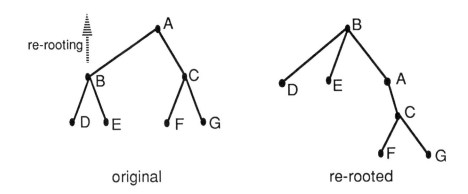

original   re-rooted

Figure 4. Re-rooting a tree.

MUE never changes the connectivity of the graph that it's displaying (which is part of Cyc), but can re-root it to form different displays. Here is a part of Cyc's class structure, which includes the graph on which Figure 2 is based:

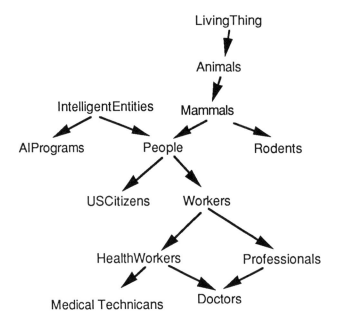

Figure 5. A class graph.

To generate a MUE display, we want to re-root the structure at the unit we are focusing on. For instance, #%People:

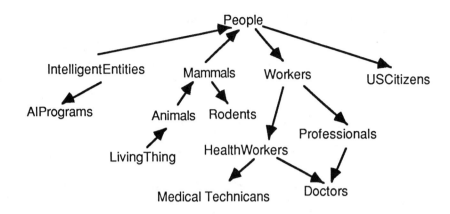

Figure 6. The same class graph, rerooted.

In the above diagram, we have preserved the original relationships and only altered their visual presentation. Some of our directed links now point upwards. To make a MUE display based on this graph, we wish to convert it to a tree-like structure with all links pointing downward (corresponding to inclusion). We can do this by replacing upward-pointing links with their inverses (in this case, replacing #%specs with #%genls). We indicate the #%genls links with shaded lines below (corresponding to the use of color in MUE):

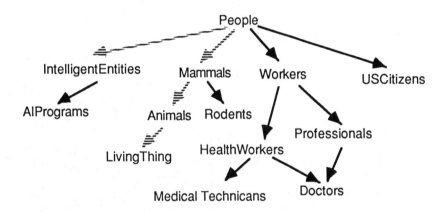

Figure 7. The re-rooted graph relabelled to form a tangled hierarchy.

This diagram could now be used to generate the MUE display in Figure 2, by presenting the relationships as inclusions (see the next section for the treatment of nodes with multiple parents).

Re-rooting allows MUE to pick any unit as the focus by making it the top of a re-rooted tree. Cyc's ability to compute the inverse of a relationship allows arbitrary graphs to be converted into trees and thus displayed via inclusion. The re-rooting process can be animated, but the resulting motion is hard to comprehend, since things are moving in many directions at once. [Lieb89] describes a similar display and animated transform using simpler structures and three-dimensional graphics.

Some units are duplicated

Note that the above diagram is not actually a proper tree: #%Doctors has two parent nodes, #%HealthWorkers and #%Professionals. Since our box diagrams must be tree structured, we can't display this directly. Instead we make two displays for #%Doctors, one inside #%HealthWorkers and one in #%Professionals. To save time, only one of these displays (arbitrarily chosen) will be recursively expanded.

A rear-view mirror metaphor helps make explain the re-rooted display

If it were possible, we'd like to maintain the consistency of the interface metaphor by putting loosenings outside the focus unit. But that would mean putting them outside the screen. Even if the focus were not the size of the screen, there may be more than one loosening of it, and it's impossible to draw two separate boxes surrounding the focus without having them intersect or having one include the other (which would convey false information).

Re-rooting provides a means for turning a neighborhood of some focus unit into a tree structure with the focus as the root and both loosenings and restrictions as subordinate, internal units. But displaying this as a tree, as in the above diagrams, is less than intuitive. We need a means of indicating to the user the difference between units that are beneath the focus in an absolute sense and those that were placed there as a result of re-rooting.

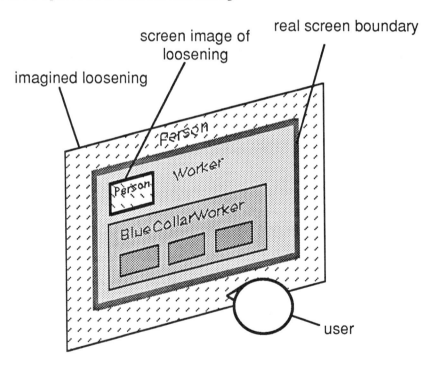

Figure 8. Viewing a MUE display through an imaginary rear-view mirror.

MUE uses position and color cues to distinguish re-rooted loosenings from restrictions. We ask the user to perform a mental inversion, and imagine that the loosenings are made visible through a "rear-view mirror" that brings them into the visible space of the display via a transform.

In Figure 8, the user is focusing on the #%Worker unit, and can see its sole loosening, #%Person, through the rear-view mirror. The rear-view mirror functions recursively as well, so that several levels of loosening can be seen in a typical display.

This layout technique has the disadvantage of having to be explained, and having no natural visual cues to remind the user what's going on. One possible solution is stereo displays that could indicate the true depth of units. Another is using head-mounted displays to generate both stereopsis and visual feedback.

EDITING IN MUE

Cyc's primary editing tool is the Unit Editor (UE) which displays units in a text-based notation (as in Figure 1). The UE can display up to four units and their slots at a time, and allows the user to explicitly edit the contents of any slot.

MUE provides an additional spatial editing capability, which can simplify certain editing tasks involving restructuring of hierarchical parts of the KB. In keeping with its use of inclusion as its primary visual metaphor, editing operations in MUE are accomplished by dragging boxes inside each other. Dragging a box will create a new link between the dragged unit and the destination, and optionally break the old link. These operations can be particularly useful when creating or modifying large class hierarchies.

In such tasks, it is often necessary to interpose intermediate classes between existing general and special-purpose classes. MUE provides a special operation, Subsume, which accomplishes this task, essentially surrounding an existing unit with a new, more general unit (we use the language of specialization and generalization in this description, although the operation can apply to any restriction/loosening type of relationship).

OTHER APPLICATIONS

This section examines the use of MUE for browsing structures other than Cyc.

Hypertext

Text Structures

MUE is useful for browsing graph-like text structures. Electronic mail conversations can form such structures by virtue of recording the links between replies and the messages they are in reply to. When the role that a message plays in a conversation is known (*i.e.*, an agreement, disagreement, or request for elaboration) the structure of the conversation becomes both more intricate and more important. Hypertext argumentation systems can benefit from the truth-maintenance approach that records justifications for facts and can propagate support, contradiction, or believability through a dependency network [Stef87].

MUE has been experimentally adapted to display mail structures based on the reply relationship. While it appears to be of some utility, it falls short of being a good visual representation, primarily because unlike Cyc units, mail messages do not have short unique identifiers to use as box headings.

Browsing Program Structure

The Symbolics Lisp environment includes facilities for recording the relationships between entities of the Lisp language [Symb88]. For a given function (or macro, type, or other named object) you can obtain a list of callers or callees. MUE has been adapted to display these relations, providing the ability to browse the structure of large Lisp programs. Lisp entities do have short unique identifiers and thus MUE's visual presentations are reasonably informative.

CONNECTING CONCEPTUAL AND TEXT STRUCTURES

Cyc has a rudimentary method of connecting conceptual and text structures by means of a special class of units called TextUnits. A TextUnit is simply a kind of Cyc unit that represents a piece of text. An AccessibleTextUnit is a TextUnit that points to text that is accessible online, thus providing an interface between Cyc and arbitrary bodies of text.

TextUnits have been used to create a conceptual index into the text of Melville's *Moby Dick*. At present this simply encodes some very basic properties of the novel. This includes its textual parts such as chapters, its characters (and which chapters they are mentioned in), and significant plot events (and which chapters they happen in and which characters are involved in them). While this effort has so far been rudimentary, this could eventually evolve into an intelligent concordance or reader's guide.

One way to think about using a KB to navigate text is by analogy to the Britannica Propaedia/Micropaedia [Pree79]. The Micropaedia consists of small articles about a great many concepts whose main function is to define and point you to a larger article in the main body of the encyclopaedia (the Macropaedia). Cyc units can fulfill a similar function of indexing text, but because the Cyc units are much more finely detailed and cross-referenced the utility would be orders of magnitude greater.

RELATIONS TO OTHER WORK

SemNet and Fisheye Views

SemNet [Fair88] has extended the techniques of network display to include three-dimensional display and sophisticated techniques for mapping node positions into display space. SemNet makes use of fisheye views [Furn86], a class of display techniques that focus on a particular point of a large structure. More detail is displayed near the focus and less detail as one moves further away. MUE's display is similar to a fisheye view in the above sense, although it does not make explicit use of an "interestingness metric" as the formal fisheye technique does. This technique offers the additional facility of defining some items (landmarks) as having an intrinsically high degree of interest, so that they are visible from a wider range of foci than normal items.

SemNet was designed around a static three-dimensional layout of knowledge and concentrated on the problems of layout and navigation within such a space. This was recognized to be inadequate for complicated networks, and some effort was made towards temporarily moving network nodes to form clusters dynamically. MUE, in contrast, has no fixed mapping into a physical space and instead emphasizes the dynamic creation of layouts based on neighborhoods as defined by the underlying knowledge base.

Nested Hypermedia Structures

Previous systems have used nested boxes to represent hypertext and other browsable structures. [Fein82] used nesting to represent tree-structured documents and could include graphics and animation. Special editors were provided for the various levels of the hierarchy: chapter, page, etc., but had no method for automatically constructing layouts from the underlying structure.

SDMS (Spatial Data Management System) [Bolt79] was an early effort to create a rich spatial browsing environment. The initial version used a tree-structured database, and allowed the user to browse by successively entering and expanding the various nodes of the tree. This was deemed to be too confusing, so later versions abandoned the hierarchical structure for a flat data space. The flat space allows the user a more natural way to use spatial navigation, but does not scale up to very large or inherently structured knowledge bases.

Boxer: Nested Boxes as a Programming Construct

Boxer [diSe86] is an interactive programming system that uses boxes and inclusion as its basic visual metaphor. Designed as a Lisp-like system, it makes use of the close analogy between inclusion of boxes and nesting of parentheses. Boxer has had some success with novice users, suggesting that inclusion is a suitable visual representation for abstraction.

Displaying the Structure and Execution of Programs

[Lieb89] has used the graphic ideas developed for MUE to display the execution of Lisp programs. The program is represented by nested boxes (in 3D) which reconfigure themselves as parts of the program get evaluated. The reconfiguration is similar to MUE's zooming process, but animated in three dimensions using size changes and rotation.

CONCLUSIONS

MUE was the result of an effort to come up with an alternative visual representation for complex knowledge structures. It embodies some new techniques for translating complex graph structure into visual representations. The system is in use by knowledge engineers but has not been evaluated as to its effectiveness in comparison with more traditional node-and-link representations. The same system has been adapted to show text and software structures. A preliminary effort has been made to use the knowledge base as a guide for navigating text.

Directions for future work include: designing richer displays that incorporate pictorial and iconic information; using other sensory cures such as sound to enhance the virtual environment; using animation and stereoscopic displays to convey the navigational processes; and closer interconnection between knowledge bases and hypertexts.

ACKNOWLEDGEMENTS

This work was undertaken as part of the Cyc project at the Microelectronics and Computer Technology Consortium. Doug Lenat and the other Cyclists contributed suggestions, a user community, and a knowledge base worth exploring. Text units were developed in collaboration with Margaret Minsky.

REFERENCES

[Alex64]   Alexander, Christopher, *Notes on the Synthesis of Form*, Cambridge: Harvard University Press, 1964.

[Bolt79]   Bolt, Richard A., Spatial Data-Management, Arhcitecture Machine Group, Massachusetts Insitute of Technology, 1979.

[diSe86]   diSessa, Andrea A. and Harold Abelson, "Boxer: A Reconstructable Computational Medium", *Communications of the ACM* 29(9), p. 859-868, 1986.

[Fair88]   Fairchild, Kim M., Steven E. Poltrock, and George W. Furnas, "SemNet: Three-Dimensional Graphic Representations of Large Knowledge Bases", in *Cognitive Science and its Applications for Human-Computer Interaction*, ed. Raymonde Guindon, Lawrence Erlbaum, Hillsdale NJ, 1988.

[Fein82]   Steven Feiner, Sandor Nagy, and Andries van Dam, "An experimental system for creating and presenting interactive graphical documents", *ACM Transactions on Graphics* 1(1), p. 59-77, 1982.

[Fole87]   Foley, James D., "Interfaces for Advanced Computing", *Scientific American*, 257 (4), p.126-135, October 1987.

[Furn86]   Furnas, George W., "Generalized Fisheye Views". *Proceedings of CHI' 86 Human Factors in Computing Systems*, p. 16-23, 1986.

[Lena84]   Lenat, Douglas B., Alan Borning, David McDonald, Craig Taylor, and Stephen Weyer, "Knoesphere: Building Expert Systems with Encyclopaedic Knowledge", *Proceedings of the IJCAI-84*, pp. 167-169, 1984.

[Lena88]   Lenat, Douglas B. and R. V. Guha, The World According to Cyc, MCC Technical Report No. ACA-AI-300-88, Microelectronics and Computer Technology Corporation, 1988.

[Lieb89]   Lieberman, Henry, "A Three-dimensional Representation for Program Execution", submitted to *Visual Languages '89*.

[Nels87]   Nelson, Theodore H., *Computer Lib/Dream Machines*. Redmond, Washington: Tempus Books, 1987.

[Pree79]   Preece, Warren E. (ed) *Encyclopaedia Brittanica (15th edition)*, Chicago, 1979.

[Stef87]   Stefik, M, Foster G, Bobrow D, Kahn K, Lanning S, Suchman L, "Beyond the Chalkboard: Computer Support for Collaboration and Problem Solving in Meetings", *Communications of the ACM*, January 1987.

[Symb88]   Symbolics, Inc, *Genera Users' Guide*, 1988.

Using Hypertext in a Law Firm

Elise Yoder

Knowledge Workshop
4750 Old William Penn Hwy.
Murrysville, Pennsylvania 15668

Thomas C. Wettach, Esq.

Reed Smith Shaw & McClay
James H. Reed Building, Mellon Square
435 Sixth Ave
Pittsburgh, Pennsylvania 15219-1886

INTRODUCTION

This paper presents an example of how hypertext can be used to support knowledge workers in their everyday work. We describe a long-term project within the law firm of Reed Smith Shaw & McClay to use hypertext for managing knowledge about intellectual property.

The Intellectual Property group of attorneys provides a demanding environment for an information management system. The attorneys use information that comes from a wide variety of sources and in a wide variety of formats. The end products of the attorneys--legal contracts, patent applications, court briefs and motions, and advice to clients--must be accurate and timely.

To help these attorneys be more effective, we are developing an application system called **HyperLex**^{TM} that will give them better tools for generating, storing, and accessing information. We are using hypertext as the core technology for the system because we believe it is a good fit with the needs of these attorneys.

Our aim in this paper is to examine how hypertext can be used in an organization like a law firm, instead of focusing on hypertext technology per se. We first give an overview of Reed Smith and its Intellectual Property group: what the attorneys do, what conditions they work under, and how their information management needs might be supported by hypertext. We then describe the HyperLex project--the underlying hypertext system, our current structure for the hypertext database, some specific applications we are building, and our scenario for expanding the use of hypertext within the Intellectual Property group and possibly into the rest of the firm. We conclude with a list of some hypertext design issues that we feel hypertext developers could address to better support this application area.

REED SMITH'S INTELLECTUAL PROPERTY GROUP

Background on Reed Smith

Established in 1877, Reed Smith is the largest law firm in Pittsburgh and the 45th largest in the United States. Reed Smith has 385 attorneys and 537 staff (as of June 1989). Of the attorneys, 275 are based in Reed Smith's main office in Pittsburgh, with the others in the Philadelphia, Virginia, and Washington, D.C. offices. Each attorney belongs to one or more of the six practice groups: Intellectual Property, Corporate, Estates Wills and Trusts, Labor, Litigation, and Tax.

Reed Smith was one of the first law firms to actively support Pittsburgh's emerging high technology community. In 1984, the firm formed a group called TECHLEX, composed of 6 attorneys (since grown to 35) from different practice groups who had expertise in the legal issues facing high technology companies. The next year, Reed Smith opened a Technology Law Center in the Pittsburgh university area to serve as the headquarters for TECHLEX. Reed Smith is also a founding member of the TechLaw Group, a consortium of 9 major law firms across the country that have substantial practices with high technology companies.

Reed Smith has made a significant investment over the years in automating their offices. In 1985 the firm replaced its ATEX word processing system with a Unix-based mainframe system from CCI (Computer Consoles International) for word processing, billing, electronic mail, file management, and relational databases. By 1986, there was a terminal on the desk of every employee. The CCI system is supplemented with personal computer systems for accounting and desktop publishing. Also, Reed Smith subscribes to on-line reference services such as LEXIS and WESTLAW in order to access large legal databases [Amer89].

The Intellectual Property group

Reed Smith's Intellectual Property group is the initial focus of our efforts. The Intellectual Property group has 16 attorneys, 4 paralegals and 8 secretaries. The group handles all forms of intellectual property including patents, trademarks, copyrights, and trade secrets. The practice involves protecting and transferring intellectual property, and also handling litigation relating to patent, copyright and trademark infringement.

The Intellectual Property attorneys produce legal advice, legal documents (contracts, patents, employment agreements), and court documents for litigation. The work has strict deadlines and time constraints. Many matters are going on simultaneously, requiring attorneys to switch quickly between tasks. During litigation, the atmosphere intensifies; often teams of attorneys collaborate on a large case.

The attorneys' information management needs

The computer systems that Reed Smith has already put in place have helped the attorneys revise legal documents much more quickly and communicate among themselves more effectively (using electronic mail) [Shep88]. However, the automation has not been as effective in helping the attorneys capture, store, and easily retrieve information.

For instance, the firm needs to make its own work products more accessible for later reference. Finished legal documents are usually archived on magnetic tapes (from which retrieval is daunting) or in printed form in the firm's law library. When attorneys start working on new documents, they have no easy way of locating existing documents that might be relevant. Frequently an attorney resorts to "query-by-email": "Has anyone out there been working on a corporate recision with significant tax implications?" Even if the attorney is in luck, and someone answers "Yes," the actual document must still be tracked down in the electronic archive or in the library.

In short, the attorneys need a system to help them find relevant information quickly and represent their ideas efficiently. The system would let them produce printed legal documents--still the medium of exchange in every courtroom--from the contents of the database. It would handle large, homogeneous sets of information, but it would serve equally well as an electronic notebook for attorneys to quickly "jot down" nuggets of information. The system would let attorneys access their documents and electronic mail on the CCI mainframe. And above all, it would be easy to learn and easy to use.

How hypertext might address their needs

We think that hypertext technology can meet many of the attorneys' information management needs. Table 1 lists some of those needs along with some capabilities of hypertext systems that address those needs. (We are not describing here any particular hypertext system; the latest-generation hypertext systems have most or all of these capabilities [Aksc88, Hala88, Kahn88]).

Intellectual Property attorneys' needs	Hypertext capabilities that address those needs
Quickly capture attorneys' ideas.	Streamlined creation of nodes, links, and comments.
Represent contents of legal documents such as patents (with their diagrams) and scanned input from printed reference documents.	Support for text, vector graphics, and bitmap images in nodes.
Articulate the structure of complex entities such as patents or legal arguments.	Ability to build structures of any form using nodes and links.
Permanently express associative relationships (such as that between a patent and the relevant pieces of prior art).	Use of links as cross-references between any nodes. Also, ability to put comments near source material so they can be viewed in context.
Efficiently build a database for large sets of information (such as a catalog of 10,000 documents to be used in a trial).	Ability to quickly build and then evolve a database and process its contents without requiring the design of a database schema.
Search for relevant information when you're not sure what's out there.	Efficient browsing, enabled by a fast response rate and streamlined interface.
Locate information you know is there, but you're not sure where.	Searching and indexing capability.
Access information at whatever level of detail is appropriate.	"Information-layering" aspect of hypertext: users can follow links to more detail according to their needs.
Switch quickly between tasks.	Ability to move quickly between parts of the database or between functions (e.g. between browsing and editing).
Collaborate with other attorneys and support staff, for general administration and on projects like large lawsuits.	Simultaneous access to a shared (possibly distributed) database.
Produce hardcopy from any portion of the database for use at home, in the courtroom, or by clients.	Ability to format and print documents from nodes and aggregates of nodes (such as hierarchies).
Ability to quickly learn the system.	Simple user interface and data model.

Table 1. Attorneys' needs and how hypertext might address them

THE HYPERLEX SYSTEM

The overall goal for the HyperLex system is to help the attorneys in the Intellectual Property group be more effective in their day-to-day work. Our strategy is to work both top-down (by creating a hypertext database to be a framework for many tasks) and bottom-up (by concentrating on several specific applications). Each of the following aspects of the project is described in a section below:

- Putting in place a multi-purpose hypertext system (KMS on Sun workstations).

- Developing a hypertext database that supports a wide range of tasks in the Intellectual Property group. Over time, we hope to assimilate more and more of the group's activities into the framework of this database.

- Developing tools for specific applications. The tools consist of customized hypertext node formats and, in some cases, customized programs that process those nodes. (We describe below two of the applications we're developing.)

- Encouraging more widespread use of the system within Reed Smith.

- Working with the developers of KMS to add capabilities as we identify the need for them.

KMS: the underlying hypertext system

The underlying hypertext system that we are using for HyperLex is KMS from Knowledge Systems, running on workstations from Sun Microsystems. Nodes in KMS (called frames) may contain any combination of text, graphics, and bitmapped images. These items can be used as links between frames. KMS provides a direct-manipulation user interface and rapid response for frame display. (See [Aksc88] for a detailed description of the KMS data model and user interface.) The database of KMS frames may be distributed across multiple servers on a network and simultaneously accessed by many users. For this reason and others, KMS is well-suited to supporting the kind of intense collaboration that the attorneys require [Yode89].

The HyperLex database

The HyperLex database provides a framework for many of the activities of the Intellectual Property attorneys. Figure 1 shows the current structure (as of August 1989) for the top levels of this database. This diagram should be viewed only as a "snapshot," since the structure is continuously evolving as the attorneys discover more types of information to include and better ways to organize it. (The diagram shows only a skeletal outline of the structure; many details have been omitted.)

As is common for KMS databases, the HyperLex database has an overall hierarchical structure that is augmented with many non-hierarchical cross-references. The top frame in Figure 1 is the point of entry for the Intellectual Property group. The frame has links to group bulletin boards, calendars, and so forth. The top frame also links to indexes of legal documents such as patents, employment agreements, contracts, and lawsuits, which are themselves represented in hierarchies of frames. Through these indexes, attorneys can refer to the work done previously by themselves and by other attorneys. They can also access the various libraries of document boilerplate (standard language that can be re-used in subsequent documents).

The top frame also links to an index of clients. For each client, there is a frame that gives access to everything related to that client: their address, correspondence, and all their legal matters. In the example shown, the fictitious client called Astro-Netics has five matters, one of which--the patent for a switching network--is shown in more detail in Figure 2. An attorney can access that patent through the client frame or through the index of patents.

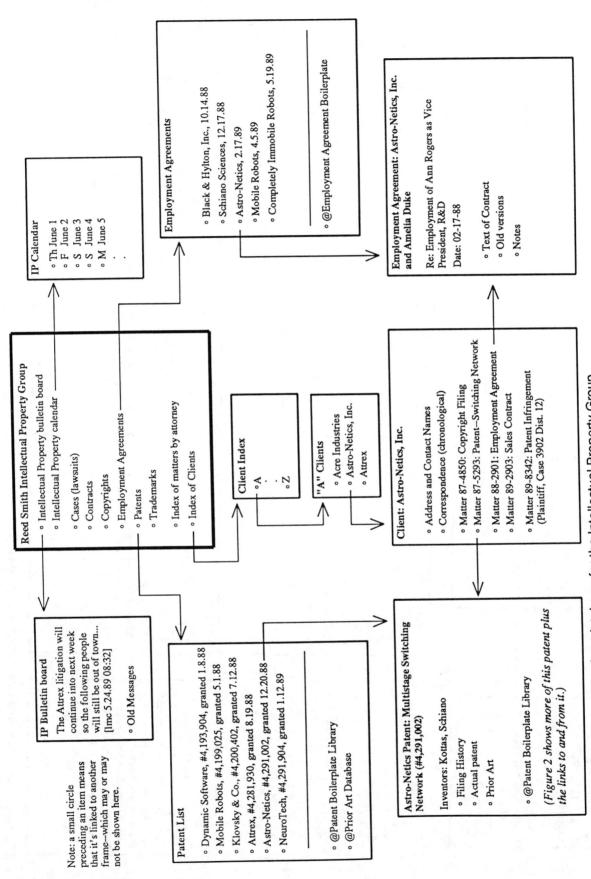

Figure 1. Top levels of the HyperLex database for the Intellectual Property Group

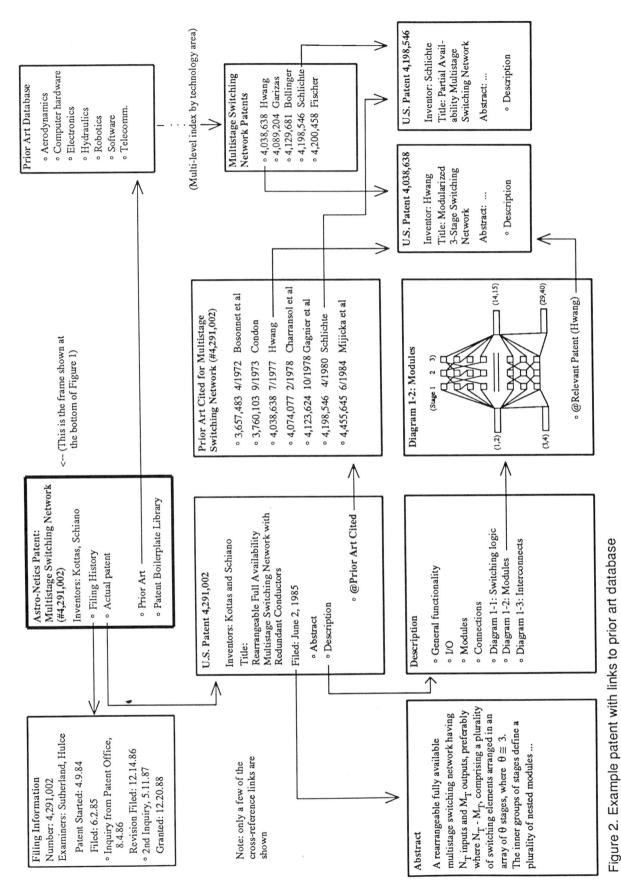

Figure 2. Example patent with links to prior art database

An example application: Patent development

When the U.S. Patent and Trademark Office examines a patent application to determine if it's patentable, they require a list of all relevant and pertinent "prior art" (published works of any form). Typically, the list contains a number of existing patents from the same technology area. Identifying the relevant prior art takes a lot of an attorney's time, especially since the volume of prior art throughout the world is growing rapidly.

One of the first parts of the HyperLex database that we developed was a database to help manage prior art information. The database indexes patents by technological category. In some cases, the entire patent is included in the database; in others, there is only the filing information and an abstract. The attorneys can locate relevant patents and browse through them at whatever level of detail is necessary. For instance, they can just scan the top frame of the patent for vital information, or they can descend into the body of the patent for more detail about the invention it describes. When they are developing a new patent application on-line, they can add cross-reference links to the relevant patents in the prior art database. Figure 2 shows an example patent with links to and from the prior art database.

Another application: Database of litigation documents

Another HyperLex application is a hypertext database that catalogs documents for a trial. In the particular trial for which we are building the database, the document production phase (in which each side requests copies of possibly relevant materials) yielded over 10,000 documents! The attorneys frequently consult these documents while they are planning the trial and during the trial itself.

In the database each document is represented by a separate KMS "catalog" frame that contains a list of 16 fields (for example, "Document Type: Memo" and "Confidential: Yes"). There are multiple frame-based indexes to the catalog frames: by court number, internal Reed Smith number, and authors. Attorneys can access the information by following a particular index or by browsing in a less directed way through the information. (We also plan to scan in the most important documents so that their entire contents--including diagrams and images--are available on-line.)

Attorneys can search the database by filling out a query frame that has the same fields as a catalog frame. The attorney specifies what is to be matched by entering desired values for the attributes. For example, someone looking for all the lab reports that are significant to the patent infringement charge would specify "Type: Lab Report" and "Infringe. Signif.: Yes". Once the search is done and the attorney reaches the document(s) he's looking for, he can add notes to that frame for future reference. He can also add cross-reference links from relevant documents to the frame. For instance, he can create a document that outlines his trial strategy and put links from that document to the pertinent catalog frames.

We should point out that there is absolutely nothing remarkable about the capability to catalog documents and retrieve them based on query values. What makes this application interesting is that it is part of a global hypertext database being used for many tasks, which means the information can be accessed more directly and the results will be readily available for use in multiple contexts.

Plans for more widespread use of HyperLex

Although our initial focus is the Intellectual Property group, we believe HyperLex may prove useful for other groups within the firm. We hope to extend the HyperLex database to encompass some of the activities of these groups. For instance, there could eventually be:

- An index to the entire firm's work product. Briefs, contracts, and written opinions could be created in the database and then indexed in multiple ways--by topic, client, chronology, etc. In this way the work done by the attorneys could become part of the firm-wide legal research library.

- A firm-wide client index and database that houses, for each client, information about all their legal matters (from all the practice groups), plus information pertaining to practice development. Such an index might also be useful when doing client conflict searches, which is an important and time-consuming task for law firms.

- A large library of approved terms and conditions for all kinds of contracts and for litigation-related documents (court briefs and motions). Each clause could be linked to information about its history, relevant court cases and other references, individual attorneys' experiences, variants for different states or for different industries, and so forth.

- Firm-wide bulletin boards (status of major cases, personnel information, schedules of marketing activities, etc.).

- An on-line index to Reed Smith's law library of published materials.

- A HyperLex interface to on-line reference databases such as LEXIS [Lamb85] and mass-storage references such as the new West CD-ROM Libraries.

It might also be possible, if there were appropriate security mechanisms, to give Reed Smith's clients access to certain parts of the database. For instance, a client company might have access to a patent that is being prepared for them so that they could work on drafts along with the attorneys rather than mailing paper versions back and forth.

Recommendations for hypertext system designers

Below are a few design areas that hypertext developers could focus on to better support this application area:

- Remote access via telephone lines for attorneys in the offices in other cities, or for attorneys who are working at home or "on the road."

- Sophisticated security mechanisms, such as the ability to define for any node (or aggregate of nodes) which categories of people can read, write, and annotate those nodes.

- Powerful database capabilities, including range-checking on values, the flexibility to revise formats in mid-stream (for instance, changing a field), and fast searching (including boolean searches and computation on values).

- The ability to automatically import, structure, and index information. This could include importing word processing files from the firm's mainframe and importing the results from searches of on-line databases.

- Support for very large scale hypertext databases with hundreds of thousands of nodes.

CONCLUSION

Our primary goal for the HyperLex project is to understand the attorneys' task environment and explore ways of supporting them in their everyday work. We have chosen hypertext as the core technology for the system because of the flexibility and simplicity that it offers. Using the KMS hypertext system, we're building a hypertext database that serves as a framework for incrementally adding applications and information sources.

Certainly, hypertext is not the best solution for any single task considered by itself. As a result, we're making the classic tradeoff of generality over power. We are forgoing the power of having specialized applications in order to have a single system that integrates a variety of tasks using a single data model.

Many of the attorneys' needs are similar to those of other types of knowledge workers. As a result, we think hypertext has potential as an integrating framework in many other environments.

REFERENCES

[Aksc88] Akscyn, R., McCracken, D., and Yoder, E. KMS: A Distributed Hypermedia System for Managing Knowledge in Organizations. *Commun. ACM 31*, 7 (July 1988), 820-835.

[Amer89] American Bar Association (ABA). Online Information: The Competitive Edge. *American Bar Association Journal, 75* (June 1989).

[Hala88] Halasz, F. Reflections on NoteCards: Seven Issues for the Next Generation of Hypermedia Systems. *Commun. ACM 31*, 7 (July 1988), 836-852.

[Kahn88] Kahn, P., and Meyrowitz, N. Guide, HyperCard, and Intermedia: A Comparison of Hypertext/Hypermedia Systems. IRIS Technical Report 88-7, Brown University, 1988.

[Lamb85] Lambert, S. Online: A Guide to America's Leading Information Services. Microsoft Press, Redmond, Wash., 1985.

[Shep88] Shepherdson, N. Computers and the Law: The Desktop Revolution. *American Bar Association Journal, 74* (August 1, 1988).

[Yode89] Yoder, E., Akscyn, R., and McCracken, D. Collaboration in KMS, A Shared Hypermedia System. In *CHI '89 Conference Proceedings*, ACM Press (April 1989), 37-42.

Hypertext Challenges in the Auditing Domain

Laura DeYoung

Price Waterhouse Technology Centre
68 Willow Road, Menlo Park, CA 94025
deyoung@pw.com

ABSTRACT

Auditing is the process by which an opinion is formed on the financial statements of a company by a group of outside professional accountants. Large numbers of documents pertaining to the company's business are examined and many more are produced during an audit in order to arrive at and provide a basis for this opinion. These documents contain a wide variety of interrelated information. Capturing these interrelationships is essential to performing an effective audit. Currently, this is accomplished by using a highly-structured, manual hypertext system. While quite effective, the system is difficult and time-consuming to maintain, and can become unwieldy when conducting an audit for a very large company.

We are in the process of developing an electronic system to meet the needs of this complex task. The complexity of the referencing system challenges current hypertext and user interface technology. At the same time, the structure of the domain affords an interesting application area within which to explore and more fully develop hypertext techniques. During the course of this project, we are exploring automatic generation of links, automatic generation of documents, hypertext path creation and access, creation of a typed-link topology for the domain, referencing of individual points and regions within documents, linking bodies of hypertext, and many other issues.

INTRODUCTION

To "audit a company" means to gather and substantiate sufficient information about a company to form an independent opinion about the accuracy of the company's financial statements. The audit is conducted by a team which varies in size and world-wide distribution according to the size and distribution of the company being audited. The audit task includes gathering and producing large numbers of documents and linking them together in ways that facilitate substantiation of their contents. These documents are gathered together in files called **Audit Working Papers**.

The Audit Working Papers have traditionally taken the shape of files of legal-sized paper, bound together with large brass clips in the upper left corner. These files include descriptions of the plan or approach used to undertake the audit, numerous forms or schedules describing procedures conducted and their findings, a wide variety of checklists with hundreds of questions, and successive summarizations of the auditors' findings and assessments.

These papers have complex interrelationships. Each piece of information is related in some way to other pieces of information within the Working Papers. The structure of these papers is inherently non-linear and quite complex. The difficulties of capturing and organizing this information in a linear format using pen and paper has been met by development of a highly stylized, manual hypertext system.

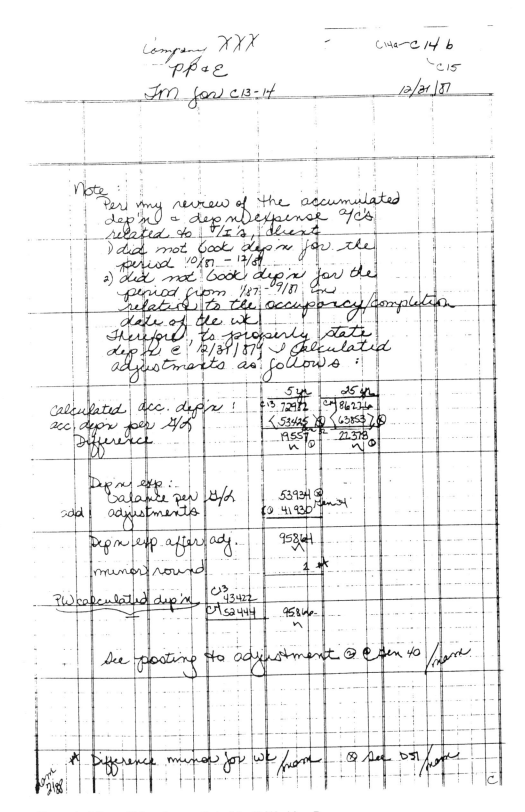

Figure 1: A Page Taken from a Set of Audit Working Papers

This system includes spatially oriented placement of references, a wide-variety of commonly used symbols for linking, and various conventions for annotation. Forward and backward referencing is complex in that it may include multiple links of various types to and from points and groups of points in documents. Figure 1, explicated below, shows an example taken from an actual set of Working Papers which gives a sense of the complexity of these references.

While the auditing task requires representation of complex interrelationships, the linking is constrained and well-defined. Also, the information in this domain is focused and constrained by the nature of what is pertinent to the audit process (e.g. dollar amounts associated with specific accounts and work being performed). Stylized ways of talking about the work being done have developed over a long period of time. For example, there are standard ways of describing procedures that are carried out and their results, and conclusions that are drawn. This provides a striking contrast to many domains to which hypertext technology has been applied, particularly those systems which strive to accommodate the general domain of human discourse, with its great diversity.

We believe we can capitalize on the well-defined nature of the information to afford much greater precision in accessing the right information at the right time than has been possible in other domains. Yet, this is a real-world problem with real-world potential gain. Internal studies suggest that approximately thirty percent of the time spent on an audit is dedicated to preparation, maintenance, and review of Working Papers. We anticipate cutting the time auditors spend on the Working Papers by a significant fraction, thereby reducing expense to the client, while providing improved functionality (e.g. being able to directly access detailed information documented in an office on the other side of the world). Therefore, the process of producing, maintaining, and reviewing working papers is an interesting and challenging candidate for automation and provides a rich application area for technical research and development, particularly in reference to hypertext, collaborative work, and powerful environments for non-technical users.

This paper continues with a more detailed look at the audit process and its inherent difficulties. The remaining sections describe why this problem is difficult, how hypertext can help as demonstrated by our Electronic Working Papers (EWP) prototype, and how the domain could provide new challenges to and ideas for advancements in hypertext technology. References to current technology and related work which can be applied to attain partial solutions are made throughout the discussion on current and future work.

REPLACING THE MANUAL PROCESS: WHY IS THIS PROBLEM HARD?

The audit process can be divided into four basic activities or phases: plan, execute, summarize, and report. Figure 2 is a simplified model of these phases and steps included in each. The flow of the audit process can be followed along the arrows shown, starting in the upper left corner of the first panel.

Each process step requires collecting and/or referencing materials and producing new documents which become part of the Working Papers. Figure 3 represents the resulting Working Papers and provides examples of the types of documents which are required or produced during analogous steps shown in Figure 2. Information in one document could potentially be related to specific information in any other document, possibly through multiple types of relationships. Types of relationships may include: support, elaboration, organization, summarization, etc. The arrows in Figure 3 represent examples of relationship types.

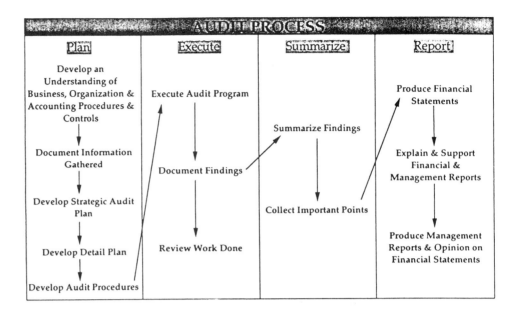

Figure 2: Audit Process. Arrows represent process flow.

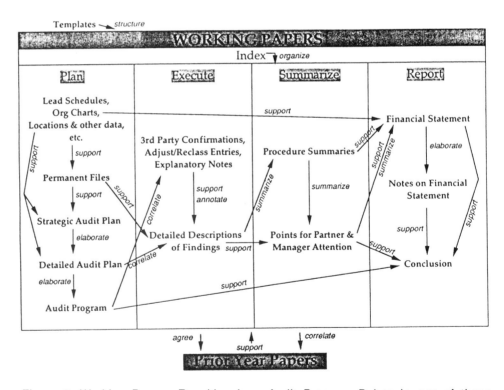

Figure 3: Working Papers Resulting from Audit Process. Points in any of these documents may be linked to specific points in any of the other documents along well-defined dimensions. Arrows represent examples of typed-links which may appear.

The Working Papers serve a variety of purposes. They serve as:

- the record of the work carried out in the audit and support for the opinion or conclusion drawn by the audit team.

- support for reports which are made to the company's management.

- the structure within which the audit is conducted.

- a source of client information, which is frequently utilized by other departments in the firm, like the tax practice.

- a basis for communication with the client.

- the common repository for work performed by various work groups.

- the focal point for communication among members of the audit team.

- a rich source of information for the next year's audit.

Some of these purposes of Working Papers are only served in a limited way by the physical system. An electronic version could provide a much richer source of information with much easier access. Certainly, processes like successive summarizations of information, copying information from one year's papers to the next, etc. could be made trivial. But our more general goals are to enhance and simplify the audit process, provide a medium for fuller communication among auditors, and enhance reporting capabilities.

Given these goals and a need to preserve and enhance the utility of the Working Papers, a number of interesting challenges arise in replacing this well-honed manual process with an electronic one. These challenges are:

1) Linking References

We need to provide an easy way to create and follow the kinds of links that appear in the physical system. Some references link specific points and groups of points or regions in various documents. Often these documents are hard copy papers which come from clients and third parties. This challenge includes providing a simple but powerful user-interface for creating, representing, and navigating through links. In addition, we must provide graphical displays which are sufficiently rich to give an auditor access to the information currently available using the physical system. This is no small task as Figure 1 shows.

At a local level, each figure or dollar amount is linked to other information which may either serve to substantiate it by pointing back to a place where the figure was derived, refer ahead to a point or points where the figure is subsequently used, or point to an explanation or annotation. Examples of these references appear in Figure 1.

On the original of Figure 1, the references appear in red to set them apart from the text. This particular page, **C14 b** as noted in the upper right, is used to elaborate on work done on pages **C13-14**. **C13** and **C14** appearing at the upper left of various figures indicate that these figures were derived from work appearing on those pages. Page references at the upper right of a number or figure, e.g. **Gen 34,** indicate a forward reference to that page, meaning the figure is used in work done or in summarizations appearing on that page. The circled number 1 at the lower right of two figures indicates that they are added together to produce a sum, referenced with a Σ **circled 1**. Sometimes circled number references can be made to another page. We can find the "posted" or logged adjustment at **circled 2** on page **Gen 40**, for instance.

Other marks of various types, circled letters, squiggles, checkmarks etc. can be found next to or below figures. These may have standard meanings (e.g. this is a sum), or an explanation or further reference might appear next to a matching mark at the bottom of the page.

It is difficult to display what is shown in figure 1 on a screen in a clear, legible way (at least for a screen of the size we expect auditors to have access to by the time a system such as this reaches the practice offices: 640 x 480). Questions arise about what should be visible, what should be referenced, whether references need to appear as explicitly as they do in the physical system, etc.

Many of the documents which auditors examine and which are included in the Working Papers are and will continue to be initially provided in hard copy form. We need to consider how to include these in the electronic system. Creating links to scanned images of hard copy documents is fairly simple, but interesting issues arise for hypertext and character recognition technologies when considering making fine-grain references into those images.

2) Maintain Physical Advantages

It is important to maintain the advantages of the physical existence of the papers to the greatest degree possible and to provide an electronic structure to replace the physical one.

Auditors have become very adept at navigating through these papers to find information. They rely not only on how the papers look but how they feel. For example, the bulk of the files indicates the amount of work completed, the sense of where one is in the papers is enhanced by seeing and feeling how many pages have been turned, different types of paper indicate types of documents and where they may have originated. An electronic version must include a good navigational system and many cues about size, location, and classification.

3) Richer Reference Paths

We want to provide ways of establishing and accessing a wider variety of complete reference paths through the working papers than are currently documented in the physical representation. This includes providing a common repository for information and ways to link pieces of the Working Papers which might be produced in isolation.

The primary concern in auditing is to insure that nothing important has been forgotten or overlooked. It is critical to make certain that points needing consideration are properly addressed, to be sure that planned work is thoroughly carried out, and to detect inconsistencies within the working papers. These represent auditing concerns with serious quality and legal ramifications. To be sure an issue was properly addressed, auditors would like to be able to easily check the evolution of its handling from the time it is raised in the Strategic Planning session through the work done to address it. Conversely, to insure consistency, they might want to follow an issue mentioned in the final summarization back through the summary process to its first point of detection and full description. Currently, if an auditor wants to check where a figure in the Financial Statement originated, he or she must manually follow a complicated path of references. At least the path exists for figures. Paths following the evolution or summarization of an issue or concept are frequently only partially complete or nonexistent even when the work is finished.

When an audit is carried out across numerous practice offices, possibly great distances apart, each practice office creates its own set of Working Papers representing the piece of the audit it is conducting. The detailed information about the work carried out in each office is, therefore, not readily available to be examined at other offices. Often, a statement of final results may be the only document linking the pieces together.

If the auditor responsible for reviewing the work would like a fuller explanation or would like to see specific documents prepared at another office, the only recourse is to use fax or phone communication.

The work on an audit is completed over months, with information coming in at random times. If paths could be established consistently as work is completed, they could also serve to indicate the progress of the work.

Information gathered along paths could be consolidated into reports providing concise descriptions of issues raised, resulting work, work progress, etc. in response to specific needs and questions. This demands an ability to consistently establish links among related issues, to consolidate work across offices, and to follow distinct, narrow paths.

4) Utilize Existing Documents

We want to provide a way to access existing documents to serve as examples for producing schedules, reports, memos, etc., along with a library of templates bearing the accepted structure and language of the business. This challenge implies the linking together of multiple sets of unrelated working papers.

The reports, memos, letters, etc. produced in an audit have a specialized structure. Also, the language used is very important in terms of communicating the exact intent and has become quite standard even though it is diverse. When an auditor wants to produce such a document, often the first step is to locate other documents of a similar type. It is preferable to make use of the existing structure and reuse portions of the language in the same way that it is preferable for a software engineer to modify an existing piece of code rather than start from scratch. Appropriate examples may be found in Working Papers of another client with a similar type of business. These documents are then used as a guide in producing the new document. Presently, there is no good way of locating appropriate or applicable documents, and there is no consistent set of templates available.

HOW CAN HYPERTEXT HELP?: OUR CURRENT SYSTEM

All the purposes served by Working Papers cited above hinge on the ability to link information. The manual process is a non-linear system as it stands. Hypertext technology can help enrich that process. The following points are made in reference to the challenges described above and describe what currently exists in our prototype.

1) Linking References

The EWP prototype provides a series of forms, supported by a general forms specification language, for recording any audit information, including information needed by the system to maintain the Working Papers. The system provides methods for linking points in these forms to other forms or scanned images of hard copy documents which vary according to the task at hand. Where it is important for a reference to be visible, links are created by typing a page reference next to the point referring to it. Other links, such as annotation links, are created automatically, linking the point, region, or page where the user initiated writing the annotation and the note. Notes on pages are available through a menu item. Notes on individual points or regions are accessed by a double mouse click on that area. Users generally need to know that references have been attached to dollar amounts, but may not care what those references are called. References to dollar amounts are indicated by enclosing the amount in stylized boxes of which the sides have indicators, like a double bar, showing that references exist. A single mouse click allows for viewing and editing links. A double click follows the link if one exists, otherwise it allows the user to create one.

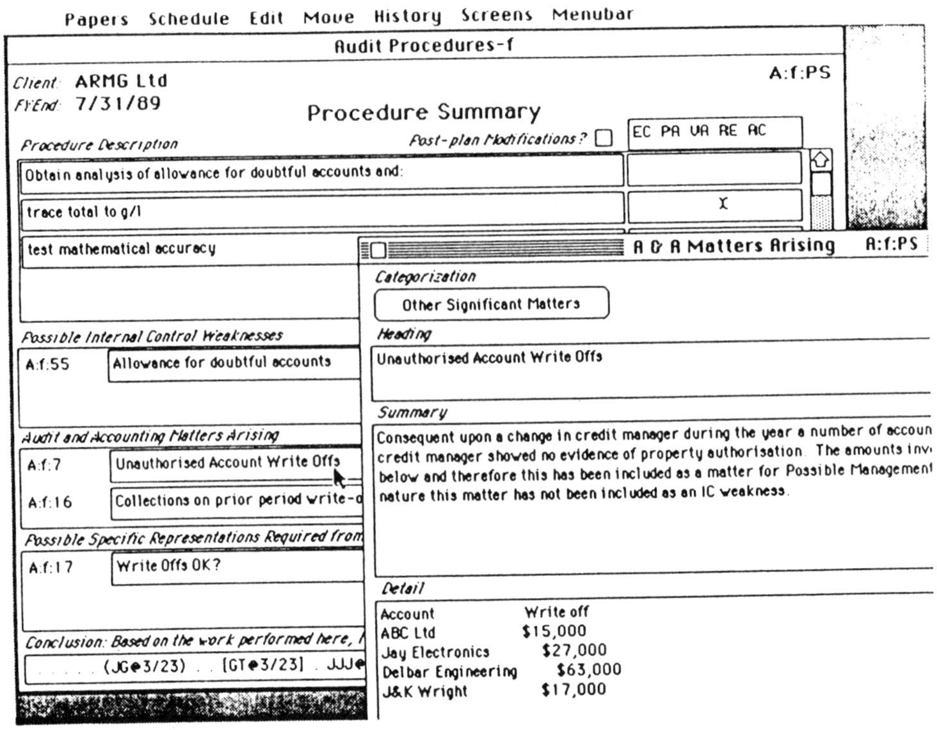

Audit Procedures-f

Client: ARMG Ltd
FYEnd: 7/31/89
Procedure Summary
A:f:PS

Procedure Description
Post-plan Modifications? ☐
EC PA VA RE AC

Obtain analysis of allowance for doubtful accounts and:

trace total to g/l
X

test mathematical accuracy
A & A Matters Arising
A:f:PS

Categorization
Other Significant Matters

Possible Internal Control Weaknesses
Heading
Unauthorised Account Write Offs

A:f:55 Allowance for doubtful accounts

Summary
Consequent upon a change in credit manager during the year a number of accoun
credit manager showed no evidence of property authorisation. The amounts inv
below and therefore this has been included as a matter for Possible Management
nature this matter has not been included as an IC weakness.

Audit and Accounting Matters Arising
A:f:7 Unauthorised Account Write Offs

A:f:16 Collections on prior period write-d

Possible Specific Representations Required from
A:f:17 Write Offs OK?

Detail
Account   Write off
ABC Ltd $15,000
Jay Electronics $27,000
Delbar Engineering $63,000
J&K Wright $17,000

Conclusion: Based on the work performed here,
. . . . . . (JG●3/23) . . . [GT●3/23] . . JJJ●

Figure 4: Procedure Summary form (back window) has a description of an audit procedure appearing in the top table with three tables below were points about "Possible Internal Control Weaknesses," "Audit and Accounting Matters Arising," and "Possible Specific Representations Required from Management" are noted. Each point has a reference code to its left linking to supporting evidence, similar to those found in physical working papers (Figure 1). Each point also has a page of description (accessed by clicking on the text of the point). Here the user has clicked on "Unauthorized Account Write Offs." The description page (front window) displays a summary of the point and detailed information as well as the heading which appears as the phrase describing the point on the Procedure Summary. The point is also categorized, here as "Other Significant Matters." This point can be gathered up with other points in this same category from anywhere in the Working Papers to appear on a summary report of such matters.

Small screen-size pages place a severe constraint on a system which traditionally uses legal-size sheets of paper, sometimes of double-width. The use of hypertext becomes even more extensive as we move detail that would have fit on a physical sheet to electronically linked pages. In this way, hypertext is becoming an important aid in dealing with limited screen real estate. Figure 4 shows an EWP page along with a page of detail which *supports* a point appearing on it.

Currently, we are conceptualizing a hypertext node as a page in the Working Papers. Pages which are forms are highly structured with various fields containing specific types of information. This structure affords the advantages of *semistructured nodes* described by Conklin in [Conk87]. Fields or regions can be referenced and subjected to specific types of processing, while the entire page is provided as context.

2) Maintain Physical Advantages

Providing sufficient context at the global level to prevent disorientation is the classical hypertext problem. Just as the browser in NoteCards is another NoteCard [Hala88], the

EWP browser looks and behaves like other forms in the system, and can be used to add new documents to the Working Papers. It provides information about the organization of the papers, as well as information about individual pages or documents, including their type (e.g. form, scanned image), and some classification information (e.g. summarization of findings, information on the progress of the audit).

The browser provides a list representing the path taken to reach a particular document, but provides no sense for where one might go or how to reach a particular place in the structure. A global map is provided for that purpose. The map is a graphical representation which describes the topology of the working papers. Since a number of pages in the Working Papers might be open at the same time (as windows on the screen, even though they may be hidden), the map highlights all those points. The map can be viewed at varying levels of granularity. As in KMS [Aksc88], some special navigational commands are also provided, allowing the user to turn pages (NEXT, PREVIOUS) through the papers or move from one instance of a particular type of document or form to another (NEXT INSTANCE, PREVIOUS INSTANCE), or GOTO any document as described by a unique reference code. These reference codes appear in the upper right corners of pages as one of the many devices which help users know where they are. The types of forms themselves help users recognize their location and how they work in much the way van Dam describes pattern recognition as one approach to preventing being "lost in hyperspace" [vanD88].

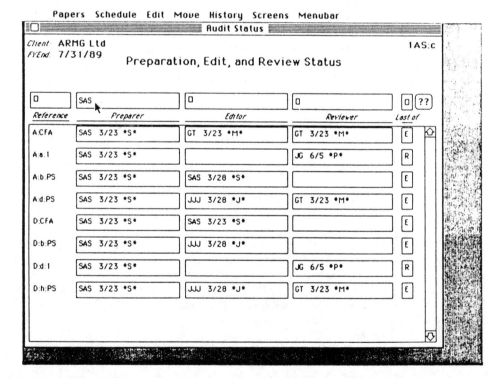

Figure 5: One of many types of report forms in EWP, this status report shows which forms or pages (references at the left) have been filled out (prepared), edited, and reviewed. Each entry displays the initials, date, and rank of the person doing the work. Sometimes it is important to know which operation occurred last (far right column showing P for Prepared, etc.) The row of boxes across the top of the form provide a simple query-by-example mechanism. Small squares are wild cards. In this example, the only entries shown are those prepared by SAS.

But as Halasz points out, "navigational access by itself is not sufficient," effective search and query mechanisms are also necessary [Hala88]. EWP provides a query-by-example mechanism for filtering and viewing information which can be gathered, based on a processing function, from any forms in the Working Papers. Figure 5 shows information which was gathered from each form about the status of the form in terms of whether it has been prepared or filled out, edited, or reviewed, when and by whom. The information in this example is being filtered by the initials of the preparer. Only reference to those forms prepared by SAS appear.

This data viewing mechanism can be used in a variety of ways, including as a means through which to view the structure of the Working Papers, perhaps filtering on the type of document.

3) Richer Reference Paths

Recognizing that the relationships between documents and points within them are very well defined in this domain, we are able to describe a typed-link topology for a set of Working Papers. There appears to be a finite number of link types necessary to describe such relationships: elaboration, summarization, annotation, summation, etc. This typed-link topology promises to provide the basis for processing much like that found in Textnet where paths can be built and text from nodes along a path can be concatenated [Conk87]. Such paths in EWP can provide reports on user-specified and constrained topics, e.g. work that was accomplished in response to a concern raised in the Strategic Plan about the obsolescence of inventory. Currently, we can provide reports following points through the summarization process, and we can provide some views into the Prior Year's Working Papers. This is a first attempt at joining two large bodies of hypertext automatically based on an understanding of content.

4) Utilize Existing Documents

The forms available within EWP can be thought of as templates which help auditors organize information and insure its completeness. Language templates for memos, proposals, conclusions, correspondence with clients, reports, etc. are also available.

HOW COULD HYPERTEXT HELP?: FUTURE WORK

1) Linking References

Future work includes answering a distinct need to access regions within scanned images of hard copy documents, as well as in forms. It is unclear whether this access should be handled by attempting to determine the structure of the document and thereby transforming it into something resembling the forms we are using; by building sufficient intelligence into the processing mechanism to determine the areas over which to process; by allowing the user to select regions, identify them, and link them to other documents; or by some combination of the above.

2) Maintain Physical Advantages

In reference to navigation and global views of the system, we plan to enhance and extend our ability to filter information and provide perspectives to include viewing information based on relationships or types of links between documents. This would include a map of the typed-link topology seen from varying perspectives.

3) Richer Reference Paths

We plan to continue to explore ways of providing paths through the Working Papers. This includes further work on joining large hypertext bodies such as sections of Working Papers which are developed separately. In order to accomplish this, it will be important to explore integration of hypertext in EWP with frame-based domain models being developed at PW [Fike88]. A model of the audit process can provide the basis for reasoning about the relationships among contents of Working Papers and automatic generation of links.

As the audit process is better understood, we will also be exploring ways in which we can support the collaborative nature of the task. There is considerable potential for employing Issue-Based Information Systems techniques to encourage conversations among audit team members [Conk87] [Bege88].

4) Utilize Existing Documents

It may also be possible, as we become more adept at linking hypertext bodies along various dimensions, to link Working Papers describing various, similar businesses in ways that allow memos and reports to be accessed based on their structure and general content, as well as specific references. This calls for extensions to the typed-link topology which include an understanding of the nature of business and will therefore depend upon ongoing work at PW on model-based reasoning in the business domain [Hams89].

CONCLUSION

The information required and produced during an audit is linked in complex, but well-structured ways. Providing a hypertext system to aid in the auditing task and afford easy access to the information raises a number of challenges including developing powerful user-interfaces which support the functionality currently available with the manual system, providing effective navigation tools, establishment of a typed-link topology to be used in building paths used to produce reports, integrating AI techniques like model-based reasoning and frame-based systems in order to link large hypertext bodies together and enhance processing capabilities. Exploring and meeting these challenges has thus far been, and promises to continue to be, an exciting area of research yielding many benefits to the auditing domain with much potential for development of hypertext and other technologies.

Acknowledgments. I want to thank: Andy Gelman, David Hirsch, Cris Johnson, and Chris Taylor for being inventive and industrious teammates on the EWP project; Jeff DeLisio, Richard Fikes, Bob Nado, Rick Taube, and Walter Hamscher for helping bridge the AI-Hypertext gap; Trisha Mount, Tom Orsi, and Geoff Thompson for doing an excellent job of transferring auditing expertise; and especially Beau Sheil for his insight and guidance.

REFERENCES

[Acke88]   Ackerman, M., Malone, T. "Intelligent Agents, Object-Oriented Databases, and Hypertext," *In Proceedings of AAAI-88 Workshop on AI and Hypertext: Issues and Directions* (August 1988).

[Aksc88]   Akscyn, R., McCracken, D.L., and Yoder, E. "KMS: A Distributed Hypermedia System for Managing Knowledge in Organizations," *Commun. ACM* 31,7 (July 1988), 820-835.

[Bege88]   Begeman, M., Conklin, J. "The Right Tool for the Job," *BYTE*, Vol. B, 10, (October 1988), 255-266.

[Camp88]   Campbell, B., Goodman, J. "HAM: A General Purpose Hypertext Abstract Machine," *Commun. ACM* 31,7 (July 1988), 856-861.

[Conk87]   Conklin, J. "Hypertext: A survey and introduction," *IEEE Computer* 20, 9 (September 1987), 17-40.

[Fike88] Fikes, R. "Integrating Hypertext and Frame-Based Domain Models," In *Proceedings of AAAI-88 Workshop on AI and Hypertext: Issues and Directions* (August 1988).

[Fris88] Frisse, M. "Searching for Information in a Hypertext Medical Handbook," *Commun. ACM* 31,7 (July 1988), 880-886.

[Hala87] Halasz, F., Moran, T., Trigg, R. "NoteCards in a Nutshell," In *Proceedings of the 1987 ACM Conference of Human Factors in Computer Systems* (CHI+GI '87) (April 1987), 45-52.

[Hala88] Halasz, F. "Reflections on Notecards: Seven Issues for the Next Generation of Hypermedia System," *Commun. ACM* 31,7 (July 1988), 836-852.

[Hams89] Hamscher, W. "Proposal for Using Explicit Representation of the Structure and Behavior of Business Entities to Assess Audit Risk," Available from author: Price Waterhouse Technology Centre, 68 Willow Road, Menlo Park, CA 94025 (April 1989).

[vanD88] van Dam, A. "Hypertext '87 Keynote Address," *Commun. ACM* 31,7 (July 1988), 887-895.

[Whal89] Whalen, T., Patrick, A. "Conversational Hypertext: Information Access Through Natural Language Dialogues with Computers," *In Proceedings of the 1989 ACM Conference of Human Factors in Computer Systems* (CHI '89) (May 1989), 289-292.

[Yode89] Yoder, E., Akscyn, R., McCracken, D. "Collaboration in KMS, A Shared Hypermedia System" *In Proceedings of the 1989 ACM Conference of Human Factors in Computer Systems* (CHI '89) (May 1989), 37-42.

Computational Hypertext in Biological Modelling

John L. Schnase and John J. Leggett

Hypertext Research Lab
Department of Computer Science
Texas A&M University
College Station, Texas 77843

ABSTRACT

This paper describes an application of hypertext to a biological research problem. An individual energetics model for Cassin's Sparrow was developed in which the computations and intellectual activities associated with each phase of the research were performed within an integrated hypertext environment. The study demonstrates the effectiveness of computational hypertext in meeting the personal information management requirements of individual researchers in the natural sciences and its ability to speed the dissemination of research results within a community of scholars. Most important, the study shows how hypertext can be "phased in" to support traditional scholarship in disciplines that are otherwise slow to respond to emerging computer technologies.

KEYWORDS

Computational hypertext, hypertext publishing, information management, collaboration, simulation modelling, natural sciences.

INTRODUCTION

Research in the natural sciences typically involves gathering data, performing computations and analyses, collaborating with colleagues, and preparing graphical and written documents for publication. In established sciences, such as biology, chemistry, and physics, these activities are influenced by long-standing traditions. Effectively managing information throughout phases of a research project can become a formidable problem to an *individual* scientist. In addition, information management poses difficulties to an entire scientific *community*. For example, the long delay between the time research results are submitted for publication and their appearance in a journal article is a frustration common to many fields.

Computer support for this type of knowledge work generally consists of an assortment of programs, interfaces, and machines -- a diverse assemblage of environments that can, at times, compound an individual's personal information management problems while doing little to speed the communication of new ideas. For proponents of hypertext, the challenge becomes how to help scientists manage their information, share their results, and accept a new medium for their scholarly activity.

The Hypertext Research Lab at Texas A&M University is exploring ways hypertext can be used to advance research and communication within scientific communities. We contend that the assimilation of emerging computer technologies by established scientific disciplines is facilitated by first demonstrating the effectiveness of a new technology in solving particular problems, then showing how the technology supports *traditional* scholarship in the discipline. Hypertext's ability to provide a uniform, integrated environment for intellectual activity promises to significantly enhance the research abilities of scientists willing to utilize the new technology.

A Case Study. In this study, an individual energetics model for Cassin's Sparrow was developed. As usual, the research dealt with many forms of information. Computer support through all phases of the research was provided entirely within a hypertext environment using the KMS hypertext system on a Sun 3/60 workstation. Field data, computations that reduce the data, the on-line, electronic form of the document, and printable, camera-ready tables, figures, and text for an article submitted to the journal *Ecological Modelling* were integrated into a single hypertext. This approach was taken to examine the effectiveness of hypertext in meeting the personal information management needs of researchers, assess its ability to speed the communication of results, and evaluate its capacity to support intellectual activites generally associated with this type of scholarship.

The work demonstrates computation within a hypertext, program code development within an integrated hypertext environment, hypertext support for distributed collaboration and authoring, an interactive, electronic journal article, hypertext support for traditional, printed journal publishing, and the ability to mail the entire hypertext over a network. Perhaps most important, the study shows how hypertext can be assimilated into a discipline's traditional methodologies to change the environment in which research occurs.

The first section of the paper provides background information useful in understanding the study. The organization and use of the hypertext is then presented. This is followed by a discussion and concluding remarks.

BACKGROUND

Hypertext. Ted Nelson introduced the term "hypertext" and described it as "... a body of written or pictoral material interconnected in such a complex way that it could not conveniently be presented or represented on paper" [Nels65], or simply, "non-sequential writing" [Nels87]. The term hypermedia, as it is commonly used, implies that information can be present in hypertexts in forms other than text. Nelson, it seems, intended "hypertext" sufficient to describe the range of media that can be present in a hypertext [Nels67]. We, likewise, tend to use the term "hypertext" to imply "hypermedia."

Hypertext Model. A set of abstractions that provide a conceptual framework for creating, storing, and retrieving information in a hypertext [Legg88].

Hypertext System. A functionally related set of computer hardware and software components that implement a hypertext model [Legg88].

Computational Hypertext. Our use of the term "computational hypertext" implies that computation *per se* is an integral component of the information contained in the hypertext.

KMS. The KMS (Knowledge Management System) hypertext system is a distributed hypertext environment for Unix workstations [Aksc88]. The KMS model is based on the abstract notion of frames interlinked in space.

Frames consist of screen-sized workspaces that contain text, graphics, image items, and space. Individual items can be linked to other frames. Users navigate from frame to frame by mouse selection, and all space in a frame can be used. There is no mode boundary between author and browser. KMS supports an interpreted action language and users can access the operating system from within the KMS system. Frames are stored as Unix files in a directory. The directories are called framesets and can be distributed across different file servers.

Cassin's Sparrow (*Aimophila cassinii*). A locally common breeding bird of mesquite-grasslands in West Texas. The natual history of arid-adapted avian species is an interesting research area to many biologists [Wolf77].

Individual Energetics Model. The biological research forming the basis of this case study deals with an energetics problem. A model was proposed to account for the daily energy expenditure of individual, adult Cassin's Sparrows. A systems analysis approach was used to formally specify the model [Gran86]. Interactive computer programs that simulate the model were also developed. The computations are based on 24-hour time-activity data collected by field observations of birds in their natural habitat.

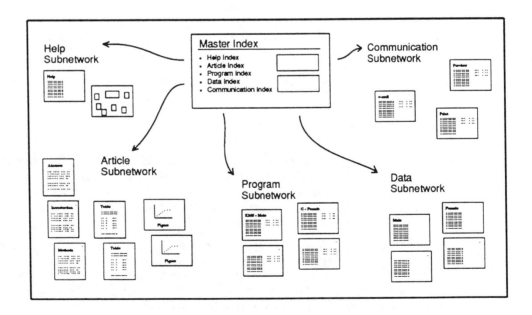

Figure 1. Organization of the Cassin's Sparrow energetics model hypertext. The Master Index provides access to five subnetworks within the hypertext.

ORGANIZATION OF THE HYPERTEXT

Figure 1 shows the overall organization of the energetics model hypertext. It consists of a network of approximately 250 frames and has a generally hierarchical structure. The Master Index is at the top of the hierarchy and allows access to five major subnetworks: Help, Article, Program, Data, and Communication.

Help Subnetwork. The Help Subnetwork contains instructions and explanations to guide the user's interactions with the hypertext. Figure 1, for example, is from a frame in the Help Subnetwork.

Article Subnetwork. The Article Subnetwork contains the electronic, on-line browsable version of the article describing the energetics model research. It includes text, tables, and figures. There is a substantial amount of interlinked information in the Article Subnetwork.

Program Subnetwork. The Program Subnetwork contains the source code for programs that simulate the energetics model. Since one of the goals of the project was to gain experience using hypertext as an environment for computation, two different approaches were taken. The Program Subnetwork consists of a KMS action language program to process the male data set and a C program that processes the female data set. Further details are provided in the following sections.

Data Subnetwork. The Data Subnetwork consists of two data sets, one for a male Cassin's Sparrow, the other for a female. It also contains KMS action language programs that extract information from the data sets for use in other applications.

Communication Subnetwork. The Communication Subnetwork contains KMS action language programs for previewing and printing the paper version of the energetics model article. It also provides an interface to the Unix mail facility that allows the entire hypertext to be sent electronically over a network.

USE OF THE HYPERTEXT

In this section, we describe the functionality of the energetics model hypertext. In doing so, we demonstrate how this hypertext, in association with the KMS system, provides an appropriate environment for the knowledge work required in the Cassin's Sparrow research project.

Entering the Hypertext. Entry to the hypertext is through the Title Frame (Figure 2) to the Master Index (Figure 3). From the Master Index it is possible to navigate to the five subnetworks in the hypertext, each of which has its own index. The Master Index also provides the context for setting model parameters and running the simulation programs.

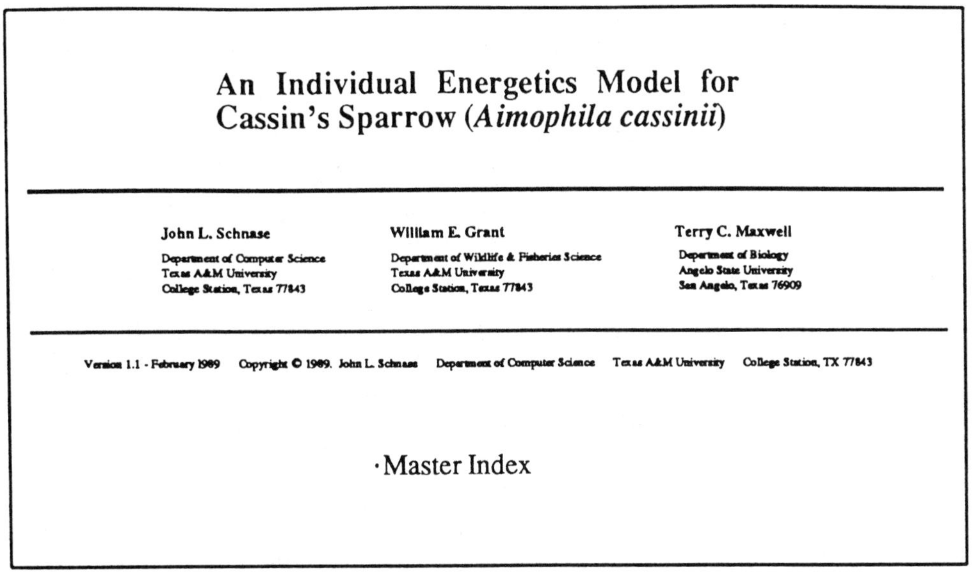

Figure 2. Title Frame of the energetics model hypertext. The Title Frame identifies the biologists who collaborated on the research and guides the user to the Master Index.

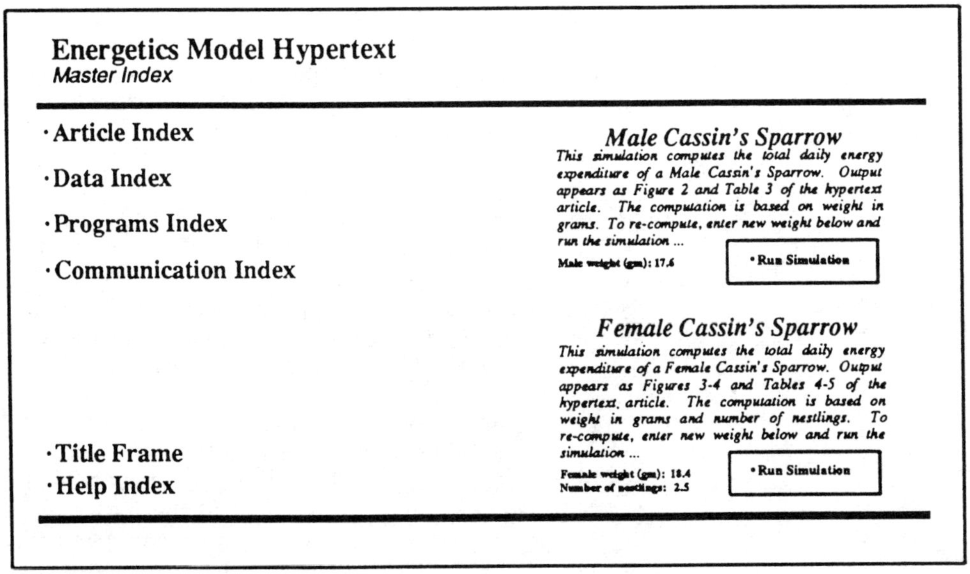

Figure 3. Master Index of the energetics model hypertext. The Master Index allows access to the five subnetworks of the hypertext. It also provides the context for interactions with the simulation program. In KMS, selectable items are denoted by the presence of a small, hollow bullet. If an action language program is attached, the bullets are filled.

Browsing, Authoring, and Annotating. Every frame in the hypertext can be browsed on-line. In KMS, the user can author, edit, or annotate anything browsable, providing permissions are appropriately set.

Figure 4 shows the Article Subnetwork Index, which allows users to navigate to sections of the on-line journal article and related tables and figures. Figure 4 also includes the actual text of the Introduction section. When the article is being browsed on-line, options on the right side of the frame allow the user to conveniently navigate to the Literature Cited section, to tables or figures referenced in the text, or to the next section of the paper.

Note in Figure 4 that the text of the article appears on the left side of a frame. KMS's facility for printing causes a tree of frames to be formatted by traversing links in a depth-first manner, assembling printable pages from only the left side of each frame. Text items preceded by "@" are ignored. Since all of the space in a KMS frame can be used, there is ample room for annotation.

Running the Simulation Programs. The KMS action language and C programs both compute the energetics model. The programs are executed by selecting "Run Simulation" from the Master Index (Figure 3). The KMS action language program reads the weight of a male bird from the Master Index frame and uses the male data file in the Data Subnetwork to compute total 24-hour energy expenditure. In a similar fashion, the C program accepts female weight and number of nestlings from the Master Index frame and performs the computation using the female data set. Changing the parameters on the Master Index frame and running the simulations cause the tables and figures to be reconstructed. As indicated in Figure 5, output generated by these programs consists of the tables and figures in the Article Subnetwork.

Program Development in the Hypertext. The simulation programs represent two very different approaches to performing computation in hypertext. In both cases, however, code development in this environment becomes another form of hypertext writing, and the resulting programs can be a complex, interlinked network of statements.

Figure 6 shows an example of the KMS action language program that simulates the male Cassin's Sparrow model. It consists of frames containing statements and comments that can be linked to other frames, just like any other text item. The semantics of the action language are oriented toward operations affecting abstractions present in the hypertext. Action language statements are interpreted by the KMS system interpreter, which sequentially processes statements in a frame and traverses links in depth-first fashion.

Hypertext can also be used as a more general program development environment. In the C program version of the simulation, a strict, top-down approach was used in writing the program. The hierarchical decomposition was realized by linking C comments in frames at one level of the hierarchy to frames at the next lower level. Leaf frames contain only C program statements. The result, as indicated in Figure 7, was a hierarchically structured hypertext C program.

In order to execute the C program, it is necessary to access the underlying operating system. KMS allows the contents of a tree of frames to be exported to a Unix file, again by following links in depth-first order. Exporting the hypertext

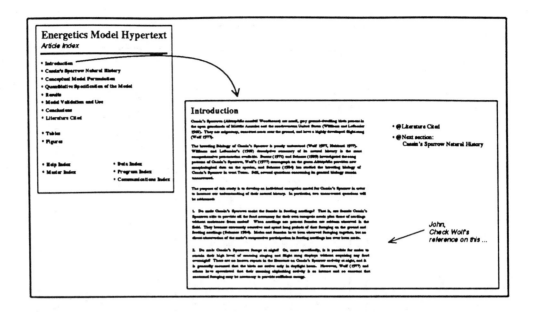

Figure 4. The Article Subnetwork Index and an example of text from the Introduction section of the Cassin's Sparrow article. Notice that it is possible to go directly to the Literature Cited section of the paper or advance sequentially to the next section. Space on the right side of the Introduction frame has been used for a personal annotation.

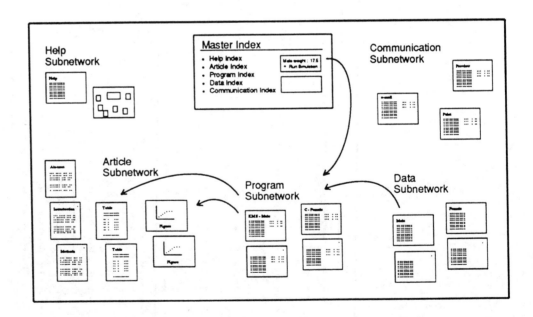

Figure 5. Computation in the hypertext. Code in the Program Subnetwork processes information contained on the Master Index and in the Data frames. Output consists of interlinked tables and figures in the Article Subnetwork. In a sense, both input and output of the computations *are* hypertext.

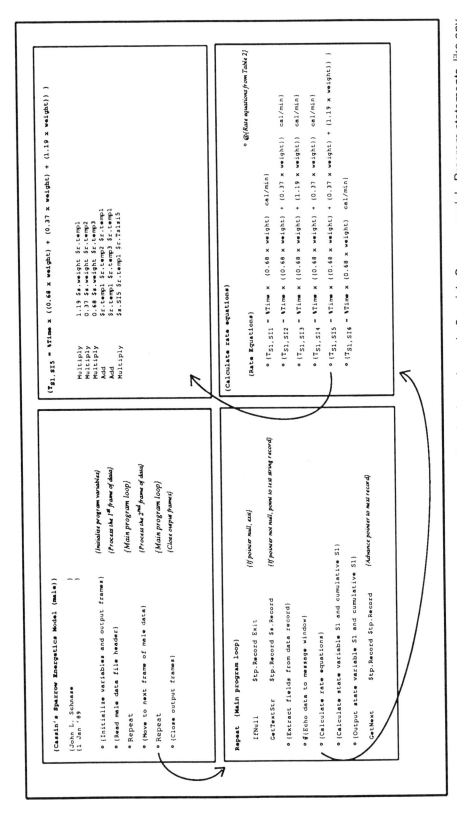

Figure 6. An example of the KMS action language program that simulates the male Cassin's Sparrow model. Program statements, like any other text item, may be linked to other frames. The KMS system interpreter processes statements on a frame in sequence and traverses links in depth-first fashion. The arrows in this example show the flow of control starting in the main program module (top left frame).

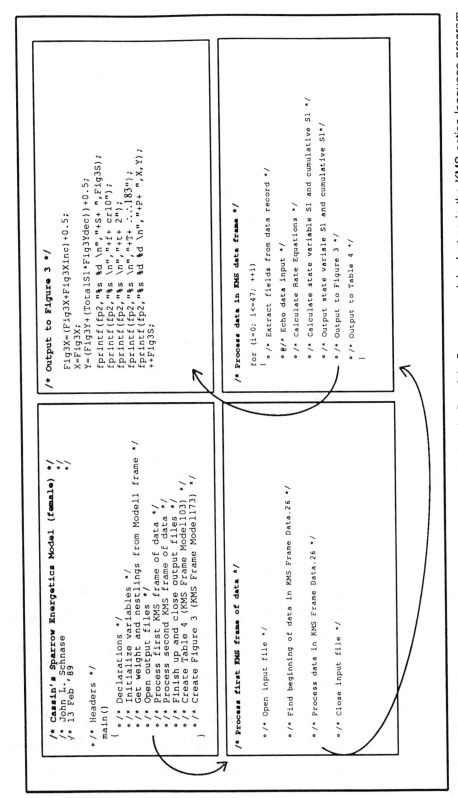

Figure 7. An example of the C program that simulates the female Cassin's Sparrow model. Just as in the KMS action language program above, a top-down approach was realized by the way the hypertext code was linked. High-level frames contain mostly linked comments, while leaf frames contain executable program statements.

C program beginning at its top frame creates a linear source file that can be processed by the C compiler. It is then a simple matter to invoke a command language interpreter of the operating system, run the compiler, and execute the resulting binary file.

Both the KMS action language program and the C program generate tables and figures that are integrated into the hypertext. The action language program does this directly, inside the hypertext. The C program, however, constructs files outside of KMS that can be accessed and displayed as frames within the hypertext.

Printing and Mailing. The KMS system allows any frame or tree of frames in the hypertext to be printed on PostScript compatible printers. In addition to this general print facility, the Communication Subnetwork contains KMS action language programs that cause only those parts of the hypertext that are relevant to a journal publication to be previewed and printed. The printed version of the article is assembled from frames in the Article Subnetwork and contains text in the appropriate format for journal submission and *camera-ready* tables and figures. In fact, it was this printed form of the article that was submitted to *Ecological Modelling*.

The Communications Subnetwork also provides a KMS action language interface to the Unix *mail* facility that allows the hypertext to be conveniently sent over a network. The user invokes this functionality by simply entering an e-mail address on the frame and selecting a "Send Hypertext Mail" option. Likewise, hypertext may be received and integrated into the user's environment by selecting a "Receive Hypertext Mail" option.

In order to mail the hypertext, a Unix *tar* file is created from the directory containing the KMS frame files. This binary *tar* file is converted into an ASCII-encoded representation by *uuencode* that can be sent using *mail*. To receive hypertext mail, the mail message is processed by *uudecode*. The frameset is then extracted using *tar*. Any networked workstation running KMS that has a local, Internet, or uucp address can have immediate access to the information, programs, data, and functionality of the energetics model hypertext.

Collaboration. The hypertext, along with the KMS system, supports collaboration in two ways. First, frames can be file-served to any networked workstation, thereby providing collaborators access to a common knowledge structure. This form of collaboration is particularly useful for authoring, editing, brainstorming, and communicating during the course of a research project. In addition, the ability to mail the entire hypertext to other interested scientists for their evaluation adds convenience and speed to an important level of dialog within a research community.

Hypertext as a Template. The energetics model hypertext can be used as a template for similar work. Copying the high-level frames and programs that define the basic structure and functionality of the hypertext provides a familiar context for managing information on a new project.

DISCUSSION

The application of hypertext to the energetics model research is, admittedly, a small-scale example. However, we believe it has important implications for the way scholarship and research are conducted in the sciences. This section describes what we consider to be the salient points to emerge from the study.

The Problem Revisited. Scientists are becoming sophisticated in the use of computers, and their research reflects an increasing dependence on computational resources. There are myriad applications available to support data collection, data reduction, statistical analysis, graphical presentations, authoring, etc. Unfortunately, the knowledge work associated with various phases of a research project can require familiarity with a wide range of programs, interfaces, operating systems, and machines. Management of the scientist's personal information space is often inconvenient and inefficient, despite the growing accessability of computing power.

There is another irony. While the increased use of computers has enabled many specific research programs, it has had less effect on improving communication within scientific communities. The time interval between submitting a paper for publication and its appearance as a journal article can be as long as 2 to 3 years for many journals in the natural sciences. The problem is compounded by the fact that traditional journal publications continue to be the principle means of communicating research results.

These problems are not unique to biology or the natural sciences. Indeed, many fields are exploring ways computers can enhance personal productivity and communication. However, established sciences have long-standing traditions that influence the way research is conducted [Kuhn70]. Some traditions, like the scientific method itself, are extremely important, while the importance of others is less obvious. These traditions confer stability and maturity on a discipline, but they can, in subtle ways, create a climate that is resistant to change.

The Hypertext Solution. Hypertext provides an intriguing solution to the information management problems faced by scientists. This study provides a concrete example of how hypertext can be used to facilitate the types of intellectual activities associated with scientific research. The following are what we consider to be the more important ideas to emerge from our experiences with the energetics model hypertext.

- *Hypertext provides an integrated, personal environment for scientific knowledge work.* All computer-supported activities associated with the research project were conducted within the hypertext. All artifacts required for reasoning about the problem were a part of the hypertext. Raw data, programs, text, figures, personal annotations -- everything in the hypertext, including the structure and functionality of the hypertext itself -- could be accessed and manipulated on an equal basis. The uniformity of the environment simplifies the personal information management problem.

- *Hypertext supports community scholarship among scientists.* The study demonstrates two ways hypertext can improve communication within scientific communities. The first is by supporting collaborative work. The effectiveness of KMS's shared-database approach to collaboration has been demonstrated in several settings [Aksc88], [Yode89]. This is likely to be most useful in the course of a research project involving more than one investigator or author. However, this application suggests an even more significant way a research community can be affected.

  The ability to electronically mail the hypertext, thereby making the entire context of a research project immediately available to others, has important implications. In addition to speeding the dissemination of new ideas, it can substantively change the nature of the dialog within a community. Not only is it possible to quickly and conveniently share results, but the context in which reasoning occured can be shared as well. Or, to quote Vannevar Bush, "The inheritance from the master becomes, not only his additions to the world's record, but for his disciples the entire scaffolding by which they were erected [Bush45]."

- *Computational hypertext is appropriate for scientific applications.* There is growing recognition of the need for computation in hypertext [Hala88]. The usefulness of hypertext in the sciences *depends* on its computational capacity. The energetics model demonstrates program development and use in a hypertext, but even more important, it shows that moving into a hypertext environment does not necessarily imply a loss of computational speed or generality.

- *Hypertext supports traditional scholarship.* One of the most important features of this application is the way it supports the *traditional* scholarly activities of scientific research. Data can be stored and easily accessed in the hypertext. Computation can be performed in the hypertext. Traditional publishing methods are supported well -- appropriate parts of the hypertext can be printed in camera-ready form appropriate for journal submission. Scientists can work in customary ways, and the benefits of an improved environment are realized without upsetting the existing order of things.

  Radical methodological changes are resisted by established sciences [Kuhn70]. Some of what is suggested by the introduction of hypertext to scientifc work would be viewed as radical. It seems that a climate of acceptance can be promoted by "phasing" hypertext into traditional patterns of scientific scholarship.

These, of course, are not new ideas. Bush [Bush45], Engelbart [Enge62], and Nelson [Nels65] were among the first to propose systems that augment the human intellect by managing information in what we now call hypertext. In fact, Bush's seminal paper was motivated in large part by his indictment of existing methods for transmitting and reviewing the results of scientific research. Even in 1945 he viewed them as "generations old and totally inadequate for their purpose" [Bush45]. There are still few examples of the use of hypertext in scientific settings.

Related Work. There are several examples of closely related work. However, most applications of hypertext have been to areas other than the natural sciences. NoteCards [Hala88], [Trig86], Neptune [Deli86a], Intermedia [Garr86], [Yank87], [Yank88], Augment [Enge84a], [Enge84b], and KMS [Aksc88], [Yode89] have all been used for collaboration and various forms of knowledge work. Brown University's IRIS Project [Garr86], [Yank87], [Yank88] is oriented toward educational applications of hypertext, and there are a number of active research programs exploring the use of hypertext in computer-aided software engineering [Bend87], computer-aided design [Deli86b], on-line help systems [Walk88], writing environments [Smit86], [Trig83], etc. However, to our understanding, most of these applications have not required the degree of integration between computation and authorship that is often seen in natural science research.

The Virtual Notebook [Gorr88] and Hypertext Medical Handbook [Fris88] support the intellectual activities of biomedical researchers and are similar to the work we are doing. Multi-media environments for personal computing are the focus of research in Carnegie-Mellon's Andrew Project [Morr86] and Bolt, Beranek, and Newman's Diamond System [Thom85], but again, specific examples of their application in scientific settings is yet to come. The Expres Project is intended to allow NSF research proposals to be developed and reviewed electronically over the Internet [Rose88]; however, there is no sense in Expres that the knowledge work involved with the research itself would occur in a fully integrated environment. Perhaps the most closely related work is Harvard's Perseus Project [Cran87] in which hypertext is being applied to traditional scholarship in the classics.

Although there presently appear to be few examples of similar applications of hypertext, the sentiments expressed by Engelbart [Enge62] in describing the Augmented Knowledge Workshop clearly reflect our own. Our research suggests ways of augmenting the knowledge work of scientific communities.

KMS's Influence. A number of hypertext systems are presently available, but few provide the range of functionality afforded by KMS [Conk87], [Schn88]. In many ways, KMS was ideally suited to this particular application. It is workstation based thereby providing access to significant computational power, a multiprogrammed operating system, and networking facilities. It is a distributed hypertext system intended to support both individual and collaborative work, and it can contain as many frames as disk space permits.

KMS's large-screen format was important. We wanted the ability to display an 8.5" x 11" page of information with room for annotations. It was also important that we be able to use all of the screen's display area for our text and graphics. The KMS user interface is extensible and allows most of the system's functionality to be invoked with a single point-and-click operation. Orientation was never a problem, since we were navigating in a familiar personal information space.

Among the frustrations we encountered using KMS, the most bothersome involved its action language. Our version (6B1) did not support arithmetic expression evaluation; those parts of the simulation program that compute formulas tend to resemble assembler code. The interpreted action language tended to run slowly, and there was no way to interrupt programs once they began executing.

An additional annoyance was the way Unix's standard output overwrites a KMS screen. This becomes a problem when KMS is being used as an interface to the operating system. Error messages from the C compiler and other utilities, for example, disrupt the visual context, which must be redisplayed. These are small complaints, and improvements are already underway.

Future plans. Future research plans include examining the use of hypertext as a front-end to large simulations running on supercomputers and studying usability issues relating to scientific hypertext environments. We also hope to begin introducing editors in the biological sciences to the concept of electronic journals.

CONCLUSIONS

It is easy for proponents of hypertext to talk about revolution. Many people have recognized its potential for nearly half a century. Now that the promises of hypertext are becoming a reality, it is important to consider how this new technology should be incorporated into our lives.

This study demonstrates the effectiveness of hypertext in addressing the personal information management requirements of scientific research. It also shows how hypertext can improve communication within a scientific community. But perhaps most important, it shows traditional scholarship occuring in the new medium of hypertext.

Advances in computing technology are often valued by their capacity to improve productivity. What perhaps is most revolutionary about hypertext is its capacity to improve *quality*. Scientists are encouraged to participate in the revolution.

ACKNOWLEDGMENTS

We thank Doug Engelbart, Rob Akscyn, Don McCracken, Steve Feiner, and Tim Oren for their comments on an early version of the hypertext. We appreciate the helpful input of ecologists Joe Folse and Bill Grant. We also thank Ed Cunnius for his assistance in designing the hypertext. This work has been funded in part by a grant from the Advanced Workstations Division of IBM Corporation, Austin, Texas, under Research Agreement 161.

REFERENCES

[Aksc88]   Akscyn, R., McCracken D., and Yoder, E.   1988.   KMS: A distributed hypermedia system for managing knowledge in organizations. *Commun. ACM*, 31, 7, (July), 820-835.

[Bend87]   Bendifallah, S., and Scacchi W.   1987.   Understanding Software Maintenance Work. *IEEE Trans. on Softw. Eng.*, SE-13, 3, (March), 311-323.

[Bush45]   Bush, V. 1945. As We May Think. *Atlantic Monthly*, 176, (July), 101-108.

[Conk87]   Conklin, J.   1987.   Hypertext: An introduction and survey. *Computer*, 20, 9, (September), 17-41.

[Cran87]   Crane, G. 1987. From the old to the new: Integrating hypertext into traditional scholarship. *Hypertext '87 Papers*, (Chapel Hill, N.C., November), pp. 51-56.

[Deli86a] Delisle, N., and Schwartz, M.   1986.   Contexts - A partitioning concept for hypertext. *ACM Trans. Off. Inf. Syst.*, 5, 2, (April), 168-186.

[Deli86b] Delisle, N., and Schwartz, M. 1986. Neptune: A hypertext system for CAD applications. *Proceedings of the ACM International Conference on the Management of Data (SIGMOD)*. pp. 132-143.

[Enge62]   Engelbart, D. 1962. Augmenting human intellect: A conceptual framework.   SRI Technical Report AFOSR-3223, Contract AF 49(638)-1024, (October).

[Enge84a] Engelbart, D. C. 1984. Collaboration support provisions in AUGMENT. *Proceedings of the 1984 AFIPS Office Automation Conference, OAC '84 Digest*, (Los Angeles, Calif., February), pp. 51-58.

[Enge84b] Engelbart, D. C. 1984. Authorship provisions in AUGMENT. *Proceedings of the 1984 COMPCON Conference, COMPCON '84 Digest*, (San Francisco, Calif., February), pp. 465-472.

[Fris88]   Frisse, M. 1988. Searching for information in a hypertext medical handbook. *Commun. ACM*, 31, 7, (July), 880-886.

[Garr86]   Garrett, L., Smith, K., and Meyrowitz, N. 1986. Intermedia: Issues, strategies, and tactics in the design of a hypermedia document system. *Proceedings of the CSCW '86 Conference*. (Austin, Tx., December), pp. 163-174.

[Gorr88]   Gorry, G. A., Burger, A. M., Chaney, R. J., Long, K. B., Tausk, C. M. 1988. Computer support for biomedical work groups. *Proceedings of the CSCW '88 Conference* (Portland Or., September), pp. 38-51,

[Gran86]   Grant, W. E. 1986. *Systems Analysis and Simulation in Wildlife and Fisheries Sciences.* John Wiley and Sons, New York.

[Hala88]   Halasz, F. 1988. Reflections on NoteCards: Seven issues for the next generation of hypermedia systems. *Commun. ACM*, 31, 7, (July), 836-852.

[Kuhn70]   Kuhn, T. S. 1970. *The Structure of Scientific Revolutions*, 2nd ed. University of Chicago Press, Chicago.

[Legg88]   Leggett, J., Schnase, J. L, and Kacmar, C. J. 1988. Working definitions of hypertext. Department of Computer Science Technical Report No. TAMU 88-020, Texas A&M University, College Station, Tx.

[Morr86]   Morris, J. H., Satyanarayanan, M., Conner, M. H., Howard, J. H., Rosenthal, D. S. H., and Smith, F. D. 1986. Andrew: A distributed personal computing environment. *Commun. ACM*, 29, 3, (March), 184-201.

[Nels65]   Nelson, T. H. 1965. A file structure for the complex, the changing, and the indeterminate. *Proceedings of the 20th National ACM Conference*, pp. 84-100.

[Nels67]   Nelson, T. H. 1967. Hypertext notes (Note 6). Unpublished manuscript.

[Nels87]   Nelson, T. H. 1987. *Literary Machines*, Edition 87.1. Available from the Distributors, 702 South Michigan, South Bend, IN 46618.

[Rose88]   Rosenberg, J., Sherman, M. S., Marks, A., and Giuffrida, F. 1988. Translating among processable multimedia document formats using ODA. *Proceedings of the ACM Conference on Document Processing Systems*, (Santa Fe, NM, December), pp. 61-70.

[Schn88]   Schnase, J. L., Leggett, J., Kacmar, C. J., and Boyle, C. 1988. A comparison of hypertext systems. Department of Computer Science Technical Report No. TAMU 88-017, Texas A&M University, College Station, Tx.

[Smit86]   Smith, J. B., Weiss, S., Ferguson, G., Bolter, J., Lansman, M., and Beard, D. 1986. WE: A Writing environment for professionals. Department of Computer Science Technical Report No. TR86-025, University of North Carolina, Chapel Hill, N.C.

[Thom85]   Thomas, R. H., Forsdick, H. C., Crowley, T. R., Robertson, G. G., Shaaf, R. W., Tomlinson, T. S., Travers, V. M., 1985. Diamond: a multimedia message system built upon a distributed architecture, *Computer*, 18, 12, (December), 65-78.

[Trigg83]   Trigg, R. 1983. A Network-Based Approach to Text Handling for the Online Scientific Community. Ph.D. dissertation. University of Maryland (University MicroFilms #8429934), College Park, Md.

[Trigg86]   Trigg, R., Suchman, L., and Halasz, F. 1986. Supporting collaboration in NoteCards. *Proceedings of the CSCW '86 Conference*, (Austin, Tx., December), pp. 153-162.

[Walk88]   Walker, J. H. 1988. Supporting document development with Concordia. *Computer*, 21, 1, (January), 48-59.

[Wolf77]   Wolf, L. L. 1977. Species relationships in the avian genus *Aimophila*. Ornithological Union Monographs No. 23.

[Yank87]   Yankelovich, N., Landow, G., and Heywood, P. 1987. Designing hypermedia "ideabases" - The Intermedia experience. Brown University IRIS Technical Report 87-4, Providence, R.I.

[Yank88]   Yankelovich, N., Haan, B., Meyrowitz, N., and Drucker, S. 1988. Intermedia: The concept and the construction of a seamless information environment. *Computer*, 21, 1, (January), 81-96.

[Yode89]   Yoder, E., Akscyn, R., and McCracken, D. 1989. Collaboration in KMS, a shared hypermedia system. *Proc. of the CHI '89 Conference*, (Austin, Tx., April), pp. 37-42.

Information Retrieval From Hypertext: Update on the Dynamic Medical Handbook Project

Mark E. Frisse and Steve B. Cousins

Medical Informatics Group
Department of Internal Medicine,
Institute for Biomedical Computing
and Department of Computer Science
Washington University School of Medicine
660 S. Euclid Avenue (Box 8121)
St. Louis, Missouri 63130
frisse@wucs1.wustl.edu

ABSTRACT

This paper attempts to provide a perspective from which to develop a more complete theory of information retrieval from hypertext documents. Viewing hypertexts as large information spaces, we compare two general classes of navigation methods, classes we call local and global. We argue that global methods necessitate some form of "index space" conceptually separate from the hypertext "document space". We note that the architectures of both spaces effect the ease with which one can apply various information retrieval algorithms. We identify a number of different index space and document space architectures and we discuss some of the associated trade-offs between hypertext functionality and computational complexity. We show how some index space architectures can be exploited for enhanced information retrieval, query refinement, and automated reasoning. Through analysis of a number of prototype systems, we discuss current limitations and future potentials for various hypertext information retrieval structures.

> *"Our ineptitude in getting at the record is largely caused by the artificiality of systems of indexing."*
>
> –Vannevar Bush, As We May Think, 1945

LARGE INFORMATION SPACES

Hypermedia may be most useful as a means for exploring large collections of information recorded in electronic form. Vannevar Bush, for example, saw the Memex as a tool which could spawn a "new profession of trail blazers, ... who find delight in the task of establishing useful trails through the enormous mass of the common record." Nelson proposes a global "public access system to be franchised like hamburger stands" [Nels87]. Trigg's thesis concerned a "network based approach to text handling for the online scientific community" [Trigg83] and Schatz's Telesophy system was envisioned as a "system for the masses" united through a "transparent WorldNet" [Schat85].

We believe that these metaphors represent a particularly desirable vision for the future of information management in medicine. Workers in pursuit of recorded biomedical knowledge must confront a literature characterized by millions of scientific articles from over 3000 worldwide scientific publications [Warr81]. Adding to the confusion, many articles are never cited, some report flawed experiments, and some make exaggerated or deceitful claims. The rate of accumulation of scientific information is expected to increase dramatically as the biomedical community embraces large-scale research endeavors like the elucidation of the structure and function of the human genome [Bilof88, Came88, Sidm88]. Without advanced information-retrieval aids, we believe that the biomedical information-seeker will resemble an inhabitant of Borges' Library of Babylon - wandering through the madness of an infinite library whose books contain every conceivable combination of letters and words.

The Dynamic Medical Handbook Project has as one of its principal goals the discovery of more effective methods for information retrieval from large-scale biomedical hypertexts. Using text from a popular medical handbook, we wish to determine the degree to which these novel software systems can facilitate the effective use of recorded medical information [Frisse88a].

LOCAL AND GLOBAL ACCESS METHODS

Many people find hypertext most useful when they examine in a sequential manner a number of separate units of text. We call these units *information units* (IUs), and we use the term *links* to identify the structures connecting IUs. We use the term *document space* to refer to that portion of the information space consisting of the information units and links, and we use the term *navigation* to refer to the process of moving along links from one IU to another. Examining one IU, the user sees within the text "buttons" with labels which represent either the semantics of a connecting link or a summary description of the IU residing at the link's distal end. We use the term *link labels* to denote information about distal information units displayed on a proximal information unit. Links can connect information units which may be far apart when viewed from the perspective of some underlying "native" document structure and the process of traversing the link allows one to traverse great "distances" in a single step. We use the term *button-based browsing* to denote the entire process of examining an IU, activating a link label icon, and travelling to a new IU (Figure 1). Button-based browsing is a *local* method of hypertext navigation.

Indexes are data structures that facilitate *global* navigation. Because indexes are in one sense a set of "pre-compiled" links, they facilitate access to a needed information unit without the need for traversal through many intermediate information units, and the time necessary to find indexed information does not increase significantly as the size of the document space increases (Figure 2).

All global methods for information retrieval appear to require the existence of a data structure "outside" the document space. We call this outside structure the *index space*, and we use the term *information space* to denote the union of the index space with the document space. In applications like HyperCard and the NeXT Digital Librarian, large and complex global index spaces are hidden from the user, giving the impression that global operations are being performed solely through manipulation of the document space. The presence of a data structure outside of the document space also allows one to retain some memory of user preferences and behavior. This memory can facilitate *learning* when the iterative models for information retrieval are adopted [Book83]. There remains much controversy over the efficacy of various methods for index-based information retrieval [Blair85a, Salt88].

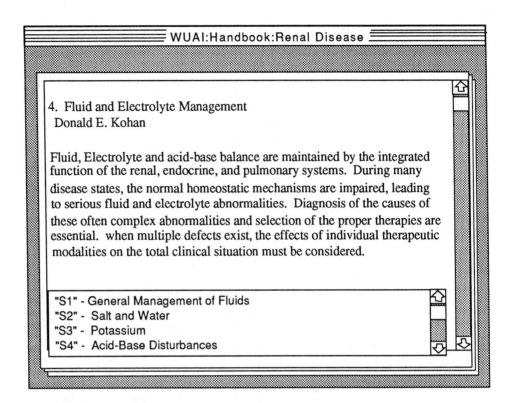

Figure 1: A typical hypertext information unit (IU) from a HyperCard medical handbook prototype. The four link labels at the bottom of the information unit represent IUs at the next immediate level of the hypertext's underlying hierarchical organization.

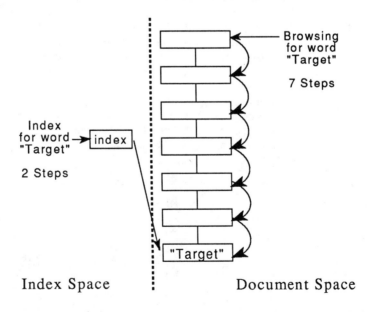

Figure 2: Local and Global methods. If button-browsing through a list, a reader at one IU can only test for the presence of a token on anotherIU by traversing the entire list because the token in question might reside only on the "last" IU examined. An index can generally answer the same question by means of a pointer which takes the user immediately to the desired IU.

Figure 3: A flat index space combined with a flat document space. This is the configuration commonly observed with an inverted index and a full-text document retrieval system. A strong sense of conditional independence is present both within the document space and within the index space. The probability that a specific document or term will appear at a specific location is independent of the location of other documents or terms.

INFORMATION SPACE CONFIGURATIONS

Configurations for both the index space and the document space can best be understood through an example. Consider first a traditional full-text document database system accessed by a conventional inverted index. The document sequence within the database generally is random and index space terms are usually arranged in lexicographic order. The lack of ordering within the document space gives testimony to the lack of explicitly stored relationships between documents. The arrangment of terms within the index space gives credit to their lexicographic ordering more than to their meaning. (Certainly the fact that the index term "ant" might immediately precede the index term "antelope" provides little insight into the order of nature!) The independence relationships observed both between documents and between index terms suggest that in traditional full-text document retrieval systems both the document space and the index space are "flat" (Figure 3). Location and meaning are not correlated. From the perspective of probability theory, knowledge about the utility of one document or index term does not provide one with information about the utility of any adjacent document or index term. This property, known as *conditional independence* explains in part the tractability of algorithms applied to full-text document retrieval systems. If two documents or index terms are independent, one can perform mathematical operations on either one without concern for the state of the other, and one generally can combine terms in a linear fashion.

The document space of the medical handbook used in our work is not flat. Our handbook, the Washington University *Manual of Medical Therapeutics*, is a hierarchically-organized document accessed in part by a traditional index [Frisse88a]. The information space of the *Manual* is characterized by a hierarchical document space and a flat index space (Figure 4).

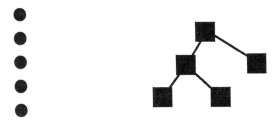

Figure 4: A flat index space combined with a hierarchical document space. This configuration exists when an inverted index is used to access a hierarchical document space

Imposing on the *Manual* the flexibility of a personalized hypertext creates a dramatic change in the structure of the document space. Incorporating cross-links into a directed hierarchy adds to the document space the potential for graph cycles, multiple parents, and multiple semantic relationships. Although some of these attributes expand capabilities for local browsing, they often do so at the expense of complexity necessary to support global access methods. By our terminology, document spaces that allow information units to have multiple parents are called " *networked spaces*".

Figure 5: A hierarchical index space combined with a networked document space. The terms in the index space are organized as a complete hierarchy. The information units in the document space are unconstrained and can be connected with multiple links.

DECOMPOSITION INTO SPACES

In our research, we have chosen to study how one can develop aids to hypertext navigation by exploiting the configurations of the index and document space of the hypertext. We believe that different conformations of index and document spaces allow for different reasoning mechanisms. To a large degree, the more complex the organization of a component of the information space, the greater the computational complexity of algorithms used to reason over the space. In this report, we summarize briefly our efforts to exploit the hierarchical document space of the *Manual*, and we discuss in detail our recent efforts to apply Bayesian reasoning techniques to hierarchical and networked index spaces in an effort to construct hypertext navigation aids that improve their performance with use (Figure 5).

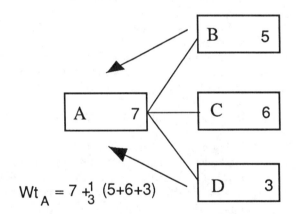

$$Wt_A = 7 + \tfrac{1}{3}(5+6+3)$$

Figure 6: Propagating Information Unit Weights Upward. Propagating weights upward biases towards information units higher in the document space. This strategy is applied to the document space to direct attention toward parent nodes of cards with high weight. This approach may be useful to identify the "best" root for a graphical browser. (See [Frisse88a] or [Cons89] for additional details)

Operations on the Document Space

When complex documents are decomposed into smaller hypertext information units, valuable contextual information can be lost. If, in a hierarchical hypertext, an information unit about "complications" is a "child" of an information unit about a "disease", one should be able to conclude that the child information unit is really about a complication of a specific disease and not about complications in general. In our previously published experiments involving manipulations of hierarchical document spaces, we proposed a method to incorporate context at the time of query by passing a fraction of an information unit's value "upward" to its parent [Frisse88a]. Parent information units would therefore be credited for their possession of valuable descendant information units (Figure 7). Consens and Mendelzon summarize this approach from the perspective of the formal query language GraphLog [Cons89].

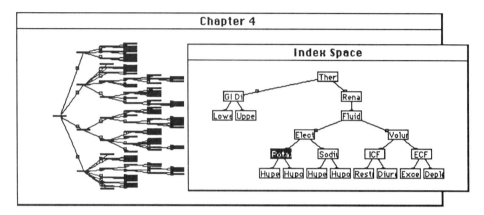

Figure 7: A portion of the index space and document space used in our experiments. The left hierarchy represents a handbook chapter. Information units (Figure 10) are accessed by activating individual nodes in the document space graph. The right hierarchy is a portion of an index space. Activating individual index space nodes displays node belief values and probabilistic relationships between nodes.

OPERATIONS ON THE INDEX SPACES

Index spaces represent a rich source of organized information about a large information space. In our current research, we are investigating how one can represent index spaces as belief networks. If index spaces are represented this way, it is reasonable to determine whether or not reader feedback can be used to manipulate the networks in a manner which will lead to a distribution belief values for topics of interest to the hypertext user.

Inference Using Belief Networks

Using a hierarchical document space and a hierarchical index space, we are exploring methods to facilitate search through a structured medical handbook (see Figure 9). In the spirit of the RUBRIC system, we arrange index terms in a hierarchical manner [McCu85]. Unlike RUBRIC, our index terms are joined by probabilistic dependencies expressed and equilibrated by the method of Pearl [Pearl88]. This method assures that new information about a reader's likes and dislikes will be transmitted recursively from all information units representing concepts upon which the user has passed judgement to all related information units present in the index space (Figure 10). For example, if our graph has an index unit node "Volume", we assign a probability which expresses our degree of belief that articles classified under the term "Volume" will be of use to the hypertext user. If index unit terms "ICF" (intracellular fluid) and "ECF" (extracellular fluid) are stated to be aspects of volume, we define between both the "Volume" and "ICF" pair and between the "Volume" and "ECF" pair some conditional probability which expresses the likelihood that if a user likes information units classified under "Volume", she will also like information units classified under the index terms "ICF" or "ECF"(Figure 8).

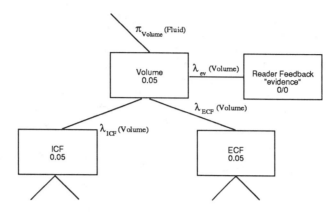

Figure 8: Probabilistic influences on node "Volume". $\pi_{Volume}(Fluid)$ represents the *predictive support* contributed by the single parent node "Fluid". $\lambda(Volume)$ represents the *diagnostic influence* contributed by the two child nodes ("ICF" and "ICF") and a single judgmental evidence node representing reader feedback. This structure is similar to the networked structures illustrated in the the work of Croft and Turtle [Crof89]. Pi and lambda messages influencing the value of other nodes are not represented in this figure. (This figure is adapted from Pearl, [Pearl88, p. 163]).

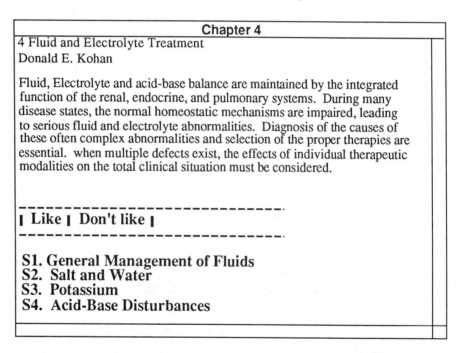

Figure 9: A typical document space information unit from a LISP handbook prototype. The lower portions of the IU represent "active text". The lower four buttons activate "child" IUs. The "Like" and "Don't Like" buttons provide feedback to the index space. This card is indexed under the terms "fluid","electrolyte", and "acid-base". Selecting the "Like" or "Don't like" button will increase by one the numerator or denominator respectively of the evidence node associated with each of the three index space nodes representing the index terms, changing the degree of belief value assigned to the corresponding three index space nodes. These changes are propagated throughout the index space network using standard Bayesian techniques. Compare this representation with that depicted in our earlier HyperCard prototype (Figure 1).

Calculating Degree of Belief in an Index Space Node

Belief networks present probabilistic relationships as a directed acyclic graph where nodes represent variables and edges represent probabilistic relationships. In many "sparse" networks, this approach significantly diminishes the worst case computational complexity because one states explicitly which variables have an effect on others. Using the methods and notation of Pearl [Pearl88], the belief distribution of the index space node "Volume" can be computed from the following three items of information:

1. The current strength of the support, $\pi_{Volume}(Fluid)$, contributed by the node "Fluid", the parent of "Volume", which in turn is dependent on all evidence (e^+) from ancestors of "Volume":

$$\pi_{Volume}(Fluid) = P(Fluid \mid e^+_{Volume})$$

2. The current strength of support, $\lambda_{Yj}(Volume)$, contributed by each of the j children of "Volume", which in turn is dependent on all evidence (e^-) from descendants of "Volume":

$$\lambda_{Y_j}(Volume) = P(e^-_{Y_j} \mid Volume)$$

$$\lambda(Volume) = \prod_j \lambda_{Y_j}(Volume)$$

3. The fixed conditional probability matrix $P(Volume|Fluid)$ that relates the node "Volume" to its immediate parent "Fluid". This relationship is needed to calculate an overall influence of "Fluid" on "Volume":

$$\pi(Volume) = \sum_{Fluid} P(Volume \mid Fluid) \, \pi_{Volume}(Fluid)$$

Because the node "Volume" "blocks" parents from children (Figure 10), these expressions can simply be combined to represent the total degree of belief in the value of an index space concept node:

$$BEL(Volume) = \alpha\lambda(Volume) \, \pi(Volume)$$

where α is a normalizing constant rendering $\Sigma \, BEL(Volume) = 1$. Similar relationships hold true for all nodes in a hierarchical network (Figure 11).

Updating Degree of Belief in an Index Space Node

If one is presented with many IUs indexed under "Volume", a favorable response to reading will increase a likelihood ratio consisting of the number of "Volume" cards read with a favorable response divided by the number of "Volume" cards read with an unfavorable response. The likelihood ratio is expressed through an evidence node associated with the "Volume" term. This evidence will increase the degree of belief that one will favor other IUs classified under the term "Volume". The conditional probability relationships associated with the "Volume" node will also increase the degree of belief that the reader will like "descendant" terms like "ICF" (intracellular fluid) and "ECF" (extracellular fluid). By similar probabilistic relationships, one will also more likely favor "ancestor" terms like "Fluid" (Figure 11).

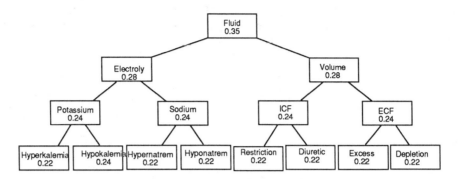

Figure 10: Reasoning over a hierarchical index space. The configuration of hierarchical index spaces allows Bayesian reasoning algorithms to compute in polynomial time. In this example, the node "volume" is the only parent of nodes "ICF" (intracellular fluids) and "ECF" (extracellular fluids). As the only parent, "Volume" *blocks* "ICF" and "ECF" from knowledge about the value of the parent node "Fluid" and all nodes in the left subtree. From a probabilistic viewpoint, complete knowledge about the value of the term "Volume" makes irrelevant knowledge about the value of all other non-descendant nodes like "Fluid" and those in the left subtree. The relationship between two nodes like "Volume" and "ICF" is represented by a conditional probability matrix. Values for the matrix are provided by observation of reader interests, empirical methods, or a heuristic function.

A change in the ratio of "favored" to "disfavored" cards indexed under "Volume" creates positive feedback by sending new lambda messages from the "evidence" node for "Volume" to the parent node "Volume". "Volume" in turn sends new lambda messages to its parent "Fluid" and new pi messages to each of its j child nodes Y_j. Pearl discusses this procedure in greater detail in Chapter four of Pearl's recent monograph [Pearl88].

$$\lambda_{evidence}(Volume) = \sum_{evidence} P(evidence|Volume)$$

$$\lambda_{Volume}(Fluid) = \sum_{Volume} P(Volume|Fluid)$$

$$\pi_{Y_j}(Volume) = \alpha\pi(Volume)\prod_{j \neq k} \lambda_{Y_k}(Volume)$$

In this case, the new evidence favoring "Volume" increases the likelihood ratio. This increases the BEL(*Volume*) to 0.79. Propagation increases BEL(*ICF*) and BEL(*ECF*) to 0.50, and increases BEL(*Fluid*) to 0.69 (Figure 12).

Negative feedback will also affect the distribution of degree of belief values over the index space. If a reader favoring "Volume" IUs now encounters many unfavorable IUs indexed by the term "Electrolyte", the resulting negative feedback will decrease the degree of belief that the reader will like other "Electrolyte" terms. Immediate effects due to belief update propagation include a decrease in the value of descendant nodes like "Potassium" and "Sodium", and a tendency to decrease the value of the ancestor node "Fluid". Because the

"Fluid" node now receives positive feedback from the "Volume" node and negative feedback from the "Electrolyte" node, its final value will depend on the relative degree of feedback from the two descendant nodes (Figure 12). In this case, a low likelihood ratio from the evidence node for "Electrolyte" decreases BEL(*Electrolyte*) to 0.13 and both BEL(*Sodium*) and BEL(*Potassium*) from 0.24 to 0.16. BEL(*Fluid*), facing opposing influences, is increased from its initial value of 0.35 to a new value of 0.51 (Figure 12).

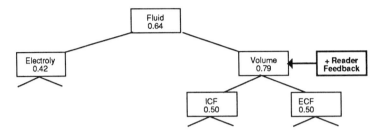

Figure 11: Positive feedback increases the likelihood ratio associated with the "dummy evidence" node associated with the term "Volume". This increase will lead to an increase in the degree of belief in the node "Volume". Increasing the belief that "Volume" is useful also increases the belief that terms near "Volume" in the index are useful. By the conditional probability relationships between "Volume" and both "ICF" and "ECF", the values of the latter two terms are increased. Because of the probabilistic relationship between "Fluid" and "Volume" the value of the term "Fluid" increases. By similar probabilistic calculations, the change in value of the term "Fluid" is propagated down through all values in the left subtree.(See Section 7.3)

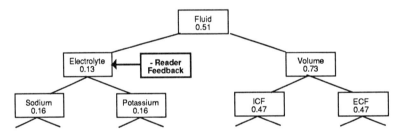

Figure 12: Negative feedback decreases the likelihood ratio associated with the "dummy evidence" child of the "Electrolyte" node. This decreases the value of "Electrolyte", which causes a corresponding decrease in the belief of neighboring terms.

Preliminary Evaluation

Our current investigations use only small information spaces but still suggest that probabilistic inference techniques can be applied to hierarchical index spaces in a manner that yields properties helpful to information retrieval from hypertext document spaces. Belief values of nodes of interest to a reader are increased in value, while nodes not of interest to the reader generally decrease in value. In some cases, the value of all nodes drifts upward, but the increase in value for nodes of interest predominates (Figure 13). In situations of repeated use, we find that personal preferences are better represented by the degree of *change* in belief values than by the *absolute* degree of belief values for index space nodes. In a sense, absolute values reflect the consensus of a group or of an individual over time. Relative changes reflect how one's current interests differ from the consensus.

Reasoning over the Index Space

...s many interesting possibilities. For example, the sharing by a col-
...g group of an index space "web" could allow a program to retrieve au-
...e portions of a new hypertext that are likely to be perceived as valuable to
...the other hand, obtaining the difference between the index space values of
an i...a and the values of a group might allow for the identification of those portions of ...e hypertext which most likely characterize the difference in interests between
the individual and the group.

Our use of belief networks differs from the method proposed by Croft and Turtle
[Croft89]. These investigators describe a network containing nodes from both the index
space and the document space. Their architecture is designed to support relationships between pairs consisting of any combination of index space term and hypertext information
unit. One elicits probabilities of the description of a concept C given a document space
node N. Probabilistic "link" representations relating pairs of document space nodes are
also supported. All other supporting information (e.g., knowledge about the meaning of
terms) is expressed as evidence nodes in a manner similar to that used in our program to
represent reader feedback from document space to index space node likelihood ratios. The
truth value of a query Q is calculated *sequentially* for each hypertext node N in the
document space. As is the case in our program, Croft and Turtle's conceptually powerful
proposal requires significant compromises to elicit probability matrix data and ensure
computational tractability.

Reasoning Over Networked Information Spaces

Several characteristics of some hypertexts lead one to believe that it will be difficult to
adapt a belief network approach to the networked information space architectures required
by many applications. First, it can be shown that applying exact Bayesian computation
methods to a complex graph is NP-complete [Coop87]. However, we believe that approximation methods like those published by Pearl and Chavez offer exciting potential for
evaluation in an information retrieval setting [Pearl86,Chav88]. Second, the incorporation of multiple semantic link types makes probabilistic computation difficult. We believe that a transformation of an index space from a semantic net representation to a predicate calculus representation allows one to perform computation using the sound foundations of probabilistic logic, but the computational complexity of this technique is equally
as intimidating [Nils86]. We believe that this problem will remain one of the challenges
facing proponents of Bayesian approaches.

Of greater concern is the broader hypothesis underlying adaptive information retrieval:
Can it be shown that a learning system will converge on the appropriate set of index
space descriptors given imprecise information? Valiant argues that in some cases the
computational complexity of this problem is insurmountable [Val84]. Our hypothesis is
that even incomplete or mildly misleading results from the index space can provide an adjunct to other information retrieval and hypertext browsing techniques. We believe that
most readers will benefit from imprecise results and that they will recognize circumstances where our algorithms are not performing effectively. The evaluation of this hypothesis awaits formal evaluation using larger hypertext information spaces.

Our approach also requires methods to assert "changing the topic". Medical use is characterized by episodic pursuit of a wide variety of topics, and it will be important to recognize when one has switched from one problem investigation to another. One will also
have to accommodate *human* learning. As we learn, we often see an abrupt change in the
desirability of information units. Information that was once invaluable can suddenly become obvious, and one must ensure that one's program recognizes when presentation of
an information unit becomes a nuisance.

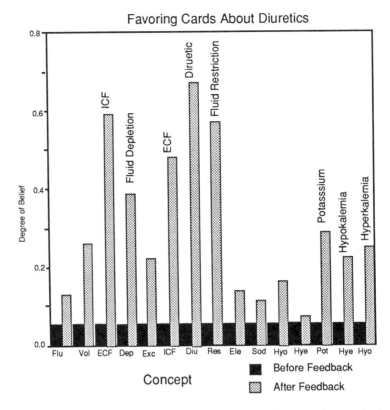

Figure 13: An Example using a Small Index Space. These data are the result of approving a number of information units concerned with diuretic therapy (See Figure 10). As expected, the preference for the "Diuretic" leaf node term is increased, as is the preference for the ancestor term "ICF" (intracellular fluid) and a sibling term "Res" (fluid restriction) . "Potassium", "ECF", and "Fluid Depletion" are increased in part because of co-occurrence in IUs and in part because of index space reasoning.

CURRENT RESEARCH STATUS

We currently are enhancing a number of prototype medical handbooks. Our current research centers on the index space, where we are attempting to provide automatic hypertext guidance by implementing algorithms of Pearl [Pearl86], Lauritzen [Spieg88], Chavez [Chav88] and Shachter [Shac86]. Our hypertext prototypes are constructed and tested using SUN-4, Macintosh, and NeXT hardware. In the near future, we will incorporate our medical hypertexts into the extensive radiology picture archiving and communications prototypes under development in the Electronic Radiology Laboratory of Washington University's Mallinckrodt Institute of Radiology [Jost89,Cox88]. Using these advanced workstations, we expect to evaluate the performance of our hypertext prototypes in "real-life" biomedical settings.

ACKNOWLEDGEMENTS

The authors wish to thank Michael Kahn, Tim Oren, Ingo A. Beinlich, H. J. Suermondt, and Steve Weyer for their helpful comments. This research is supported in part by the New Medical Foundation and through an equipment grant from Apple Computer, Inc. Dr. Frisse is a Teaching and Research Scholar of the American College of Physicians.

REFERENCES

[Belew86]   RK Belew. Adaptive information retrieval: Machine learning in associative networks. PhD thesis, University of Michigan, Ann Arbor, Michigan, 1986.

[Bilof88]   H Bilofsky. The genbank genetic sequence data bank. **Nucleic Acids Research**, 16:1861 - 1863, March 11, 1988.

[Blair85a]   D Blair and M Maron. An evaluation of retrieval effectiveness for a full-text document retrieval system. **Communications of the ACM**, 28:289 - 299, March 1985.

[Book83]   A Bookstein. Information retrieval: A sequential learning process. **Journal of the American Society for Information Science**, 34:331 - 342, September 1983.

[Came88]   G Cameron. The EMBL data library. **Nucleic Acids Research**, 16:1865 - 1867, March 11 1988.

[Chav88]   RM Chavez and GF Cooper. A fully polynomial randomized approximation scheme for the bayesian inference problem (working paper). Technical report, Stanford University, Stanford California, Fall, 1988.

[Cons89]   MP Consens and AO Mendelzon. Expressing structural hypertext queries in GraphLog. In **Proceedings of Hypertext 89**, Pittsburgh, Pennsylvania, 1989.

[Coop87]   GF Cooper. Probabilistic inference using belief networks is NP-hard. Technical Report KSL-87-27, Medical Computer Science Group, Stanford University, Stanford, California, 1987.

[Cox88]   G Cox and SJ Dwyer. Picture archival and communication systems. In **RISC Ninth Conference on Computer Applications in Radiology**, June 1-4, 1988.

[Croft89]   WB Croft and H Turtle. A retrieval model incorporating hypertext links. In **Proceedings of Hypertext 89**, Pittsburgh, Pennsylvania, 1989.

[Frisse88b]   ME Frisse. From text to hypertext. **Byte**, 13:247 - 253, October, 1988.

[Frisse88a]   ME Frisse. Searching for information in a hypertext medical handbook. **Communications of the ACM**, 31:880 - 886, 1988.

[Heck86]   D Heckerman. Probabilistic interpretations for MYCIN's certainty factors. In L Kanal and J Lemmer, Editors, **Uncertainty in Artificial Intelligence Artificial Intelligence**, pages 11 - 22, Amsterdam, 1986. North Holland.

[Jost89]   R Jost, W Wessel, G Blaine, J Cos, and R Hill. PACS - Is there a light at the end of the tunnel? In **Conference on Medical Imaging III**, SPIE, pages 1093 - 1125, Newport Beach, California, January 29 - February 3 1989.

[McCu85]   BP McCune, RM Tong, JS Dean, and DG Shapiro. RUBRIC:a system for rule-based information retrieval. **IEEE Transactions on Software Engineering**, SE-11:939 - 945, September 1985.

[Nels87]   T Nelson. **Literary Machines**, 87.1 edition. Project Xanadu, 8480 Fredricksburg #138, San Antonio, Tx. 78229, 1987.

[Nils86]   N Nilsson. Probabilistic logic. **Artificial Intelligence**, 28:71 - 87, 1986.

[Oren87]   T Oren. The architecture of static hypertexts. In **Proceedings of Hypertext87**, pages 291 - 306, University of North Carolina, Chapel Hill, November 13-15 1987.

[Oren88]   T Oren. The CD-ROM connection. **Byte Magazine**, 3:315 - 320, December 1988.

[Pearl88]   J Pearl. **Probabilistic Reasoning in Intelligent Systems: Networks of Plausible Inference**. Morgan Kaufmann, San Mateo, CA, 1988.

[Pearl86]   J Pearl. Evidential reasoning using stochastic simulation of causal models. Technical report, University of California, Los Angeles, Los Angeles, California, September, 1986.

[Salt88]   G Salton. Another look at automatic text-retrieval systems. **Communications of the ACM**, 29:648 - 656, July, 1988.

[Schat85]   BR Schatz. Telesophy. Technical Report Bellcore TM-ARH-002487, Bell Communications Research, 445 South Street, Morristown, NJ. 07960-1910, 1985.

[Shac86]   R Shachter. Evaluating influence diagrams. **Operations Research**, 34:871 - 872, 1986.

[Shas85]   D Shasha. Netbook - a data model to support knowledge exploration. In **Proceedings of the Eleventh Conference on Very Large Databases**, Stockholm, August, 1985.

[Sidm88]   K Sidman, D George, W Barker, and L Hunt. The Protein Identification Resource PIR. **Nucleic Acids Research**, 16:1869 - 1871, March 11, 1988.

[Spieg88]   S.L.Lauritzen and D Spiegelhalter. Local computations with probabilities on graphical structures and their application to expert systems. **J. Royal Statistical Society**, 9:157 - 224, 1988.

[Trigg83]   R Trigg. A network based approach to text handling for the online scientific community. PhD thesis, University of Maryland, Department of Computer Science, College Park, Maryland, November 1983. Technical Report 1346.

[Val84]   L Valiant. A theory of the learnable. In **Proceedings of the 16th Annual ACM Symposium on the Theory of Computing**, Washington D.C., April, 1984.

[Warr81]   KS Warren, Editor. **Coping with the Biomedical Literature**. Praeger Publishers, New York, 1981.

A Retrieval Model for Incorporating Hypertext Links

W. Bruce Croft and Howard Turtle

Computer and Information Science Department
University of Massachusetts
Amherst, MA 01003

INTRODUCTION

The field of Information Retrieval (IR) has focused on the development and evaluation of retrieval models for text documents, such as those found in bibliographic databases [Rijs79,Salt83,Belk87]. These retrieval models specify strategies for evaluating documents with respect to a given query, typically resulting in a ranked output. Hypertext researchers, on the other hand, have emphasized flexible organizations of multimedia "nodes" through connections made with user-specified links, and interfaces that facilitate browsing in this network of links. A number of approaches to the integration of query-based retrieval strategies and browsing in hypertext networks have been proposed. The I^3R system [Crof87,Thom89] and a medical handbook system described by Frisse [Fris88], for example, use query-based retrieval strategies to form a ranked list of candidate "starting points" for hypertext browsing. The I^3R system also uses feedback during browsing to modify the initial query and locate additional starting points. The important issue from an IR perspective is the choice of a retrieval model, and consequently a retrieval strategy, for hypertext. This choice will have an impact on the effectiveness of retrieval and on the system implementation. A retrieval model can also provide a more formal specification of the meaning of some hypertext links.

It may appear that the highly connected structure of a hypertext database and the variety of link types that may be used to make those connections distinguishes it from a conventional text database. Network structures are, in fact, not new to IR and retrieval models have been proposed that use automatically and manually generated links between documents and the concepts or terms that are used to represent their content. *Document clustering*, for example, is a retrieval model based on links between documents that are automatically generated by comparing similarities of content [Will88]. *Citations* are another form of link between documents that has been studied [Smal73]. Links between terms can be derived from *term clustering* [Spar70,Rijs77] or the information in a manually-generated thesaurus [Hump87]. Network representations that attempt to integrate this information have been developed [Oddy77,Crof87], but these have been used primarily for browsing. Recent studies have shown that retrieval effectiveness may be improved by combining the evidence represented by the different link types in a network representation

[Crof89], and our approach has been to develop a retrieval model to formalize this approach. In this paper, we describe a model based on Bayesian inference networks [Pear89] that appears to capture the major aspects of previous probabilistic IR models [Rijs79] and can easily be extended to include hypertext links. The possibility of such a model was also referred to by Frisse [Fris88].

In the next section of the paper, we will illustrate how multiple sources of evidence can be used to answer a query and how various types of hypertext links can be regarded as forms of evidence. This will be done using a deductive database representation of the problem. We will then describe a non-deductive or plausible inference approach to retrieval. In particular, we will describe how a Bayesian inference network can be constructed from the information in a hypertext database and how this is used to answer queries. In the final section of the paper we discuss alternative approaches and implementation issues.

Throughout this paper, we shall be discussing the effectiveness of retrieval techniques. In contrast to measures of retrieval efficiency based on space and time requirements, measures of effectiveness are based on how successful a technique is in locating the relevant documents for a query. The usual effectiveness measures are *recall* and *precision*, which are, respectively, the proportion of relevant documents that are retrieved and the proportion of retrieved documents that are relevant. These measures and a variety of others are described extensively in the IR literature [Rijs79].

RETRIEVAL AS INFERENCE

Retrieval involves a comparison of the things to be retrieved (in this case, hypertext nodes) and a query. During browsing, the query remains implicit and the comparison is done by the searcher. We are primarily concerned here with the situation where an explicit query exists and the comparison is done by an automated retrieval mechanism. In simpler systems, such as those based on string matching, the comparison tests equality of strings contained in the query and node representations. In general, however, determining that the query and a node are related will require an inference mechanism. To illustrate this, consider the deductive database (i.e. Prolog-like [Cloc81]) representation of a hypertext database shown in Figure 1. The first part of the database specifies facts about the nodes. In particular, the about predicate is used to "index" the nodes. That is, we represent the content of the node by associating it with particular concepts. This association can be established in a variety of ways, including manual term selection or automatic assignment based on statistical or natural language processing techniques [Spar74,Lewi89]. Note that in our example we have used generic concepts such as concept2 rather than concepts actually derived from text. The second part of the database specifies the current links between nodes. These are of various types, including:

- Links between nodes derived by statistical "nearest neighbor" measures - nn

- Links between nodes derived from citations in the text - cites

- Links between nodes that represent a structural hierarchy - part_of

```
about(node1,concept2).
about(node1,concept23).
about(node1,concept34).
about(node2,concept4).
about(node2,concept34).
about(node3,concept15).
    .   .
    .   .
synonym(concept2,concept8).
synonym(concept23,concept56).
is_a(concept12,concept3).
nn(concept3,concept12).
nn(concept34,concept17).
    .   .
nn(node2,node34).
nn(node14,node12)
cites(node5,node45).
cites(node5,node22).
links_to(node2,node41).
links_to(node20,node26).
links_to(node2,node3).
part_of(node5,node36).
    .   .
    .   .
about(Node,ConceptX)  :- about(Node,ConceptY),
                            synonym(ConceptX,ConceptY).
about(Node,ConceptX)  :- about(Node,ConceptY),
                            nn(ConceptX,ConceptY).
about(Node,ConceptX)  :- about(Node,ConceptY),
                            is_a(ConceptX,ConceptY).
    .   .
about(NodeX,Concept)  :- about(NodeY,Concept),
                            nn(NodeX,NodeY).
about(NodeX,Concept)  :- about(NodeY,Concept),
                            cites(NodeY,NodeX).
about(NodeX,Concept)  :- about(NodeY,Concept), %hypertext rule 1
                            links_to(NodeY,NodeX).
about(NodeX,Concept)  :- about(NodeY,Concept), %hypertext rule 2
                            part_of(NodeX,NodeY).
```

Figure 1: A Hypertext Deductive Database

- Other links between nodes specified manually - links_to

The last two link types are those found in a typical hypertext database, whereas the other two are more typical of bibliographic retrieval systems. The database also specifies a variety of relationships between concepts, such as those derived from a thesaurus (synonym, is_a), that may not be represented as links in a hypertext database.

The remainder of the deductive database specifies rules that can be used to derive additional facts about nodes from the stated facts. For example, the rule labelled "hypertext rule 1" can be used by a deductive inference engine to derive facts about connected nodes such as node2 and node41. In this case, we can derive the facts about(node41,concept4) and about(node41,concept34). In other words, the meaning of a node is partially derived from the nodes connected to it. We shall refine this "definition" of a hypertext link in the next section. Note that some types of hypertext link may not participate in the retrieval process. A link type that connects the nodes in a particular sequence, for example, might be used only for browsing the database and not for direct retrieval.

A query in a deductive database is of the form $\{N|W(N)\}$, which can be read as "Retrieve all nodes N such that $W(N)$ can be shown to be true in the current database". For simplicity, we are assuming that N is the only free variable in the formula W. In our Prolog-like syntax, an example query might be

```
?- about(N,concept15), about(N,concept34).
```

The only N that satisfies this query is node3, which will be retrieved. Note that the links_to rule was used to prove the query is true for this node.

In general, proving the query and thereby retrieving nodes may involve the use of all the rules specified in our example database. Removing a rule associated with a particular link type may result in some nodes not being retrieved. Each of the link types that are used in rules, therefore, can be regarded as a form of evidence that is used by the retrieval mechanism. Effective retrieval requires combination of multiple sources of evidence.

Is deductive retrieval an appropriate retrieval model for hypertext? There is, in fact, considerable evidence that such a model would have poor effectiveness [Salt83]. The major problem lies in the uncertainty associated with natural language. This uncertainty affects all aspects of our deductive database example, including the facts (is concept2 an accurate description of node1?), the rules (some rules may be more certain than others), and even the query (some parts of the query may be more important than others). A retrieval model must take this uncertainty into account to produce effective results. For this reason, we are looking at retrieval models based on *plausible* or non-deductive inference. In the next section we shall describe one such model that incorporates uncertainty and allows combination of multiple sources of evidence.

BAYESIAN INFERENCE NETWORKS

A number of approaches to plausible inference have been proposed [Spie86]. These include heuristic certainty measures, non-standard logics, Bayesian inference networks [Pear89], the Dempster-Shafer model of evidential reasoning, and symbolic representations [Cohe87]. We have chosen to use Bayesian inference networks, primarily because information retrieval research has had considerable success with simple probabilistic models [Rijs79,Belk87] and because Bayesian networks are similar to the representations used in some advanced IR systems (e.g. I^3R).

A Bayesian inference network is a directed, acyclic dependency graph in which nodes represent propositional variables or constants and arcs represent dependence relations between propositions (see [Pear89] for a complete treatment of Bayesian nets). For hypertext applications, the roots of the dependency graph are hypertext nodes; interior nodes and leaves represent concepts. If a proposition represented by a node p directly implies the proposition represented by node q, we draw a directed arc from p to q. If-then rules in Bayesian nets are interpreted as conditional probabilities, that is, a rule $A \rightarrow B$ is interpreted as a probability $P(B|A)$. The arc connecting A with B is labelled with a matrix that specifies $P(B|A)$ for all possible combinations of values of the two nodes. The set of matrices labelling arcs pointing to a node characterize the dependence relationship between that node and the nodes representing propositions naming it as a consequence. For the class of rule bases we are interested in, these link matrices are fixed by the rule base and do not change during query processing. Given a set of prior probabilities for the roots of the DAG, these compiled networks can be used to compute the probability or degree of belief associated with the remaining nodes.

Different restrictions on the topology of the network and assumptions about the way in which the connected nodes interact lead to different schemes for combining probabilities. In general, these schemes have two components which operate independently: a predictive component in which parent nodes provide support for their children (the degree to which we believe a consequent depends on the degree to which we believe the antecedents of the rules naming it), and a diagnostic component in which children provide support for their parents (if our belief in a proposition increases or decreases, so does our belief in the antecedents that name the proposition as a consequent). The propagation of probabilities through the net can be done using information passed between adjacent nodes.

To see how a Bayesian network relates to the underlying probabilistic model, consider the simple network shown in Figure 2 which represents a database where there are no connections between the hypertext nodes (i.e. simple document retrieval). In this network, the nodes labelled N1 to N4 represent propositions that a hypertext node has a particular content. The specific content is that of the corresponding hypertext node. The nodes labelled C1 to C7 represent propositions that a hypertext node is represented (indexed) by a particular concept. The directed links from an N node to a C node represent the conditional probability $P(C|N)$, which is the probability that a particular concept represents a hypertext node given that the node has a particular content.

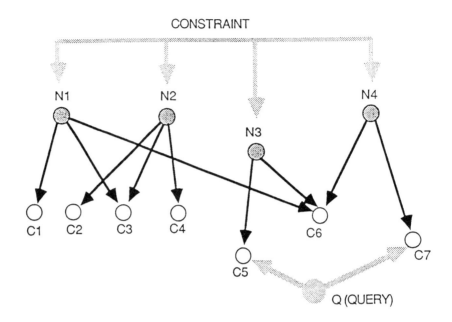

Figure 2: A Simple Bayesian Network

The query node Q represents a conjunction of C propositions. During retrieval, a constraint is applied to the network that restricts a single N node to be initially true. The network is then used to compute the probability of Q being true given this particular content (or hypertext node). This constraint is applied to each N node in turn (conceptually, at least) and the end result is a ranking of hypertext nodes according to the values of $P(Q)$. Note that retrieval, as in the deductive database example, is implemented as a form of inference. In the particular forms of Bayesian inference networks used here, we could in fact regard $P(Q)$ as the probability that Q could be proved true.

We can also describe this use of the network in terms of an explicit probabilistic model. It can be shown that, given certain assumptions, the optimum retrieval effectiveness will be obtained by ranking nodes (or text documents) according to estimates of $P(Q|N)$, which is the probability that the query is true given a particular hypertext node [Robe77]. This *Probability Ranking Principle* is usually expressed in terms of probability of *relevance*, but we believe that this formulation is actually more precise. The probability $P(Q|N)$ can be tranformed into an expression that involves the indexing concepts using standard probability theory as follows:

If we use $R_i = (C_1, C_2, ..C_m)$ to refer to a particular indexed representation of a node, or in other words an assignment of concepts to a node (C_i is true when assigned), then

$$P(Q|N) = \sum_i P(Q|R_i, N)P(R_i|N)$$

and since Q and N are conditionally independent with respect to R,

$$P(Q|N) = \sum_i P(Q|R_i)P(R_i|N)$$

Now we apply Bayes' theorem,

$$P(Q|N) = \sum_i \frac{P(R_i|Q)P(Q)}{P(R_i)} P(R_i|N)$$

At this point, we can use various approximations to estimate these probabilities. The most common assumption is independence, e.g.

$$P(R_i|Q) = \prod_{j=1}^{m} P(C_j|Q)$$

although we shall see that the inference network can represent dependencies between concepts. Given the independence assumptions, we get

$$P(Q|N) = P(Q) \prod_{j=1}^{m} (\frac{P(C_j|Q)}{P(C_j)} P(C_j|N) + \frac{1 - P(C_j|Q)}{1 - P(C_j)} (1 - P(C_j|N))$$

This expression is the basis of the network shown in Figure 2. When the appropriate estimates for the probabilities in this expression are introduced, a function for ranking nodes is produced. In this case, the ranking function is approximately equivalent to giving each node a score that is the sum of the weights of matching query terms, where the weights depend on the frequency of occurrence of a term in each hypertext node and in the entire collection of hypertext nodes (Salton's *tf.idf* weight [Salt83]).

As more complicated models are introduced, the inference network becomes a more convenient representation for calculation of the probabilities. For hypertext databases, the most important extension to the simple retrieval model is to introduce dependencies that represent the links between hypertext nodes. In terms of the probabilistic model, this means that we introduce probabilities of the form $P(N_j|N_k)$ in the expression

$$P(C_i|N_k) = P(C_i|N_j)P(N_j|N_k)$$

Intuitively, this means that if hypertext node j is indexed by a particular concept and is linked to hypertext node k, there is some probability that hypertext node k should also be indexed by that concept. This is the non-deductive form of the hypertext link rules in the example deductive database in section 2.

Figure 3 shows the simple Bayesian inference network extended to include dependencies between hypertext nodes and between concepts. The probabilities of the

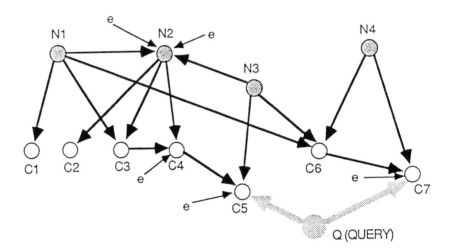

Figure 3: Bayesian Inference Network Incoporating Node and Concept Dependencies.

form $P(C_j|C_k)$, which capture the thesaurus and statistical information mentioned in the deductive database example, allow us to calculate $P(Q|N)$ more accurately than the simple model assuming independence. We have introduced *evidence* nodes (those labelled e) in this network to show that the dependencies between hypertext nodes and concepts are of the form $P(N_j|N_k, e)$. The evidence is the facts stored in the database, such as linked_to(Node1,Node2). When several pieces of evidence relate to a conclusion, such as mutiple links between the same hypertext nodes, a model of disjunctive interaction [Pear89] can be used.

The extended model has a significant impact on the hypertext nodes that are retrieved. Consider two hypertext nodes that are ranked equally according to their own contents. If one of these nodes is connected to other nodes and the other is not, then the extended model will rank the connected node higher. This is a desirable property for a retrieval strategy that is designed to find starting points for browsing. The other advantage of the extended model is that the higher ranked documents will be more likely to satisfy the user's information need, or in other words, the effectiveness of retrieval will improve.

Another extension that can be made to the network is to allow uncertain queries.

The easiest way to understand this is to imagine that users express their information needs in the form of text. It will then be possible to derive a range of queries from this text in the same way that different indexed representations of hypertext nodes can be derived from their contents. The network can then be regarded as computing $P(I|N)$, or the probability that a textual information need is satisfied given a particular node. More specifically, we can develop the extended model as follows:

Starting with the expression derived previously and replacing Q with I we get

$$P(I|N) = \sum_i \frac{P(R_i|I)P(I)}{P(R_i)} P(R_i|N)$$

If we now include the intermediate variable Q as was done for the node representations, the expression becomes

$$P(I|N) = \sum_i (\frac{P(I)}{P(R_i)} P(R_i|N) \sum_j P(R_i|Q_j)P(Q_j|I))$$

The probabilities could then be estimated using independence assumptions as before.

The practical use of this extension is to allow users to specify which parts of their query are more important, as was done in the I^{3}R and OFFICER systems [Crof88]. This amounts to allowing them to estimate $P(Q_j|I)$.

IMPLEMENTATION ISSUES

The retrieval model we have described is of theoretical interest since it integrates and extends existing retrieval models, but its practical significance depends upon the degree to which it allows us to improve retrieval in real hypertext applications. In this section we review basic implementation approaches and open research issues.

As described previously, a hypertext network is similar to advanced document databases that have been used in various experimental settings. Existing automated indexing techniques can be used to create the set of concept nodes and link them to hypertext nodes. Similarly, techniques exist for generating nearest neighbor, citation and other types of links.

The links and nodes of the Bayesian inference net can be handled either as new hypertext nodes and links that are normally invisible to the user or as a separate network that is used as an index to the hypertext database. An integrated hypertext/inference network would allow the retrieval engine to make direct use of hypertext links already present, whereas a separate inference network is probably easier to implement with existing hypertext systems. Further, the information associated with a link in the inference network is different than that typically associated with a hypertext link (i.e. a probability matrix).

Other open issues are:

- Topology restrictions. Inference networks cannot contain directed cycles (a node cannot support itself). This restriction limits the class of recursive rules and predicates that can be represented. For example, a rule like

```
about(NodeX,ConceptY) :- about(NodeX,ConceptX),
                         synonym(ConceptX,ConceptY).
```

  can be represented because it has a finite extension and need not introduce a cycle, but mutually recursive predicates are not allowed, nor are base predicates that would induce a cycle (e.g., `cites(NodeX,NodeY)` and `cites(NodeY,NodeX)`).

- The networks are computationally simpler when they are singly connected (i.e. when each path from the document node to the query has no shared intermediate nodes). When the paths are not distinct, special techniques are required to augment the basic belief propagation rules. While several techniques are known, we will need experience with real hypertext databases to determine how often they are required, which techniques work best in practice, and what computational burden they impose.

- While most queries handled by conventional retrieval systems can be answered using the precompiled network, some important query forms cannot. In particular, queries which involve evaluable predicates (e.g. `greater`, `less`) or multiple document variables present problems. This suggests that deductive and non-deductive inference will need to be integrated in practical systems.

While the practical utility of inference networks has yet to be established, it is important to note that they represent extensions to current IR practice. We know, for example, that we can successfully represent large collections of text documents and produce effective rankings of those documents based on automatically derived probability estimates. Further work is required to validate this new retrieval model in a hypertext setting and to compare the effectiveness of retrieval techniques based on inference networks to those based on simpler probabilistic models.

ACKNOWLEDGMENTS

This work was supported in part by OCLC Online Computer Library Center, by Rome Air Development Center and Air Force Office of Scientific Research under contract F30602-85-C-0008, and by NSF Grant IRI-8814790.

References

[Belk87] Belkin, N. and Croft, W.B., "Retrieval Techniques". *Annual Review of Information Science and Technology*, Edited by M.E. Williams, Elsevier Science Publishers, 22, 110-145, 1987.

[Cloc81] Clocksin, W.; Mellish, C. *Programming in Prolog*. Springer-Verlag, New York, 1981.

[Cohe87] Cohen, P.R.; Kjeldsen, R. "Information Retrieval by Constrained Spreading Activation in Semantic Networks", *Information Processing and Management*, 23, 255-268, 1987.

[Crof89] Croft, W.B., Lucia, T.J., Cringean, J, and Willett, P. "Retrieving Documents by Plausible Inference: An Experimental Study", *Information Processing and Management*, (in press).

[Crof88] Croft, W.B.; Krovetz, R. "Interactive Retrieval of Office Documents", Proceedings of the ACM Conference on Office Information Systems, 228-235, 1988.

[Crof87] Croft, W. B.; Thompson, R., "I^{3}R: A New Approach to the Design of Document Retrieval Systems", *Journal of the American Society for Information Science,* 38, 389-404, 1987.

[Fris88] Frisse, M.E., "Searching for Information in a Hypertext Medical Handbook", *Communications of the ACM*, 31, 880-886, 1988.

[Hump87] Humphrey, S.M.; Miller, N.E., "Knowledge-Based Indexing of the Medical Literature: The Indexing Aid Project", *Journal of the American Society for Information Science*, 38, 184-196, 1987.

[Lewi89] Lewis, D., Croft, W.B. and Bhandaru, N., "Language-Oriented Information Retrieval", *International Journal of Intelligent Systems*, (in press).

[Oddy77] Oddy, R.N. "Information Retrieval Through Man-Machine Dialogue", *Journal of Documentation*, 33, 1-14, 1977.

[Pear89] Pearl, J., *Probabilistic Reasoning in Intelligent Systems.* Morgan Kaufmann, California, 1989.

[Rijs77] Van Rijsbergen, C.J., "A Theoretical Basis for the Use of Co-Occurrence Data in Information Retrieval", *Journal of Documentation*, 33, 106-119, 1977.

[Rijs79] Van Rijsbergen, C.J., *Information Retrieval.* Butterworths, London, 1979.

[Rijs86] Van Rijsbergen, C.J.. "A Non-Classical Logic for Information Retrieval". *Computer Journal*, 29, 481-48, 1986.

[Robe77] Robertson, S.E. "The Probability Ranking Principle in IR", *Journal of Documentation*, 33, 294-304, 1977.

[Salt83] Salton, G. and McGill, M., *An Introduction to Modern Information Retrieval*, McGraw-Hill, New York, 1983.

[Salt83] Salton, G.; Fox, E.A.; Wu, H. "Extended Boolean Information Retrieval", *Communications of the ACM*, 26, 1022-1036, 1983.

[Smal73] Small, H. "Co-Citation in the Scientific Literature: A New Measure of the Relationship Between Two Documents". *Journal of the American Society for Information Science*, 24, 1973.

[Spar70] Sparck Jones, K. *Automatic Keyword Classification for Information Retrieval.* Butterworths, London, 1970.

[Spar74] Sparck Jones, K. "Automatic Indexing", *Journal of Documentation*, 30, 393-432, 1974.

[Spie86] Spiegelhalter, D.J. "A Statistical View of Uncertainty in Expert Systems", in *Artificial Intelligence and Statistics*, 17-55, Addison-Wesley, Reading, 1986.

[Thom89] Thompson, R. and Croft, W.B., "Support for Browsing in an Intelligent Text Retrieval System", *International Journal of Man-Machine Studies*, 30, 639-668, 1989.

[Will88] Willett, P., 'Recent Trends in Hierarchic Document Clustering: A Critical Review', *Information Processing and Management*, 24 (5), 577-598, 1988.

The Use of Cluster Hierarchies in Hypertext Information Retrieval*

Donald B. Crouch, Carolyn J. Crouch and Glenn Andreas

Department of Computer Science
University of Minnesota - Duluth
320 Heller Hall
Duluth, Minnesota 55812

ABSTRACT

The *graph-traversal approach* to hypertext information retrieval is a conceptualization of hypertext in which the structural aspects of the nodes are emphasized. A user navigates through such hypertext systems by evaluating the semantics associated with links between nodes as well as the information contained in nodes. [Fris88] In this paper we describe an hierarchical structure which effectively supports the graphical traversal of a document collection in a hypertext system. We provide an overview of an interactive browser based on cluster hierarchies. Initial results obtained from the use of the browser in an experimental hypertext retrieval system are presented.

INTRODUCTION

Information retrieval is concerned with the representation, storage and retrieval of documents or document surrogates. Information retrieval activities are routinely conducted on-line under the control of search intermediaries or end users who have been trained to use somewhat complex user-system interfaces. However, poor query formulations and inadequate user-system interaction still occur even with skilled users. For example, Cleverdon has noted that "if two search intermediaries search the same question on the same database on the same host, only 40 percent of the output may be common to both searches." [Clev84]

What is being done to aid users of information retrieval systems? The most common approaches are generally directed either toward the development of aids based on sophisticated user interfaces or toward the development of expert system techniques for the more complex operations of text retrieval systems. [Crou89] Research involving sophisticated user interfaces is primarily concerned with system functioning and convenience as it relates to the user; its goal is to facilitate the use of the system by providing computerized aids previously available only to the search intermediary in non-computerized forms. Among the facilities normally included in systems of this type are vocabulary displays, thesaurus expansion of vocabulary items designed to add related terms to already existing search words, the construction and storage of search protocols, operations with previously formulated queries, etc. While this type of research is warranted and its results encouraging, it has not necessarily produced more effective retrieval but instead has generated tools for *effortless* learning and use of an information retrieval system.

The other major area of research in the development of user aids for information retrieval is concerned with the design of expert systems that facilitate access to the stored

---

*This work was supported by the National Science Foundation under grant IRI 87-02735.

collections. The goal of such research is to capture the expertise of search intermediaries in formulating Boolean queries and in dealing with other types of retrieval services. The expert approach is based on the use of domain-specific knowledge that covers the topic areas represented by the collection, a language analyzer that can understand natural language queries and translate them into appropriate internal forms, and rules for search formulation and search strategy designed to choose search methods based on user criteria. It may eventually become feasible to generate search formulation criteria in the form of rules that do in fact reflect the expert knowledge of trained search intermediaries. However, for the time being, one has reason to be careful in accepting many of the currently unevaluated design proposals for expert system approaches as effective solutions to the retrieval problem.

We submit that a viable alternative to using either very sophisticated user interfaces or expert systems as a solution to the retrieval problem consists of using only simple user-system interactions which enhance the effectiveness of retrieval operations through the addition of properly designed user friendly features. These features allow the user to function in an active role, replacing the full natural language comprehension which is desirable yet currently unavailable in an automatic search expert.

This approach to interface design is inherent in the concept of hypertext information retrieval. Hypertext supports a user's exploration of informational data items by representing data as a network of nodes containing text, graphics and other forms of information. [Smit88] A user may navigate through the hypertext system by following the links between nodes. The path a user follows is determined by his/her analysis of the information contained within the nodes and the semantics associated with links between the nodes. [Fris88]

In hypertext information retrieval, each node is generally assumed to be a single document. Links exist which connect each document to other documents having keywords in common with it; the semantics of the links between nodes are keywords (document index terms) or some descriptive information representing the connected documents. In this paper we introduce an hierarchical structure which provides additional semantic information within and between nodes. This structure seems particularly well suited to the user's exploration of a document collection in a visual context. The user may browse among the data items by analyzing a graphical display of the structure itself as well as the semantic links between nodes.

In the next two sections, we briefly describe the retrieval model and the characteristics of the hierarchy on which our structure is based. We then describe a prototype of a hypertext retrieval system utilizing the cluster hierarchy and present the initial results of an experiment comparing retrieval performance of the hypertext system with that of an automatic retrieval system.

INFORMATION RETRIEVAL MODELS

The most common information retrieval models are the Boolean retrieval model and the vector space model. These two models are briefly described and their use in conventional information retrieval systems examined.

Boolean Retrieval Model

Most retrieval systems are based on the *Boolean model*. Queries are expressed as a set of terms connected by the Boolean operators *and, or* and *not*. Such systems retrieve information by performing the Boolean operations on the corresponding sets of documents containing the query terms. Although the Boolean model can be used effectively in automatic text retrieval (in fact, a query can be formulated to retrieve any particular subset of items), imprecise or broad requests utilizing the *or* relation can result in the retrieval of large numbers of irrelevant texts while narrow or overly precise queries utilizing the *and* relation can exclude many relevant items. In practice a compromise is often obtained by the use of a query formulation that is neither too broad nor too narrow. [Salt86]

Although the Boolean model has been widely accepted, it does have its problems:

- Boolean queries are difficult to construct; intermediaries are generally required to add terms not originally included, provide synonyms or alternate spellings, drop high-frequency terms, etc. [Fox86],

- Boolean systems generally do not provide for the assignment of term weights,

- the size of the subset of documents to be returned is difficult to control, and

- the retrieved documents are usually presented in a random order (no ranking based on an estimate of the query-document relevance is provided).

The difficulties associated with the construction of Boolean queries are well known. One author recently commented that "research and development in information retrieval since the 1950's has concentrated on methods which can provide better retrieval without the need for Boolean queries." [Colv86]

Vector Space Model

The *vector space model* is conceptually the simplest retrieval model and is better suited for use in hypertext retrieval systems than the Boolean model. In the vector space model, the content of each document or query is represented by a set of possibly weighted content terms (i.e., some form of content identifier, such as a word extracted from the document text, a word phrase, or concept class chosen from a thesaurus). A term's weight reflects its importance in relation to the meaning of the document or query. Each informational item (document) may then be considered a term vector, and the complete document collection becomes a vector space whose dimension is equal to the number of distinct terms used to identify the documents in the collection. [Rijs79, Salt83]

In the vector space model, it is assumed that similar or related documents or similar documents and queries are represented by similar multidimensional term vectors. Similarity is then generally defined as a function of the magnitudes of the matching terms in the respective vectors.

A vector representation of documents and queries facilitates certain retrieval operations, namely:

- The construction of a clustered document file (consisting of classes of documents such that documents within a given class are substantially similar to each other). In clustered collections, an automatic search can be limited to the documents within those clusters whose class vector representations are similar to the query vector.

- The ranking of retrieved documents in decreasing order of their similarity with the query.

- The automatic reformulation of the query based on relevance assessments supplied by the user for previously retrieved documents. The intent of *relevance feedback* is to produce a modified query whose similarity to the relevant documents is greater than that of the original query while its similarity to the nonrelevant items is smaller.

The vector processing model also exhibits certain disadvantages, namely:

- Some model parameters, such as the query-document similarity function, are not derivable within the system but instead are chosen a priori by the system designer.

- Terms are assumed to be independent of one another.

- Term relationships are not expressible within the model.

A recent characterization of the vector space model is contained in [Wong84].

CLUSTERED DOCUMENT ENVIRONMENTS

A principal advantage of the vector space model for use in hypertext information retrieval is that algorithms exist for structuring a document collection in such a manner that similar documents are grouped together. A cluster hierarchy is represented by a tree structure in which terminal nodes correspond to single documents and interior nodes to groups of documents. In a hypertext system based on a clustered environment, the user can readily focus his/her search on those groups (clusters) that are likely to contain documents which are highly similar to the query. Additionally, the cluster hierarchy is beneficial as a browsing tool in that it makes it possible easily to locate neighboring items with related subject descriptions.

Agglomerative Cluster Hierarchy

Voorhees [Voor85] has shown that retrieval effectiveness may be enhanced in automatic retrieval systems when a type of clustering, known as *agglomerative hierarchic clustering*, is used to generate a cluster structure. In such a clustering method, each document in the collection is considered initially to be a singleton cluster. The two *closest* clusters are successively merged until only one cluster remains. The definition of *closest* depends on the actual clustering method being used.

Fig. 1 contains an example of a hierarchy for the *single link* agglomerative clustering method. In the single link method the similarity between two clusters is the maximum of the similarities between all pairs of documents such that one document of the pair is in one cluster and the other document is in the other cluster. It may be noted that in the hierarchy documents may appear at any level and that clusters overlap only in the sense that smaller clusters are nested within larger clusters.

Each cluster in Fig. 1 is labelled with the *level of association* between the items under it. The clustering level determines the association strength of the corresponding items. Thus the similarity between items B, C and D in Fig. 4 is 0.9. On the other hand, the similarity between item A and the cluster containing items B, C and D is only 0.7. The level of association is a useful link semantic in a hypertext system.

Searching a Clustered Environment

To retrieve documents automatically in a clustered environment, comparisons are generally made between the query vector and document vectors using one of the standard measures of similarity. A cluster search simplifies the search process by limiting the search to subsets of documents. For example, with an agglomeratively clustered tree such as that shown in Fig. 1, a straightforward, narrow, *depth-first* search starts at the top of the tree and calculates the similarity between the query and each of its children. The child most similar to the query is selected, and the similarity between the query and each of the non-document children of that node is calculated. The process is repeated until either all the similarities between the query and the non-document children of some node are less than that between the query and the node itself, or all the children of that node are document nodes. The documents comprising the cluster represented by that node are returned. The search may be broadened by considering more than one path at each level. The broadest search considers all paths and abandons them as they fail certain criteria.

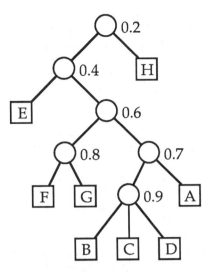

Fig. 1 A sample single link hierarchy

A *bottom-up* search may also be performed on such a tree. The cluster at the lowest level of the tree whose centroid is most similar to the query is chosen as the node at which the search will start. The search continues up the tree until the similarity between the query and the parent of the current node is smaller than the similarity between the query and the current node. The documents contained in the cluster corresponding to the current node are returned. The bottom-up search is often more effective due to the uncertainty involved at high levels of the hierarchy. [Crof80]

Cluster hierarchies have been used effectively in automatic searches. Such hierarchies are also useful in performing searches based on browsing operations. These types of operations, we believe, can produce significant improvement in retrieval performance. Automatic cluster searches are highly structured; the next link in the search path is determined solely on the basis of the similarity between the query vector and the vector representation of the node being evaluated. By displaying suitable portions of the hierarchy during the course of the search operations and letting the user choose appropriate search paths at each point, the output obtained should be superior to that obtained by automatic cluster searching. For example, in a hypertext system with an interactive browser, following evaluation of items B, C, and D in the sample tree of Fig. 1, the user has the choice of exploring either a tightly clustered structure containing items F and G (which are very similar to each other with a similarity value of 0.8) or of staying in the same cluster and evaluating item A (at a lower similarity level of 0.7). In contrast, the control mechanism of the automatic search procedure may terminate the search at the node labelled 0.7 and never evaluate the cluster containing items F and G. The effectiveness of this type of user-directed, interactive browsing is determined by comparing the results of such interactive searches to those obtained by automatic cluster searches.

THE INTERACTIVE BROWSER

A browser incorporating the cluster hierarchy as its primary network structure was implemented on a Macintosh IIx computer using HyperCard. The Macintosh is connected via a local area network to a SUN System on which the SMART information retrieval system [Salt71] resides. The SMART system provides packages for textual analysis, clustering, performance evaluation, etc.

To conduct a search using the browser, a user initially specifies a natural language query which is subsequently transformed into a term vector representation via the SMART retrieval system. The hypertext system then displays a window containing the original query and its corresponding term vector (Fig. 2). As suggested by the annotated display of

Fig. 3, a user may obtain the word stem associated with each concept in the term vector as well as the document frequency of that term by clicking on a concept number in the vector. At any point during the search process, the user may add or delete concepts from the query vector representation or completely re-specify the query itself. The query window also contains a list of identifiers representing the documents which the user has determined to be relevant to the query. Initially this list is empty; however, as the user conducts the search process, he/she enters documents into the list.

To begin (or continue) a browse in the clustered environment, the user clicks on the *Use Query* button. The interface presents a display of the clustered document space represented as a complete link hierarchy. A user may begin an exploration of the cluster tree at any point, for example, at the root node for a top-down approach or at a leaf node (document) for a bottom-up approach. The user may prefer to initiate a search at an interior node (a cluster) which contains one or more documents known to be similar to the query.

In general, a tree representation of a clustered collection is too large to be displayed in its entirety. Therefore, a user is presented with two views of the cluster tree simultaneously: a local view containing the subtree within which the user is currently browsing (see Fig. 4) and a global view, a more comprehensive view of the tree containing a significantly larger number of nodes than the local view (see Fig. 5). A user-directed traversal among the nodes is simultaneously reflected in both displays. The global view permits the user to observe where the search is being conducted in relation to the entire tree while the local view provides the user with more detailed information about a specific subtree.

As may be noted, many links and informational items are provided by the interface system to aid the user during the browsing process. As suggested by Fig. 4, the local view of the tree:

- Uses different iconic representations to distinguish interior nodes (clusters) from leaf nodes (documents).

- Displays for each interior node the level at which the documents cluster. The clustering level represents the degree of association between the items under it.

- Lists the number of documents contained within the subtree defined by each node as well as the number of children of that node. This information can also be obtained by counting the nodes in the global view of the tree.

- Lists the value of the correlation measure of the query vector with either the centroid vector or the document vector associated with each node in the subtree. During the search process the user may change the correlation measure being calculated by means of the Correlation Measure pop-up menu. At present, the system provides a choice of several measures including vector product, inner product, Tanimoto, cosine and overlap.

- Provides a listing of the concepts contained within the query vector (see also Fig. 6). This information is also displayed in the query window; however, in the tree display, the concepts in the query are displayed in ascending order of document frequency. The user may alter the query by adding or deleting concepts from the query vector during the search process without returning to the query window.

- Uses different iconic representations to distinguish relevant documents from the other documents in the tree. A list of the documents which the user has chosen as relevant to the query is maintained in the display. The user may freely insert document identifiers into and delete items from this list. The icons of the documents in this list are then highlighted in the tree representation.

- Lists document identifiers represented by the leaf nodes of the tree.

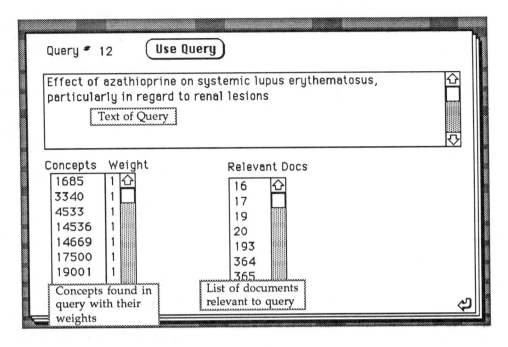

Fig. 2 A sample query card and its parts

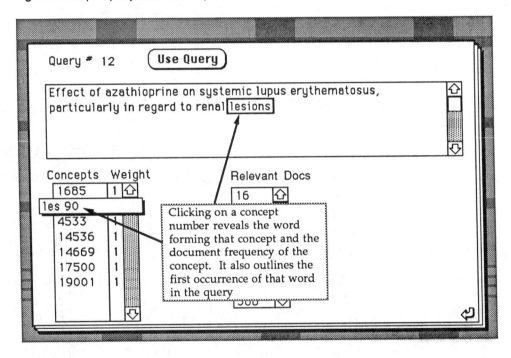

Fig. 3 Clicking on a concept number

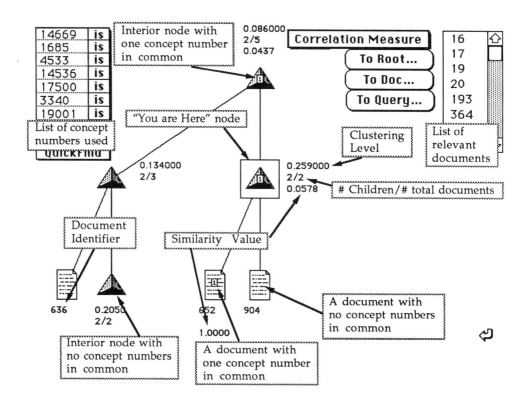

Fig. 4 The browser and its parts

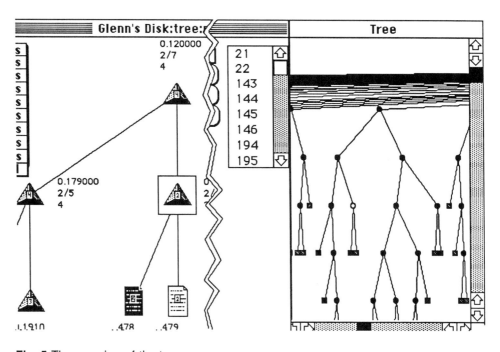

Fig. 5 The overview of the tree

One can obtain additional information from the local tree display by clicking on various items contained within the display. For example, by option clicking on a node which has terms in common with a query, the selected node's icon is replaced with an informational window listing the terms in common and the weights associated with these terms (Fig. 7). Choosing a concept number in the query vector results in a display of the textual description of the chosen term and its document frequency (Fig. 6). Clicking on a terminal node (a document icon) results in the display of additional information associated with the document. An example of a document window is contained in Fig. 8. One can also review the query or enter a new query by selecting the *To Query* button. It should be noted that each of the display windows has informational features associated with them which support the visual search process.

The global view of the tree (Fig. 5) has few items associated with a node, since the purpose of this display is to assist the user in locating his/her position within the tree during the navigation of the cluster space. The three types of icons used in the global view distinguish the following types of nodes:

- A document classified as relevant by the user. As previously noted, identifiers of the relevant documents are highlighted in the local view.

- A document which has not been classified as relevant.

- The node corresponding to the central node in the local view of the tree.

These nodes are color coded to facilitate a quick review of the tree at large.

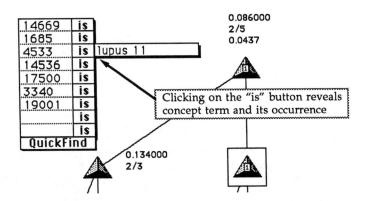

Fig. 6 Finding the term for a concept number in the browser

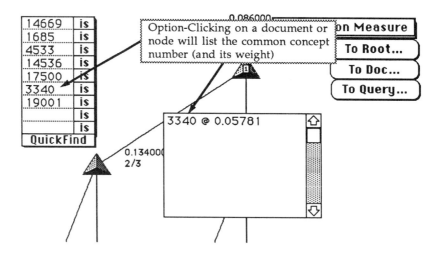

Fig. 7 Getting common concept number information

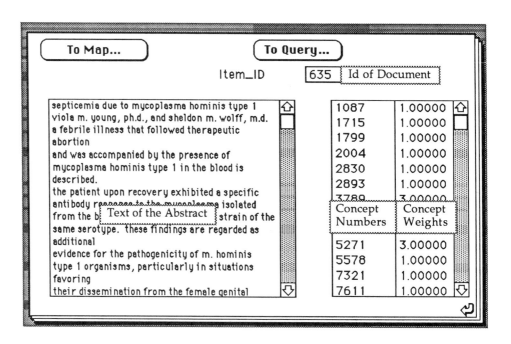

Fig. 8 Document card and its parts

The user may view (move to) other portions of the tree not currently in the local or global windows in one of several ways:

- By scrolling up or down or left or right in the global display window. The window moves across the tree in the global view in the direction represented by the scrolling action of the mouse.

- By clicking on a node in the local view. In this case, the chosen node becomes the central node in the local view. Such an action effectively moves the local view up or down one level of the tree.

- By clicking on the *To Root* button in the local view. This action causes the interface system to redraw the local view of the tree with the central node becoming the root node.

- By clicking on the *To Doc* button in the local view. The To Doc button allows the user to view the document window associated with any document in the collection. To obtain a document window, the user must specify the document's identifier. Clicking on the To Tree button in the document window returns the user to a local view of the tree with its central node corresponding to the parent node of the document contained in the document window.

The tree displays described above and the informational windows associated with items contained in the displays are effective for representing a local cluster arrangement for a small collection or a local area of a larger collection.

EVALUATION OF THE BROWSER

The SMART information retrieval system provides a general framework for conducting retrieval experiments. SMART has fully automatic iterative search methods with automatic relevance document classification. The means exist within the system for evaluating the effectiveness of the retrieval process; the effectiveness of any interactive system can be established by comparison with automatic search procedures contained in the SMART system. SMART also provides collections of documents and corresponding sets of queries which may be used for experimentation. Relevance assessments have been produced by persons knowledgeable of the subject matter in the collections.

In order to develop a general search strategy which a user may employ in the hypertext retrieval system, we focused on the MEDLARS Collection, a somewhat homogeneous collection generated by the National Library of Medicine. A user-controlled cluster search technique which performs well in a homogeneous collection will perform as well or generally significantly better in a heterogeneous collection. MEDLARS consists of 1,033 documents in the medical field and a corresponding set of 30 queries. The document vectors were generated from an analysis of the abstracts of the documents. The MEDLARS collection was then clustered using a complete link clustering algorithm, resulting in a very wide tree. The cluster hierarchy contains 76 subtrees at the root node, and the maximum depth of the tree is ten.

To assist in the development of a method for conducting a visual interactive search of a clustered collection, we divided the MEDLARS query collection into two subsets. One set of queries (the base set) was used to aid in the development of the methodology; the other set was used to estimate the performance of the interactive search process.

We performed an interactive search in the hypertext system for each query in the base set to determine the optimal search a user would follow in order to retrieve the known relevant documents of the query. By conducting this process for each of the 15 queries in the base set, we were able to observe and define the common threads linking relevant documents to the cluster tree. Our observations and the resulting search method that evolved are reported in [Andr89].

An important point about both phases of the experiment is that the actual text of the document (as shown in the document cards) was never examined during the interactive search process to determine document relevance. Doing so would of course have substantially improved retrieval performance in an actual user-controlled search process. However, one of our objectives when conducting this experiment was to apply some of the insight gained from the interactive visual search to an automated system. An automated search system does not consult actual text during the search process; it uses only a vector representation of the document. We are now performing extensive testing with larger collections which does not place such a severe constraint on a user.

Once we had developed some search guidelines, the fifteen remaining queries in the Medlars collection were processed using the developed search procedures. The list of relevant documents was of course initially empty at the beginning of each search process. The companion global tree viewing program was not needed in a search, since a frequent user of the browser system has little problem with navigation of the search tree; novice users would certainly want to use the companion program, however. For each query, the query text was initially inspected prior to the navigation, and the resulting query vector edited as needed. Depending on the intermediate results obtained and the general feedback gained from the browsing process, the query vector was often modified to produce additional relevant documents.

On an average, we were able to retrieve 55% of the relevant documents for the queries in the test set. The automatic retrieval system had a recall value of only 32%. Thus, even without taking full advantage of the information linked to a node (namely, the document abstract itself), use of the interactive browser yielded a significant improvement over automatic cluster searches. Additionally, use of the hypertext system resulted in the return of slightly fewer irrelevant documents; with the browser, 25% of the documents found were irrelevant compared to 28% in the automatic system.

CONCLUSION

Our immediate objective in this work was to produce a retrieval system that allows easy and accurate searching and browsing of a document collection. The representation of a collection as a cluster hierarchy was shown to provide a solid basis on which to build a hypertext retrieval system. The interactive browser is believed to be sufficiently comprehensive and flexible enough to support a variety of experiments designed to evaluate the effects of user control, user intervention, and the visual analysis of graphical data representation on retrieval performance during the cluster search process. The dynamic nature of the HyperCard environment on which the browser is based is well suited to meet the need of flexibility required for these tasks.

REFERENCES

[Fris88]   M. E. Frisse, Searching for Information in a Hypertext Medical Handbook. *Communications of the ACM*, **31:7** (1988), pp. 880-886.

[Clev84]   C. W. Cleverdon, Optimizing Convenient On-Line Access to Bibliographic Databases. *Information Service Use*, **4** (1984), pp. 37-47.

[Crou89]   D. B. Crouch and R. Korfhage, The Use of Visual Representations in Information Retrieval Applications. In *Visual Languages and Applications*, R. Korfhage (ed.), Pergamon Press, New York (1989).

[Smit88]   J. B. Smith and S. F. Weiss, Hypertext. *Communications of the ACM*, **31:7** (1988), pp. 816-819.

[Salt86]   G. Salton, Another Look at Automatic Text-Retrieval Systems. *Communications of the ACM*, **29:7** (1986), pp. 648-656.

[Fox86]   E. A. Fox, Information Retrieval: Research into New Capabilities. In *CD ROM*, S. Lambert and S. Ropiequet (eds.), Microsoft Press, Redmond, Washington (1986), pp. 143-174.

[Colv86]   G. Colvin, The Current State of Text Retrieval. In *CD ROM*, S. Lambert and S. Ropiequet (eds.), Microsoft Press, Redmond, Washington (1986), pp. 131-136.

[Rijs79]   C. J. Van Rijsbergen, *Information Retrieval, Second Edition*. Buttersworth, London (1979).

[Salt83]   G. Salton and M. J. McGill, *Introduction to Modern Information Retrieval*. McGraw-Hill Book Company, New York (1983).

[Wong84]   S. K. M. Wong and V. V. Raghavan, Vector Space Model of Information Retrieval: A Reevaluation. In *Research and Development in Information Retrieval*, C. J. van Rijsbergen (ed.), Cambridge University Press, London (1984), pp. 167-186.

[Voor85]   E. M. Voorhees, The Effectiveness and Efficiency of Agglomerative Hierarchic Clustering in Document Retrieval. Ph. D. Thesis, Department of Computer Science, Cornell University, Ithaca, New York (1985).

[Crof80]   W. B. Croft, A Model of Cluster Searching Based on Classification. *Information Systems*, **3** (1980), pp. 189-195.

[Salt71]   G. Salton, *The SMART Retrieval System*. Prentice-Hall, Englewood Cliffs, New Jersey (1971).

[Andr89]   G. Andreas, Visual Analysis of the Search Process in a Clustered Document Environment. Technical Report, Department of Computer Science, University of Minnesota - Duluth (June, 1989).

The Matters that Really Matter
for Hypertext Usability

Jakob Nielsen

Technical University of Denmark
Department of Computer Science
Building 344
DK-2800 Lyngby Copenhagen
Denmark
email: datJN@NEUVM1.bitnet

ABSTRACT

We compare 92 benchmark measurements of various usability issues related to hypertext which have been published in the hypertext literature in order to find which ones have shown the largest effects.

INTRODUCTION

By now, a fair amount of empirical research has been done on the usability of hypertext and of various options in hypertext design. Many of the studies have focused on understanding and optimizing a single system or design option and do not always generate results which can be used for quantitative comparisons. Many other studies, however, have indeed compared two or more approaches to some problem and have measured various usability parameters for these conditions. When faced with this confusing "market place" of human factors results, practitioners may be excused if they find it hard to know what actions they should take on the basis of the usability research literature. To alleviate this problem, we here look at a broad set of empirical results in a uniform way to determine which usability effects are the most important to pay attention to for hypertext designers.

When examining the research literature, we have to note that the issues being studied are not always those the authors believe are the ones with the largest effects on usability. Some studies are conducted for more or less "political" reasons because various funding agencies want certain effects measured. In other cases, researchers may find great theoretical motivation for studying issues which only have minor impacts on the overall usability of systems considered as a whole. These reasons may explain the somewhat peculiar mixture of results we have found in the research literature.

META-ANALYZING EXISTING BENCHMARK RESEARCH

The traditional approach to meta-analysis is to take a number of studies which have addressed the same issue and compare them to find an over-all conclusion with respect to that issue. Unfortunately, the empirical literature about hypertext is currently much too sparse to allow such an approach. If the trend towards empirical studies of navigation seen at the British *Hypertext II* conference continues [Nielsen 1989c], we may have sufficient many studies of navigation in hypertext available in a few years to allow a thorough meta-analysis of navigation.

For the time being, we cannot do detailed meta-analyses, so instead we have conducted a broader analysis of the spectrum of issues related to hypertext usability. Of course, the various papers summarized here have measured several different usability parameters, such as ease of learning or efficiency of use. To some extent it is not reasonable to compare such different measurements, but we will do so anyway. To use the analogy of "comparing apples and oranges", that is exactly what a Polar explorer had to do to determine which provisions to bring to minimize the risk of scurvy. In the same way, a hypertext designer working under a given set of resource limitations cannot attend to *all* the options with a potential usability impact. Therefore it is necessary to know which aspects of hypertext usability have the largest effects so that one can make sure to take them into account.

A fair amount of previous research has resulted in benchmark numbers comparing the usability of various approaches to accessing text online. Not all the studies have looked at hypertext explicitly but there are some studies of non-hypertext systems which are relevant for the usability of hypertext and which are also reported here.

We have identified 92 results comparing various usability aspects of interest for hypertext from 30 different papers in the scientific literature. These results are summarized in Table 1 converted into a uniform format where our interest is not so much the numbers which were measured but the relative effect of the various conditions tested. All effects have been normalized to a single relative scale where 100 indicates that the two conditions scored exactly the same on whatever usability parameter was measured.

For reasons of space it has not been possible to give a full survey of all 30 papers here. For such a survey, the reader is referred to [Nielsen 1989] which also contains a discussion of the relationship between usability parameters for traditional human-computer interaction studies and hypertext usability studies.

Benchmark Summary Table

The following table summarizes the 30 research studies on hypertext usability. For each benchmark comparison we list a single number showing the relative performance of the first condition relative to the second (or control) condition in the experiment. The numbers are given in percent, so a listing of 100 would indicate that the two conditions tested out identically while a listing of 150 would indicate that the first condition was 50% better than the second and a listing of 50 would indicate that the first condition was only half as good as the second. The column "N" indicates the number of subjects on which the benchmark comparison is based. The column "Literature reference" refers to the list of references at the end of this paper but for reasons of space only lists the first author even in the case of a paper with multiple authors.

The usability parameters measured in the various experiments have been converted to a performance scale where bigger is better to the extent that larger numbers indicate more usable systems - i.e. higher speed, fewer errors, more user satisfaction, better grades, etc. Figure 1 shows an overview of the distribution of the magnitudes of the benchmark effects listed in this table.

	Performance (% of control)	N	Literature reference
Comparisons between various hardware devices			
Reading time from CRTs vs. paper			
Traditional screen	73*	32	Wright 1983
Traditional screen	78*	24	Gould 1984
High-res 60 Hz screen, anti-aliased font	99°	12	Gould 1987
Error frequencies when proof-reading from CRTs vs. paper			
After 10 minutes of reading	88*	24	Wilkinson 1987
After 50 minutes of reading	64*	24	Wilkinson 1987
Proportion of effort spent attending to the medium itself rather than on solving task			
Revising text on a computer vs. with pen and paper	507*	8	Haas 1989
Effect of screen size: Time to answer questions			
34 lines vs. 18 lines, Hyperties on Holocaust	116°	12	Shneiderman 1987
60 lines vs. 22 lines, text editor with program text	135*	16	Reisel 1987
120 lines vs. 22 lines, text editor with program text	206*	16	Reisel 1987
Effect of screen size: Full page workstation display vs. PC-sized display			
Writing speed in wpm when writing a letter	95°	15	Hansen 1988
Length of the letter	121°	15	Hansen 1988
Quality of the letter	135*	15	Hansen 1988
Effect of color coding			
Text A on color-coded paper vs. non-colored paper	116*	32	Wright 1988
Text B on color-coded paper vs. non-colored paper	85*	16	Wright 1988
Color-coded text on screens vs. non-colored screen text	92°	16	Wright 1988
Pointing device used to activate Hyperties anchors			
Mouse vs. arrow keys as "jump keys", short distance	85*	16	Ewing 1986
Mouse vs. arrow keys as "jump keys", long distance	95*	17	Ewing 1986
Touch screen activation strategies in Hyperties:			
Take-off vs. land-on activation, task time for first task	95°	30	Potter 1989
Take-off vs. land-on activation, blank space errors	339*	30	Potter 1989
Take-off vs. land-on activation, wrong hit errors	144°	30	Potter 1989
First-contact vs. take-off activation, task time	116°	30	Potter 1989
First-contact vs. take-off activation, total errors	94°	30	Potter 1989
Touch screen activation strategies in a non-hypertext text system			
First-contact vs. take-off activation, task time	124*	24	Potter 1988
First-contact vs. take-off activation, total errors	55*	24	Potter 1988
Various basic software aspects of the user interface			
Using multiple windows vs. a single-window display			
Time to read text, novice users	92*	16	Tombaugh 1987
Time to read text, experienced users	95°	32	Tombaugh 1987
Time to find previously read text, novices	85°	16	Tombaugh 1987
Time to find previously read text, experienced users	130*	32	Tombaugh 1987
Effect of fast (3 sec.) vs. slow (11 sec.) response times			
Time to complete task	200*	16	Patterson 1987
Frames retrieved per user decision	150*	16	Patterson 1987
Comparisons between hypertext and other computer systems			
Hypertext without overview map vs. scrolling text file			
Time to answer questions about a Pascal program	72*	20	Monk 1988
Hypertext with overview map vs. scrolling text file			
Time to answer questions about a Pascal program	101•	20	Monk 1988
Hierarchical hypertext vs. linear text file			
Concepts from general interest article recalled	57*	12	Gordon 1987
Concepts from technical article recalled	107°	12	Gordon 1987
Users' subjective preference	50•	24	Gordon 1987
Hypertext vs. traditional menu access to same info			
Number of questions answered in 15 minutes	125*	35	Shneiderman 1987
Users' subjective preference	140*	35	Shneiderman 1987
Hypertext vs. command-based database access			
Different nodes of information seen	108°	?	Canter 1985
Proportion of different nodes to total nodes visited	49*	?	Canter 1985
Spikes (user retracing route by backtracking)	321*	?	Canter 1985
Rings (user returning to previously visited data)	216*	?	Canter 1985

Hypertext vs. expert systems for diagnosis			
Proportion of problems solved correctly	121•	12	Peper 1989
Time to solve problems	82•	12	Peper 1989
Comparisons between hypertext and printed paper			
Hyperties vs. paper article, time to answer questions			
Question about fact in start of article	52*	20	Shneiderman 1987
Question about facts in body of article	88°	20	Shneiderman 1987
Question about facts requiring search in two articles	100°	20	Shneiderman 1987
SuperBook vs. printed book			
Search time, words from heading	80°	20	Egan 1989b
Correct responses, words from heading	113°	20	Egan 1989b
Search time, words from running text	174*	20	Egan 1989b
Correct responses, words from running text	183*	20	Egan 1989b
Search time, words not in text at all	86*	20	Egan 1989b
Essay quality scored by judge	161*	20	Egan 1989b
Facts included in essay	146*	20	Egan 1989a
"Discriminating" facts included	225*	20	Egan 1989a
Guide vs. paper documentation for diagnosing costomer problems at ICL			
Proportion of customer calls handled correctly	129•	?	Brown 1989
Students taking a poetry course taught on hypertext system vs. on paper			
Improvement in ability to analyze poems			
Students in class using hypertext vs. in regular class	117•	17	Catano 1979
Two other classes, hypertext class vs. regular class	55•	20	Catano 1979
Subjective preconceptions			
Online manuals vs. printed manuals	125•	81	Nielsen 1986
Online textbooks vs. printed textbooks	83•	81	Nielsen 1986
Online fiction vs. printed fiction	24•	81	Nielsen 1986
Online manuals with reader annotation vs. without	135•	81	Nielsen 1986
Online textbooks with reader annotation vs. without	191•	81	Nielsen 1986
Online fiction with reader annotation vs. without	94•	81	Nielsen 1986
Various hypertext facilities			
Hypertext with overview map vs. hypertext without map			
Time to answer questions about a Pascal program	141*	20	Monk 1988
Hypertext with various overview mechanisms,			
Exploratory with vs. without map, answer accuracy	112•	16	Hammond 1989
Exploratory with vs. without index, answer accuracy	104•	16	Hammond 1989
Directed with vs. without map, task time	104•	16	Hammond 1989
Directed with vs. without index, task time	105•	16	Hammond 1989
Exploratory with vs. without map, new-to-old ratio	163*	16	Hammond 1989
Exploratory with vs. without index, new-to-old ratio	149*	16	Hammond 1989
Directed with vs. without map, new-to-old ratio	152*	16	Hammond 1989
Directed with vs. without index, new-to-old ratio	167*	16	Hammond 1989
User ratings of the hypertext buttons in Guide			
Note vs. average button, easy to understand	115°	25	Nielsen 1989b
Replacement vs. average button, easy to understand	115°	25	Nielsen 1989b
Reference vs. average button, easy to understand	78*	25	Nielsen 1989b
Note vs. average button, improves document	122*	25	Nielsen 1989b
Replacement vs. average button, improves document	97°	25	Nielsen 1989b
Reference vs. average button, improves document	88°	25	Nielsen 1989b
Effect of size of hypertext nodes			
Many small nodes vs. few large, time on questions	142*	16	Kreitzberg 1988
Iterative design of the SuperBook user interface			
SuperBook version 2 vs. 1, search time	141•	20	Egan 1989c
SuperBook version 2 vs. 1, correct responses	109•	20	Egan 1989c
Issue-based argumentation networks built in the hypertext system gIBIS			
Links "supporting" positions vs. links "objecting to"	236•	32	Conklin 1988
Effect of the task and individual user differences			
Effect of user's task on choice of navigation mechanism			
New-to-old node ratio, exploratory vs. directed task	141*	80	Hammond 1989
Use of index, exploratory vs. directed task	33*	16	Hammond 1989
Use of guided tour mechanism, exploratory vs. directed	337*	16	Hammond 1989
Effect of age on moving from just looking at a hypertext system to actually using it			
Young (≤20 years) vs. older users/on-lookers	1150•	500	Baird 1988

Effect of level of expertise on time required to complete task			
Users with 30 min windows skill vs. complete novices	170•	24	Tombaugh 1987
Effect of level of expertise on approach to solving task			
Use of table of contents on third day vs. first day	25•	12	Joseph 1989
Effect of users' motivation, activity level, etc. on number of new nodes created			
Most active vs. modal participant (in subnet B)	633•	2	Conklin 1988
Most active vs. modal participant (in subnet A)	1000•	4	Conklin 1988
Effect of users' spatial visualization abilities on time to find answers in a hypertext			
High visualization score (19) vs. low visualizationscore (2)	193*	12	Campagnoni 1989
Effect of fatigue			
Error frequencies after 50 min vs. 10 min. screen use	64*	24	Wilkinson 1987

* = difference from the control group's 100% mark reported by the author to be statistically significant
° = difference from the control group's 100% mark reported by the author not to be statistically significant
• = the author did not report test of statistical significance, so we don't know for sure

Note: "Performance" has been calculated so that bigger is better in all cases. For e.g. "time to complete task", a higher score means that the task was completed faster, for error-rates, higher scores mean fewer errors.

Table 1. Summary of 92 benchmark comparisons of usability measurements related to hypertext from 30 papers in the research literature.

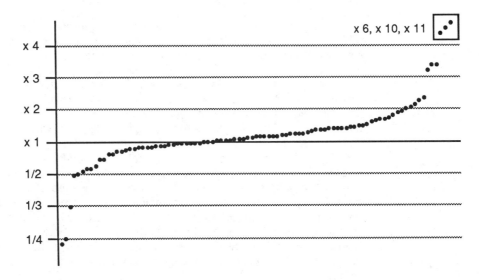

Figure 1. Each of the 92 benchmark measures have been plotted sorted according to the distance of the measured effect from the neutral point of 100%.

DISCUSSION: THE MATTERS THAT MATTER

It is obvious from Figure 1 that there are a few of the conditions listed in Table 1 which give rise to really big effects while the majority of the effects are less than a factor 2. This does not mean that the smaller effects are not important, since anybody would certainly gladly take advantage of, say a 20% performance increase if possible. Furthermore, there are lots and lots of these smaller effects so their cumulative effect might be large, even though very little is known about how the individual aspects of a user interface design interact to form a whole. The figure does indicate, however, that there are some effects which are so much larger than the others that one needs to consider them with extra care. Therefore Table 2 lists the conditions which gave rise to an effect of at least a factor of 2, sorted according to the magnitude of the effect measured.

The "winner" is the score of 1150 for proportion of young people (20 years or younger as judged by Baird et al.) compared to the proportion of older people who went from looking at Glasgow Online to actually using it [Baird et al. 1988] at a field installation. This difference between the two age groups of more than an order of magnitude makes all the 20 to 50% differences so carefully measured in other studies pale in comparison. This indication of the importance of age in the acceptance of new technology is a lesson we should take seriously, especially when considering that most of the other studies reported here have been conducted with young college students as subjects. This result also corresponds with general studies of the impact of age on attitudes towards new technology [Breakwell and Fife-Schaw 1988] where older people have been found to have increased feelings of inability to master technology.

The two "runner-ups" are also individual differences in the form of two cases of the activity level in posting new nodes in gIBIS which score 1000 and 633. The sixth item in Table 2 is also related to individual differences in the form of user expertise. So we conclude that individual differences are the most important effect for hypertext usability.

Egan [1988] summarized studies of individual differences in use of non-hypertext computer systems and found that the differences in text editing performance was typically a factor of about 5 while the differences in information search performance varied between a factor of about 3 in some studies and a factor of about 10 in other studies. Finally, individual differences in programming performance was typically a factor of 25. On the basis of these results, we should not be surprised to find factors of about 10 for individual differences in hypertext use.

Of the ten effects with an impact of a factor 3 or more, four are related to individual differences, and two are related to differences in the user's task. So we furthermore conclude that the user's task is another issue which should be looked at carefully. For example Hammond and Allinson [1989] found that hypertext users who were given two different kinds of task used various hypertext facilities very differently. Users who were exploring the hypertext structure to try to learn about the subject it covered, made heavy use of a guided tour facility and not very much use of the index, while users who were trying to answer specific questions behaved in the opposite way.

Finally, we note that items 4, 9, 12, 13, and 15 in Table 2 are related to users behaving differently in the use of hypertext compared to the use of paper or other computer systems, indicating the importance for hypertext people of not relying too much on usability results from those other domains. For example, Haas [1989] counted the proportion of users' protocol statements which referred to the editing medium itself rather than to the text being edited. This proportion was significantly larger when the subjects used a computer than when they used pen and paper, thus indicating that pen and paper is still the most transparent even though the test users all had at least 4 years of computer experience.

A similar conclusion can be drawn from comparing the two studies of touchscreens by Potter et al. [1988 and 1989]. When testing touchscreen strategies for non-hypertext applications, there were significant differences between a first-contact strategy and the lift-off strategy [Potter et al. 1988], but these two strategies turned out to have about the same usability in the Hyperties hypertext application where the active areas in the form of hypertext anchors tended to be larger areas [Potter et al. 1989]. These two studies taken together again show the danger of blindly transferring usability results from other computer applications to hypertext.

We should stress that the effects reported here were calculated with respect to the usability parameters studied in the individual research papers which form the source of the data in Table 1. It is not necessarily the case that all of these parameters are of true importance in the real world. For example, it may well be the case that it is harder to get older people to use hypertext on a voluntary basis, but that would be of no importance to us if we were designing a hypertext system for use in, say elementary schools. If we had some way to force users to use the system, we might also have less interest in users' voluntary behavior even though we would of course have an ethical obligation to take special care to introduce older users to our system in as painless a way as possible.

Furthermore, it might be the case that the actual *impact* of certain usability parameters are disproportionate to their measured effect. By "impact" we mean the change in the real world resulting from the design or use of the system. It is often the case, for example, that a design choice which objectively tests out to have only a minor impact on users' performance has a major effect on their subjective decision on whether or not to adopt the system. It could also be the case that certain usability parameters have little or no impact on users' performance on real world tasks because their effect is not felt very much during the execution of those tasks.

Unfortunately, extremely few studies exist of the real world impact of using hypertext systems, possibly because hypertext has not been used all that much yet for real world tasks. One of the few such studies was reported by Peter Brown [Brown 1989; summarized in Nielsen 1989c] in his invited speech at the Hypertext II conference. Guide is being used at the British computer company ICL for the task of diagnosing the fault when a customer calls for service. This task is called "laundering" and the proportion of customer calls handled correctly was 68% when the launderers used a paper representation of the information and 88% when they used hypertext.

No.	Phenomenon studied	Factor	Reference
1	Effect of age on moving from just looking at a hypertext system to actually using it Young (≤20 years) vs. older users relative to on-lookers	11.5•	Baird 1988
2	Effect of users' motivation, activity level, etc. on number of new nodes created: Most active participant vs. modal participant in subnet A	10.0•	Conklin 1988
3	Effect of users' motivation, activity level, etc. on number of new nodes created: Most active participant vs. modal participant in subnet B	6.3•	Conklin 1988
4	Proportion of effort spent attending to the medium itself rather than on solving task Revising text on a computer vs. with pen and paper	5.1*	Haas 1989
5	Subjective preconceptions: Online fiction vs. printed fiction	4.2•	Nielsen 1986
6	Effect of level of expertise on approach to solving task: Use of table of contents on third day vs. first day	4.0•	Joseph 1989
7	Touch screen activation strategies in Hyperties: Take-off vs. land-on activation, blank space errors	3.4*	Potter 1989
8	Effect of user's task on choice of navigation mechanism: Use of guided tour mechanism, exploratory vs. directed task	3.4*	Hammond 1989
9	Hypertext vs. command-based database access: Spikes (user retracing route through data by backtracking)	3.2*	Canter 1985
10	Effect of user's task on choice of navigation mechanism: Use of index, exploratory vs. directed task	3.0*	Hammond 1989
11	Issue-based argumentation networks built in gIBIS: Links "supporting" positions vs. links "objecting to"	2.4•	Conklin 1988
12	SuperBook vs. printed book: "Discriminating" facts included	2.3*	Egan 1989a
13	Hypertext vs. command-based database access: Rings (user returning to a previously visited piece of data)	2.2*	Canter 1985
14	Effect of screen size: Time to answer questions 120 lines vs. 22 lines, text editor with program text	2.1*	Reisel 1987
15	Hypertext vs. command-based database access: Proportion of different nodes visited to total nodes visited	2.0*	Canter 1985
16	Effect of fast (3 sec.) vs. slow (11 sec.) response times response times: time to complete task	2.0*	Patterson 1987
17	Hierarchical hypertext vs. linear text file: Users' subjective preference	2.0•	Gordon 1987
* = *difference from a factor of one reported by the author to be statistically significant* • = *the author did not report test of statistical significance, so we don't know for sure*			
Note: The effects have been calculated so that bigger is better in all cases. For e.g. "time to complete task", a higher score means that the task was completed faster, for error-rates, higher scores mean fewer errors.			

Table 2. List of the 17 effects which are larger than a factor 2. These are the "matters that really matter".

CONCLUSIONS

Most of the effects measured in the usability studies in the research literature are comparatively small. You should of course take advantage of these results anyway to improve the usability of your hypertext system, but the two most important issues to consider are

• Individual differences among users - so make sure to test with subjects who are representative of your intended users, since different people will perform very differently. What is best for one group of users may not be best for another.

• The effect of different tasks: People having different tasks will use hypertext systems in different ways, so different hypertext mechanisms are needed to support different tasks.

Because of these two observations, there is little hope for a single, universal hypertext user interface design which will be optimal to everybody.

We have also seen that one cannot always rely on having the results of usability studies of non-hypertext computer systems transfer to apply also to the usability of hypertext systems, so you are advised to exercise caution if you try to do so.

Acknowledgements

Terry Mayes, Gary Marchionini, and Pat Wright provided helpful comments on an earlier version of this paper.

References

Baird, P., Mac Morrow, N., and Hardman, L.: "Cognitive aspects of constructing non-linear documents: HyperCard and Glasgow Online", *Proc. Online Information 88* (London, UK, 6-8 December 1988), pp. 207-218.

Breakwell, G.M. and Fife-Schaw, C.: "Ageing and the impact of new technology", *Social Behaviour* **3**, 2 (June 1988), pp. 119-130.

Brown, P.: "Keynote address", presented at the *Hypertext II Conf.* (York, UK, 29-30 June 1989).

Campagnoni, F.R. and Ehrlich, K.: "Information retrieval using a hypertext-based help system", *Proc. ACM SIGIR Conf.* (Cambridge, MA, June 1989).

Canter, D., Rivers, R., and Storrs, G.: "Characterizing user navigation through complex data structures", *Behaviour and Information Technology* **4**, 2 (April-June 1985), pp. 93-102.

Catano, J.V.: "Poetry and computers: Experimenting with the communal text", *Computers and the Humanities* **13** (1979), pp. 269-275.

Conklin, J. and Begeman, M.L.: "gIBIS: A hypertext tool for exploratory policy discussion", *ACM Trans. Office Information Systems* **6**, 4 (October 1988), pp. 303-331.

Egan, D.E.: "Individual differences in human-computer interaction", In: Helander, M. (Ed.): *Handbook of Human-Computer Interaction*, Elsevier Science Publishers, 1988, pp. 543-568.

Egan, D.E., Remde, J.R., Landauer, T.K., Lochbaum, C.C., and Gomez, L.M.: "Acquiring information in books and SuperBooks", *Proc. Annual Meeting American Educational Research Assoc.* (San Francisco, CA, 27-30 March 1989). a

Egan, D.E., Remde, J.R., Landauer, T.K., Lochbaum, C.C., and Gomez, L.M.: "Behavioral evaluation and analysis of a hypertext browser", *Proc. ACM CHI'89* (Austin, TX, 30 April-4 May 1989), pp. 205-210. b

Egan, D.E., Remde, J.R., Gomez, L.M., Landauer, T.K., Eberhardt, J., and Lochbaum, C.C.: "Formative design-evaluation of "SuperBook"", *ACM Trans. Office Information Systems* **7** (1989). c

Ewing, J., Mehrabanzad, S., Sheck, S., Ostroff, D., and Shneiderman, B.: "An experimental comparison of a mouse and arrow-jump keys for an interactive encyclopedia", *Int.J. Man-Machine Studies* **24**, 1 (January 1986), pp. 29-45.

Gordon, S., Gustavel, J., Moore, J., and Hankey, J.: "The effects of hypertext on reader knowledge representation", *Proc. Human Factors Society 32nd Annual Meeting* (1988), pp. 296-300.

Gould, J.D. and Grischkowsky, N.: "Doing the same work with hard copy and with cathode ray tube (CRT) computer terminals", *Human Factors* **26** (1984), pp. 323-337.

Gould, J.D., Alfaro, L., Fonn, R., Haupt, B., Minuto, A., and Salaun, J.: "Why reading was slower from CRT displays than from paper", *Proc. ACM CHI+GI'87* (Toronto, Canada, 5-9 April 1987), pp. 7-11.

Haas, C.: "Does the medium make a difference? Two studies of writing with pen and paper and with computers", *Human-Computer Interaction* **4**, 2 (1989), pp. 149-169.

Hammond, N. and Allinson, L.: "Extending hypertext for learning: An investigation of access and guidance tools", *Proc. BCS HCI'89* (Nottingham, UK, 5-8 September 1989).

Hansen, W.J. and Haas, C.: "Reading and writing with computers: A framework for explaining differences in performance", *Commun. ACM* **31**, 9 (September 1988), pp. 1080-1089.

Joseph, B., Steinberg, E.R., and Jones, A.R.: "User perceptions and expectations of an information retrieval system", *Behaviour and Information Technology* **8**, 2 (March-April 1989), pp. 77-88.

Kreitzberg, C.B. and Shneiderman, B.: "Restructing knowledge for an electronic encyclopedia", *Proc. Intl. Ergonomics Association 10th Congress* (Sydney, Australia, 1-5 August 1988).

Monk, A.F., Walsh, P., and Dix, A.J.: "A comparison of hypertext, scrolling, and folding as mechanisms for program browsing", In: Jones, D.M. and Winder, R. (Eds.): *People and Computers IV*, Cambridge University Press 1988, pp. 421-435.

Nielsen, J.: "Online documentation and reader annotation", *Proc. 1st Conf. Work With Display Units* (Stockholm, Sweden, 12-15 May 1986), pp. 526-529.

Nielsen, J.: "Survey of hypertext usability", appendix to the tutorial notes for the *Hypertext'89 Tutorial on Evaluating Hypertext Usability,* 5 November 1989, Pittsburgh, PA. (this is a draft of a chapter to appear in J. Nielsen: *Hypertext and Hypermedia,* Academic Press, 1990). a

Nielsen, J. and Lyngbæk, U.: "Two field studies of hypermedia usability", *Proc. Hypertext 2 Conf.* (York, UK, 29-30 June 1989). b

Nielsen, J.: "Trip Report: Hypertext II", *ACM SIGCHI Bulletin* **21**, 2 (October 1989). c

Patterson, J.F. and Egido, C.: "Video browsing and system response time", In: Diaper, D. and Winder, R. (Eds.): *People and Computers III,* Cambridge University Press, Cambridge, UK, 1987, pp. 189-198.

Peper, G., Williams, D., Macintyre, C., and Vandall, M.: "Comparing a hypertext document to an expert system", *manuscript submitted for publication 1989, IBM Dept. 77K, Bldg. 026, 5600 N 63rd St., Boulder, CO 80314.*

Potter, R.L., Weldon, L.J.., and Shneiderman, B.: "Improving the accuracy of touch screens: An experimental evaluation of three strategies", *Proc. ACM CHI'88* (Washington, DC, 15-19 May 1988), pp. 27-32.

Potter, R., Berman, M., and Shneiderman, B.: "An experimental evaluation of three touch screen strategies within a hypertext database", *Int.J. Human-Computer Interaction* **1**, 1 (1989).

Reisel, J.F. and Shneiderman, B.: "Is bigger better? The effects of display size on program reading", In G. Salvendy (Ed.): *Social, Ergonomic and Stress Aspects of Work with Computers,* Elsevier Science Publishers, 1987, pp. 113-122.

Shneiderman, B.: "User interface design and evaluation for an electronic encyclopedia", In G. Salvendy (Ed.): *Cognitive Engineering in the Design of Human-Computer Interaction and Expert Systems,* Elsevier Science Publishers, 1987, pp. 207-223.

Tombaugh, J., Lickorish, A., and Wright, P.: "Multi-window displays for readers of lengthy texts", *Int.J. Man-Machine Studies* **26**, 5 (May 1987), pp. 597-615.

Wilkinson, R.T. and Robinshaw, H.M.: "Proof-reading: VDU and paper text compared for speed, accuracy and fatigue", *Behaviour and Information Technology* **6**, 2 (April-June 1987), pp. 125-133.

Wright, P. and Lickorish, A.: "Proof-reading texts on screen and paper", *Behaviour and Information Technology* **2**, 3 (July-September 1983), pp. 227-235.

Wright, P. and Lickorish, A.: "Colour cues as location aids in lengthy texts on screen and paper", *Behaviour and Information Technology* **7**, 1 (January-March 1988), pp. 11-30.

Expanding the Notion of Links

Steven J. DeRose

Summer Institute of Linguistics
7500 W. Camp Wisdom Road
Dallas, TX 75236

INTRODUCTION

Research in the humanities, particularly in text-oriented fields such as Classics and Religious Studies, poses particular challenges to hypertext and hypermedia systems. The complex set of primary and secondary documents form an intricate, highly interconnected network, for the representation of which hypertext is ideal. The variety and quantity of links which are needed pose challenges especially for data structures and for display and navigation tools. The specific needs arise in other contexts as well, particularly those with very large or complicated document collections.

In this paper I shall classify and discuss these needs, with illustrations from the CD-Word project at Dallas Theological Seminary,[1] the Perseus Project at Harvard University,[2] and a variety of other hypermedia systems.

ISSUES IN SUPPORTING SCHOLARLY TEXT RESEARCH

Classical and biblical documents, like other natural language texts, have *more than one structure*: (a) a logical or linguistic structure, with units such as chapters, paragraphs, sentences, etc.; and (b) a physical or layout structure, with pages, lines, etc. Although the logical structure is more important, for certain purposes the layout is also needed (see below). Both structures are largely hierarchical, but they cannot readily be reconciled into one hierarchy. This poses difficulties for many systems (such as Guide) which constrain document structures and links to a single hierarchy. Even worse, many systems do not support hierarchies *per se* at all, though one can usually build fortuitously hierarchical structures; the fact that hierarchies are a real part of text structure means that completely free-form systems such as HyperCard, NoteCards, HyperGate, and so on tend to miss an important aspect of documents.

---

[1]CD-Word gathers a range of primary and secondary documents for biblical studies into a Guide-based environment intended to facilitate the work of students, researchers, and clergy. It is being developed by Dallas Theological Seminary through private financial sponsorship, with the assistance of Owl International and Fulcrum Technologies Inc. I serve as a consultant to the CD-Word project, but the opinions expressed here are my own and do not necessarily reflect the views of the project or other staff. I would like to thank Robin Cover and Gary Simons for numerous helpful comments on this paper, and the Brown University Computing in the Humanities Users' Group, especially David Durand, Andrew Gilmartin, Elli Mylonas, and Allen Renear, for many enlightening discussions of hypertext.

[2]Perseus [Hugh88, Cran87] is a major project which gathers many classical Greek texts and some reference works, plus images of architecture, artifacts, and so on into a hypertextual database for pedagogy and research. Perseus, under the guidance of Greg Crane, Elli Mylonas, and others, has also produced a number of text analysis and search utilities which are being integrated into Perseus' hypermedia environment.

In addition to these two commonplace hierarchical structures, ancient documents often have an unbounded number of additional structures (some hierarchical, some not), which reflect the analytical decisions of exegetes and other textual scholars. Furthermore, many important texts have formal naming schemes which scholars use in order to "link" to pieces of the documents; the named pieces usually match elements of the main structures.

Ancient documents have another complexity: they exist in many *versions*, creating through repeated copying and in some cases editing. This is similar to the problem of document versions which has recently received attention. However, unlike with newly-authored documents, we do not know the sequential or genetic relationships between the extant copies of ancient texts; inducing them is itself a scholarly pursuit, for which the ability to compare and associate different versions, is needed. Low-end systems completely ignore version control, some even (as does HyperCard) foregoing "Undo." FRESS [Cata79, vanD71] introduced "Undo," but only to one level, with no permanent record. Many systems support linear "audit trails," but assume there is only one successor to each version. Nelson's Xanadu design allows for multiple successors, but appears to fail when a single successor element has multiple sources. To my knowledge, no hypermedia system yet handles the degree of multiple inheritance required for manuscript research.

The documents of interest to literary scholars also frequently exist in versions of another kind: *translations*. A translation is characterized by having much the same document structure as its original (and, hopefully, the same meaning), but little or none of the same concrete content (at the word and character level). Of course, readers often wish to see translations in co-ordination with originals. Various classes of annotations, such as part of speech labels, are similarly relevant, but tend to apply at the low levels of structure, in contradistinction to translations. CDWord is one of the few systems so far which coordinates simultaneous display of translations.

Literature in general differs from more technical material in that it requires deeper interpretive skills; whereas a technical manual aims to be very explicit, this may not be a significant goal for a novel. Because of this, the desired paths of exploration and methods of annotation cannot be defined in advance for literature (even by the author); therefore sophisticated search, retrieval, and annotation tools are required.

Because most ancient documents are in unfamiliar languages, many users need help from dictionaries and other aids, as well as tools for locating desired passages, when skimming, especially when skimming or retrieval is impractical.

A TAXONOMY OF LINKS

These corpora show that links involve much more complicated theoretical and design issues than may at first appear. This section will describe these linking needs in terms of several sorts of links that differ not only in purpose but in structure, function, and preferred means of implementation.

Figure 1 presents the taxonomy of links which I will discuss. The precise divisions could be expressed in different ways, but I suggest that this set of relationships is useful to the user as a framework for understanding the capabilities of a system, and to the designer when planning user interfaces and data structures.

On paper I can only approximate this taxonomic structure in the arrangement of the discussion, by choosing some particular order in which to describe its components. Ideally, however, I would create a hypertext which mirrored the taxonomic structure itself.

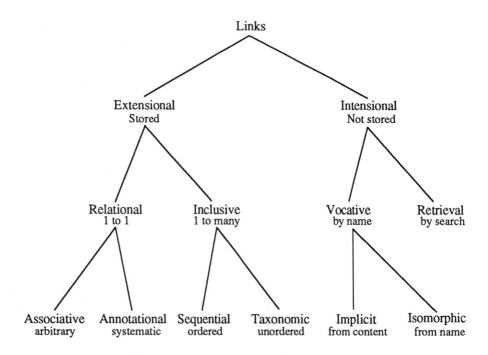

Figure 1: A taxonomy of links

1: Extensional links

Extensional links are idiosyncratic, tying various parts of the docuverse together in unpredictable ways. They must be stored individually. Extensional links have received much more attention than *intensional* links, which are discussed below as class number 2.

1A: Relational links

The first subdivision of extensional links includes *relational* links (Conklin uses the term "referential" [Conk87]). These connect single locations together. By writing "locations" I do not wish to prejudice the question of whether points, markup elements, arbitrary spans of text, or even discontiguous spans are linkable. The distinction is rather that each of the two ends of a relational link is one conceptual unit, not many.

1A1: Associative links

A relational link which is entirely unpredictable is called an *associative* link. Such links are the usual stock in trade of hypertext systems. Since they attach arbitrary pieces of documents, they cannot be replaced by retrieval algorithms, or even by unilateral creation on the part of an author. Rather, every user must be able to create them on the fly and to organize them in whatever ways seem appropriate.

Because these links serve many purposes, they are usually labelled according to type. Trigg has proposed a taxonomy that insightfully covers a large range of needs [Trig83]. However, no closed taxonomy is likely to be adequate for all future purposes, so coining new types should be possible.

There is, nevertheless, a problem with an unrestricted set of types: the problem of standardization. If users can create their own type-names, they will certainly eventually produce a situation in which one cannot effectively choose links based upon type. In a worldwide community of users there is the problem of language, but even in a single language users will find many names for the same thing, and the same name for distinct things. How, then, can one resolve the semantics of link types?

The same problem occurs in electronic mail forums, bulletin boards, etc.: systems that do not enforce a list of topics quickly bog down in inconsistency. Similar problems in library cataloging led to using standard subject taxonomies.

In the same way, new types must be possible, yet lack of standardization has its own dangers. I advocate allowing any user to add to a standard taxonomy, but only by choosing to make each new type a sub-type of one which already exists. This solution has many of the same advantages (and limitations) as type inheritance systems in object oriented programming systems.

1A2: Annotational links

An *annotational* link differs from an associative link in that one of its ends is (in principal) predictable. That is, the existence of a link from each of a class of locations is predictable, but the targets of those links are not.

Thus, part of speech marking is an annotational link, because it cannot be reliably predicted merely from a word's form; dictionary lookup is not, because the target is relatively predictable. Annotational links are very similar to isomorphic links (see below), but represent connections from portions of a text to *information about the text*, such as the presence of linguistic, thematic, or other phenomena. They also tend to originate from very low level elements (e.g., from every word), although they can originate from larger units as well.

Often an annotation is selected from a fixed set of items, such as {noun, verb, adjective, adverb, particle}. It is useful if a system can enforce such user-defined constraints, but I have seen no hypermedia system which can (but see [Simo88]).

One difficulty with annotational links is that they are likely to be attached to every word of a text. In such a case the user probably does not want to see an inline button or link marker after every word! Instead, such links should either remain invisible until requested, or perhaps be followed automatically and displayed interlinearly. In CDWord they are available through ever-present menus.

1B: Inclusion Links

Extensional links which connect one originating location to many target locations, not just one, are called *inclusion links*, and are similar to Conklin's "organizational" links [Conk87:34]. They function mainly to represent super-ordinate/sub-ordinate relationships between document elements. They are of two sub-types: sequential and taxonomic.

1B1: Sequential links

A *sequential* link has multiple, ordered target locations. *Paths* are a simple example: it should be possible to associate a path with a given location, so the path is accessible from it as a matter of course, and this feature follows immediately from viewing paths as sequential links.

However, the most important example of the sequential link is the *structure-representing* or *s-r* link, which represents those aspects of document structure commonly encoded via descriptive markup in word processing. For example, a section links to the sequence of its sub-parts, which may include subsections, paragraphs, block quotes, emphatic elements.... Most sequential links are of this kind, and represent hierarchical structures of the text (see [Coom87]).

A major identifying feature of these structure-representing ("s-r") links is that they provide a basis for presenting the text in linear form when needed. Some documents exist that need never be formally linearized. However, millions of documents already exist in linearized form, whose authors thought carefully about that constraint when composing them, and so we ought to provide for them.

Card-oriented hypertext systems seldom support s-r links, thus avoiding real complexities of document structure by implementing an impoverished model of text. Some systems (such as Xanadu [Nels87]) treat structural relationships as merely a special case of associative links. However, s-r links deserve special treatment by hypermedia systems, for several reasons (cf [DeRo87]):

First, s-r links usually require specialized display, for example being traversed automatically in order as the user scrolls, rather than followed only on request. That is, one should not have to follow links in order to see successive verses of the Bible, speeches within an ode, or paragraphs of a chapter; rather, one should see a smooth and uninterrupted view of the *document*.

Second, s-r links express many useful and standard hierarchies. Although systems like NoteCards allow hierarchical organizations, they do not provide support for defining *specific* structures which authors consider standard, such as outline levels, chapters/sections/subsections, etc. The user who needs non-hierarchical documents is of course not constrained, since many other kinds of links are available; but by knowing about formal structures, a system can (see also [Barn88]):

1)   assist in generating useful links between related structural elements (for example, collecting all section-title elements into a table of contents linked to the contents);

2)   perform more effective retrieval (for example, weighing words in titles more heavily than words in running text);

3)   help prevent anomalous documents (for example, those whose paragraphs contain chapters).

Third, s-r links characteristically point to sequences of other s-r links and not to arbitrary spans of text. For example, a section may be a sequence of paragraphs; it is not merely a sequence of ranges of characters. Representing a section in the latter fashion would not express that certain ranges are also the targets of successive paragraph-links, and that this is not mere chance; as Conklin points out ([Conk87:36], some elements "are much more tightly bound together than. . . nodes are to each other."

Fourth, unlike associative links, the set of s-r link types is fairly constrained. Standardization of types is important, as for associative link types. However, even with a carefully planned standard (e.g., [AAP86]), new or forgotten uses will continue to arise.

1B2: Taxonomic links

A *taxonomic* link leads to multiple target locations, but does not impose an order on them. Such links generally associate lists of properties with particular document elements. For example, one may associate examples of some literary phenomenon with commentary about it, or attach keywords indicating relevance, importance, secrecy requirements, etc. (FRESS was probably the first hypermedia system to support such information). One may create an unordered path connecting passages of interest, otherwise like the paths created with sequential links. Another application is to connect related groups of data in a lexicon, such as cross-references between words.[1] Taxonomic links are very similar to annotational links, but tend to originate from higher-level elements.

2: Intensional links

Opposed to all the extensional link types already discussed, are the *intensional* link types. These have in common that they follow strictly from the structure and content of the documents they link, and so need not be stored one by one by the hypertext system. In other words, the destination of an intensional link is defined by some *function* that finds the desired ends, rather than being a *list* of known ends. Because of this, intensional links are in principle unidirectional, although in some cases a function may be invertible, making it possible to reverse some intensional links. They may also have multiple ends. Conklin [Conk87:35] mentions a broad notion of "keyword links" in passing, and notes they are "yet to be fully explored."

2A: Vocative links

Some intensional links are called *vocative* because they invoke a particular document element *by name*. Many document elements do not have names useful to humans. However, many also do. For example, each entry in a dictionary has its main entry word. Reference works in general are distinguished by their use of element names, but other documents also name some elements ("Chapter 3" or "Figure 27"), and many ancient texts have standard reference methods. In all these cases, certain links may be inferred, and thus need not be stored.

2A1: Implicit links

A vocative link which exists because its target element's name appears within the *content* of the source document is called an *implicit* link. The most obvious example is dictionary look-up. Dictionaries should be available from every word in every text; this clearly requires too many links to store or display explicitly, especially when many dictionaries are involved.

In the simplest case the system need merely extract a selected word and use it as an index key (or element name) of the referenced document. However, complexities arise:

1) There may be many dictionaries for a language. New ones may be added at any time, and should not require lengthy processing before being used.

2) The word form found in the text may not be the same as the index key for the dictionary; in some languages (those with complex morphology) this problem can be nearly intractable.

3) Implicit links may be used to access many other kinds of documents and sub-documents in addition to dictionaries. For example, online maps of all the world's countries ought to be accessible from any instance of a country name in any text (similar to features in Perseus [Hugh88]).

---

[1]An obvious but incorrect application of taxonomic links would be to encode formatting information. Formatting should (except perhaps in particular rare cases) be a consequence of element *types*, not of element *instances*; otherwise consistency of formatting and of format-changing is lost, and the user can be tempted to discard the role of author for that of typesetter, seldom a good use of an author's time.

4)   Implicit links may attach not just to words, but to any elements of the text; if they are too frequent to have individual link markers, a clear way must be provided for choosing what element to use.

Because implicit links can are so frequent, and can go to such a wide variety of places, a means for choosing where in the docuverse implicit links are to lead is required. In CDWord, users can select a word in a text, and then choose dictionary lookup, map lookup, or other options via a menu. Since there are multiple reference works in each category, users can choose a preferred work in each category, which will then be the one accessed.

Standardized reference methods constitute a second kind of implicit link. Appearing in print, "Matt 1:10" is a link to chapter one, verse ten of Matthew's Gospel. It is an abstract link, leading to a structural element that transcends the particular manuscripts, versions, translations, and other documents that instantiate the notion "Bible." The reader reasonably expects that every such reference in any online text links to the correct verse in any document sharing certain aspects of the Bible's structure, even if the author has not created an associative link, or even marked up the reference as such. These links may be handled in much the same manner as dictionary look-ups. As Crane has pointed out, such links have an advantage over typical associative links, in that they communicate to the user some indication of their destination [Cran87:53].

Bibliographic and similar references constitute a third kind of implicit link. Internal references may be as brief as "see chapter 10." References to other works may appear in many different forms as dictated by the kind of document referenced and by personal and editorial tastes. Nevertheless such cross-references should function as implicit links. At present this is not so serious a problem, because only a small portion of literature is available in electronic form. As the docuverse becomes a reality, however, it will become crucial to standardize the syntax of bibliographic references.

Implicit links are used all the time on paper, so they will be an important part of what users desire for some time to come. As already noted, references found in printed originals pose the particular problem that they commonly point to page numbers. There will also be many occasions for making references from the docuverse out to paper documents, and so online document systems must support page references.[1]

Implicit links, finally, may come directly to the user's mind. A user should be able to request a particular dictionary entry, Bible verse, or journal article by name at any time. Most hypermedia systems allow this in some form: some require an arcane name, such as a card id; some (e.g., FRESS) have provided explicit naming operators and an index space; in cases where conventional names exist, they should be directly usable as well.[2]

2A2: Isomorphic links

A vocative link which exists because its target element's name appears as an element *name* in the source document (rather than as content) is called an *isomorphic* link. Isomorphic links are most useful in cases where different documents share much or all of their logical structure. They define the correspondences among large structures of elements, usually entire documents.

---

[1]Perhaps even more difficult is the problem of referring to elements of an online hypertext from paper, since pages are not meaningful, and element identifiers do not seem intuitive.

[2]This is harder than it may seem; for example, verses of the Psalms are numbered differently in Greek and Hebrew versions, yet must be interconnected.

I have already described the many documents that share the element structure of the Bible; documents which exist in several versions sharing most of their structure pose a similar problem. A hypertext system that includes such documents should provide for connecting the corresponding elements, so that users can compare and relate them.

A distinguishing characteristic of isomorphic links is that they tie together like-named (not "like-positioned") document elements. Despite superficial variations there exists an abstract (meta-) document we call the "Bible," represented by thousands of concrete manuscripts, editions, and translations. These documents share a structure of abstract elements. By providing the ability to name document elements similarly despite their existing in diverse documents, the needed level of abstraction can be achieved.

In reading meta-documents, the most common need involves viewing simultaneously several concrete instances of a particular text phenomenon. Parallel, synchronized windows or panes are the usual solution. For documents with entirely commensurable element names this solution is relatively easy, but there are usually deviations from perfect isomorphism. For example, certain elements may be missing in some versions, or re-ordered; numbered groups of elements may be divided or counted differently; elements may correspond to higher or lower level elements in other versions. Also, corresponding elements may differ drastically in size, in which case it is important for a hypertext system to align and move text intuitively.

2B: Retrieval links

Retrieval links are very similar to vocative links. However, where vocative links find their target by a formal name, retrieval links find their target by its content, or perhaps by both name, structure, and content. A retrieval link invokes a process to search a portion of the docuverse for something. The process may be of arbitrary complexity, and may in principle involve name-based, structure-based, and content-based decisions. Whereas implicit links are defined globally (for example, it can be a system universal that words are linked to dictionary entries), retrieval links originate only at particular locations.

The list of locations found by the process associated with a retrieval link constitutes the destination; thus the destination may change over time. So long as the universe of potential link ends does not change, and so long as the list is known to be complete, a list and a retrieval produce the same result; but the retrieval link survives changes more effectively.

Retrieval links could be subdivided into *nominal* links, which search the structure of named elements in their target document(s), and *content-based* links, which search the content. However, there will be cases in which a single retrieval link must refer to both types of information, so I do not think this distinction is salient.

CONCLUSIONS

Just to support the features of typical paper versions of the Bible, we must include hundreds of thousands of links. The large number of links required would, if kept explicit, severely tax the capabilities of any hypertext system. Thus the dense and complex interconnections of the biblical studies materials clearly demonstrate the need for more sophisticated linking methods in hypermedia. A fundamental requirement is support for intensional linkage, where an unbounded set of links is supported by indexing and retrieval rather than by exhaustive cataloging. Moreover, a wide range of link kinds should be supported, most of which do not readily fit into the usual associative linking paradigm.

Biblical, classical, and literary scholars regularly require such complex tools, and have devised means to the same ends on paper. Designers of hypermedia systems would do well to take these problems into account, for they will probably arise in all fields, differing only in priority and guise.

BIBLIOGRAPHY

[AAP86] American Association of Publishers. 1986. *Reference Manual on Electronic Manuscript Preparation and Markup.* Washington, DC: AAP Electronic Manuscript Project.

[Barn88] Barnard, David T., Cheryl A. Fraser, and George M. Logan. "Generalized Markup for Literary Texts." *Literary and Linguistic Computing* 3 (1): 26-31.

[Cata79] Catano, J. 1979. "Poetry and Computers: Experimenting with Communal Text." *Computers and the Humanities* 13(9): 269-275.

[Conk87] Conklin, Jeff. 1987. "Hypertext: An introduction and Survey." *IEEE Computer* 20 (9): 17-41.

[Coom87] Coombs, James H., Allen H. Renear, and Steven J. DeRose. 1987. "Markup Systems and the Future of Scholarly Text Processing." *Communications of the Association for Computing Machinery* 30 (11): 933-947.

[Cran87] Crane, Gregory. "From the Old to the New: Integrating Hypertext into Traditional Scholarship." In *Proceedings of Hypertext '87.* Chapel Hill: Department of Computer Science, University of North Carolina.

[DeRo87] DeRose, Steven J. 1987. "Hypertext and Scholarship in the Humanities." Position paper in *Proceedings of Hypertext '87.* Chapel Hill: Department of Computer Science, University of North Carolina.

[Hugh88] Hughes, John. 1988. "Studying Ancient Greek Civilization Interactively—The Perseus Project." *Bits and Bytes Review* 2 (1): 1-12.

[Nels87] Nelson, Theodore H. 1987. *Literary Machines.* Edition 87.1. South Bend, Indiana: The Distributors.

[Simo88a] Simons, Gary F. 1988. "The Computational Complexity of Writing Systems." In *Proceedings of the Fifteenth LACUS Forum.* Lake Bluff, Illinois: Linguistic Association of Canada and the United States.

[Simo88b] Simons, Gary F. and John V. Thomson. 1988. *How to Use* IT: *Interlinear Text Processing on the Macintosh.* Edmonds, Washington: Linguist's Software.

[Trig83] Trigg, Randall H. 1983. "A Network-based Approach to Text Handling for the On-Line Community." Ph.D. dissertation, University of Maryland.

[vanD71] van Dam, Andries and David E. Rice. 1971. "On-line Text Editing: A Survey." Computing Surveys 3 (3): 93-114.

Hypertext and "the Hyperreal"

Stuart Moulthrop

Department of English
Yale University
P.O. Box 7355 Yale Station
New Haven, Connecticut 06520

I. INTRODUCTION

As the technology of hypertext matures and becomes widespread, the changes it brings to textuality will affect all fields of writing, including those associated with literature. Using an important recent work of hypertextual fiction as a focal point, this paper offers a perspective on hypertext informed by literary and social criticism. It invokes Jean Baudrillard's distinction between technologies of displacement (the "robot") and technologies of augmentation (the "automaton") to argue for the design of texts and systems that are accessible and enabling rather than opaque and objectifying.

II. HYPERTEXT AND DECONSTRUCTION

The arrival of hypertext is more than an advance in information technology. Seen from the viewpoint of textual theory, hypertext systems appear as the practical implementation of a conceptual movement that coincides with the late phase of modernity. This movement rejects authoritarian, "logocentric" hierarchies of language, whose modes of operation are linear and deductive, and seeks instead systems of discourse that admit a plurality of meanings, where the operative modes are hypothesis and interpretive play and hierarchies are contingent and local. The editors of a recent collection of post-structuralist literary criticism strike a characteristic note when they announce that each of the essays in their volume "develops an insistent coherence of its own that drives toward conclusive and irrefutable assertions. But it does this while holding open the possibility of a multiplicity of competing meanings, each of which denies the primacy of the others" (Mach87, 7).

Until recently this deconstruction of discursive authority seemed to have only limited relevance to society at large. Critical debates over literary texts, however vigorous, never seemed to have much bearing on the future of information systems or the political economy of the west. But hypertext offers to make the interpretive agenda of post-structuralist literary theory a matter of general textual practice. Now every instance of written discourse, from the corporate memo to the visionary novel, lies open to deconstruction in actu. Since any writing can be linked or woven into a de-centered matrix of information, its affiliation with a specific, identifiable speech act comes into question. Issues that were once of concern mainly to philosophers of language thus have begun to present themselves to theorists of information technology under the guise of problems in groupware design, versioning, and on-line publishing. While it may at first seem that deconstruction and the creation of distributed electronic text systems are incommensurable parts of the same phenomenon, in fact they are united in principle. The changes that have come to the technology of writing take us out of the realm of self-validating truths and decrees and place us instead in a context that requires negotiation, cross-reference, and a constant awareness of diversity. This fundamental change in our discursive practices cannot help but have effects on social institutions beyond the domains of literature and media. If we are to respond intelligently to these developments it is essential that we begin a dialogue between theorists of literature and theorists of information technology, and that ideas emerging out of this collaboration be implemented both in technical and artistic practice — categories which may in fact tend strongly to converge in the next decades.

In order to approach hypertext from some ground common both to literature and information technology we require a broader view of technology and social change. The perspective adopted here draws on the work of Jean Baudrillard, a social theorist who has written extensively on the phenomenon of simulation. Baudrillard uses this term both in reference to specific technologies, such as the creation of "artificial realities" in military training applications, and to more general cultural practices, such as the political influence of "silent majorities" and other demographic inventions. According to Baudrillard, simulation subverts reality: "Simulation is no longer that of territory, a referential being or a substance. It is the generation by models of a real without origin or reality: a hyperreal" (Baud83, 2).

Needless to say, this notion of "hyperreality" is highly problematic and the objections to Baudrillard's views have been many (see for instance Jame86, 85; Krok88, 14-16; Hutc88, 223). Like Marshall McLuhan, whom Baudrillard occasionally and grudgingly accepts as a precursor, Baudrillard seems to posit an unfallen state -- McLuhan's "unified sensorium," Baudrillard's pre-simulation "reality" -- into which the serpent of postmodern technology has crept. This view is of course perilously naïve: no definition of "reality" can divorce itself so neatly from technology. "Reality," however defined, depends in large measure on technologies of perception and representation. Baudrillard's conflict of "reality" and "the hyperreal" is really a struggle between competing technologies or modes of cognition — the same struggle between authoritative, serial processes and de-centralized, parallel processes whose traces can be seen in the development of hypertext. Hence, in spite of its naïveté, Baudrillard's commentary on "the precession of simulacra" can be essential in an understanding of hypertext and its larger social implications. This paper is an attempt to outline such an understanding through examination of one hypertext system, Bolter, Joyce, and Smith's Storyspace, and scrutiny of a work of narrative fiction written as a demonstration of that system, Michael Joyce's "Afternoon."

III. FICTION MACHINES

According to Jean Baudrillard, the rise of simulation threatens an apocalypse:

> Here comes the time of the great Culture of tactile communication, under the sign of the technico-luminous cinematic space of total spatio-dynamic theatre.... This is a completely imaginary contact-world of sensorial mimetics and tactile mysticism; it is essentially an entire ecology that is grafted on this universe of operational simulation, multistimulation and multiresponse (Baud83, 140).

Baudrillard has clearly seen something terrifying on the horizon, but it is hard to say exactly what that might be. Perhaps it is a new technology of entertainment ("feelies" or "simstim"), perhaps a global information order ("noösphere" or "matrix"), perhaps it is some sinister extension of the present media ecology combining all of the above. Whatever it may be, Baudrillard's bogey has not yet caught up with us. In spite of the apparent dominance of reality-as-representation or "the hyperreal," the organization of political and economic life in the west has not yet become an artificially determined feedback circuit. If it had, after all, Baudrillard's warning would have been pre-empted: the self-referential mechanisms of representation would be invisibly woven into the fabric of reality, beyond all critique.   It is still possible to isolate and criticize self-generating sign systems. We retain the ability to examine the implications of "a universe of operational simulation" and to adopt countermeasures should these implications prove as dangerous as Baudrillard suggests. A "total spatio-dynamic theatre" might be well and good so long as the emergency exits were clearly marked; but such totalizing structures often provide no outlets, or tend to collapse into a singularity from which nothing can escape. It follows that we must carefully scrutinize changes in communications media, particularly where those changes affect the scope of imagination and expression. This scrutiny seems especially appropriate to recent changes in the possibilities for literature, particularly in the domain of hypertextual narrative and interactive fiction, for it is there that the foundations of Baudrillard's globe-theatre may even now be taking shape.

David Porush has identified a genre of "cybernetic fiction" in which authors confront the importance of the machine by playing on the recognition that "their texts are constructed of words, that words are part of the larger machinery of language, and that language is shaped the still larger machinery of their own consciousness...." But this play is not to be taken too seriously; for all their gestures toward immachination, these writers are careful to register the fact that their texts are products of human agency (Poru85, 19). These writers regard fictional mechanism strictly as a metaphor, but as Porush observes, the metaphor tends to escape the bounds of the figural. Cybernetic fiction is the first step toward the construction of actual fiction machines.

Such fictive engines have existed for some time, both as experimental novels (e.g., Cortazar's *Hopscotch* or Pavic's *Dictionary of the Khazars*) and more recently as electronic fictions (e.g., Disch's *Amnesia* or Pinsky's *Mindwheel*). All of these mechanized narratives set out to revolutionize the traditional economy of story (or narrative potential) and discourse (or actual telling). Instead of offering a single, exclusive arabesque through a universe of possibilities, these fictions allow readers to choose among multiple paths. Given divergent choices, the narrative may differ markedly from one reading to the next. The discourse of the moment emerges through an asynchronous exchange between reader's desires and writer's designs — hence works of this sort are often called 'interactive fiction,' even though strictly speaking that is a misnomer. As one forthright writer of such fictions confesses: "There are grounds for arguing that no truly interactive system of any sort exists — except perhaps implanted pacemakers and defibrillators — since true interaction implies that... initiatives taken by either user or system alter the behavor of the other" (Joyc89, 7).

The greatest obstacle to interactivity in fiction resides in the text-to-reader leg of the feedback loop. The narrator of Tristram Shandy proclaims that good writing "is but a different name for conversation," but his claim is disingenuous. In true social interaction the interlocutor must be free to range in any discursive direction, but writersof fiction exercise such liberty only at the expense of coherence and intention, qualities which even post- or anti-modernists have a hard time abandoning. The cleverest "interactive" systems, like the simulated raconteur RACTER, put no constraints on the reader-to-text leg of the loop, but all impose limits on the text's response.

Hence experiments in multiple narrative find themselves flanked by problematic alternatives. On one hand lies the text as trackless expanse, which is the dangerous topography Milorad Pavic stakes out in his "lexicon novel in 100,000 words," *Dictionary of the Khazars*. The book is a collection of documents concerning a vanished Central European people, spanning twelve or thirteen centuries and comprising dozens of characters and narrative lines. As in any encyclopedia, there is no predefined sequence of reading nor is it easy to infer any single, hierarchical assembly of the data. The reader needs a great deal of curiosity and resourcefulness to survive in this unknown territory and no doubt none but the very brave will attempt the journey. This is perhaps the ironic point of the epigraph that appears just inside the title page: "Here lies the reader / Who will never open this book. / He is here forever dead" (Pavi88, 3).

If we proceed in the opposite direction from Pavic's wilderness of signs we come to the text as Cretan labyrinth, where the reader must either penetrate to the center or be liquidated by some pre-emptive fate. The first generation of "electronic novels," most of them heavily indebted to role-playing games, present this sort of geography. In Pinsky, Hales, and Mataga's *Mindwheel*, for instance, reading consists of an interrogative journey through four electronically preserved minds. The reader is dispatched by a guide ("Dr. Virgil") in search of a "wheel of power" that will save humankind from self-destruction.

Readers who fail to follow the right set of clues, or who cannot elicit these clues from the programmed "minds," draw this response from Dr. Virgil: "Perhaps you are not the right one for this quest.... Whatever you did, it seems to have been particularly senseless for somebody trying to save a planet. Oh well, do you want to try again?" (Pins87, 75).

The expected answer in this case is of course "yes" — readers are meant to cycle through a series of experimental assaults until they solve all the verbal puzzles presented by the text, and any reader can succeed eventually; all enigmas here have solutions. As their earliest critics observed, electronic texts like Mindwheel are informed by "the optimism of the scientist at least as much as the mystery of art" (Nies84, 122). They are thus necessarily committed to certainty and singularity, since readers are rewarded for eliminating alternatives and zeroing in on the most successful strategy. Such empirical entertainments have their value, of course, and I would argue vigorously for their importance as a genre; but it would be wrong to suggest that they exhaust the possibilities of interactive fiction.

IV. AFTERNOON OF THE SIMULACRA

There is a course open to hypertextual narrative which leads neither to the puzzle palace nor to the wilderness. In 1985, setting out to write a "test file" for a new interactive text program, the novelist Michael Joyce produced a variably structured fiction called "Afternoon," a piece that marks an important innovation in interactive narrative. Joyce's story, loosely inspired by Cortazar and Antonioni, invites the reader to circulate digressively among a matrix of characters and events that are never quite what they seem on first presentation. "I want to say that I may have seen my son die this morning," an unspecified speaker confides in many versions of the narrative, disclosing a rich field of fictive possibility. But the narrative produced by "Afternoon" will not validate or disprove either the speaker's desire or his perception. Like the *Dictionary of the Khazars*, "Afternoon" is a "mystery" only in the older sense of that word, the sense of ritual or hieratic procedure. But unlike Pavic's openwork encyclopedia, "Afternoon" does provide some overt structure, wherein lies its importance for cybernetic fiction.

In the first generation of electronic fictions, the reader's 'interaction' with the narrative is controlled by a parser: a routine that scans anything the reader types on the prompt line, searches for certain strings of characters, and identifies the chunk of text indexed to a given string. This response convention is the most pernicious kind of referendum — it solicits 'free' responses but is in fact able to respond only to a very restricted set of constructions. Unhappy with this arrangement, Joyce introduces a different convention in "Afternoon," built around "words that yield." A word in the text "yields" when it cues the next discursive move. For instance, in the phrase "I may have seen my son die this morning," "son" or "die" lead to an accident site, where the narrator finds skid marks and a school report on "The Sun King." Under the convention of yield words, Joyce's text becomes a scattering of fragments which may be reassembled by verbal association. Yet this implied re-weaving of the text does not mean that "Afternoon" is driven by a desire for wholeness and singularity.

The notion of "words that yield" replaces a fraudulent referendum with a fairly straightforward multiple choice. This is still a reductive structure, but Joyce limits tendencies in this direction by making the entire process of selection optional. Almost every textual node in "Afternoon" carries a default link triggered when the reader either enters some word without a specific yield or simply sends a blank response. This means that any response will generate movement through the text, and it therefore also means that the reader usually will not know if a transition was activated by a yield word or by default. This design decision effectively removes "Afternoon" from the problem-solving genre. There are no grail quests here; to read "Afternoon" is to wander and explore, not to seek and appropriate. The text preserves a more or less coherent linearity, but it does not sacrifice associative freedom. It therefore represents, I would argue, the most successful current application of "hypertext" (or "non-sequential writing") to fictional narrative.

"Afternoon" redefines the limits of its genre, suggesting that electronic fiction may be about to come into its own as a form of literature. But because it defines the state of the art, Joyce's text also reveals some inherent problems in hypertextual fiction — problems whose implications need serious attention. Considered from the point of view of an ordinary reader, "Afternoon" seems an elegant compromise of formality and free play. But an ordinary reader's perspective is of only limited value here. No hypertext is ever identical with its functional product, and there is much more to "Afternoon" than meets the reader's eye. Above the network of interwoven, intersecting stories is a hypertext system called Storyspace (Joyc88, 10). The relationship of "Afternoon" to this unseen structure is peculiar, and it suggests that the tension between determination and randomness in hypertextual fiction may not be so easily resolvable.

The description of Joyce's "yield" scheme given above omitted an important detail. The transition from one place in the text to another is governed in some cases not just by the reader's current response, but also by the history of her previous responses. The linking mechanism in Storyspace allows the writer to specify both the verbal content that will trigger the link and a list of places which the reader must have visited beforehand. Unless both conditions are satisfied, the "yield" link is replaced by the "default" link. With this system in operation, "Afternoon" resembles an automated railway in which the points keep switching of their own accord. Since the story is heavily recursive, readers may find themselves frequently returning to the same textual locales; but a yield word that took them from "son" to "Sun King" on the first iteration may now lead somewhere else entirely. The text can seem to have a mind of its own and readers may easily feel lost within its shifting circuitry — an outcome consistent with the nondeterminist principles of the text. Joyce has said that "Afternoon" has "no flow chart" and that there is no sense in trying to map its complexities. The mysteries of the text's design and function are not meant to be penetrated; it comes to us already deconstructed, designed for reception as process, not product.

And yet Storyspace contains a facility that could help to demystify such complexities: a function that generates graphic representations of structures created within it. The program can at least approximate a map or architectural outline (if not a circuit diagram) of "Afternoon" — in fact it does so automatically whenever one opens the text with the structure editor as opposed to the separate reading module. Jay David Bolter, co-designer of Storyspace, contends that hypertext frameworks represent an evolutionary step in the technology of writing (Bolt89, 12). These systems for "topographical writing" are intended to satisfy the impulse writers have always felt to move beyond the two dimensions of linear text into the three dimensions (and more) of text-as-network. Obviously readers cannot follow meaningfully into this "writing space" unless they are provided with some sort of navigational aid, so a mapping facility becomes essential, if only for orientation (Land87, 331). But the map display in Storyspace is not just a visual index. Changing the appearance of the map, for instance by redrawing a link line so that it points to a different locale, changes the actual organization of the text, in this case rerouting a pathway from one place to another. The map is not only an aid to navigation but a tool for reshaping the text. Reading space becomes writing space.

This sort of sympathetic or as Jorge Luis Borges called "partial" magic, whereby the map becomes a metaleptic surrogate for the thing it represents, brings us back to the discourse of simulation. Baudrillard's essay on the subject begins with a reference to Borges, in whose vision the map-as-territory decays, leaving only the gross physicality of the real behind. Baudrillard inverts Borges' parable, arguing that it is the real that has decayed, allowing its artificial, cartographic double to take its place. We no longer have access to reality, only to a systematic representation —hyperreality, which now recursively maps itself.

Applying Baudrillard's analysis to Storyspace, one might at first suspect that the idea of mapping textual space is an analog for the encroachment of hyperreality. In this view, Bolter's topographic writing space would represent an alienation of prose from its 'proper' procedures, a step toward the ultimate simulation of narrative. Hypertext, one might claim, threatens to replace the 'reality' of books with a 'hyperreality' of information networks whose complexities will give rise to uncontrolled self-reference and involution.

But this critique grossly misapplies the idea of simulation. In order to understand the true import of topographic writing, we must once again rewrite the parable of the map. For it appears that a map, when applied not to physical space but to textual or storyspace, does not represent a conspiracy to mimic and usurp prior structure. The textual map in Bolter's writing space is not a simulacrum or doppelganger, it is an empowering abstraction. The difference lies in the fact that its techno-magical influence over the text is extensive rather than intensive. Baudrillard's map-as-simulation is sinister because it subsumes "the real" into an autonomous system. But the map of writing space cannot be self-governing because it lacks a feedback loop. It can transform the text but at least in versions of the program I have seen, it cannot spontaneously transform itself. The map exists only in order to pass information to and from the writer/reader. The terms of Baudrillard's parable are thus re-inverted: this map acts not to guarantee the closure of an information system, but to open the system to change.

But the map, as we have seen, is not the only ordering principle available in Storyspace. The system of conditional "yields" developed in "Afternoon" employs a very different kind of structure, one that does contains a feedback loop: "Afternoon" is able to modify its current behavior by referring to a record of its previous behavior. More important, it performs this process in relative invisibility. Ordinary readers, who are concerned only with narrative discourse, are unaware of the logical transactions that underlie each textual jump. Set free to wander through the spaces of the story, they remain more or less unaware of the way the text is anticipating and controlling their movements. It is the logic of "yields," then, and not the map, that most closely resembles Baudrillard's spectre of supreme simulation.

V. ROBOTS AND AUTOMATA

The two ordering techniques we have under consideration here, the visible map as against the invisible protocol of transitions, stem from two different approaches to artificial systems, or as Baudrillard would have it, two different "orders of simulacra," the automaton and the robot: "The automaton is the analogy of man and remains his interlocutor.... The [robot] is man's equivalent and annexes him to itself in the unity of its operational process." (Baud83, 92-93). Bolter's topographic writing system does indeed present an analogy of discursive consciousness (the ancient analogy from which spring 'places of invention' and 'memory palaces'), and it is meant to augment rather than supplant human imagination. On the other hand, while the inner machinations of "Afternoon" would be hard to pass off as an artificial intelligence, they do operate as a sort of narrator-equivalent, and their tendency is definitely to "annex" the reader to their process.

Compared to its precursors, "Afternoon" is undoubtedly a kinder, gentler form of electronic fiction, and it would be ludicrous to present it as a pernicious mechanization of narrative: "Afternoon" is no plague vector for robotic literature. Indeed, Joyce's preference for esoteric over exoteric structure has the weight of western literary tradition behind it. As he puts it, "a fiction is essentially a selfish interaction for both its author and its reader," and it is hard to gainsay him this (Joyc89, 7). The problems of structure in "Afternoon" spring from causes rooted deep in the postindustrial imagination, indicating that our understanding of narrative, and of imaginary creations more generally, is approaching a crisis. The nature of this crisis is not hard to specify. There is a third order of simulacra in Baudrillard's scheme, comprising "models from which proceed all forms according to the modulation of their differences" (Baud83, 100). It is in this order that we find the real terrors of simulation, chiefly the prospect of totalizing, self-governing systems that would be capable of dictating the terms of cultural, political, and economic survival.

One vision of the third order is William Gibson's cybernetic "matrix," a "consensual hallucination" representing the sum of electronic knowledge/capital (Gibs84, 51-52). The world governed by this global simulacrum tends toward the dystopic — "like an experiment in social Darwinism, designed by a bored researcher who kept one thumb permanently on the fast-forward button" — but out of narrative necessity if nothing else, Gibson's world leaves some room for human agency. A starker and perhaps more accurate view of third-order simulation occurs in "Aliens," a shrill but provocative short story by David Leavitt. Leavitt puts his prophecy in the mouth of a sixteen-year-old game hacker who announces "the great computer age when we won't need dungeon masters. A machine will create for us a whole world into which we can be transported. We'll live inside the machine — for a day, a year, our whole lives — and we'll live the adventures the machine creates for us. We're at the forefront of a major breakthrough — artificial imagination. The possibilities, needless to say, are endless" (Leav86, 86-87).

Truer words have hardly ever been imagined. When the human propensity for world-building embraced the culture of the machine, it begat first cybernetic fictions and then fiction machines. Michael Joyce's "Afternoon" has redeemed electronic fiction from adolescence, lifting it up from the dungeon of linear game quests into the relative liberty of Storyspace. But electronic fiction now finds itself at a decision point. If future developers pursue "robotic" structures like the esoteric machinery behind the "yields" in "Afternoon," then the genre is likely to move toward seamless simulations that are less interactive than manipulative. Taken in this direction, electronic fiction could indeed provide the genetic material out of which "artificial imagination" might evolve. The suggestion that a few eccentric fictions could lead to the triumph of global simulation may seem to be paranoid fantasy, but assuredly it is a fantasy which the military-entertainment complex takes very seriously. And sometimes paranoia becomes parable. The greatest of such parables is Borges' short story, "Tlön, Uqbar, Orbis Tertius," in which a secret cabal of faceless men produce the encyclopedia of an imaginary planet. Through a process of insidious subversion the culture and history of the imaginary world come to replace those of the real world: "The contact and the habit of Tlön have disintegrated this world. Enchanted by its rigor, humanity forgets over and over that it is a rigor of chess masters, not of angels" (Borg62, 17).

I submit that hypertextual fiction has the potential to instantiate such rigorous and un-angelic games. But if future writers and system designers turn their attention to 'automated' structures like the topographic analog of Storyspace, the genre could evolve toward a literature not of "selfish interaction" but of genuine mutuality. It might contribute not to the further precession of simulacra but to more critical forms of social discourse. In an influential recent essay on postmodern aesthetics, the critic Frederic Jameson half-blindly foresees such a possibility:

> An aesthetic of cognitive mapping — a pedagogical political culture which seeks to endow the individual subject with some new heightened sense of its place in the global system — ...will have to hold to the truth of postmodernism... the world space of multinational capital — at the same time at which it achieves a breakthrough to some as yet unimaginable new mode of representing this last, in which we may again begin to grasp our positioning as individual and collective subjects and regain a capacity to act and struggle which is at present neutralized by our spatial as well as our social confusion. The political form of postmodernism, if there ever is any, will have as its vocation the invention and projection of a global cognitive mapping, on a social as well as a spatial scale. (Jame86, 92)

Jameson's skepticism about a politically relevant postmodern art ("if there ever is any") may have much to do with the fact that he has not yet encountered hypertext. Nevertheless Jameson's projection is important, if nothing else because it underscores the fact that the changes in textuality with which we are concerned have important social and political implications — a fact that seems undeniable even if one does not share

Jameson's ideological agenda. The model of textual relations invoked in this "aesthetic of cognitive mapping" might well be an implementation of Roland Barthes' dream of writing as "that social space that... allows no enunciative subject to hold the position of judge, teacher, analyst, confessor, or decoder" (Bart79, 81). Such a writing space presumes a new community of readers, writers, and designers of media — a community in which these roles would be much less sharply differentiated than they are now. There are signs that hypertext and hypertextual narrative are moving in this direction. HyperCard, for all its imperfections and despite its egregious lack of a map-driven structure editor, has introduced thousands to the basic concepts of distributed textuality. And more important, the likelihood that HyperTalk will become the scripting language of future Macintosh Systems suggests a future in which "robotic" design decisions will be easy enough to circumvent with the help of HyperTalk "automata." The HyperCard world may constitute the low end of the hypertext enterprise, but it has nonetheless stimulated a number of projects which redefine the idea of interactivity in narrative. Robyn Miller's "Manhole" (Prolog Software, 1988), situates its reader (interagent?) in a spatialized, object-oriented environment that invites a relatively free exploration of a three-dimensional space. John McDaid's fiction-in-progress, "Uncle Buddy's Phantom Funhouse," allows its user to manipulate as well as explore the constraints of its textual space. If one looks beyond HyperCard and the PC world, more sophisticated systems such as Joseph Bates' "Oz" hold the potential for further exploration of truly user-collaborative narrative — though with the prospect of "simulated realities" the Baudrillardian spectre once again presents itself.

The evolution of a new writing space or an "aesthetic of cognitive mapping" asks a lot of the future, but then, there is much indeed at stake. One way or the other, hypertext fiction appears destined to lead us toward a world "where we won't need dungeon masters anymore" — but such an outcome could arise just as easily from the perfection of the dungeon as from its abolition, from the immanence of the masters as well as their eradication. It remains to be seen which world hypertext will ultimately allow us to produce.

VI. REFERENCES

[Bart79]   Barthes, Roland, "From Work to Text," in *Textual Strategies*, Josué Harari, ed., Cornell University Press, Ithaca, NY, 1979., pp. 73-81.

[Baud83]   Baudrillard, Jean, *Simulations*, trans. Paul Foss, Paul Patton, and Philip Beitchman Semiotext(e), New York, 1983.

[Bolt89]   Bolter, Jay David, *Writing Space*, Lawrence Erlbaum Associates, New York, 1989 (to appear).

[Borg62]   Borges, Jorge Luis, *Labyrinths: Selected Stories and Other Writings*, trans. Donald A. Yates and James E. Irby, New Directions, New York, 1962.

[Gibs84]   Gibson, William, *Neuromancer*, Berkeley Books, New York, 1984.

[Hutc88]   Hutcheon, Linda, *A Poetics of Postmodernism: History, Theory, Fiction*, Routledge, New York, 1988.

[Jame86]   Jameson, Frederic, "Postmodernism, or The Cultural Logic of Late Capitalism," *New Left Review* 146 (1984): 53-71.

[Joyc88]   Joyce, Michael, "Siren Shapes: Exploratory and Constructive Hypertexts," *Academic Computing*, November 1988.

[Joyc89]   "Selfish Interaction: Subversive Texts and the Multiple Novel," in Barton D. Thurber, ed., *Literacy in the Computer Age*, Paradigm Press, New York, 1989 (to appear).

[Krok88]   Kroker, Arthur and David Cook, *The Postmodern Scene: Excremental Culture and Hyper-Aesthetics*, 2nd ed., St. Martins, New York, 1988.

[Land87]   Landow, George P., "Relationally Encoded Links and the Rhetoric of Hypertext," *Hypertext '87 Papers*. Hypertext '87 Conference, Chapel Hill, 1987.

[Leav86]   Leavitt, David, "Aliens," in Debra Spark, ed., *20 Under 30*, Scribner's, New York, 1986.

[Mach87]   Machin, Richard and Christopher Norris, "Introduction," in *Post-Structuralist Readings of English Poetry.*, ed. Richard Machin and Christopher Norris, Cambridge: Cambridge University Press, 1987.

[Nies84]   Niesz, Anthony J. and Norman Holland, "Interactive Fiction," *Critical Inquiry* 11 (1984): 104-112.

[Pavi88]   Pavic, Milorad, *Dictionary of the Khazars: A Lexicon Novel in 100,000 Words*, trans. Christina Pribicevic-Zoric, Alfred A. Knopf, New York, 1988.

[Pins87]   Pinsky, Robert and P. Michael Campbell, "Mindwheel: a Game Session," *New England Review/Bread Loaf Quarterly*, 10 (1987): 70-75.

[Poru85]   Porush, David, *The Soft Machine: Cybernetic Fiction*, Methuen, New York, 1985.

Expressing Structural Hypertext Queries in GraphLog

Mariano P. Consens
Alberto O. Mendelzon

Computer Systems Research Institute
University of Toronto
Toronto, Canada M5S 1A4

ABSTRACT

GraphLog is a visual query language in which queries are formulated by drawing graph patterns. The hyperdocument graph is searched for all occurrences of these patterns. The language is powerful enough to allow the specification and manipulation of arbitrary subsets of the network and supports the computation of aggregate functions on subgraphs of the hyperdocument. It can support dynamically defined structures as well as inference capabilities, going beyond current static and passive hypertext systems.

The expressive power of the language is a fundamental issue: too little power limits the applications of the language, while too much makes efficient implementation difficult and probably affects ease of use. The complexity and expressive power of GraphLog can be characterized precisely by using notions from deductive database theory and descriptive complexity. In this paper, from a practical point of view, we present examples of GraphLog queries applied to several different hypertext systems, providing evidence for the expressive power of the language, as well as for the convenience and naturalness of its graphical representation. We also describe an ongoing implementation of the language.

INTRODUCTION

Hypertext systems are intended to support the organization and manipulation of networks of text nodes (or multimedia nodes, for hypermedia) connected by typed links. As current systems start getting more use, several limitations in the basic approach are becoming apparent. In a recent survey [Hala88], seven key issues are identified as requiring work for the next generation of hypertext systems. The first five of these are:

This work has been supported by the Information Technology Research Centre of Ontario and the Natural Science and Engineering Research Council of Canada. The first author was also supported by the PEDECIBA – United Nations Program for the Development of Basic Sciences, Uruguay.

1. **Search and query facilities.** Current systems are heavily oriented towards browsing and network navigation. They lack powerful query languages that allow the specification and manipulation of arbitrary subsets of the network.

2. **Augmenting the basic node and link model.** The directed graph model is too low level to support complex ways of organizing the information in a network.

3. **Virtual Structures.** Hypertext systems support only manual changes to the contents or structure of a network, making them relatively static in practice. It would be desirable to have dynamically defined structures that can make the network reconfigure itself automatically in response to changes.

4. **Computation over graphs.** Current systems are passive; for example, they do not include inference engines that may actively derive new information from what is explicitly stored.

5. **Versioning.** When hypertext technology is applied to the maintenance of large technical documents, or to computer assisted engineering, it is essential to have mechanisms for managing versions and configurations and to control concurrent access reliably.

In this paper we describe a powerful query language for hypertext, called `GraphLog`, that addresses all points 1 to 5 above. Point 3 is addressed by allowing the definition of virtual links, point 4, by supporting computation of aggregate functions on subgraphs of the document graph, and point 5, versioning, by using `GraphLog` to specify versioning policies. Finally, `GraphLog` can be easily extended to more elaborate object-oriented models that address point 2.

`GraphLog` queries are visually oriented; they are formulated by drawing with a graph editor the patterns that are to be searched for in the hypertext network. Halasz distinguishes in [Hala88] between *structural* and *content based* search. Content based searches will find nodes that contain certain patterns; structural searches look for whole subgraphs of the overall graph that have a certain structure. `GraphLog` emphasizes structural queries, although in the conclusions we suggest the integration of structural and content-based queries in a single language.

An important issue in the design of such a language is expressive power: too little power limits the applications of the language, while too much makes efficient implementation difficult and probably affects ease of use. We have two sorts of arguments for the adequacy of the expressive power of `GraphLog`. Elsewhere, we have used notions from deductive database theory and descriptive complexity to characterize from a theoretical point of view the class of queries that can be formulated in the language[1][Cons89]. In this paper, from a practical point of view, we survey several existing hypertext systems and queries described by their authors and show how they can all be expressed in `GraphLog`.

---

[1]In fact, the name of the language comes from its close relationship to Datalog, in turn a relative of Prolog.

THE QUERY LANGUAGE

The graph-based query language G^+ provided a starting point for `GraphLog`. We have extended G^+ by adding negation and changing the semantics to make the definition of the language simpler. In `GraphLog`, an interrelated collection of documents – a hyperdocument – is viewed as a directed labelled graph. A *query* is a graph pattern containing one distinguished edge. The effect of the query is to find all instances of the pattern that occur in the hyperdocument and for each one of them define the "virtual link" represented by the distinguished edge. Graph patterns are themselves graphs, and they can be specified by drawing them on a screen.

The formal semantics of the language is given in [Cons89]. Each query is given a precise meaning by associating it with a set of recursive Horn clauses defined on the relations that make up the graph. Instead of giving the full definition of the language here, we will introduce it by a series of examples and informal explanations.

Consider a hierarchical document where there are nodes for each chapter, section, subsection, etc., and edges labelled `contains` relate each part to its subparts. The query in Figure 1 defines a virtual link `top` that points from each component of the document directly to the top-level component. In this case the pattern is a pair of nodes connected by an arbitrary sequence of `contains` links such that the second node has no incoming `contains` link. For each such pattern, the query defines a `top` link between these nodes. Note the regular expression `contains`$^+$ labelling a dashed edge in the query. This means the pattern to be found is a path composed of any number of edges, each one labelled with `contains`. In general, any regular expression may be used; for example, if instead of `contains`, the graph used several different link types such as `has-chapter`, `has-section`, `has-subsection`, we could replace the regular expression `contains`$^+$ with (`has-chapter` | `has-section` | `has-subsection`)$^+$. The crossed-out edge in the query means that a node only qualifies as a `top` node if there is *no* `contains` edge coming into it.

This simple example already shows that `GraphLog` can express queries that are not expressible in conventional database languages such as relational algebra. The dashed edge, standing for a path of arbitrary length, corresponds to an arbitrarily long sequence of "join" operators, and there is no single relational algebra query equivalent to it, as is well known in database theory [Aho79].

What can we do with a virtual link such as `top` once we have defined it? We have three possibilities. First, we may wish to treat it simply as the answer to a query, that is, to display it to the user in some form and then forget it. Second, we may wish to incorporate it into the document, treating it as a *snapshot*. In this case, the link as computed by the query will remain in the document, but it will not be affected by future changes. Finally, we may make it into a *view*, meaning that not only does it get incorporated to the document, but it is also kept dynamically up to date, so that if, say, a new leaf node is added to the tree, its `top` link is automatically inserted. This choice is independent of the query language and would be made by the user interface in consultation with the user.

From the point of view of a user, once a link is created it can be manipulated in the same ways no matter whether it is a snapshot, a view, or a manually created set

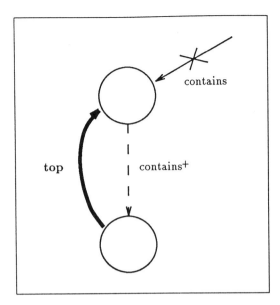

Figure 1: Defining a virtual link.

of edges. As an example of this, suppose that after creating the **top** link we realize that the network is not really a hierarchy, because there are nodes that belong to more than one document. We now want to link explicitly all top level nodes that share a component document. The query in Figure 2 generates a **shares-with** link between any two top nodes that have a common sub-document.

So far we have shown edges labelled only with a property name. This is the simplest case, and the label corresponds to the type of the link. In general, an edge may be labelled with a literal of the form $p(c_1, ..., c_n)$, associating n atomic values with the relationship between the endpoints.

Consider for example a rather different hyperdocument that might be used by a travel agency. The nodes contain textual and pictorial information about cities. One type of link between cities represents flights. We could then have edge labels of the form flight(Airline,Departure,Arrival). Another type of link gives distance information. Edge labels for this kind of links have the form dist(Distance). These values can be used in queries in many ways. Figure 3 shows a query that defines a link ind-dist(D) between Toronto and Vancouver by adding the Toronto-Calgary distance to the Calgary-Vancouver distance. Note that we are modelling node attributes such as city name by edges going to rectangular nodes. This is just to keep the data model as simple as possible; it is straigthforward to incorporate node attributes explicitly if we wish.

This last example was somewhat artificial; it would make more sense, if we do not know the distance between Toronto and Vancouver, to estimate it as the *smallest* sum of distances from Toronto to some city C and from C to Vancouver. Figure 4 shows how the *aggregate operator* min can be used in GraphLog to express this. The distinguished edge will be labelled by ind-dist(S) where S is the smallest of all sums defined above. The fact that the intermediate node is doubly circled is

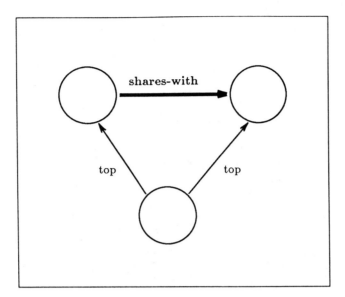

Figure 2: Documents that share a component.

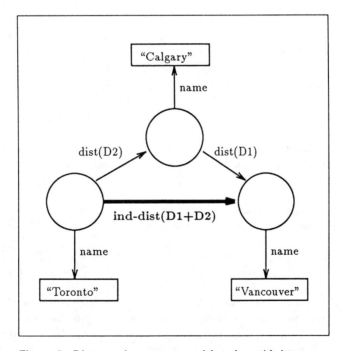

Figure 3: Distance between two cities via a third one.

meant to suggest that we are computing an aggregate over all possible choices of this intermediate node.

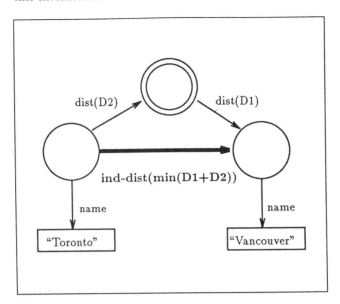

Figure 4: Distance between two cities via any third one.

Next, as the reader may expect, we are going to generalize Figure 4 to compute the *shortest distance* between Toronto and Vancouver independently of how many intermediate cities we go through. Instead of simply adding two distances, we now need to be able to add all distances appearing along a path of arbitrary length between Toronto and Vancouver. The dashed edge in Figure 5 between the two cities represents these paths. The distinguished edge will be labelled with the minimum over all paths of the sum of the distances along each path. Note the label on the path between Toronto and Vancouver is dist($\{D\}$)$^+$, not dist(D)$^+$. This is because a label dist(D)$^+$ would mean we are looking for paths such that, for some distance D, all hops along the path are of length D, which is not what we want. The notation $\{D\}$ is meant to suggest that we want to collect the *set* of all distances because we are going to apply the *path summarization operator* sum to them.

EXPRESSIVE POWER

The expressive power of `GraphLog` can be characterized precisely from a theoretical point of view by relating it to the language of function-free Horn clauses called *Datalog*. Ignoring aggregate operators, `GraphLog` turns out to be equivalent to what is called *piecewise-linear, stratified Datalog*, a version of Datalog in which recursive rules are restricted to use the predicate being defined only once in its definition and negation is allowed in a controlled way [Ullm88]. Interestingly, the queries expressible in the language are exactly those than can be computed in space logarithmic in the size of the database. `GraphLog` with aggregate operators is more expressive than the relational algebra and calculus with aggregates of [Klug82]. We

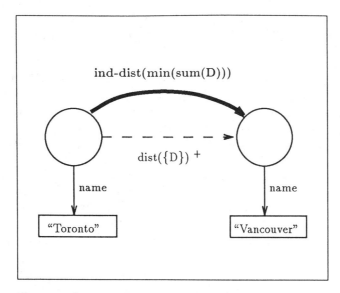

Figure 5: Shortest distance between two cities.

will not present these results here; see [Cons89] for the details.

From a practical point, we will now present examples of how `GraphLog` could be used in the context of several different hypertext systems, providing evidence for the expressive power of the language, as well as for the convenience and naturalness of its graphical representation.

NoteCards

NoteCards [Hala87] is an "idea processing" hypertext system. Nodes in NoteCards are the electronic analog of the 3×5 familiar paper notecard. A web of typed links interconnect the note cards in a hyperdocument.

An application of the NoteCards system described in [Hala87] consisted in authoring a public policy research paper. One kind of link used by the author, *supports* links, connected notecards with supporting arguments. The next two examples illustrate the possibilities of `GraphLog` in an idea processing hypertext system.

Example 1: Assume that in addition to linking notecards with supporting arguments, the author indicated her belief in the strength of the support by assigning it a number between 0 and 1. The strength could be represented by an edge label of the form supports(S).

The graphical query in Figure 6 defines a virtual link most-reliable(R) that connects notecard N1 to the notecard N2 containing its most reliable unsupported argument, and also gives the reliability R of this argument. A notecard N2 not supported by any other card is defined to be the most reliable unsupported argument for N1 if the weakest link in the chain of arguments from N2 to N1 is stronger than the weakest link in any other such chain. Making this connection into a virtual link would keep it updated as the author's beliefs change and new arguments are incorporated or old ones deleted.

Note there are two boxes in this query. The first one defines a property of nodes called supported; the bottom one uses this property to find most reliable unsupported arguments. The two queries could have been combined into one box in this case; in general, it is convenient to be able to break a query down into several steps, defining at each step intermediate links that can be used in subsequent steps. The user need not be concerned with the exact order in which the different steps are executed; the system will determine an ordering that ensures each link is computed before it needs to be used, as long as there are no cycles in this ordering. Sets of queries with cyclic orderings are syntactically forbidden. □

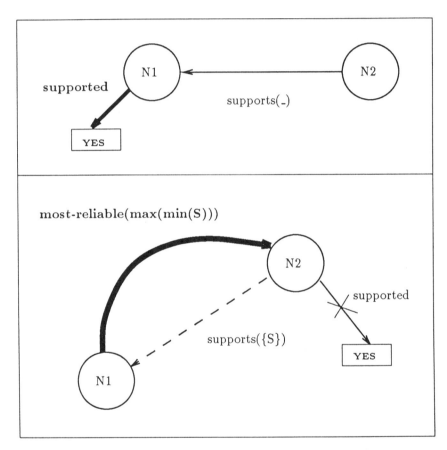

Figure 6: Creating a virtual link to the most reliable unsupported evidence.

Example 2: Suppose an author is writing a collaborative research paper and need to see what cards have been created recently by her co-authors. Figure 7 shows the query graph that defines a set of nodes with the notecards created by someone other than the author in the last three days (the constant TODAY is a "system provided" value for the current date). Note that, instead of defining any new links, we simply highlight one of the nodes in the query to indicate that we just want the resulting set of nodes as the answer. ☐

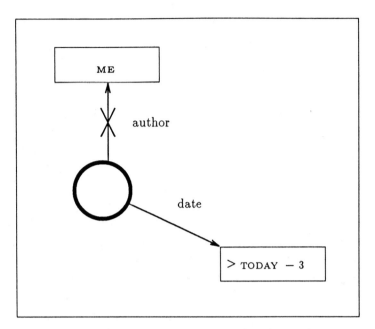

Figure 7: Nodes created by someone else in the last three days.

gIBIS

The gIBIS hypertext system has a specific objective: "to provide a systems design team with a medium in which all of their work can be computer-mediated and supported" [Bege88]. It provides a hypertext environment for the IBIS design methodology. IBIS supports the constructive discussion of the issues that arise during the design process by presenting positions that respond to the issues and arguments that support or object to the positions.

Nodes in gIBIS are of three kinds: they hold either an issue, a position or an argument. There is also a fixed number of link types. For example, a position responds-to an argument and an argument either supports or objects-to its position.

Example 3: Figure 8 shows the graphical query that finds the issues with at least two positions without arguments (another example query from [Hala88]). ☐

Example 4: This example illustrates the use of GraphLog in a typical "ad-hoc" query: how popular are an author's positions in a gIBIS hyperdocument? We will break this query down into three steps. The first two associate with each position P two links called count-s and count-o that point to nodes containing respectively

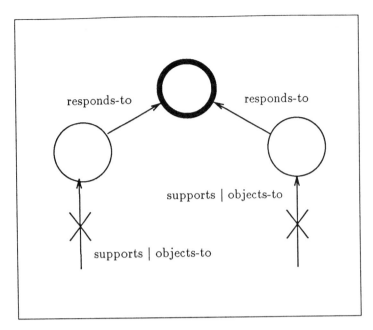

Figure 8: Issues with at least two positions without arguments.

the total number of arguments that support P and the total number of arguments that object to P. The third step computes the average of the support-to-objection ratio for the author's positions and stores this average as the "popularity" of the author. Figure 9 shows the graphical query that results. □

In gIBIS, a user can also group an issue together with its positions and corresponding arguments into what constitutes an IPA (issue-position-argument) composite node. This IPA composite node is used to record the decision reached on an issue. GraphLog would allow a flexible selection of what nodes should be grouped in a composite.

History Mechanism

A very useful aid to avoid dissorientation when browsing a hyperdocument is the history mechanism. Systems that support a history mechanism (like ZOG/KMS and HyperCard) provide the user with virtual links that connect in sequence the last nodes visited.

A slightly more sophisticated history mechanism would create attributes for the nodes in the history trace, recording for each node the time at which the user opened and closed the node. The following example illustrates a GraphLog query that uses the history mechanism to locate previously neglected relevant information.

Example 5: After a couple of hours of working within a hyperdocument, a user realizes that while avoiding distractions by not following links named digression he

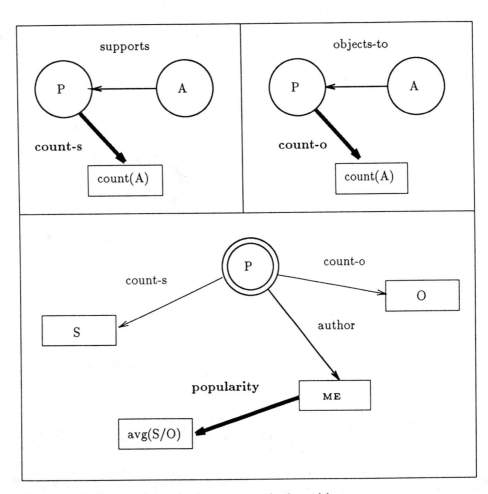

Figure 9: Finding out how popular are an author's positions.

probably missed some important point. He wonders:

> "Where did I see a link labelled "digression"? I remember that it was between 2 and 3 hours ago."

Figure 10 shows the query graph that helps the user to trim down the search. The constants HERE and NOW are "system provided" values for the currently open node and the current time, respectively. Note how the arithmetic comparisons "<" and ">" are represented by links like any other relationship between nodes, although both the links and the nodes to which they point are virtual in this case. □

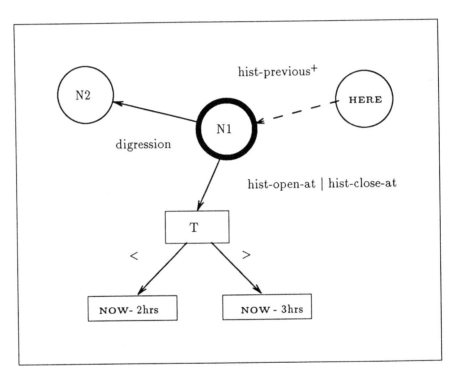

Figure 10: Searching back the history mechanism.

DynamicDesign

DynamicDesign [Bige87, Bige88] is a CASE (Computer-Aided Software Engineering) environment for the C programming language implemented as a front-end to the HAM hypertext storage system.

The nodes store all the components of a software engineering project. A node attribute, project-component, takes values that indicate the kind of component stored in the node: requirement, specification, object-code, source-code (one C function is stored per node), library, comment, dictionary (i.e., symbol table), etc.

The links are used to relate the different components. A link attribute, relation, describes the kind of relationship between nodes: calls (between functions stored in source code nodes), refers-to (from a function to a dictionary; it describes the C variable referred to in the function and has an additional attribute with the name of the C variable), in-library (from functions to libraries), implements (from functions to specifications), follows-from (describing the linear order between nodes when printed or compiled), etc.

DynamicDesign answers some queries on the structure of the hyperdocument of a software engineering project:

- What does a function do? (follows comments, implements)

- Who (directly) calls this function? (follows calls)

- What is this variable used for? (follows comments)

- Who (directly) uses this variable? (follows refers-to(V))

The importance of these queries is clear. It is also clear that there are several other relevant queries (e.g., who directly or indirectly uses this function?), and that not all of them can be anticipated and "built into" the environment.

Adding GraphLog to DynamicDesign allows dynamic specification of queries that were not anticipated by the system designers. The different values of the relation link attribute can be used to define GraphLog virtual links calls, follows-from, in-library, implements and refers-to(V), where V is a C variable name. The example below illustrates one application of GraphLog in the DynamicDesign hypertext system. It also introduces a new feature of the language, link inversion.

Example 6: Figure 11 shows the query graph that finds the functions F1 that share a variable with some function F2 implementing (directly or indirectly) the io-spec specifications, but not belonging to the syncio library nor calling any function in it. The refers-to(V) links from nodes F1 and F2 to node D means that variable V, defined in dictionary D, is referenced in both nodes. Note the "− calls" label on the path from F2 to io-spec. We are looking for a path from function F2 to some specification whose name is io-spec. The path may be a direct one, in which case we do not use the "− calls" part, or it may be that F2 is at the end of a chain of functions G_1, G_2, ..., G_n, such that G_1 implements io-spec and each G_i calls G_{i+1}, and G_n calls F2. The edges from G_i to G_{i+1} go in the opposite direction to the path; this is the purpose of the inversion operator "−". Similarly, the in-library link is inverted in the path from F2 to syncio. Notice that the node labelled with variable D is not strictly necessary; it could have been omitted by using a link from node F1 to node F2 labelled "refers-to(V) − refers-to(V)". □

The HAM versioning mechanism is particularly useful for a CASE application. The next example illustrates a query that uses a link next-version to locate a specific piece of code.

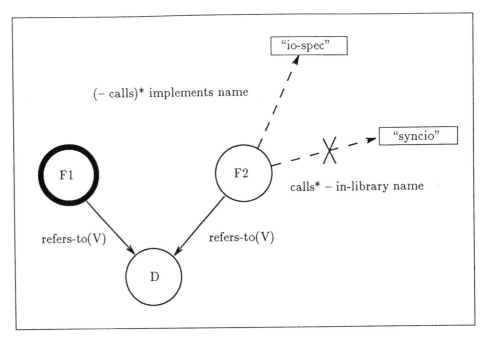

Figure 11: Finding code in hypertext CASE.

Example 7: Suppose a programmer has to find the code for a particular function, and she gives the following information:

> "I am looking for the last version of a function that implements the security-spec; the first versions were done by myself; then Dennis took charge of it; I do not remember the authors that followed him; maybe Dorothy or Chris were in charge before Jeff, who I am sure wrote the current version."

The graphical query of Figure 12 finds the functions satisfying the above description. The first graph simply adds to the existing link between two successive versions a new link indicating who is the author of the second version. The second graph looks for the current version of functions F1 that implement, directly or indirectly, the security-spec specification and are preceded by a chain of versions satisfying the rather vague criteria the user has in mind. Note that, even though the system does not support approximate search, the flexibility of regular expressions does provide some of the power of approximate matching. In particular, the ocurrence of an underscore in a regular expression involving closure means that we are looking for an arbitrary sequence of values along a path. □

HAM Versioning

Versioning is an important feature in hypermedia systems [Hala88, Garg88]. The specific details of versioning mechanisms differ from system to system. An advantage

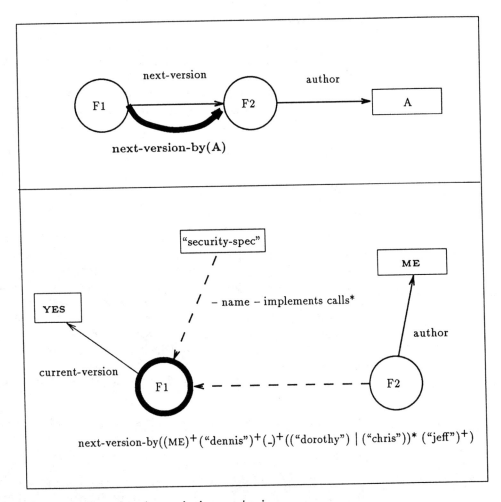

Figure 12: Querying the versioning mechanism.

of a query language like `GraphLog`, that has the capability to describe revision sequences, is that it can specify quite clearly these details as well as implement variations of the versioning policies originally provided by the hypertext system.

Example 8: In the HAM, a link may or may not keep linking the most recent versions of the nodes it connects. This is a user's choice, selected by setting to YES or NO a keep-up-to-date link attribute defined by the system. Keeping links up to date is the default policy, while not doing so is useful to retain links between previous (fixed) node versions.

Figure 13 describes the "keep up to date" policy for link versions in the HAM. To simplify the graphical query, current-version is defined simultaneously for links and nodes in the first query graph. The second query graph defines the from relation between a link and its start-point node to be kept up to date with the last node (and link) version if the keep-up-to-date attribute is set to YES. The third query graph contemplates the situation where no "keeping up to date" is desired. □

Dynamic Medical Handbook

In the Dynamic Medical Handbook [Fris88b, Fris88a] a content-based query is given as a set of keywords and the sectioning structure of the hyperdocument is used to help find the best starting points (i.e., either a chapter, section, subsection, and so on) for the interested reader. This search mechanism constitutes an interesting and non-trivial example of the combination of content-based and structural search. The algorithm first assigns an intrinsic weight for each card and keyword that is directly proportional to the number of keyword occurrences in the card and inversely proportional to the total number of occurrences of a keyword in the whole hyperdocument. Then a total weight is recursively propagated from the leaves to the root of the sectioning structure. The contributions of subsections to sections decrease exponentially with their distance in the sectioning hierarchy.

Example 9: The selection of the best starting points for the content-based query (i.e., those nodes with highest total-weight) can be expressed in `GraphLog` as shown in Figure 14.

We assume that a weight is associated with each node by the link weight and that the relation section-of describes a tree. Note the notation [C] following the section-of* expression. This means that variable C will store the length (number of edges) of each path that matches the regular expression. With this in mind, the query can be interpreted as follows. For each document component N2, for each section or sub-section N1 of N2 that is at distance C from N2 in the document tree and has weight W, add $W/(2^C)$ to the total weight of N2. □

Note that, as our queries become more ambitious, their representation in `GraphLog` becomes more complex. We do not envision an end user composing queries like the ones in Figures 13 or 14; rather, `GraphLog` could be used as a tool to allow a system

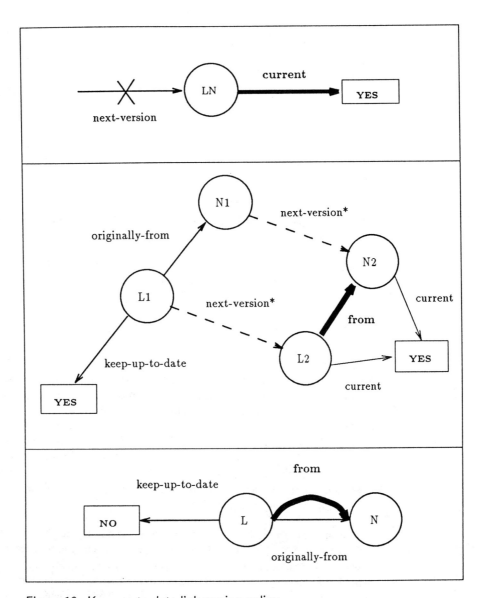

Figure 13: Keep up to date link version policy.

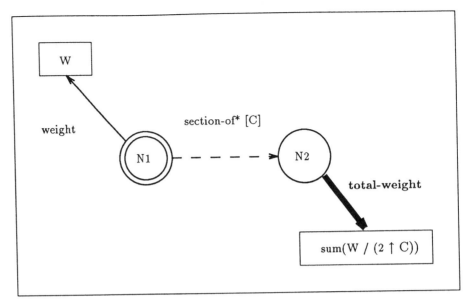

Figure 14: Selecting the optimal starting points in content-based search.

designer to provide a useful repertoire of "canned" queries, in much the same way that database query languages are used in large information systems.

HyperCard

We conclude this section by considering the application of GraphLog to the extremely simple model of Apple HyperCard. Stacks are composed of cards, and cards are related by links whose only property is the icon associated with the "button" at the start-point of the link. An interesting version of GraphLog can be adapted to this model that, although limited, will be a convenient improvement to the information retrieval capabilities of HyperCard. Instead of using symbolic labels on the edges, we can label them with the iconic button corresponding to the link. Regular expressions can be used as before. In addition, nodes in query graphs denoting stacks can be represented by the corresponding icons rather than by simple circles or rectangles.

This simple "GraphLog on HyperCard" query language has potential for two important extensions. The first is combining HyperCard content search with the structure search represented by a query graph; i.e., strings that must be present in the text fields of cards can be associated with the corresponding nodes in the query graph. The second extension is to allow, in addition to the specification of strings that must be present in cards, the invocation of an arbitrary HyperTalk script[2] in association with a node in a query graph that will allow the specification of more complex conditions that must be satisfied by the corresponding cards.

---

[2] HyperTalk is a special purpose programming language that provides extensibility to the HyperCard system.

PROTOTYPE IMPLEMENTATION

This section describes an ongoing implementation of `GraphLog`. The prototype is actually based on the earlier language G^+ and is being extended to handle full `GraphLog`. We refer to this system as the G^+ Prototype.

The original effort consisted in the specialization of a Smalltalk-80™ [Gold83, Gold84] graph editor product (NodeGraph-80 [Adam87]) for editing query graphs and displaying database graphs. The resulting editor supports graph "cutting and pasting", as well as text editing of node and edge labels, node and edge repositioning and reshaping, storage and retrieval of graphs as text files, etc.

Once the Graph Editor was available, the Query Evaluation component was developed to support G^+ edge queries. These are simple queries containing two nodes with one (possible dashed) edge connecting them, labelled with an arbitrary regular expression. The algorithms used to search the database for answers are discussed in [Mend89].

In Figure 15 the small G^+ GraphEditor window at the top of the screen contains an edge query. The large G^+ Graph Editor window shows the flights hypertext database mentioned in the section that introduced `GraphLog`.

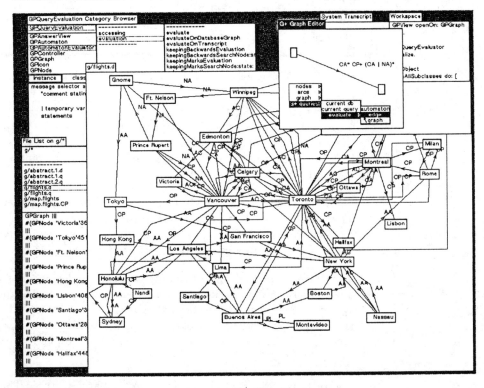

Figure 15: Invoking the evaluation of a G^+ edge query.

Figure 16 shows a screen dump displaying one of the answers of the query in Figure 15 by highlighting one path described by the query on the database graph.

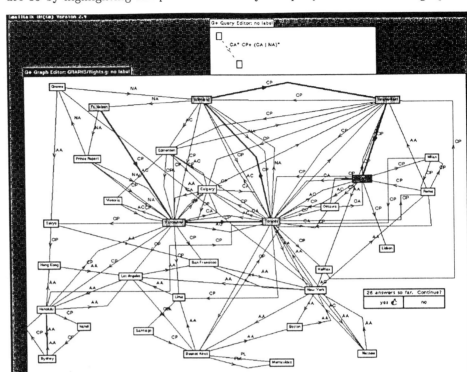

Figure 16: Displaying the answers of a G$^+$ edge query.

Rather than viewing the answers superimposed on the database graph, the user may choose to view them in a separate window called a graph collection browser. Figure 17 shows one such window. The left pane contains a list of paths that were found to satisfy the query, represented by their end points, and one such path is being displayed in the right pane.

Finally, the user may select to collect all the answers together into one new graph. This graph in turn may be queried, providing a mechanism for iterative filtering of irrelevant information until a manageable subgraph is obtained. Figure 18 shows an answer graph in which only American Airlines flights have been retained.

The current state of the prototype consists of the ongoing implementation of a query interface for the GraphLog query language on top of the Neptune hypertext system front-end to the Hypertext Abstract Machine (HAM) [Deli86]. The HAM is a general-purpose, transaction-based, multi-user server for a hypertext storage system. The HAM model is general enough to implement any current hypertext system [Camp87].

Figure 19 is a diagram of the G$^+$ Prototype architecture. The G$^+$ Query Interface and the G$^+$ Query Evaluation constitute the implementation of the G$^+$ Prototype. So far, the evaluation is being prototyped as a Smalltalk-80 program running as a client of the HAM within the Neptune environment. A more mature implementation

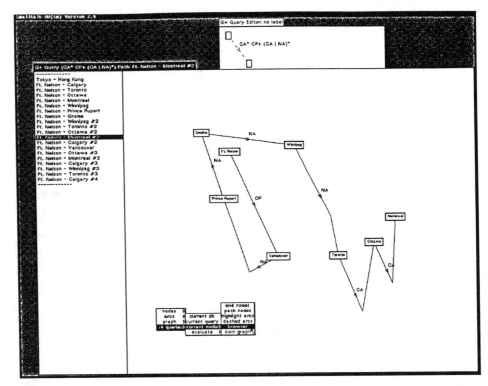

Figure 17: Displaying the answers in a browser.

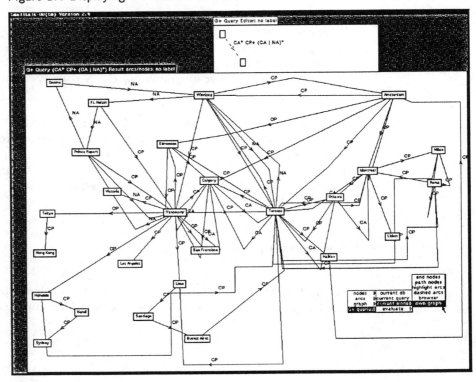

Figure 18: Displaying the answers in a single graph.

will have the evaluation components down-loaded to the HAM server.

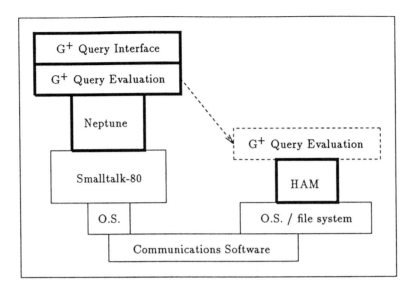

Figure 19: G$^+$ Prototype architecture.

CONCLUSIONS

We have described a powerful structural query language for hypertext. The language can express a large variety of queries that arise naturally in several different hypertext systems. It has a sound theoretical basis taken from the theory of database query languages and logic programming, but is visually oriented and avoids explicit use of logic formulae or recursion.

The next step in the development of GraphLog should be to integrate structure-based search with content-based search. Since regular expressions are already an essential part of the language, it is natural to do this by allowing each node in a query graph to be qualified by searching its contents for substrings matching a regular expression. This can be combined with value-based queries on node attributes for a completely general query language.

ACKNOWLEDGMENTS

The authors are grateful to Fred Lochovsky for his helpful comments and to Christine Knight and Frank Eigler for their contributions to the prototype.

REFERENCES

[Adam87] Sam S. Adams. *NodeGraph-80 Version 1.0*. Knowledge Systems Corporation, 1987.

[Aho79]   A.V. Aho and J.D. Ullman. Universality of data retrieval languages. In *Proc. 6th ACM Symp. on Principles of Programming Languages*, pages 110–120, 1979.

[Bege88] Michael L. Begeman and Jeff Conklin. The right tool for the job. *BYTE*, pages 255–266, October 1988.

[Bige88] James Bigelow. Hypertext and CASE. *IEEE Transactions on Software Engineering*, pages 23–27, 1988.

[Bige87] James Bigelow and Victor Riley. Manipulating source code in DynamicDesign. In *Hypertext'87 Workshop*, pages 397–408, 1987.

[Camp87] Brad Campbell and Joseph M. Goodman. HAM: A general-purpose hypertext abstract machine. In *Hypertext'87 Workshop*, pages 21–31, 1987.

[Cons89] Mariano P. Consens. Graphlog: "real life" recursive queries using graphs. Master's thesis, Department of Computer Science, University of Toronto, 1989.

[Deli86] N. Delisle and M. Schwartz. Neptune: A hypertext system for CAD applications. In Carlo Zaniolo, editor, *Proceedings of ACM-SIGMOD 1986 International Conference on Management of Data*, pages 132–142, 1986.

[Fris88a] Mark Frisse. From text to hypertext. *BYTE*, pages 247–253, October 1988.

[Fris88b] Mark Frisse. Searching for information in a hypertext medical handbook. *Communications of the ACM*, 31(7):880–886, 1988.

[Garg88] Pankaj K. Garg. Abstraction mechanisms in hypertext. *Communications of the ACM*, 31(7):862–879, 1988.

[Gold84] Adele Goldberg. *Smalltalk-80: The Interactive Environment*. Addison-Wesley, 1984.

[Gold83] Adele Goldberg and David Robson. *Smalltalk-80: The Language and its Implementation*. Addison-Wesley, 1983.

[Hala88] Frank G. Halasz. Reflections on NoteCards: Seven issues for the next generation of hypermedia systems. *Communications of the ACM*, 31(7):836–852, 1988.

[Hala87] F.G. Halasz, T. P. Moran, and H.R. Triggs. NoteCards in a nutshell. In *ACM Conference of Human Factors in Computer Systems*, pages 45–52, 1987.

[Klug82]   Anthony Klug. Equivalence of relational algebra and relational calculus query languages having aggregate functions. *Journal of the ACM*, 29(3):699–717, 1982.

[Mend89]   A.O. Mendelzon and P.T. Wood. Finding regular simple paths in graph databases. In *Proc. 15th International Conference on Very Large Data Bases*, 1989.

[Ullm88]   J.D. Ullman. *Principles of Database and Knowledge-Base Systems*, volume 1. Computer Science Press, Potomac, Md., 1988.

VISAR: A System for Inference and Navigation in Hypertext

Peter Clitherow, Doug Riecken and Michael Muller

Bellcore
444 Hoes Lane
Piscataway, NJ 08854

Abstract

Hypertext systems have traditionally been constructed by hand. This process can stand improvement in several aspects: it is laborious; requires a human to understand the text and infer all the relationships between the concepts/topics; and while the resulting hypertext may be traversed by a reader in an arbitrary fashion, s/he may still find it difficult to understand the concepts as expressed by the builder of the hypertext.

We present a knowledge-intensive assistant for building hypertext fragments from a knowledge base customised both explicitly and implicitly by a user. Such a presentation may clarify relationships between concepts that were present implicitly in multiple sources of information. In the domain of an intelligent information retrieval system, we show how such an assistant may render customised views of knowledge extracted in a manageable form.

While the presentation medium of the original system is graphic, we also speculate that presentation of the information in alternative hypermedia appears to be straightforward.

1 Introduction and Problem Statement

If we are ever to fulfill the promise of a global hypertext network covering all the world's literature, it seems clear that machine assistance will be needed in both its construction and access. Machine accessible material generally falls into two general categories: that of traditional database records, accessible through full text searching and information retrieval systems; and hypertext systems with their own access mechanisms, sometimes encompassing full text search and keyword retrieval. Neither of these offers the scalability and utility needed for such a large-scale project.

Halasz [11] has noted that typical hypertext systems such as NoteCards are deficient in navigation aids for unfamiliar heterogeneous networks. Typically, users develop a feel for a network simply by exploring it --- however, this is obviously not practical for hypertext networks consisting of tens of thousands of nodes, or those that will be created dynamically. The development of structural queries and compositional nodes are also identified as interesting --- such things would be powerful aids to navigation in the network.

Salton [21] presents a glimpse of a future hypertext system derived from analysis of the structure of a document (sections, paragraphs, etc.) and he notes that vocabulary matching methods and link traversal algorithms (spreading activation) can be used to retrieve related parts of a document (corresponding to related nodes in a hypertext network). However, this kind of approach only works well on documents with predefined structure, such as manuals.

In the evolution of hypertext systems to more semantic rather than syntactic approaches, we find that the access and retrieval mechanisms must also reflect this change. Hypertext systems may learn from the research in Information Retrieval (IR). While classic IR techniques perform statistical computations on words to categorize a document (perhaps corresponding to many hypertext nodes), decide whether or not it was relevant to a query, and return a match index, there are more recent methods that:

o   determine relevance through a deliberately approximate eigenvector representation based on the entire information space and performed in advance of the query [6]

o   decompose a linear document into a fish-eye view with user-controlled dynamically changeable depth and breadth [7]

o   collect reference objects in a relatively "passive" or "grazing" manner for later review by the user [8]

o   use knowledge-based techniques to maintain user profiles to improve completeness and selectivity of retrieved information [15]

o   perform aliased keyword matches across a distributed network of heterogeneous data objects [22]

o   find relationships between two concepts through their being referenced in the same document. [23]

All these approaches promise to perform better than "raw" keyword retrieval algorithms, yet they still do not allow the system to give the intelligent assistance that is surely needed for *manipulating* the results --- they are unable to give an account of *why* a certain citation was deemed appropriate, and so on.

We present a prototype of such a system --- VISAR,[1] that addresses some of these problems --- in particular, the inference and navigation aspects. VISAR constitutes a step along the path of gradual evolution from purely classic "syntactic" Hypertext systems, to more complex Hypertext with "semantics", after systems such as Thoth-II [4].

2 Overview and domain of VISAR

The VISAR system has been created to serve the function of an intelligent assistant for a research practitioner in the spirit of Knoesphere [12]. VISAR's specific purpose is to perform an initial survey of some field of interest to a researcher, presenting relationships between concepts that enable such an expert to focus on particular aspects to be explored in research. Traditionally, a researcher performing such a task undertakes a literature survey --- either by hand using the various abstracts journals, or with an online service, directly or through a professional intermediary. Both these approaches suffer from major problems, such as:

---

[1]James Hogan provided the inspiration for the name VISAR. While the system's goals are less ambitious than those of its namesake in *Giant's Star* (Ballentine Books, New York) we feel our use of the name parallels his intention.

o Problems of scale --- a typical response to a query from an information retrieval system might be "there are 571 hits: do you wish to see them all?".

o Precision problems, when the output returned has low actual relevance.

o Recall problems, such as not getting all (or even most) of the information relevant to your needs that's in the data base actually returned to you.

Several studies, such as [20], document these shortcomings more completely. The VISAR prototype is an attempt to solve some of these problems.

VISAR takes a request from a user and returns a set of citations (from a knowledge base) that seem to be related to the user's needs. However, VISAR differs in two important respects from existing systems that perform similar tasks:

o It allows a user to specify *relationships* between *concepts* rather than boolean combination of keywords for input.

o Instead of returning a ranked list of titles of citations in return, it presents a personal information representation (*perinrep*), that is a conceptual reduction of the relationships between concepts found that seem to be related to the request. A perinrep is a form of hypertext fragment --- the concepts involved, without the traditional associated body of text.

This last feature allows a user to gather an "overview" of what the retrieved citations convey in a conceptual sense.

Briefly, then VISAR:

1 takes a textual request from a user,

2 fleshes this out with related concepts from a default perinrep, giving a request perinrep,

3 performs inference in the Cyc knowledge base to find "matching" conceptual relationships,

4 applies concept reduction strategies to present manageable quantities of information.

This is illustrated in figure 1. The system and its features are elaborated in the following sections.

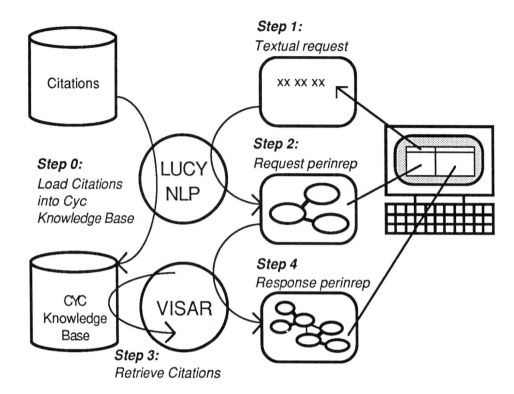

Figure 1. Functional Diagram of VISAR.

3 The *Perinrep* concept

A perinrep is simply a (small) slice of the semantic network, which VISAR has chosen to present to the user. Users obtain information by manipulating perinreps as described in section 6.2. For the moment, we will state that a perinrep is displayed on a bitmapped screen as a graph structure linking nodes which represent concepts. The lower right hand window of figure 2 shows the way in which a perinrep is presented to the user by VISAR.

There are two perinreps of interest here --- the request perinrep and the retrieval perinrep. The request perinrep is a graph representing the user's current *focus of attention*. It is created in two ways:

o   by merging a textual request with a previously existing perinrep, or

o   by direct manipulation of the request perinrep itself by the user.

We use [13] to represent and manipulate perinreps and citations. Cyc may be viewed as a vast semantic net containing the beginnings of "consensus reality" implemented with sophisticated representation and inference languages [14].

Initially, a default perinrep is created (or retrieved) for the user. This is a form of generalization of the "user profile" concept, in that it contains relationships between Cyc concepts, rather than lists of keywords. The default perinrep contains information relating to social groupings (organizational culture in a corporation for instance), professional interests, recreational interests, educational background, and context from previous interactions with VISAR. Each of the entities in the default perinrep has associated with it a "relevance", e.g., high, low and so on. (These are actually proper units pertaining to relative value in Cyc.)

This is combined with the specific conceptual relationships being sought by a user to give the "request perinrep" (lower left screen of figure 2) --- section 5 explains this process in detail.[2]

The retrieved perinrep is an abstraction of the concepts and their relationships that VISAR considers appropriate responses to a user request. It's important to reduce the complexity of the information to be presented by abstraction (simply) to make large quantities of information more digestible. Another way of thinking about this (due to Rau in [19]), is that the retrieved perinreps are isomorphic (as sub-graphs) in some way (depending on how closely related the concepts are) to the request perinrep sub-graph --- VISAR is being used to perform a kind of sub-graph matching.

4 Initial acquisition of the citations

Before VISAR can perform the work described in this paper, it is initialized with a corpus of technical citations (typically journal and conference articles, rather than books[3]), in standard ASCII format. The titles of these are parsed by the LUCY natural language processing system (NLP) [24], into a syntactic structure which relates the components in a functional way, corresponding to their positions as subjects and objects in the syntactic structure of the sentence. Though we have tested this process separately, it is not integrated with the rest of VISAR yet --- most of the citation titles in our test knowledge base have been entered by hand. Further details of the parsing process are recorded in [2].

Of course, this approach is predicated on the assumption that a title accurately conveys the contents of the whole paper. A much more accurate assessment could be done if we were to use NLP to process the whole document. Unfortunately, this is well beyond the capabilities of current discourse analysis systems, but is an ongoing topic of interest to researchers.

Syntactic words can have mappings onto Cyc concepts (units in Cyc terminology --- e.g., Cyclist), e.g.,

connectionist <-- Cyc unit *NeuralNetworkSoftwareArchitecture*

From this, VISAR can deduce "who's doing what to whom". For instance, the sub-title of the paper you are currently reading, "A System for Inference and Navigation in Hypertext", can be parsed into:[4]

"A instance of a computer program that facilitates two specific activities, namely inference and navigation, in a specific domain, hypertext."

The actual representation follows the example given above.

Moreover, these concepts themselves have a relationship in the Cyc ontology, from which we can infer relationships to still other concepts that may be of interest to a user. For instance, *Hypertext* has a specific relationship to *PublishedMaterial* and

---

[2] This mechanism might fulfill some of the promise of Rich's work [17].

[3] This is because such articles usually handle a small number of concepts in depth, rather than a large number less deeply, hence are arguably more likely to be a reference source of choice for the researcher.

[4] This is one of the two parses LUCY generates.

ComputerProgram. (This is not to claim that Cyc has as well connected a network as humans do of course)

Thus, the knowledge present in VISAR is more akin to that in knowledge bases used in AI, rather than traditional hypertext systems. We see this as a necessary transition if hypertext systems are to fulfill their promised utility as systems to assist humans, rather than to present more data. VISAR's task can be seen as that of assisting a user searching through a vast semantic hypertext network, extracting and presenting small digestible parts of it.

5 Inference in VISAR

Using the process above we have incorporated representations of citations in our Cyc-based knowledge base. A inference process is used to decide which of the represented citations should be presented to the user; there are others that are obtained "for free" because of the Cyc concept representation used in VISAR. To perform these inferences, we have on hand three objects: the default perinrep, a textual request and the Cyc knowledge base itself. Let us suppose that a user has typed a request:

"Search for cognitive model of music"

We use the same LUCY technology described above to parse this into relationships between Cyc units, the salient parts of which are expressed in the left window of figure 2.

Now, the units explicitly requested by the textual request are combined with those of the default perinrep using the HCC function (see section 6.1), by finding concepts in the perinrep that are more general than those in the explicit request. The purpose of this process is to "flesh" out a request with implicit information (in a way analogous to the process of anaphora resolution), so as to aid the inference proper. Thus, in the above request, the Cyc unit *CognitiveModel* might be related to other concepts implicit in a user's context, such as *AIProblemSolving*.

Our process of inference is a form of matching of the request perinrep (a graph structure) with structures in the knowledge base that seem to share features. Starting from the concepts in the perinrep with the highest "relevance", e.g., those derived explicitly from the text, "Cognitive Model" *CognitiveModel* etc, we search for citations explicitly talking about those concepts --- a la keyword retrieval. So we will find citations explicitly talking about "Cognitive Model of Music". The next step, is to look further, at parts of the request perinrep connected to those primary topics. At this stage, we might be searching for "AI used in Music", or "Models of Composition". This process is repeated, each time moving "further" from the concepts actually specified for originally, and gathering citations that could be of interest. This process is stopped when one of three things happens:

o   A predetermined number of citations have been found.

o   A predetermined amount of effort (e.g., CPU time) has been expended.

o   The concepts found have fallen below a predetermined threshold of "relevance".[5]

---

[5] All these quantities are part of the default perinrep for a user, and can be modified per retrieval or session.

This process is somewhat similar to the "spreading activation" model used in GRANT [3]. It is more powerful though, in that one can combine arbitrary concepts in relationships with one another, which eliminates the problem the GRANT approach has with using the same keyword in different contexts.

In our test knowledge base, the above example might yield the following citations:

1   *Music, Memory, and Thought*

2   *An Expert System for Computer-Assisted Composition*

3   *Music, Mind, and Meaning*

4   *An Expert System for Schenkerian Synthesis of Chorales*

5   *Vivace: A Rule Based AI System for Composition*

6   *An Expert System for Music Perception*

7   *Problem Reduction in Musical Composition*

8   *Neural Net Modelling of Music*

9   *Connectionist Models of Musical Thinking*

10 *Cybernetics, Art, and Ideas*

These were found by VISAR using a default limit on relevance. Obviously, this limit could be lowered, and more citations would be found, but there is a point of diminishing returns: the complexity of the retrieved perinrep would increase and eventually we would be presenting all the citations stored in Cyc. Note that many of these citations would not have been found in traditional boolean keyword based information retrieval or hypertext navigation systems. In particular, the last citation in the list above illustrates something of the serendipity normally associated with happy discoveries in a library. The paper claims from its title to be isomorphic in two sense to the first paper, and so is presented as a potentially interesting candidate for perusal. Perhaps this can be considered an example of teh kind of "non-linear" thinking described by Beeman and others in [1].

6 Managing Information in VISAR

The other novel feature of VISAR is that it presents these without getting users lost in a bird's nest of links and nodes. Researchers have grappled with this problem for some time. In SemNet [9] for instance, various ways of presenting the contents of a knowledge base in three dimensions are explored. We chose not to follow such examples, because such an interface seems to limit the application to a graphical mode of interaction; we wish VISAR to be accessible through other media. Furthermore, as the authors of SemNet point out, although the Fisheye Views are successful in reducing the complexity of the information, users may become disoriented in passing certain invisible boundaries.

We are less interested in making random leaps through the concept space that such systems provide, than in allowing a structured exploration of the concepts. To provide this, we have adapted ideas from the Cyc Museum Unit Editor [14] to display concepts and related super-concepts. We show concepts and their relationships as icons displayed on a two dimensional graphics screen. They are connected by either lines or arrows, depending on the *function* relationship implied by a given citation. For instance, in the citation, "Neural Net Modelling of Music", there is a clear semantic dependency between "music" and "modelling" for instance. This is conveyed in the direction of the arrow connecting the Cyc concepts derived from the words. However, "Music, Mind and Meaning" gives no such functional relationship, hence VISAR will connect them with simple lines.

George Miller's studies [16] show that human short-term memory seems to have a capacity of "the magical number 7 plus or minus two" --- we present a graph structure to the user in a perinrep that has at most seven interrelated concepts. If there are more, then the concept reduction strategies outlined below are applied until this threshold is reached. Once this has been done, the remaining concepts are drawn (in somewhat arbitrary places) on the screen. Ultimately of course, the threshold should be part of the requested perinrep, customizable by a user.

6.1 Concept Reduction --- Perinrep Construction

Concept reduction in VISAR is a process by which different concepts derived from the title of a citation are determined and then are reduced to the retrieved perinrep. For example, Cyc might have a citation entitled, *"Goal Formulation in an Expert System"*. From this, a conceptual relationship between the Cyc units *ExpertSystemProblemSolver* and *ProblemGoal* might be derived. Now, Cyc has a substantial taxonomy of units, ranging from the very general e.g., *PhysicalObject* to the very specific, e.g., *MusicalConductor*. Each unit in Cyc is related to many others through generalization and specialization of set membership, as well as individual properties of the concepts. So, if the cited paper conveys a relationship between *ExpertSystemProblemSolver* and *ProblemGoal* it certainly also conveys a relationship between generalizations of those concepts, such as *ProblemSolver* and *Problem*.

A function HCC returns the *Highest Common Concept* of two Cyc units, by applying one or more of three reduction operators, that we call *concept generalization, concept factoring* and *concept chaining*. Generalization, as implied, searches up a Cyc generalization hierarchy for a common ancestor --- the example in the previous paragraph illustrates this. Concept factoring is simply the joining of two or more sub-graphs through common concepts. Concept chaining is the process of relating concepts through slots other than the generalization/specialization slot. For instance, the concept *RuleBase* is related to *ExpertSystemProblemSolver* by being a *ComponentOf* it. Obviously, not all slots should be chained along --- currently, we choose from a list of "appropriate" slots gathered heuristically.

The concept reduction process VISAR performs is the following:

1   VISAR constructs the set L of all (unique) concepts from the retrieved sub-graphs.

2   Each of the concepts is indexed on the Cyc taxonomy --- this is a process of describing the navigation operations to reach the concept from the root concept of Cyc. The list L is sorted on this value.

3   VISAR applies function HCC on the the last two elements in L replacing them with the new super-concept. This concept is indexed and the list sorted again.

4   Step 4 is repeated until the length of the list $n <= 7$ (the magical number).

5   VISAR then defines links between the n concepts in list L based on the respective relationships between these concepts as recorded in the original retrieved graphs.

This procedure is applied exhaustively to all ten retrieved structures to give the perinrep as presented to the user in the lower right window of igure 2.

The above procedure is used to present to the user an overview of the requested conceptual relationships retrieved from the literature citations Cyc has stored. We note that there will come a day when these citations are not just abstract structures stored in Cyc for ease of manipulation, but full fledged concepts just like other Cyc units.

6.2 Manipulation of Perinreps

The user may access any given node in the concept graph to explore information of related subconcepts, in the following ways:

1   expanding the concept into its subconcepts (these have been remembered from the time they were reduced).

2   perusing the citations that underlie the concept --- these are the texts of the citations that were originally parsed into the system to give the retrieved concepts.

3   collapsing a set of subconcepts into the single superordinate concept, i.e., performing the algorithm described above.

This permits users to move from one high-level concept to another, and to explore one or more of these concepts to any desired depth. Any window can be expanded to fill the screen so as to accommodate more detail. In addition, the user can change to a new focus, or revisit a previously selected focus (where *focus* refers to a high level concept which is used to organize an initial display for the user). Finally, the user can copy interesting titles for subsequent reporting or requesting of the full text of the citation.

The menu bar at the top of the screen gives access to several other services which we hope users will *not* need. These include a sorted index of concepts and a sorted index of titles. Of course, if VISAR is successful, users will prefer to use our graphical display instead of poring through textual lists.

6.3 Turning things around

We have emphasized that, in contrast to a traditional retrieval/searching system, which just returns "hits", VISAR returns something more akin to a continuum of concepts. This is rather like taking a large hypertext network, and extracting a small network from it. A user can manipulate the retrieved perinrep to gather information that would normally require another query and a further trip to the database. However, when a user expands a part of the retrieved perinrep that was presented as being only of peripheral interest, obviously such a user is asking for the system to refocus the view.

At this stage, it seems that VISAR should gather concepts related to the new focus of attention, because there may well be concepts that would now show up, close in relevance to the new focus, that were not presented before. In a future version of VISAR, this will be implemented automatically, i.e. mousing on such a concept will trigger a new retrieval. For the moment, a user must do this explicitly with the interface.

Perhaps we could use a "depth of research" measure, of how thoroughly the system digs around to find distant analogues. This is dependent on how much time a user (and the CPU) is prepared to spend on the search. But this can be quantified in a reasonable manner.

7 Summary and future research

While much work remains to be done on VISAR, we believe current results justify some optimism. VISAR seems to be a first step in the direction of constructing coherent large hypertext networks from multiple sources, in which we can perform deductions about what portions of the network will be of interest to a user in a given situation. The prototype has only been evaluated with a relatively small number of test citations, so we obviously need to do further study with larger samples to find out if this approach with the perinrep reduction mechanism truly enables users to understand large hypertext structures. Of course, our "hypertext" is a bare bones structure without the text normally found in such systems, though the citations themselves are associated with each node. An interesting extension, would be to have the source text of the articles (which the citations point to) read into our system. (But see Nilson [16].)

VISAR's ultimate large-scale utility depends on LUCY parsing things correctly, which in turn depends on the content of the Cyc KB, and lexical matching use of citations to automatically acquire knowledge. There will of course be situations in which LUCY and/or VISAR will be stumped, e.g.,

"Space TeleRobotics: A few more hurdles"

The difficulties lie in two places here: unknown words such as "telerobotics" which an intelligent human could guess at but are unlikely to be in a computer lexicon, and idioms such as "more hurdles" that require interpreting in a larger context. The Cyc project at MCC was started specifically to handle these kinds of problems involving broad general knowledge to perform such guesswork. We hope to utilize their results in future generations of LUCY.

One attractive possible project is to create a daemon to "monitor" a researcher's field, providing for a more passive or "grazing" style of information gathering [8]. This might work by creating a perinrep from processing the titles of papers the researcher has written in the field, and then from time to time, retrieving the relevant citations in the VISAR knowledge base (Assuming that VISAR is being updated with new citations as they arrive).

While we have designed our interface to be graphical, it does not seem difficult to exploit other media. Cyc units have names chosen to assist the human knowledge ontologists; in ambiguous cases, or those where the concept is very general, English text is provided with each unit to assist a user. It would not seem difficult to generate natural language text to document the relationship between the concepts displayed, particularly as there are at most seven shown on the initial screen. This text might alternatively be sent to a speech synthesizer.

We believe VISAR makes visible connections between related work (possibly spanning multiple citations) that were not explicit before (such as the case with the interesting citation on "Cybernetics, Art and Ideas"), and additionally, provide some measure of the happy serendipity that has traditionally accompanied browsing in libraries.

Although much of VISAR's power comes from the Cyc knowledge base, we have only just begun to exploit the breadth and depth of the relationships that Cyc encodes. We foresee a much more useful version of VISAR being able to interpret a user request in terms of matching it up against models of research in a field, and returning the *arguments* a citation makes in support of its claims, for instance. Such a tool would be of inestimable value to researchers.

Bibliography

[1] Beeman, W.O., *et al.*, "Hypertext and Pluralism: From Linear to Non-linear Thinking", in *Proceedings of Hypertext-87*, University of North Carolina, Chapel Hill NC, November 1987.

[2] Clitherow, P.A., *et al*, *VISAR: An Intelligent Interface Agent for Information Retrieval*, in preparation, July 1989.

[3] Cohen, P.R., Kjeldsen, R., "Information Retrieval Constrained Spreading Activation in Semantic Networks", *Information Processing & Management*, **23**(4), 1987.

[4] Collier, G., "Thoth-II: Hypertext with Explicit Semantics", in *Proceedings of Hypertext-87*, University of North Carolina, Chapel Hill NC, November 1987.

[5] Croft, W.B., "Approaches to Intelligent Information Retrieval", *Information Processing & Management*, **23**(4), 1987.

[6] Dumais, S.T., Furnas, G.W., Landauer, T.K., Deerwester, S., and Harshmann, R., "Using latent semantic analysis to improve access to textual information", in *CHI'88 Conference Proceedings: Human Factors in Computing Systems*, ACM, Washington DC, May 1988.

[7] Egan, D. "Superbook: Behavioral evaluation and analysis", In *Proc. Bellcore End User Computing Symposium* 1989, Piscataway NJ: Bellcore, in press.

[8] Egido, C., Bussey, H., Kaplan, A., and Rohall, S., "PIGS: A passive information grazing system", Poster presented at SIGCHI '89, Austin TX.

[9] Fairchild, K.M., Poltrock, S.E., Furnas, G.W., "SemNet: Three-Dimensional Graphic Representations of Large Knowledge Bases", in *Cognitive Science and its Applications for Human-Computer Interaction*, Guindon, R. (Ed), Lawrence Erlbaum, Hillsdale, NJ, 1988.

[10] Fox, E.A., "Development of the CODER System: A Testbed for Artificial Intelligence Methods in Information Retrieval", *Information Processing & Management*, **23**(4), 1987.

[11] Halasz, F.G., "Reflections on NoteCards: Seven Issues for the Next Generation of Hypermedia Systems", in *Proceedings of Hypertext-87*, University of North Carolina, Chapel Hill NC, November 1987.

[12] Lenat, D.B., *et al*, "Knoesphere: Building Expert Systems with Encylopedic Knowledge", in *Proceedings of IJCAI-83*, Karlsrue, FRG, 1983.

[13] Lenat, D.B., Prakash, M., Shepherd, M., "CYC: Using Common Sense Knowledge to Overcome Brittleness and Knowledge Acquisition Bottlenecks", *AI Magazine*, **6**(4), 1986.

[14] Lenat, D.B., Guha, R.V., *The World According to CYC*, MCC Tech Report, ACA-AI-300-88, September 1988.

[15] Miller, G.A., "The magical number seven, plus or minus two: Some limits on our capacity for processing information", *Psychological Review*, **63**, pp. 81-97, 1956.

[16] Nilson, M.E., "A Knowledge-Based Approach to Information Filtering", IEEE International Workshop on Telematics, Denver, CO 1989.

[17] Rich, E., "Users are Individuals", *Intl. Journal of Man-Machine Studies*, **18**, 1983.

[18] Pollitt, S., "CANSEARCH: An Expert Systems Approach to Document Retrieval", *Information Processing & Management*, **23**(2), 1987.

[19] Rau, L.F., "Knowledge Organization and Access in a Conceptual Information System", *Information Processing & Management*, **23**(4), 1987.

[20] Salton, G., "Another look at automatic text-retrieval systems", *CACM*, **29**(7), 1986.

[21] Salton, G., "Automatic Text Indexing using Compex Identifiers", in *Proc. ACM Conference on Document Processing Systems*, Santa Fe, NM, December 1988.

[22] Schatz, B., "Telesophy: System support for the abstract model of an information space", in *Proceedings of Bellcore End User Computing Symposium*, Bellcore, Piscataway NJ, November 1988, in press.

[23] Wiesner, S.J., "Two-&-Two, a high-level system for retrieving related pairs of documents", *SIGOIS Bulletin*, **9**(4), 1988.

[24] Wittenburg, K., *Natural Language Parsing with Combinatory Cetegorical Grammars in a Graph-Unification-Based Formalism*, Ph.D. thesis, University of Texas, Austin, TX, 1986.

What To Do When There's Too Much Information

Michael Lesk

Bellcore
445 South St
Morristown, NJ 07960-1910

Hypertext systems with small units of text are likely to drown the user with information, in the same way that online catalogs or bibliographic retrieval systems often do. Experiments with a catalog of 800,000 book citations have shown two useful ways of dealing with the "too many hits" problem. One is a display of phrases containing the excessively frequent words; another is a display of titles by hierarchical category. The same techniques should apply to other text-based retrieval systems. In general, interactive solutions seem more promising than attempts to do detailed query analysis and get things right the first time.

1. Problem

As larger and larger quantities of material are entered into computer systems, users are overwhelmed with information. Hypertext aggravates this because it breaks the material up into small units, thus increasing the total number of items. Increasing the total number of items makes it more difficult to find any particular item. Builders of hypertext system are faced with unappetizing alternatives:

• having only a few links, so that many of the interesting and relevant frames are not accessible;

• having many links, including perhaps full text search to locate any item, but causing users to retrieve more items than they can handle.

The problem of "information overload" isn't new: the effect of high-speed, easy-to-use information systems has made this obvious with electronic mail as well as bibliographic retrieval systems. What is needed, both in hypertext and conventional retrieval systems, is a way to let users select from a large space of retrieved items. In hypertext, the lack of an overall sequence (the inability to line up items in a row, as is done with the pages of a conventional book) makes finding specific items more difficult than in conventional systems. One answer is text searching. Text retrieval as a hypertext option has been proposed many times, e.g. see [Hala88] and [Fris88]. However, users are likely to be overwhelmed by the amount of material retrieved in really large collections, unless some kind of structure can be introduced.

To put this in perspective, consider the possibilities of searching a large on-line catalog by looking for individual words. A library catalog is a good model for a hypertext system because it contains many small items, each of which is described by specific fields such as author, subject heading, classification number, publisher and so on; and each of which can be thought of as linked to the other items which contain an identical field, e.g. one can consider that an entry for a book by *Boris Pasternak* is linked to all other entries which also have *Boris Pasternak* as the author. In practice this is generalized, so that the user can also look for *Pasternak* as a subject heading or a title word (e.g. for biographies or literary criticism dealing with him). Large numbers of book descriptions are available for testing.

In a catalog of 800,000 books (provided by OCLC), mostly 1980s English-language monographs, it may not be surprising to find that *history* is not very selective (81,000 instances); but even terms like *nuclear, theology, drug,* and *Scotland* appear more than 3000 times. This is not apparent to users in ordinary catalogs where each book title is only accessible by the first word; in full-text retrieval, every instance of a word in a subject heading or title can be found.

How can this be dealt with? Some of the problems that result from multiple occurrences are caused by ambiguous words. For example, there are 491 instances of *Stern,* representing well over 100 different personal names and 16 instances of *stern* as a word (in all cases meaning *rear,* not *rigorous* — the primary use is in *stern-drive* engines for boats). Even the rarer name *Sterne* appears 63 times, representing both Laurence Sterne and George Sterne. But sorting these problems out is not enough: the primary difficulty is simply large numbers of books on the actual subject the reader has requested. For example, *industrial* has nearly 8000 instances and *productivity* more than 1000; so *industrial productivity* retrieves 369 documents almost all of which are using the words as intended. In order to placate the user without lots of spare time, it is necessary to improve the selectivity of the search.

Needless to say, this quantity problem also has a bad effect on those searching for completeness. For example, how many searchers, having dug through 1331 entries for *airplane,* are going to remember that some of these books were written by British authors, and take the trouble to find out that there are 85 entries for *aeroplane,* of which 69 are new (16 entries contain both spellings).

This paper describes various methods for dealing with the information overload problem, with the intent of helping the user select from a variety of possibilities. They are demonstrated in the context of a catalog retrieval system, with 800,000 citations. The system runs on a Sun 3/75 and is written in C. It includes some simple suffixing and other searching aids [Lesk88]. All the samples shown are taken from screen dumps, and most deal with the word *screen.* In general, it has been necessary to abbreviate the displays for the format of this proceedings; they normally contain contain either more resolution or more information A straightforward search on the word *screen* would retrieve 481 documents, two of which, for example, are:

```
Type some kind of search query, one line:
Query: screen
```

```
T: Screening in cancer : a report of a UICC international workshop,
   Toronto, Canada, April 24-27, 1978
A: Miller, A. B. (Anthony B.)
$: 20.00F
C: Geneva
I: International Union Against Cancer,
D: 1978.
P: 338 p. :
S: Cancer -- Diagnosis -- Congresses.
S: Medical screening -- Congresses.
#: C270
d: 16.99/4075
```

```
T: Batik, tie dyeing, stenciling, silk screen, block printing ; the har
   decoration of fabrics
A: Kafka, Francis J.
C: New York,
I: Dover Publications
D: [1973, c1959]
P: 198 [13] p. :
S: Textile printing.
S: Textile design.
#: NK9500 .K3 1973b
```

Mo

In these two documents *screen* appears in the context of *screening for cancer*, and *silk-screen printing*, not to mention *movie screen* and *television screen*. If one of these meanings is correct, the user could add words (or use relevance feedback to do it automatically) that would clarify the query and improve retrieval. However, the intended meaning (eg *Japanese screen painting* or *Plants for hedges and screens*) may not be in the first few. Consulting a dictionary may help; here is the Merriam-Webster 7th New Collegiate definition for *screen:*

Nouns:

1a   a device used as a protection from heat or drafts or as an ornament

1b   a nonbearing partition often ornamental carried up to a height necessary for separation and protection

2a   something that shelters, protects, or conceals, specifically a body of troops, ships, or planes thrown to protect a command, an area, or larger force

2b   a shield for secret usu. evil practices

3a   a perforated plate or cylinder or a meshed wire or cloth fabric usu. mounted and used to separate coarser from finer parts.

3b   a system for examining and separating into different groups

3c   a piece of apparatus designed to prevent agencies in one part from
affecting other parts (optical, electric or magnetic screens).

3d   a frame holding a usu. metallic netting used esp. in a window or door to exclude insects

4a1   a flat surface upon which a picture or series of pictures is projected

4a2   the motion-picture industry

4b   something that receives or retains a mental image or impression

4c   the surface upon which the image appears in a television or radar receiver

5   a glass plate ruled with crossing opaque lines through which an image is photographed in making a halftone screen

Verbs:

1   to guard from injury or danger

2a   to give shelter or protection to with or as if with a screen

2b   to separate with or as if with a screen.

3a   to pass (as coal, gravel, ashes) through a screen to separate the fine part from the coarse; also: to remove by a screen

3b1   to examine usu. methodically in order to make a separation into different groups

3b2   to select or eliminate by a screening process

4   to provide with a screen to keep out insects

5a   to project (as a motion-picture film) on a screen

5b   to present in a motion picture

6   to appear on a motion-picture screen

7   *hide* 9

However, the relative frequencies of the words used in the particular collection represented by a hypertext or other retrieval system are not those in a general dictionary. For example, *halftone screen* does not appear at all, and *screening coal* appears only twice. Metaphorical uses of words are also a problem: *bolt* is neatly sorted by the dictionary into its sense of *running* and its sense of *fastening* but the typical use is in the phrase *A nuts and bolts guide to* ..., which is semantically almost useless. What is needed is some method of selection that reflects the particular retrieved set for a given word.

2. Useful techniques.

When the problem is a search on an overly frequent word, one straightforward procedure is to display the phrases containing the frequent word in question. Here are the significant words that precede and follow *screen* in the collection:

```
Type some kind of search query, one line:
screen


       Here are some words that abut the word you used
Can I interest you in..
         medical screen (35)     screen congress (28)
              ii screen (24)     screen writer (26)
            drug screen (20)     screen process (25)
          report screen (19)     screen print (19)
            mass screen (15)     screen study (17)
           stage screen (14)     screen test (13)
             skp screen (10)     screen method (12)
         genetic screen (8)      screen paint (8)
   developmental screen (8)      screen infancy (8)
        neonatal screen (7)      screen phase (6)
        Mark (with right mouse button) or type the words you want added, then hit retu:
```

If the user chooses *screen printing* as the correct phrase, the result is shown below.

```
Type some kind of search query, one line:
Query: screen
```

```
T: Batik, tie dyeing, stenciling, silk screen, block printing ; the hand
   decoration of fabrics
A: Kafka, Francis J.
C: New York,
I: Dover Publications
D: [1973, c1959]
P: 198 [13] p. :
S: Textile printing.
S: Textile design.
#: NK9500 .K3 1973b
```

```
T: Textile/garment screen printing
A: Kosloff, Albert.
C: Cincinnati, Ohio
I: Signs of the Times Pub. Co.,
D: 1980.
P: 153 p. :
S: Screen process printing.
S: Textile printing.
S: Decorated fashion apparel.
#: TT273 .K67 1980
d: 667/.38
```

```
T: Screen printing techniques
A: Murrell, Graham.
$: $5.95
A: Turner, Silvie, 1946-
C: New York
I: Taplinger Pub. Co.,
D: 1979, c1976.
P: 118 p. :
S: Screen process printing.
#: TT273 .T87 1979
d: 746.6
```

Note that this has reduced the 481 documents to 33 and that they are all relevant. This technique has the advantage of being applicable to all collections; whatever the text used, it is straightforward to extract adjacent words and display them. The phrases are precomputed and thus can be displayed immediately with no delay. For the 800,000 book file, which requires 235 Mbytes to store in full, the phrase list is only 13 Mbytes.

The disadvantage of a phrase display is that it gives little organized sense of the information distribution. For example, it is often the case that the same adjacent word appears in both the "before" and "after" lists; for example, an author's name such as *Walt Whitman* will appear both in the normal form (where it is referenced in a title) and in the form *Whitman, Walt* on the author line. As an example here is the phrase display for *Whitman*:

```
   walt whitman (63)    whitman walt (94)
  peggy whitman (6)     whitman john (16)
  state whitman (6)     whitman county (11)
 marcus whitman (5)     whitman massacre (11)
narcissa whitman (3)    whitman dale (9)
 joseph whitman (2)     whitman narcissa (9)
richard whitman (2)     whitman dougla (9)
modernist whitman (2)    whitman robert (9)
 emerson whitman (2)    whitman marcus (8)
           whitman richard (6)
```

It is clear that *Walt Whitman* dominates all the others, but the balance of topics is less clear than it might be. The display does not clearly distinguish, for example, between the personal names such as *Richard Whitman* or *Narcissa Whitman*, the geographic or historical names such as *Whitman county, Washington* and the *Whitman massacre*, and the phrases such as *Emerson, Whitman, and the American muse*. Some of this could be improved by sorting the phrases by field of occurrence (title, author, subject heading) but at the cost of increasing complexity for the user. In the case of *screen* note that some meanings of the word did not appear at all, because they were not reflected by frequent phrases.

An alternative is to show the occurrences of words in titles by subject category. Since nearly all the books in this catalog are in the hierarchical LC classification, it can be used to show occurrences of items by subject class. This presents a display indicating the various subject areas in which books appear and the relative frequency of occurrence of book titles in each display.

The size of the subject categories used is varied by the number of categories retrieved and the amount of screen space available. For a relatively frequent or ambiguous word that spreads across many LC categories, the first display can only show the main headings. For example, here is a display of the instances of the word *screen* by LC divisions (initial letters).

```
Type some kind of search query, one line:
Query: screen
Occ. Subject                        Title (No. found 199)
143 P/Language and Literature       The face on the screen and other stor
 99 R/Medicine                      Toxicity screening procedures using b
 51 T/Technology                    "Environmental stress screening, spen
 50 M/Music                         Broadway to Hollywood /Can't help sin
 30 L/Education                     Finland /Screen design strategies for
 21 H/Social Sciences               National ethnic survey, 1980 /Mexican
 17 N/Arts                          The technique of screen & television
 12 --/--                           Alfalfa seed screenings as a feed for
 10 Z/Bibliography                  Screen process printing photographic
  8 Q/Science                       NOS version 2 screen formatting refer
  5 --/--                           Screening inductees/An analysis of th
  5 S/Agriculture                   Climbing and screening plants /The Co
  5 U/Military Science              "V{ 3}ara landsm{11}an" /"Vara landsm
  4 D/History -- Old World          The star-spangled screen /A scrap scr
  4 K/Law                           Medical screening of workers /State 1
  3 B/Philosophy and Religion       The Hutt adaptation of the Bender-ges
  3 C/History -- Auxiliary          Screening in cancer /Modulation trans
  3 E/American history              Northwest Coast Indian graphics /Nort
  3 G/Geography                     North Dakota resource management plan
  2 J/Political Science             Neonatal screening /Screening federal
  2 V/Naval Science                 Police management--recruit screening/
  1 A/General works                 Analysis of the mean spherical approx


Which category should be expanded? (n for none):
```

This shows clearly that the main uses are movies and medical screening, but also indicates a few odd items, such as smoke screens in military contexts. If the user then chooses *agriculture*, looking for items like *climbing and screening plants*, the result is

```
Type some kind of search query, one line:
Query: screen
Occ. Subject                        Title (No. found 199)
  2 SB427/Climbing plants.          Climbing and screening plants /The Co
  1 SB437/Hedges.                   Hedges, screens & espaliers
  1 SF961/Cattle -- Diseases.       Blood protein screening in healthy an
  1 SH153/Fish-culture --           Efficiency tests of the primary louve


Which category should be expanded? (n for none):
```

Since there are so few books, the individual category labels are shown. If there had been more, the LC classes might only have been displayed at the two-letter level. The user, now seeing what the LC category for *hedges* is, can search directly for that category; the result is a set of specific books about hedges and screens, such as:.

```
Type some kind of search query, one line:
Query: sb437
```

```
T: Shelter effect; investigations into aerodynamics of shelter and its
   effects on climate and crops.
A: Jensen, Martin.
C: Copenhagen,
I: Danish Technical Press,
D: 1954.
P: xi, 264 p.
S: Windbreaks, shelterbelts, etc.
#: SB437 .J4
```

```
T: Evergreens. (Added feature: Azaleas-rhododendrons)
A: Gillespie, Norvell.
C: San Francisco,
I: California Chemical Co.,
D: 1961.
P: 48 p.
S: Evergreens.
S: Azaleas.
S: Rhododendron.
#: SB437 .G7
```

Note that these titles do not include the word *screen*, although other books in this category do. This is the equivalent of looking at the shelves in a normally arranged library, once the user has figured out which categories are relevant.

The same thing can be done in the Dewey system, although only about half the books have Dewey listings, so often the most common category is "none" (represented by two dashes). Depending on the subject, either LC or Dewey may happen to provide a more useful breakdown. Note that the LC and Dewey category assignments are usually done by different catalogers and may represent a different choice of the primary subject for a particular book. For example, the title *Selling Mother's Milk: The Wet-Nursing Business in France, 1715-1914'* was judged by the LC classifier to belong under "Infant Nutrition" (RJ216) while the Dewey classifier put the book in 338.4, "Economics — Production — Secondary industries" (and "Economic History — France" is another defensible choice). Furthermore many books are classified more than once; a book of songs about American railway accidents, *Scalded to Death by the Steam*, was published in both the United States and Great Britain. The US edition is classified as a song book (Dewey 784.6, LC ML3351), while the British edition is considered a book about railway accidents (Dewey 363.1, LC HE1780). Without both editions in hand, of course, it is possible that such choices reflect changes when the book was republished in a different country or different edition. In any case, the alternative classifications present additional chances to move around and to improve the recall of the search.

The problem with this technique, of course, is that a hierarchical classification may not be available for a particular document collection. There are techniques involving statistical methods for attempting to cluster documents although so far none of them is in common use; see Salton and McGill [Salt83], who have encouraged the use of document clustering, and van Rijsbergen [Rijs79] who is more skeptical. An easier problem than *ab initio* clustering is to put new documents into an existing classification system by comparing them with existing material. Note that if the only purpose of a classification is to assist in retrieval, items may be put in more than one category (unlike a library, which has to assign books to unique categories to shelve them).

It is possible, of course, to merely search for subject classes without using word search at all, as opposed to the system described which uses subject classes to sort out retrievals from a previous word search. However, since most users are not familiar with the existing classification systems, such searches are not generally popular [Gell83].

3. Further possibilities.

Two-dimensional displays of information can be made on suitable workstations. For example, here is a display of LC vs. Dewey number, with each title plotted about where it should be.

```
Type some kind of search query, one line:
Query: screen                                    (481 found, 26 shown)

              ┌The technique of screen &┐
         ┌VAX BASIC for business┐          ┌Handbook of screen┐
016      └                     ┘           └                  ┘
155                ┌Programming tools for the IBM PC┐
228      ┌Type A behaviour, stimulus┐     ┌Handbook of screen┐
331               ┌Turbo C┐
353                      ┌Screening for children with┐
370           ┌Screening out the past┐
384
47                       ┌Climbing and screening┐
614      ┌Screening for children with special┐  ┌Information┐
618
621      ┌Economic appraisal of rural roads┐   ┌Screening and test┐
628               ┌Body sense┐
646                ┌Screening and surveillance for┐
652
667      ┌Alfalfa seed screenings as a feed┐  ┌Screening of soft┐
693      ┌Raisin by-products and bean┐    ┌Hedges, screens &┐
741               ┌vi--the UNIX screen editor┐
755
764      ┌Practical method of measurement for┐  ┌The step-by-step┐
790           ┌Fortieth Western New York┐
794      ┌An account of the high altar screen┐  ┌57 How-to-do-it┐
812
820
842   HG    LB    PN163 PS35  RC268 RJ399 TE228 Z249
942 E78    KF    N      PN207 QH545 RG304 SB437 TN816
```

The intent is to spread out the documents in space so that the user can see various groups. The most popular subjects will pile up, and the rarer subjects (eg the agricultural uses, or the book *VAX BASIC for business: a screen-based approach*) will show through the "holes" where few other books are. Since most users are not familiar with the classification systems in detail, however, this plot is not terribly clear. In addition, only a sample of the titles (and of the text in each title) can be displayed, which also makes it more difficult to interpret such plots.

To deal with the screen limits, all of the titles can be represented by replacing them with squares, as shown below.

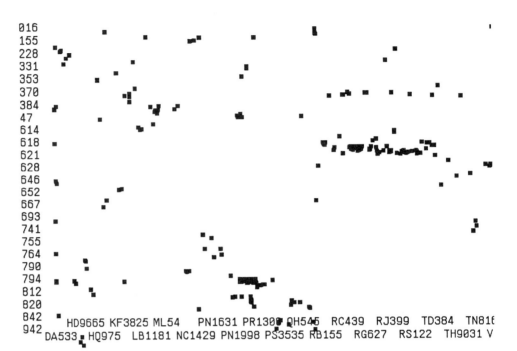

This shows the mapping between LC and Dewey, again for the books retrieved for a query on *screen*. It is also relatively hard to interpret. If all catalogers made the same decisions about the subject matter of the books, and if the LC and Dewey systems both had complete coverage divided in the same ways, this would be a functional plot showing a one-to-one correspondence between the two classification systems. In reality it serves mostly to demonstrate the "hot spots": the books at Dewey 790 and LN PN (the Hollywood books) and the books in LC R-categories and Dewey 610, the medical screening.

Perhaps more interesting is the following attempt to use as axes LC class and readability; as a surrogate for readability, syllables per word are used. The hope was that this measure would give some indication of genre:

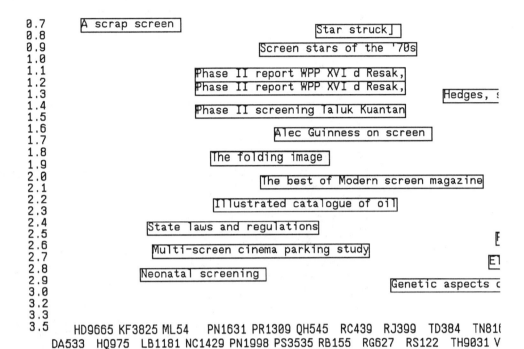

In this plot the movie books tend to be at the top, and the technical books at the bottom. It is easy to display any other coordinates in the book record, whether LC number, Dewey number, number of pages, author name, or whatever. The scales are stretched as necessary to spread across the set of items picked. The difficulty is to find neatly scalable parameters which will help the user locate the desired information. Many of the parameters are not intuitively meaningful to the reader, and some which are, such as number of pages, do not provide a particularly useful distinction between different books.

Not all queries, of course, result in information overload. *Hypertext* itself occurs only twice, for example. And sometimes, even in this very large collection, a user may request a word that does not appear at all. A possible solution to this inverse problem is to use a dictionary, and find related words by looking at words defined with the same terms. For example, below *aspic* is replaced by a list of words either used in the definition of *aspic* or sharing defining terms with *aspic* in the Oxford Advanced Learner's Dictionary of Current English. Note that this does find books on cooking; although not the best solution to the problem of missing words, it is better than the alternative of merely reporting "no hits."

```
Type some kind of search query, one line:
Query: aspic
          Expanding to:   aspic chicken jel blancmange cranberry gel gela
```

```
T: The effect of varying proportions of sucrose to crystalline high
   fructose corn syrup on the color, gel strength, flavor intensity an
   sweetness perception of grape jelly
A: Hetzel, Barbara A.
D: 1987.
P: xiii, 111 leaves ;
S: Sucrose.
S: Corn syrup.
S: Jelly.
S: Fructose.
#: LD5171.S715h H479
```

```
T: Chicken & in love
A: Goldberg, Natalie.
$: $2.50
C: Minneapolis
I: Holy Cow] Press,
D: 1980.
P: 58 p. ;
#: PS3557.03583 C47
d: 811/.54
```

In the long run, it will also be possible to include material from the table of contents and text of books, it is hoped. The software here can display either just titles as shown here,

```
Type some kind of search query, one line:
Query: information retrieval

Information retrieval and processing  / Doyle, Lauren B., 1926-  / 1975
Design and implementation of computer-based information systems  / Szyp
Guidelines for the building of authority files in / Di Lauro, Anne.  /
Career information in counseling and career development  / Isaacson, Le
Computer representation and manipulation of chemical information  / Wip
Recent trends in geographic information processing in the National / Ta
Accounting information systems  / Hicks, James O.  / 1981.
File management and information retrieval systems : a manual for / Gill
Information policy for the 1980's : proceedings of the Eusidic /  / 197
EURIM 3 : a European conference on the contribution of users to plannin
Subject and information analysis  / Dym, Eleanor D.  / 1985.
Videotext : the coming revolution in home/office information retrieval
Information systems for health services  / McLachlan, Gordon.  / 1980.
Methods of analysing information requirements applied to physical / Noo
Theoretical issues in information retrieval : proceedings of the Fourth
Year of the oceans : science of information handling  / Grundy, R. L. (
Cost control and information systems : a complete guide to effective /
Directory of United Nations databases and information systems, 1985  /
Insurance information systems  / Krause, H. Thomas.  / 1985.
```

citations (as shown in several earlier figures), pictures of the dust jackets,

```
Type some kind of search query, one line:
Query: austen garden
```

```
T: The Ordnance Survey Guide to
   Gardens in Great Britain
E: Robert Pearson
E: Susanne Mitchell
E: Candida Hunt
D: 1986
I: Newnes Books (Country Life Books)
I: Ordnance Survey
C: Twickenham
P: 320
```

```
T: Pride and Prejudice
A: Jane Austen
I: Penguin
D: 1972
P: 398
C: Harmondsworth
```

or even display the full text of a book, in those cases where the text is available, as shown here for *Pride and Prejudice*.

```
<T PRIDE AND PREJUDICE><V I><C I>
IT is a truth universally acknowledged, that a single man in
possession of a good fortune, must be in want of a wife.
However little known the feelings or views of such a man
may be on his first entering a neighbourhood, this truth is so
well fixed in the minds of the surrounding families, that he is
considered as the rightful property of some one or other of
their daughters.
"My dear Mr. Bennet,' said his lady to him one day, "have
you heard that Netherfield Park is let at last?'
```

At present only citations are available except for special demonstration examples. When more information can be obtained, it will be possible to find much better links between items and use them to help suggest new items to a user.

4. Conclusions

As hypertext increases the resolution of searching by storing many small items, it increases the complexity of searching by having more items. Traditional libraries solve similar problems by agglomeration, e.g. binding loose issues of journals. Electronically, we need similar ways to display context and organization for hypertext units. Systems with large amounts of information are going to require ways to help users sort out what they want. Two methods are proposed and demonstrated on a test collection of 800,000 book citations.

Both
(1)   displays of phrases involving frequent words and
(2)   displays of items by subject category are useful.

Generalizations of these techniques should be effective in other hypertext environments.

The assistance of OCLC (the Online College Library Center, including particularly Martin Dillon and Martha Lindeman), Merriam-Webster, the Oxford Text Archive, Oxford University Press, and the British Library is gratefully acknowledged.

[Fris88]   Mark Frisse, "Searching for Information in a Hypertext Medical Handbook," *Commun. ACM* vol. **31**, no. 7, pp. 880-886, 1988.

[Gell83]   V. J. Geller and M. E. Lesk, "User Interfaces to Information Systems: Choices vs. Commands", *Proc. 6th Int. ACM SIGIR Conference*, Bethesda, Md. pp. 130-135, June 1983.

[Hala88]   Frank Halasz, "Reflections on Notecards: Seven Issues for the Next Generation of Hypermedia Systems", *Commun. ACM* vol. 31, no. 7, pp. 836-852, 1988.

[Lesk88]   Michael Lesk, "Word Manipulation in Online Catalog Searching: Using the Unix System for Library Experiments," *Proc. 1988 EUUG Meeting*, London, England, April 1988.

[Rijs79]   C. J. van Rijsbergen, **Information Retrieval**, Butterworths, London, 1979.

[ßalt83]   Gerard Salton and Michael McGill, **Introduction to Modern Information Retrieval**, McGraw-Hill, New York, 1983.

The Role of External Representations in the Writing Process: Implications for the Design of Hypertext-based Writing Tools

Christine M. Neuwirth and David S. Kaufer

English Department
Carnegie Mellon University
Pittsburgh, PA 15213

ABSTRACT

The long-range goal of the research reported here is to study the role of hypertext-based external representations in augmenting performance on a cognitively complex task, in particular, on a synthesis writing task. The production of a written synthesis is a challenging task that requires managing large amounts of information over an extended period of time. Thus, synthesis writing is a task that is well-suited for testing the potential of hypertext technologies to support work on complex tasks.

From a case study of experts and novices, we have developed a theory of the cognitive processes involved in producing a written synthesis. We have also developed a preliminary theory of the role of external representations in the writing process. We have drawn upon these two theories to design several hypertext-based external representations that we believe will augment writers' performance on a written synthesis task. The hypertext-based applications include a general graph object and a table object; these objects form the foundation for a set of specialized tools to support synthesis writing, namely, a summary graph, synthesis grid and synthesis tree.

INTRODUCTION

From the beginning, hypertext researchers have been concerned with the role of external representations in complex tasks such as writing. For example, Douglas Engelbart, an influential hypertext pioneer, explicitly envisioned the computer as a tool for augmenting human intellect through "automated external symbol manipulation [Enge63]." Even earlier, Vannever Bush, a visionary who is generally credited with proposing the first hypertext (which he called a "memex"), conceived of it as an external representation of human associative memory that would augment our ability to work with the world's scientific literature. Bush saw the role for such an external representation of memory as improving upon the encoding performance of the human memory system, with associative links providing more speed and flexibility of retrieval than traditional external stores, albeit still not equal to the speed and flexibility of the human system:

> One cannot hope to equal the speed and flexibility with which the mind follows an associative trail, but it should be possible to beat the mind decisively in regard to the permanence and clarity of the items resurrected from storage [Bush45].

The basic vision that Bush described for creating associative links, representing them, and following them has been pursued in many actual implementations of hypertext systems. An implicit assumption shared by such systems was that a good representation for performing the process of retrieval from an external memory would be one that provided a mechanism to mimic the associative links of human memory. This assumption has been called into question by the problem of users "getting lost in hypertext," a disorientation problem in which users forget where they are in the hypertext network, forget how to get to another place in the network, or forget what is in the network [Char87, Foss89]. Conklin characterizes the root of the problem as follows:

Of course, one also has a disorientation problem in traditional linear text documents, but there are only two options about where the desired passage is: earlier or later in the text. Hypertext offers more degrees of freedom [than traditional linear documents], more dimensions in which one can move, and hence a greater potential for the user to become lost or disoriented. In a network of 1000 nodes, it is easy to imagine that information could become hard to find or even forgotten altogether [Conk87a].

Ironically, the very potential strength of hypertext, namely improving the management of loose collections of relatively unstructured information, turned out to be a major potential weakness. Not surprisingly, numerous efforts have been undertaken to create more adequate mechanisms for managing the loose collections of unstructured information that are characteristic of hypertext, including mechanisms for accessing, organizing and filtering it. These efforts fall into two camps: those who are developing general mechanisms and those who are developing task-specific mechanisms. General mechanisms that have been developed include, among others, graph views of the hypertext network [Hala87b], user-defined paths through the network [Trig83] as well as dynamically generated system paths [Robe81, Shne86], and context-dependent displays [Gold80, Gold84, Yank85]. Task-specific development efforts abound. For those explicitly concerned with writing tasks, mechanisms have included, among others, hierarchical structures [Enge68, Trig83, Neuw87, Smit87], special link types for authors and reviewers [Trig83], and hypertext interfaces for authoring and linear interfaces for reading [Walk87]. In systems with sufficient flexibility, users themselves have evolved task-specific interfaces [Trig87, vanL85]. Indeed, Marshall argues that sufficiently flexible hypertext systems are well-suited for supporting the process of developing task-specific external representations [Mars87].

Although concern for external representations has occupied one of the central places in hypertext research, little is known about what makes one external representation better than another. Competing external representations have received only informal evaluations. This paper will report on a project whose aim is to study the role external representations can play in augmenting human performance on a complex task, in particular, on a synthesis writing task. As part of the project, we are exploring a framework, based on a model of the architecture of human cognition, for comparing external representations. The framework is intended to provide a foundation for more formal evaluations of competing external representations. Such a foundation is needed for empirical studies of how external representations can augment human performance on complex tasks. In the next section we outline why writing, and in particular, synthesis writing, is a good task for studying external representations. In section three, we present aspects of synthesis writing that are important for understanding the research we are describing. In section four, we present a cognitively-based framework for answering the question "When is one external representation better than another?" In section five, we outline the interface design for a set of hypertext-based applications and describe what cognitive role we see them playing in the process of synthesis writing. In section six, we discuss related research. Finally, we outline some general implications for the design of hypertext systems.

THE IMPORTANCE OF EXTERNAL REPRESENTATIONS IN WRITING TASKS

Is writing an appropriate task for studying the potential of hypertext-based representations for augmenting performance on complex tasks? In this section, we review some of the features of the writing that, we believe, make it appropriate.

Task Difficulty

Many writing tasks are sufficiently difficult that even experienced, highly skilled writers frequently

> – focus on details at the expense of larger goals and attend to information that plays no role in later problem-solving
>
> – forget information that would have been useful
>
> – need to search for information that they could only partially retrieve
>
> – select incorrect operators and paths and need to backtrack
>
> – engage in trial search
>
> – lose track of goals

As we shall argue in this paper, hypertext-based external representations have the potential to significantly reduce these difficulties.

The Role of Partial Products

Writing is an open-ended design task. A *design* task is a task that involves creating a product: an architect designs a building, a software engineer designs a computer program, a writer designs a paper. An *open-ended* task is one in which the task specifications do not sufficiently constrain the end-state. In open-ended design tasks, problem solvers must further constrain the task in order to build the final product. The partially completed product plays an important role in this process: The partially completed product becomes part of the task environment and constrains the subsequent course of the design. For example, writers frequently re-read portions of the text they have produced so far to provide constraints for the next segment of text that they want to produce [Flow81, Kauf86]. Thus, writing is a task in which new, interactive external representations of partial products can be expected to have a profound impact.

The Role of Planning

To construct a finished, polished product is expensive, so we usually associate design with planning, especially planning with the aid of representations and models. In this sense of design, an architect's task is a prototype design task because steel, bricks and concrete are too unwieldy and costly to be good media for planning; the architect *must* work with the aid of drawings and models. Although less prototypical, it is relatively expensive for a software engineer to produce syntactically correct program code, and for a writer to produce polished formal sentences. Indeed, a study by Glynn, Britton, Muth and Dogen indicated that generating polished formal sentences early in the process of writing depressed the quality and quantity of ideas that writers produced [Glyn82]. Presumably, interactive external representations that offer writers more alternatives to formal sentences could significantly facilitate planning.

Synthesis Writing

The production of a written synthesis is a challenging task that requires managing large amounts of information over an extended period of time. As such, it is a task that is well-suited for testing the potential of hypertext for supporting work on complex tasks.

Moreover, providing tools to support the production of written syntheses is of significance in its own right. In every discipline, constructing a synthesis of previous research is a crucial step in carrying out new research. In all areas of scientific endeavor, a researcher must provide a context for his or her contribution, both when contemplating new studies and when communicating new results with colleagues.

A PRELIMINARY MODEL OF THE PROCESS OF SYNTHESIS WRITING

Constructing a written synthesis has many elements in common with other writing tasks as well as some points of difference. In this section, we sketch some aspects of synthesis writing that are important for understanding the research we are undertaking.

The primary purpose of a written synthesis is to describe the structure and relationships among various authors and to simplify those relationships in such a way that general statements can be made, statements that can lead to economies of memory, to the description of general laws, or to the generation of insights such as hypotheses for research or solutions to problems [Soka74].

To examine the processes involved in producing a written synthesis, we collected thinking-aloud protocols from people at two skill levels, expert and novice. Our model of synthesis writing is based on data from a larger task – writing an original argument from sources. This set of protocols formed a rich data base of evidence about the problem-solving processes involved in writing a synthesis because subjects produced a written synthesis as part of their original essays.

Subjects and Materials

Five of the subjects were experienced writers. They included three professors of philosophy and two Ph.D. students. Two subjects were novices. Both were undergraduate students recruited from a writing class.

We asked subjects to read eight articles on the issue of paternalism and to write an essay that made an original contribution to the issue. The issue of paternalism can be summed-up by the question, "When is it right, if ever, for a society or an individual to limit another person's freedom for that person's own good?" We chose this task because it offers an open-ended challenge, yet it does not require knowledge of highly specialized domains that would fall outside the competence of some subjects; that is, subjects could construct a reasonable essay using only the techniques taught in a writing class.

Writers wrote at their own pace, taking up to fifty hours to complete the task. We analyzed a subset of the subjects' protocols in detail; we examined others more cursorily to find corroborating evidence [Geis86]. In analyzing the protocols, we did not take it as our task to develop a model of the entire writing process. Instead, we focused on aspects of particular importance to argument. In the following sections, we limit the analysis even further and discuss the similarities and differences among subjects as they relate to producing a written synthesis.

Because of the small number of subjects, the model that we will sketch must be viewed as preliminary and open to significant revision. The model will have served its purpose in this paper, however, if it provides the level of detail about cognitive processes in writing that we believe is necessary in order to discuss the role of external representations.

Processes of Synthesis

In working on the synthesis writing task, our experts employed the following, identifiable processes:

1. A *selection* process that identifies important information in individual source texts. In what follows, we refer to the knowledge structures that this process produces as a *summary* of each author. The knowledge structures built by this process provide a representation of a single source text.

2. An *aggregation* process that groups authors according to similarities/differences on relevant attributes. We refer to the knowledge structures that this process produces as a *synthesis grid*.

3. A *hierarchy-building* process that organizes the authors according to degree of similarity/difference and provides an analysis of the causes of those differences. We refer to the knowledge structures that this process produces as a *synthesis tree*.

4. A *generation* process that produces a written synthesis in an organizational pattern that can be seen as a traversal of the synthesis tree.

In contrast to the expert subjects, the novice subjects can best be characterized as decomposing the synthesis writing task into two subtasks:

1. A *selection* process that identifies important information in individual source texts.

2 A *generation* process that produces a written synthesis by the juxtaposition of the summaries.

In sum, expert subjects interpreted the synthesis writing task as an opportunity to create new knowledge that allowed them to position authors in the issue. Novices, however, interpreted the synthesis writing task as a report on the reading that simply included information from all the sources.

Task Decomposition

The experts carried out these subtasks in ways that can be characterized both as opportunistic [Haye79] and as decomposed into minimally interacting subsystems. For example, it was not uncommon for experts to make an aggregation statement while in the course of selecting important information from a single source text. We consider this behavior to be opportunistic. However, after reading all the source texts most of the experts also spent some time in aggregating authors and building a hierarchy.

In *Sciences of the Artificial*, Simon argues that a useful way to study a complex system is to decompose it into nearly independent subsystems, subsystems that can be studied in relative isolation from each other [Simo69]. This "divide and conquer" strategy has been observed in subjects working on other complex information processing tasks such as programming [Jeff81]. Not all decompositions are equally effective. A poor task decomposition will leave many significant interactions between subtasks. When subtasks interact significantly, the work accomplished in one subtask will have to be substantially redone when working on another subtask. Subjects sometimes had to redo their work.

The selection process, aggregation process and hierarchy-construction process, working in a structured, yet flexible, flow of control, are central to the representations in our interface design. In the following paragraphs, we describe these processes in more detail.

The Selection Process: A Schema-Theoretic View

In our analysis of the expert protocols, we hypothesize that experts encode an argumentative text with a problem-solution schema. A schema is an abstract knowledge structure that summarizes what is known about a variety of cases that differ in many particulars [Ande84]. The theoretical challenge for researchers is to specify the form and substance of schemata and the processes that use the knowledge structured by the schema.

The experts we studied seem to encode an argumentative text as an author's directions for proceeding through an issue, from problem to solution. To understand an argument is to be able to follow the author's directions as the author moves from "What's the issue about?" (see the issue), to "What's the root tension in the issue?" (define the problem), to "How do we resolve this tension?" (choose a solution). Although we studied arguments of policy, we expect to see a similar schema for other genres such as research.

When reading, experts devoted little time to the consideration of statements that did not fit the issue-problem-solution schema. Moreover, experts demonstrated an impressive, though by no means perfect, ability to retrieve and apply information that fit into this schema. In contrast, novices often could not see the forest for the trees, spending more time on statements that are peripheral to the author's main argument than experts. In addition, they had difficulty distinguishing the author's position from the author's discussion of an opponent's position.

The Aggregation Process: A Class Formation View

The goal of the aggregation process is to find a set of dimensions of similarity/difference across the multiple authors.

For the most part, subjects did not take the original source texts as input to the process of aggregation. Rather they worked with a subset of information generated by the selection process. Moreover, for our expert subjects, this subset was often not a direct quotation from the source text; more frequently, it was a gist that seemed to remind them of the source. As noted earlier, novices did not exhibit a strong aggregation process.

Subjects did not always articulate the attributes on which they were basing their aggregation. Experts seemed to search for statements on which authors disagreed. Sometimes these disagreements were explicit; sometimes the experts inferred them. Novices, on the other hand, seemed to suppress disagreement among authors. Experts sometimes attempted to generate characterizations of the groupings, that is, they tried to make general statements that described a group in a way that distinguished it from other groups.

Construction of a Hierarchy

The aggregation process only builds similarities and differences on single propositions. The hierarchy-construction process seeks to connect propositions into a hierarchy. The goal of the hierarchy-construction process is to find the most important unresolved disagreements among authors. We hypothesize that experts use these unresolved differences as starting points for discovering their own contribution to the issue.

We hypothesize that experts begin by examining the knowledge structures built in the aggregation process. If one of the propositions in these structures can be identified as important, unresolved, and most deserving of further discussion, the search may end. If none of the propositions meet these criteria, then the expert will try to construct a proposition which does. Regardless of whether the proposition arrived at is found or constructed, experts treat it as the pivotal proposition and use it to form the start of their synthesis tree. They build the rest of the synthesis tree by positioning authors on branches that are backward or forward from the propositional disagreement at the pivotal point.

Evidence for this hierarchic construction from our case studies is suggestive but far from conclusive. Invariably our experts, in combination with the aggregation process, set the goal of trying to identify the most important or pivotal propositional disagreement in the issue. They often nominated and rejected many such disagreements in the course of arriving at one. Whenever they nominated a disagreement as pivotal, they would search for the underlying agreements that channelled into that disagreement. They would also search for disagreements among authors who agreed in their response to the pivotal proposition.

A FRAMEWORK FOR STUDYING THE ROLE OF REPRESENTATIONS

In this section, we draw on an architectural model of human cognition developed by Anderson [And83] to explore the space of interactions between external and internal representations and to develop a framework for understanding the ways in which one representation may be better than another. This framework will serve as the methodological ground in studying the role of hypertext-based external representations in complex tasks.

To study the role of external representations, we need to define more precisely what we mean by a representation and to develop criteria for making a judgment that one representation is better than another. Following Bobrow, we define a representation as the result of a selective mapping M from a world W at time t: $W_t ->_M R_t$.1

We first must distinguish external representations from internal representations and define their interactions. Internal representations are stored in memory; external representations are stored on paper or some other medium. Internal representations, of course, are not directly observable. When we speak of an internal representation encoding particular units and relations, we mean that the particular internal representation is postulated in order to account for subjects' observable behavior.

In the remainder of this section, we discuss the interactions of internal and external representations in terms of the following components of human cognition: encoding processes, storage and retrieval processes, match and execution processes, and control of cognition. The discussion forms the basis for answering the question "When is one representation better than another?"

Encoding Processes

Encoding processes create an internal representation from an external representation and deposit the internal representation into working memory. The resulting internal representation may or may not be informationally equivalent to the external representation, where two representations are informationally equivalent if all of the information in one is also inferable from the other, and vice versa [Simo78]. There is considerable evidence that the encoding processes for external representations do not always create an informationally equivalent internal representation. For example, the encoding processes for sentences do not seem to encode the temporal sequence of words in most cases [Bran72]. Given the limits of the number of elements in working memory, it is probably adaptive for subjects not to encode elements that are usually irrelevant to processing tasks.

---

1   Where W can also be a representation [Bobr79]. If W has a set of actions that change the state of W to W', then we may define a set of operations, R_O, on R that operate on R in order to change R to R' in response to W-->W' instead of mapping from W' to obtain R'.

Although the encoding processes do not necessarily produce an internal representation that is informationally equivalent to the external representation, they can. Indeed, in a recent article on external representations, in particular, on the role of diagram versus words, Larkin and Simon ground their discussion in the hypothesis that the encoding processes for diagrams and words produce informationally equivalent internal representations, but that the internal representations for diagrams are not computationally equivalent to the internal representations for words, that is, the set of processes that operate on the diagrammatic versus verbal internal representations do not carry out those operations with equivalent ease and speed [Lark87]. A study by Santa provides evidence for their hypothesis [Sant77]. Santa presented subjects with a spatial configuration of verbal elements and a spatial configuration of geometric elements. Santa predicted that subjects would encode the verbal material serially in the normal left-to-right, top-to-bottom reading order; he predicted that subjects would encode geometric material in a way that preserved spatial information. If this prediction were the case, then the internal representations would be informationally equivalent but computationally inequivalent. Subjects were asked to verify whether a test array contained the same elements as the study array. Some test arrays were identical to the study array, others arrayed the elements linearly. Subjects' reaction times confirmed Santa's prediction: For the verbal material, subjects made judgments more quickly when the test array was linear rather than identical; for the geometric material, subjects made judgments more quickly when the test array was identical rather than linear.

The Santa study also demonstrates that in the absence of other information (e.g., what the external representation is going to be used for), the encoding processes are influenced by the type of elements (e.g., verbal, geometric) that are being encoded. An experiment by Bower and Springston demonstrates that the encoding processes are strongly influenced by properties of the representation such as time, color, size, and so on [Bowe70]. Subjects were induced by pauses or variations in size and color to miss encoding a set of letters into familiar chunks (e.g., IC BMF BIU SAOK instead of ICBM FBI USA OK). Subjects remembered fewer letters from the hard to encode lists than from the easy to encode lists. It is reasonable to suppose that encoding processes are both data-driven and context-driven (e.g., to a certain extent, the same representation may be encoded in different ways for use in different problem-solving contexts); it is also reasonable to suppose that encoding processes themselves change in response to problem-solving experience.

In addition to evidence that some representations are encoded in computationally inequivalent representations, there is also evidence that the computational inequivalence of representations can significantly influence subjects' problem-solving performance [Haye77, Paig66, Simo76]. For example, Paige and Simon documented that in some problems, crucial relationships among components of a problem are easier for subjects to discover with an external diagrammatic representation than with an external verbal representation [Paig66]. The verbal and diagrammatic external representations were informationally equivalent. If we assume that the internal representations that subjects encoded were also informationally equivalent, then the effect can be plausibly explained if it is attributed to the computational inequivalence of subjects' internal representations: Subjects operating with the internal verbal representation, in which the relationship is not explicitly represented, fail to make the inferences necessary to discover the crucial relationships; subjects operating with the internal diagrammatic representation do not need to infer the relationship, since it is represented explicitly.

This discussion suggests that we can compare external representations as follows:

1. One external representation can be better than another if it helps a subject encode more elements that are relevant to a particular problem-solving activity than another, or fewer elements that are irrelevant.

2. One external representation can be better than another if the subject's encoding processes produce informationally equivalent internal representations, but the subject has a set of processes that operate more easily and efficiently on one internal representation than another.

Storage and Retrieval Processes

Storage processes create permanent records in declarative memory of the contents of working memory. Retrieval processes access internal representations in long term, declarative memory and deposit them in working memory.

The elements that the encoding processes deposit into working memory act as sources of activation in memory. These elements stay active for a period of time. An element that is a source of activation by direct perception, however, only becomes inactive after it is no longer directly perceived. By keeping an element in direct perception, external representations can affect the duration of an element in working memory. How does duration in working memory affect storage and retrieval?

Although an element in working memory that is still being directly perceived remains in working memory, there is evidence that the duration in working memory is not related to whether the element will be stored permanently [Crai73]. Thus, it is unlikely that the continued activation of elements in the presence of external representations by itself will improve memory for the element.

Although duration in working memory does not affect whether an element is stored, it may affect how and where the element is stored. Permanent declarative knowledge is stored in chunks (or cognitive units). Broadbent has suggested that the ability to combine elements into chunks depends on the ability to access those elements in working memory [Broa75]. An external representation that keeps otherwise widely separated elements in working memory may increase the likelihood that they will be stored as a unit. For example, in an argumentative text, the elements that subjects need to identify as instances of *see-the-issue*, *define-the-problem*, and *propose-a-solution* may occur at widely separate locations. Subjects who lack strong schema for argumentative texts are unlikely to activate the schema upon encountering an element. However, if the elements needed for the schema are represented externally and, as a result, are still in working memory, the likelihood of activation will be increased. Although this explanation was not suggested, it is consistent with Dansereau et al.'s findings of a facilitative effect for less skilled readers of external, network representations of texts [Dans79].

Because elements in the external representation that are perceived remain active and do not need to be retrieved, we might expect that the external representation could reduce retrieval failures if it helps people maintain the elements needed in processing in working memory. In addition, the elements in working memory can act also as primes for associative activation, facilitating retrieval of related elements. It is interesting to note that representations that are informationally equivalent can serve this role. For example, a study by Glynn and DiVesta found facilitative effects on retrieval in the presence of an external, structured outline [Glyn77].

These observations allow us to add to our developing understanding of the ways in which one representation might be better than another:

3. One external representation can be better than another if it increases the likelihood that the element will be stored in a chunk that will be useful in problem-solving; since elements in a chunk are retrieved together, such chunking can reduce search upon retrieval, that is, it can reduce the time needed for associative activation of the chunked elements.

4. One external representation can be better than another if it reduces the need to retrieve the element, either because the element is currently being perceived and is already in working memory or because the element is easily re-encodable through a perceptual scan of the external representation.

5. One external representation can be better than another if it primes related elements for retrieval and these elements are needed for problem-solving.

Match and Execution Processes

A matching process puts data in working memory in correspondence with the conditions of productions. Productions consist of condition-action pairs. The condition specifies a set of features that must be in working memory. The action specifies a set of structures that will be deposited in working memory. When the condition of a production matches a set of structures in working memory, the production is selected to apply and the execution processes deposit the action side in working memory. Since the structures that the actions of productions deposit in working memory compete with other elements, external representations can clearly be useful as memory aids for helping to store intermediate results of operations.

Control of Cognition

The matching processes control the major processes of cognition including perception, attention, and motor control. Although a major source for the control of cognition is data-driven, another major source of control is the goals that the actions of productions can deposit into working memory. These goals then act as sources of activation; activation spreading from the current goal will maintain closely linked goals in working memory as well. The rest of the goals, however, will have to be retrieved from long term memory. Given the limitations of long term memory retrieval, there will be many failures to retrieve goals. An external representation of goals could be expected to have a facilitative effect on maintaining goals. Burtis et al. report that experienced writers often use notes of their goals to keep themselves on task [Burt83]. Singley reports a facilitative effect of an external representation of goals for novice LISP learners [Sing87]. External representations then can be useful for keeping track of goals.

In performing under the control of a goal structure, problem solvers can encounter points where insufficient information exists to achieve the next goal. In this case, a problem solver must often choose to guess or to postpone an action and set an intention to deal with it later (delay execution). Because human ability to maintain prior states of control in problem solving is severely limited [Gree74], we can expect a facilitative effect for a representation of goals that the problem solver intends to return to later.

These observations allow us to add again to our picture of the ways in which one representation can be better than another:

6. One external representation can be better than another if it is a better medium for storing intermediate results of operations.

7. One external representation can be better than another if it helps to maintain the activation of the current goal or to retrieve the next goal.

8. One external representation can be better than another if it helps the problem-solver to maintain a set of goals that must be returned to when the problem-solver has more information.

APPLYING OUR THEORY TO INTERFACE DESIGN

The framework just outlined does not, unfortunately, *generate* user interfaces for tasks. It does, however, provide a heuristic by which to think about the role of external representations and to compare them. This section describes the design of interfaces to augment writers' performance on a written synthesis task and analyzes them with the aid of our theory of the cognitive processes involved in synthesis writing and our heuristic framework for studying the role of external representations. For the purposes of description, it is useful to start with our representational theory of the knowledge structures writers build as they design a synthesis. The names of these knowledge structures correspond to the names of individual tools that will assist writers in building them. We call these tools Notes, Summary Graph, Synthesis Grid, and Synthesis Tree.

To make the work of these representations clear and to sketch how they communicate with one another, we ask the reader to follow a hypothetical writer using these programs to write a synthesis of essays on the issue of animal experimentation.

The Summary Environment

Notes

Figure 1 depicts a screen from a note-taking program we have already implemented called Notes [Neuw87].[2] The program allows writers to take notes on source texts, either hard copy or stored as computer files. The left portion of Figure 1 shows a source text, C.R. Gallistel, "Bell, Magendie, and the Proposals to Restrict the Use of Animals in Neurobehavioral Research." To the right, in a region labeled *All Notes List*, is a list of notes that a writer has been taking on the Gallistel article. Further to the right, in the region labeled *View Notes*, are the contents of those notes. Above the *All Notes List*, in a region labeled *Classes*, is a set of user-defined classes by which users can categorize their notes.

The Notes program is intended to augment writers' performance in encoding source texts and retrieving what they have encoded, and in encoding and retrieving their responses, reactions, and evaluations of those texts.

---

[2] The Notes program supports work in a variety of reading and writing courses on the CMU campus. The other interfaces described in this section are currently being designed as part of a project entitled "The Work-in-Preparation" (PREP) Editor: Support for Co-Authoring and Commenting," James Morris, David S. Kaufer, Christine M. Neuwirth, Ravinder Chandhok, Principal Investigators, NSF Grant No. IRI-8902891.

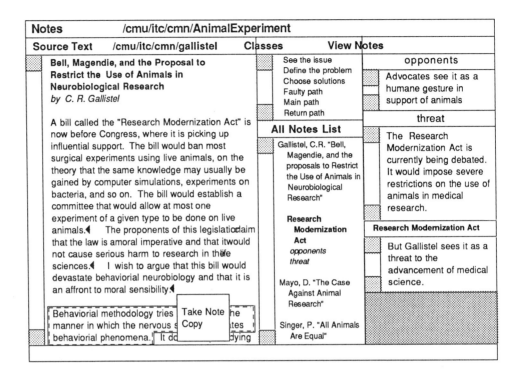

Figure 1. The Notes program.

Summary Graph

Figure 2 depicts a Summary Graph, a representation of the schema we hypothesized experts employ for encoding an argumentative text, namely, as a path through an issue, from seeing it, defining it and choosing a solution. The main path represents the position of the author of the argumentative text. Faulty paths represent the positions of those that the author opposes. Return paths represent the author's reasons for rejecting positions on the faulty paths. An author's linear text may contain all of the schema elements depicted in Figure 2, but in a different order, or it may leave out some elements altogether. But, we hypothesize, experts can be usefully described as instantiating a linear text within this schema.

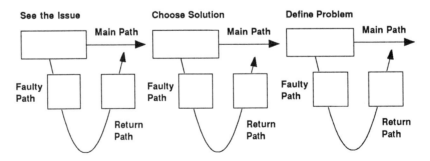

Figure 2. A Summary Graph.

Figure 3 depicts a portion of a Summary Graph for Gallistel on the issue of animal experimentation. The graph is a competing external representation for the information depicted in the Notes interface in Figure 1.

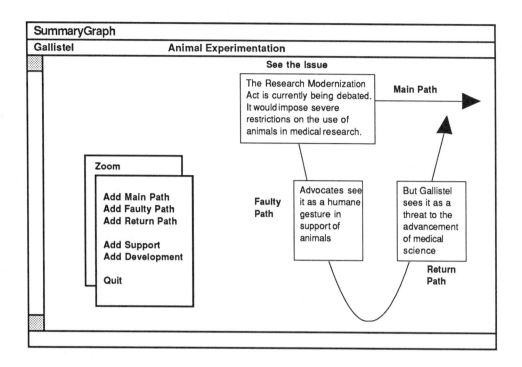

Figure 3. A portion of an instantiated Summary Graph

The Summary Graph may help writers, particularly novice writers, encode more elements that are relevant to synthesis writing–and fewer irrelevant ones–than the Notes program interface. Unlike the Notes program, it may focus novice writers' attention explicitly on the elements that experts focus upon.[3] Likewise, the representation may help novice writers maintain goal activation. An empty cell in the graph may help them to notice that they have missed encoding some part of the author's position on the issue.[4] On the other hand, expert writers already seem to encode relevant elements and exhibited little trouble in maintaining goals in this part of the task, so the Summary Graph may not be superior to Notes for them in this regard. Indeed, since the Notes program allows writers to record their own elaborations of the source text material while they are encoding the source itself, Notes may be a better encoding interface than the Summary Graph for experts. On its face, it is a better medium for storing a wider variety of the intermediate results that experts generated during this reading-to-write task.

The Summary Graph may also provide writers, both novices and experts, with more help than Notes in working with the relationships among the argumentative elements. Note that in the Summary Graph, the relationships among faulty path, return path and seeing the issue are represented explicitly whereas they have only an implicit representation (via the class mechanism) in Notes. The two representations may be informationally equivalent, but writers may be able to operate more easily and efficiently on the representation which depicts the relationships explicitly. For example, such an encoding may help writers when they are drafting summaries of the argument. Likewise, the Summary Graph may increase the likelihood that the argumentative elements will be stored as a single chunk, reducing search upon retrieval.

---

[3] Of course, novice writers must be taught to understand the meanings of these elements and to recognize them in source texts. See [Kauf89] for a textbook.

[4] In one instance, when a source text omitted an explicit discussion of "seeing-the-issue," we observed an expert trying to infer what the author might have said, based on what would be consistent with the rest of the source text.

The Synthesis Environment

Synthesis Grid

Figure 4 depicts a Synthesis Grid on the issue of Animal Experimentation.

The purpose of this structure is to let writers explore points of local similarity and difference across authors. The first column of the grid depicts the names of authors–Cohen, Gallistel, etc.–summarized in previously constructed Notes or Summary Graphs. This column is automatically generated. The remaining columns depict authors' responses to abbreviated propositions (e.g., Results Important, Alternative Means, etc.), responses which relate or distinguish them on the dimension of similarity/difference. Discovering these dimensions (column headings) is the goal of building a synthesis grid.

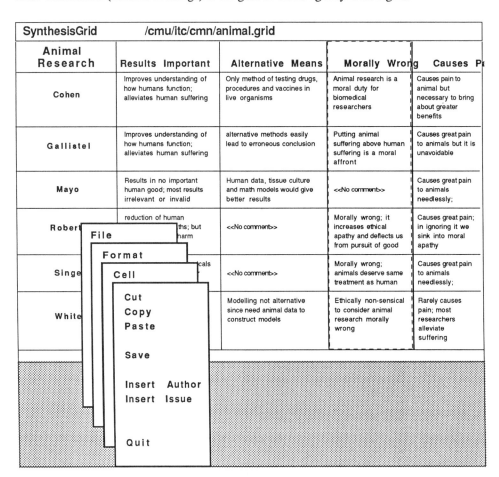

Figure 4. A Synthesis Grid.

To discover these dimensions, writers can automatically route their summary notes into the cells of this grid. The grid starts with columns for each milestone: "see the issue," "define the problem," "choose a solution." Summary notes sorted across authors and indexed at the same milestone can be shuffled and reshuffled under that column heading until the writer is ready to decompose the "see the issue" column into more specific dimensions. The writer can edit the summary notes so that they look like responses to the propositions. For example, in the summarizing space, the note on Cohen under the column heading "Morally Wrong" is not phrased as a response to the proposition, "The results of animal research are morally wrong." But now, as part of the synthesis grid, a writer, to make progress toward a synthesis, might come to view this note as a response to that proposition – and edit it accordingly.

We hypothesize that the Synthesis Grid will be superior to the Notes or Summary Graph representations in producing a synthesis because the processes of searching for similarities/differences across authors operate more efficiently on this representation: Elements needed by those processes are more easily retrieved through a perceptual scan of the external representation. Like the Summary Graph, the Synthesis Grid representation can cause writers to notice that they have missed encoding an author's position on some part of an issue. For example, the cell Mayo/Morally Wrong may be empty because the writer failed to notice Mayo's position when reading the original source text (cf. [vanL85]).

Synthesis Tree

Figure 5 depicts a Synthesis Tree. The Synthesis Tree goes a step beyond the Synthesis Grid. Whereas the Grid enables writers to index their notes on authors around common propositions, there are no relationships holding across propositions (column headings) and so no guarantee that anything but *local* similarities and differences across authors are being represented. What is needed is a way to index authors within a structure that explicitly represents hierarchies of *overall* agreement and disagreement. Agreements or disagreements high in the hierarchy propagate down and so are more important than agreements or disagreements lower in the hierarchy.

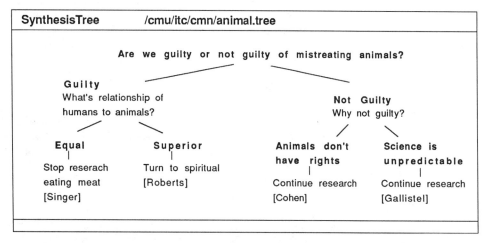

Figure 5. A Synthesis Tree.

A synthesis tree is a data structure that allows writers to index authors within this hierarchy of overall agreement and disagreement. Writers build the tree in three steps. First, they design what they perceive to be the most salient division among authors. Without labeling this split, they make a binary (sometimes tertiary) sort of authors according to where they fall along this division. The system then creates two (or three) branches sprouting from a root with the authors sorted according to branches. The writer is now prompted to label the branches. This labeling completes the major division (the crux) of the issue. Writers then design the tree both above the crux and below it. To design *up* from the crux, they are directed to search their synthesis grid for agreements across authors who occupy different branches at the crux. These agreements are called preliminary agreements because they represent commonalities between authors before they split at the crux. To design *down* from the crux, writers are directed to search their synthesis grid for disagreements across authors who occupy the same branch at the crux. These disagreements are called minor disagreements because they represent splinterings that arise between authors who occupy the same node at the crux. The division at the crux is a one time decision. Designing preliminary splits above and minor splits below the crux are iterative decisions.

In Figure 5, a writer has represented the division at the question "Are we guilty or not guilty of mistreating animals?" as the crux of the issue. The authors Singer and Roberts both fall on the same branch at the crux. They are opposed to Cohen and Gallistel on this same question. However, subsequent to their agreement at the crux, Singer and Roberts part company on the question of the relationship of humans to animals. And Cohen and Gallistel part company on their explanation as to why we are not guilty of mistreating animals. The Synthesis Tree provides an overall design structure for the written synthesis. That is, this tree can be linearized into a plan for a formal synthesis paper.

We expect the Synthesis Tree to be a better representation than the Grid for writers who are trying to find the most important unresolved differences among authors. It provides a medium for storing writers' intermediate decisions about importance of disagreement. In addition, writers can scan the tree and see, at a glance, the relationships among authors. For example, it is easy to see that the disagreement between Singer and Roberts is a disagreement "among friends."

Cognitive Control

Representation of Goals

Figure 6 depicts a goal tree for the synthesis writing task. The goal tree program will allow writers to traverse the tree in a depth-first order via a **Next** option or in a user-defined order. In addition, the program will allow writers to mark a goal as suspended. Marking a goal as suspended will put the goal on a Return List, a list of goals that the writer wants to be reminded to return to later.

Support for Backtracking

The processes of synthesis writing that we have been sketching require writers to abstract from the original source texts. Such abstractions are often open to significant revisions as the writer's understanding of the issue evolves. In a hypertext environment, these abstractions can be linked to their supporting locations in the source texts.[5] When writers need to return to the source texts to check their abstractions for accuracy against their current understanding, such links reduce search upon retrieval.

Such backtracking is a characteristic of open-ended design tasks. Thus, an architectural requirement for the system is support for backtracking. In particular, the system must allow users to trace information that they have transformed from the original source text to notes to summary to synthesis and so on. For example, whenever the user takes a note, the Notes program creates a link that links the passage in the source text to the note. As the information is viewed and perhaps altered in different viewing environments (e.g., in the Synthesis Grid), the system must maintain links to its history in those environments. At any time, the user can request to see the representation of that information in different environments, perhaps to check its accuracy, its placement in relation to other propositions, and so on. Figure 7 illustrates a writer selecting the menu option "History As Source Text." This click opens up a window with Gallistel's original source text. It highlights and activates passages of Gallistel's text that lie in the scope of the currently activated notes.

---

5 For offline texts, abstractions can be linked to supporting quotations and page numbers.

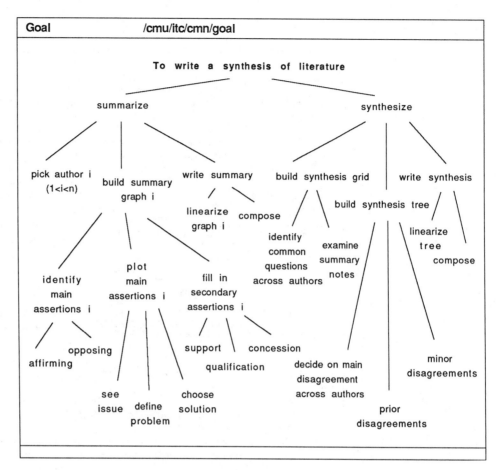

Figure 6. A Goal Tree.

Our case studies suggest two reasons why writers need to backtrack. First, they need to explore previous paths in order to get a perspective on their current progress. Second, they need to search for decisions they want to undo. The need to undo many of these decisions only reveals itself after progressing further through the task. Thus a writer will often learn that the notes and summaries taken are nonoptimal only *after* entering the synthesis space. Previous views don't simply inform current views; current views can also inform previous ones as well. Building tools that support such backtracking will allow us to explore whether writers will be less prone to premature closure in their search for good solutions [Perk81], and if so, whether more search translates to better solutions.

Support for Bottom-up and Top-down Planning

Writing actual prose represents a bottom-up planning procedure. As in other complex tasks, our experts engaged in a combination of top-down and bottom-up planning. It is unclear, however, whether writers need to plan bottom-up or whether bottom-up planning results from failure to retrieve goals. Thus, another architectural requirement is support for bottom-up and top-down planning. For example, the system must support movement from prose to notes as easily as writers can at the present time convert notes to prose.

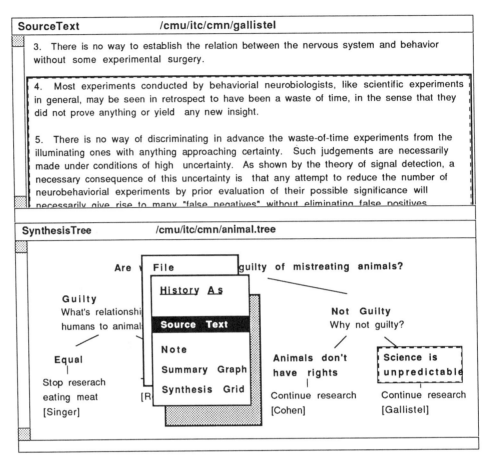

Figure 7. Support for backtracking.

RELATED WORK

Smith, Weiss, and Ferguson have been developing WE, a Writing Environment to support professional writers [Smit87]. WE provides two major external representations, "Network Mode" and "Tree Mode," and two subordinate ones, "Editor Mode," through which the user associates text with nodes in the network or tree, and "Text Mode," by which the user can see a linearization of the nodes and text in Tree Mode, where the nodes represent headings, subheadings, and so forth. Like WE, we advocate a general graph object. But we advocate task- and user-specific instantiations of graph objects to support specific cognitive processes (e.g., SummaryGraph for encoding relevant elements in arguments of policy). Like WE, we advocate a general tree object. But again, we advocate task- and user-specific uses for the tree. For example, the SynthesisTree represents a *plan* for a written synthesis, but the nodes do not represent headings, subheadings, and so forth of a linear document. The work we have described here is complementary to WE, since the sort of mechanisms provided by WE's Network Mode and Tree Mode could be useful for a writer who is drafting a written synthesis after having used Notes, Summary Graph, Synthesis Grid, and Synthesis Tree to create a design for one.

Numerous projects are involved in representing arguments by displaying views of the relationships among various elements. Conklin and Begemen are developing gIBIS, a hypertext system to support the collaborative construction of Issue Based Information Systems [Conk87b]. Again, the work we describe here is complementary. For example, gIBIS assumes that users know what the issue is, and provides them with a structure for representing an issue's elements. In contrast, our work has been focused on discovering what the issues are across a range of sources. Also, the external representations we are developing may prove useful in synthesizing networks like those in gIBIS. Smolensky,

Bell, Fox, King and Lewis are developing EUCLID, a hypertext system designed to represent the logical structure of philosophical arguments [Smol87]. Their development effort has focused on developing alternative representions of argumentative texts themselves, whereas ours has focused on analyzing cognitive processes of authors working with traditional linear representations of argumentative texts and providing support for those processes. Marshall has been using the Xerox's NoteCards system [Hala87b] to develop a methodology for exploring representation issues for various application areas, including argumentation [Mars87]. Like EUCLID, the representations are of argumentative texts themselves, in this case, legal arguments.

IMPLICATIONS FOR THE DESIGN OF HYPERTEXT

The external representations we envision have a couple implications for the design of hypertext systems to support them. First, our framework for comparing external representations implies that the "best" external representation depends intimately on the cognitive processes that the user is performing and upon the user's own knowledge and skills. This suggests that the flexibility needed to allow users to view hypertext networks through multiple representations, to move from one representation to another, and to tailor representations for themselves will continue to be an important issue in the design of hypertext systems [Hala87a].

Another implication concerns the issue of types of nodes the system supports, in particular, types of composites. Halasz defines the semantics of composites as inclusion 'by reference' rather than 'by value.' In inclusion by reference, changes to the components of a composite node are reflected in the composite and changes in the composite would actually change the components [Hala87a]. In inclusion 'by value,' changes made in the composite are not automatically reflected in the component, nor vice versa. In an application such as the Synthesis Grid, however, it would be useful to define another composite type in which the component would be included 'by value, ' but with the links from the composite to the components retained. Note that the 'by value' component needs itself to be includable in other composites. For example, the revisions a writer creates in a Summary Graph (a composite of selections from the source texts) need to be able to work as components of a composite in the Synthesis Grid.

FUTURE PLANS

In conjunction with the development of these hypertext-based external representations, we plan to conduct a set of studies to help us answer three research questions. In this section, we briefly outline these questions. The framework for studying the role of external representations will both guide these studies and itself be put to the test as to its usefulness in guiding research on user interface.

Question 1: Are the assumptions about representation that our interface design makes warranted? This is a question of the validity of our knowledge representations for writing. It would be foolish to implement representations that don't matter to high quality summaries and syntheses or that writers are unable to use effectively.

Question 2: Do our hypertext-based interfaces effectively support the building of knowledge structures they are designed to support? This is a question of formative evaluation.

Question 3: What is the effect of our writing environment on the quality of a written synthesis and the time it takes to complete one? How will writers using our tools compare to writers using a simple text-editor? Does it make a difference if the writer is an expert? A novice? This is a question of summative evaluation.

ACKNOWLEDGMENTS

The ideas presented here were developed during many discussions Dick Hayes, Jim Morris and Rob Chandhok. Thanks to Terilyn Gillespie for her assistance with all aspects of this project and to Soo-Tsu Leng for his assistance with the illustrations. Thanks also to the Hypertext '89 reviewers for their helpful comments.

REFERENCES

[Ande83]   Anderson, J.R. *The Architecture of Cognition*. Cambridge, MA: Harvard University Press, 1983.

[Ande84]   Anderson, R.C., & Pearson, P.D. A schema-theoretic view of basic processes in reading comprehension. In P.D. Pearson, (Ed.), *Handbook of Reading Research*, pp. 255-291. New York: Longman, 1984.

[Bobr79]   Bobrow, D.G. Dimensions of Representation. In D.G.Bobrow & A. Collins (Eds.), *Representation and Understanding*, pp. 1-34. NY, NY: Academic Press, 1979.

[Bowe70]   Bower, G.H., & Springston, F. Pauses as recoding points in letter series. *Journal of Experimental Psychology* , 83, 1970, 421-430.

[Bran72]   Bransford, J.D., Barclay, J.R. , & Franks, J.J. Sentence memory: A constructive versus interpretive approach. *Cognitive Psychology*, 3, 1972, 193-209.

[Broa75]   Broadbent, D.E. The magical number seven after fifteen years. In R.A. Kennedy & A. Wilkes (Eds.), *Studies in Long-term Memory*. New York: Wiley, 1975.

[Burt83]   Burtis, P.J., Bereiter, C., Scardamailia, M., & Tetroe, J. The development of planning in writing. In G. Wells & B. Kroll (Eds.) *Explorations in the Development of Writing*. Chichester, England: JohnWiley and Sons, 1983.

[Bush45]   Bush, V. As we may think. *Atlantic Monthly*,176, July 1945, 101-108.

[Char87]   Charney, D. Comprehending non-linear text: The role of discourse cues and reading strategies. *Hypertext '87 Papers,* The University of North Carolina, Chapel Hill, NC, November 13-15, 1987, 109-120.

[Conk87a]   Conklin, J. *A survey of hypertext*. MCC Technical Report STP-356-86, Rev. 1, Microelectronics and Computer Technology Corporation, February, 1987.

[Conk87b]   Conklin, J., & Begeman, M.L. gIBIS: A hypertext tool for team design deliberation. *Hypertext '87 Papers*. The University of North Carolina, Chapel Hill, NC, November 13-15, 1987, 247-252.

[Crai73]   Craik, F.I.M., & Watkins, M.J. The role of rehearsal in short-term memory. *Journal of Verbal Learning and Verbal Behavior*,12, 1973, 599-607.

[Dans79]   Dansereau, D. F. et al. Development and evaluation of a learning strategy training program. *Journal of Educational Psychology* 71(1), 1979, 64-73.

[Engle3]   Engelbart, D.C. A conceptual framework for the augmentation of man's intellect. In P.W. Howerton & D.C. Weeks (Eds.) *Vistas in Information Handling*, Vol. 1. London: Spartan Books, 1963.

[Enge68]   Engelbart, D.C., & English, W.K. A research center for augmenting human intellect. *Proceedings of 1968 Fall Joint Computer Conference*, 33 Part 1, Montvale, N.J.: AFIPS Press, 1968, 395-410.

[Flow81]   Flower, L., & Hayes, J.R. The pregnant pause: An inquiry into the nature of planning. *Research in the Teaching of English*, 15, October, 1981, 229-243.

[Foss89]   Foss, C.L. *Detecting lost users: Empirical studies on browsing hypertext.* INRIA Technical Report No. 972, L'institut National de Recherche en Informatique et en automatique, Sophia-Antipolis, 2004 Route des Lucioles, 06565 Valbonne, France, February, 1989.

[Geis86]   Geisler, C. Taking control of the text: Transforming issues through reading and writing. Paper presented at the American Educational Research Association, San Francisco, April 1986.

[Glyn77]   Glynn, S.M., & DiVesta, F.J. Outline and hierarchical organization aids for study and retrieval. *Journal of Educational Psychology* 69(2), 1977, 89-95.

[Glyn82]   Glynn, S.M., Britton, B.K., Muth, K. D., & Dogen, N. Writing and revising persuasive documents: Cognitive demands. *Journal of Educational Research* 74(4), 1982, 557-567.

[Gold80]   Goldstein, I.P., & Bobrow, D.G. Descriptions for a programming environment. *Proceedings of the First Conference AAAI*, August 1980.

[Gold84]   Goldstein, I.P., & Bobrow, D.G. A layered approach to software design. In D. Barstow, H. Shrobe, & E. Sandewall (Eds.) *Interactive Programming Environments*. McGraw-Hill, 1984, 387-413.

[Gree74]   Greeno, J.G., & Simon, H.A. Processes for sequence production. *Psychological Review* , 81, 1974, 187-198.

[Hala87a]   Halasz, F.G. Reflections on Notecards: Seven issues for the next generation of hypermedia systems. *Hypertext '87 Papers*. The University of North Carolina, Chapel Hill, NC, November 13-15, 1987, 345-366.

[Hala87b]   Halasz, F., Moran, T., & Trigg, R. NoteCards in a nutshell. *CHI+GI*, Toronto, Ontario, April 5-9, 1987, 45-52.

[Haye79]   Hayes-Roth, B., & Hayes-Roth, F. A cognitive model of planning. *Cognitive Science*, 3, 1979, 275-310.

[Haye77]   Hayes, J.R., & Simon, H.A. Psychological differences among problem isomorphs. In N.J. Castellan, D.B. Pisoni, & G.R. Potts (Eds.), *Cognitive Theory*, Vol. 2, pp. 21-41. Hillsdale, NJ: Lawrence Erlbaum Associates, 1977.

[Jeff81]   Jeffries, R., Turner, A.A., Polson, P.G. & Atwood, M.E. The processes involved in designing software. In J.R. Anderson (Ed.), *Cognitive Skills and Their Aquisition*, pp. 255-283. Hillsdale, NJ: Lawrence Erlbaum Associates, 1981.

[Kauf86]   Kaufer, D.S., Hayes, J.R., & Flower, L. Composing written sentences. *Research in the Teaching of English* 20(2), May, 1986, 121-140.

Kauf89]   Kaufer, D.S., Geisler, C., & Neuwirth, C.M. *Arguing from Sources: Exploring Issues through Reading and Writing*, San Diego: Harcourt Brace Jovanovich, 1989.

[Lark87]   Larkin, J.H., & Simon, H.A. Why a diagram is (sometimes) worth ten thousand words. *Cognitive Science,* 11, 1987, 65-99.

[Mars87]   Marshall, C.C. Exploring representation problems using hypertext. *Hypertext '87 Papers.* The University of North Carolina, Chapel Hill, NC, November 13-15, 1987, 253-268.

[Morr86]   Morris, J.H., Satyanarayanan, M., Conner, M.H., Howard, J.H., Rosenthal, D.S., & Smith, F.D. Andrew: A distributed personal computing environment. *Communications of the ACM* 29(3), March, 1986, 184-201.

[Paig66]   Paige, J.M., & Simon, H.A. Cognitive processes in solving algebra word problems. In B. Kleinmuntz (Ed.), *Problem Solving: Research, Method and Theory.* New York: John Wiley, & Sons, Inc., 1966.

[Perk81]   Perkins, D.N. *The Mind's Best Work.* Cambridge, MA: Harvard University Press, 1981.

[Robe81]   Robertson, G., McCracken, D., & Newell, A. The ZOG approach to man-machine communication. *International Journal of Man-Machine Studies,* 14, 1981, 461-488.

[Sant77]   Santa, J.L. Spatial transformations of words and pictures. *Journal of Experimental Psychology: Human Learning and Memory,* 3, 1977, 418-427.

[Shne86]   Shneiderman, B., & Morariu, J. The interactive encyclopedia system (TIES), Department of Computer Science, University of Maryland, College Park, MD 20742, June 1986.

[Simo69]   Simon, H.A. *The Sciences of the Artificial.* Cambridge, MA: The MIT Press, 1969.

[Simo76]   Simon, H.A., & Hayes, J.R. The understanding process: Problem isomorphs. *Cognitive Psychology,* 8, 1976, 165-190.

[Simo78]   Simon, H.A. On the forms of mental representation. In C.W. Savage (Eds.), *Minnesota studies in the Philosophy of Science. Vol IX: Perception and Cognition: Issues in the Foundation of Psychology.* University of Minnesota, Minneapolis, 1978.

[Sing87]   Singley, K. The effect of goal-posting on operator selection. Paper presented at the Third International Conference on AI and Education, Pittsburgh, May 1987.

[Smit87]   Smith, J.C., Weiss, S.F., & Ferguson, G.J. A hypertext writing environment and its cognitive basis. *Hypertext '87 Papers.* The University of North Carolina, Chapel Hill, NC, November 13-15, 1987, 195-214.

[Smol87]   Smolensky, P., Bell, B., Fox, B., King, R., & Lewis, C. Constraint-based hypertext for argumentation. *Hypertext '87 Papers.* The University of North Carolina, Chapel Hill, NC, November 13-15, 1987, 215-246.

[Soka74]   Sokal, R. R. Classification: purposes, principles, progress, prospects. *Science*, 185, 1974, 115-123.

[Trig83]   Trigg, R. *A network-based approach to text handling for the online scientific community*, PhD Thesis, Dept. of Computer Science, University of Maryland, 1983.

[Trig87]   Trigg, R.H., & Irish, P.M. Hypertext habitats: Experiences of writers in NoteCards. *Hypertext '87 Papers.* The University of North Carolina, Chapel Hill, NC, November 13-15, 1987, 89-108.

[vanL85]   van Lehn, K. *Theory reform caused by an argumentation tool.* Xerox Palo Alto Research Center Technical Report, ISL-11, 1985.

[Yank85]   Yankelovich, N., Meyrowitz, N., & van Dam, A. Reading and writing the electronic book. *IEEE Computer*, October, 1985.

From Ideas and Arguments to Hyperdocuments: Travelling through Activity Spaces

Norbert A. Streitz, Jörg Hannemann, and Manfred Thüring

Integrated Publication and Information Systems Institute (IPSI)
Gesellschaft für Mathematik und Datenverarbeitung mbH (GMD)
Dolivostraße 15
D-6100 Darmstadt
F. R. Germany (F.R. Germany)

INTRODUCTION

Discussing relevant issues for the next generation of hypermedia systems, Halasz [Hala88] provides also a classification along the following three dimensions: scope, browsing vs. authoring, and target task domain. In this paper, we will especially discuss aspects of the second dimension focussing on support for idea processing and authoring in hypertext systems. Although one cannot classify existing systems by assigning them exclusively to one category of this dimension[1] hypertext systems are primarily discussed from the reading and browsing point of view and as support for retrieval. This is also reflected in attempts to transform existing (linear) text sources into hypertext structures in order to profit from their additional interactive branching capabilities.

On the other hand, if one really wants to make use of the full concept of hypertext structures as described by Conklin [Conk87], this offers new and exciting possibilities for writing and for ways to support this activity. From our point of view [Stre88b], writing is a complex problem solving and design activity with multiple constraints. The final product - in terms of a hyperdocument - can be viewed as an externalized representation of internal knowledge structures which have been developed by the author. Thus, authoring tools which are especially geared to the preparation of hyperdocuments will offer much better facilities for conveying the message and intention of authors. This way, they can communicate knowledge in a format which is closer to their knowledge structures than it was possible with traditional documents. Integrating additional information about the author's intentions and knowledge structure and shipping it to the reader as part of an electronic document facilitates more comprehensive processing on the recipient's side. It implies that documents produced with these tools keep authors' knowledge structures alive by preserving their argumentation and rhetorical structures which then can be used for subsequent processing. This improves not only reception by human readers but also by text analysis components for machine translation or automated abstracting. While it is very difficult today to analyse argumentative and rhetorical aspects of natural language texts, these documents would contain this information explicitly. We will provide examples of this additional information when discussing the activity and document type "argumentation" which we selected as our task domain.

Another starting point for our research is the observation that almost all hypertext systems are - especially with respect to authoring - passive systems, i.e. they do not offer active (intelligent) support to the author by providing feedback, advice, or guiding. Of

---

[1] A clearcut distinction has been employed only with the separation of Concordia and the Document Examiner [Walk87].

course, the realization of this goal requires the integration of knowledge-based capabilities in a hypertext system. This implies that the architecture of the authoring tool includes components which permit monitoring and analysis of the author's activities. They are necessary to build up knowledge bases about authors and semantic structures of documents. But these provisions are rarely found in existing systems.

Based on this assessment of the current situation of hypertext systems, we are developing an active, knowledge-based authoring and idea processing tool for creating and revising hyperdocuments. The system - SEPIA: Structured Elicitation and Processing of Ideas for Authoring - will represent a major portion of the functionality we expect from an author's workbench of the future. The research presented in this paper represents only a part of it and must be viewed within this framework.

System design and prototype development of SEPIA is determined by two main objectives. Our first and overall objective is to build a cognitively adequate system. To accomplish this, we employ the approach of user-oriented and task-driven system design based on the principle of cognitive compatibility [Stre87]. This requires to use results derived from models about cognitive processes in writing and more general in problem solving. The second more ambitious objective is to build an active system. Especially by setting our focus this way, it was necessary to cut down the complexity of the general problem of active systems. We selected a finite but not trivial subset of authoring activities and document types: argumentation and argumentative texts. The activity as well as the document type are very well defined and exhibit structures which offer excellent starting points for monitoring and guiding.

AUTHORING SYSTEMS AND WRITING IN HYPERTEXT ENVIRONMENTS

As already mentioned in the introduction, hypertext systems can be distinguished by their primarily intended use: retrieving (browsing and searching) vs. authoring (creating and designing). This distinction does not exclude that some systems can be used for both purposes, e.g. KMS [Aksc88] or Intermedia [Yank85], but most of them differ in the extent of support for these two activities. Examples of the first type are HyperTIES [Marc88] with its usage in interactive museum exihibits and the Document Examiner [Walk87] as the on-line presentation of technical documentation from Symbolics. Although it also allows to create and organize personally structured selections of the total information offered it is a read-only system. The corresponding authoring tool (Concordia) has been made available separately.

Systems primarily designed for writing focus on tools for creating nodes and links, organizing them into network structures and revising these structures as well as the content of their nodes. Examples of authoring tools are: TEXTNET [Trig86] and NoteCards [Hala87] for idea processing, Writing Environment [Smit87] for document preparation or Neptune [Deli86] for supporting the design and documentation of large-scale software systems. Since Neptune is meant to support software engineering it also stresses versioning and node/link attributes. Systems as e.g. Guide [Brow87], HyperCard [Will87] and HyperTIES also show some limitations as they do not offer a graphical representation of the node-link structure of the hypertext network. This deficit results in a number of crucial problems connected with support for navigation (disorientation problem) and for personal information structuring. A special but for our intended research relevant application is to map argumentation structures onto hypertext structures. One of the rare examples is the gIBIS-system [Conk87b], a hypertext tool for team design deliberation.

Two general problems for authoring in hypertext environments can be identified. First, the problem of "cognitive overhead" [Conk87a] which results from the requirement to label nodes, links and structural relationships at a very early stage. NoteCards [Hala88] forces the user to label and link his nodes right away which often results in premature organization. This conflicts with a "natural" way of generating ideas and writing initial segments of text when structures are less definite in the beginning. Most of the time, they are not explicitly spelled out, exist only in the mind and evolve in a flexible way much later. Second, almost all authoring tools for hypertext are rather passive storage and retrieval systems, i.e. they do not provide active support compatible with the activities of the authors. By "active" we mean that the authoring tool should be able to monitor and guide authors in their problem solving activity.

In general, one can state that the issue of providing cognitively adequate support for authors of hypertext documents has not been addressed as much as is desirable. One exception is the approach connected with the development of the Writing Environment (WE) [Smit87, Smit88]. In this case, design decisions were based within a cognitive framework of writing. This approach is a very promising one, but the specific implementation is lacking some features of the full hypertext concept. Although WE provides a linking mechanism in the network mode the resulting structure is not preserved in the final document. Beyond this, there are more basic deficits in hypertext research with respect to writing. Research is not really addressing the crucial problem that writing a non-linear text might require very different concepts of creating, revising, and composing documents and therefore different kinds of support. On the other hand, the publishing situation to date does not really provide the external conditions and demands for having hypertext as the final document structure. This is also reflected in reports about authors using e.g. NoteCards for idea processing and structuring but turning to outliners and traditional text processing tools when writing the final document [Trig87].

DEVELOPMENT OF AUTHORING TOOLS AND THEORIES OF WRITING

A prerequisite for information retrieval - not only in hypertext systems - is that this information must have been produced some time before. While publishing is communicating knowledge, authoring and in particular writing is knowledge production and transformation. It can be observed that the construction of writing tools is mainly based on intuition and first-order task analysis. What is lacking is a sound theoretical foundation for building cognitively compatible interfaces which provide intelligent support for writing. Kintsch forecasts that the progress in this field will remain restricted unless a sufficient cognitive theory of writing is developed [Kint87]. This deficit is not surprising because cognitive processes of writing as opposed to reading and comprehension was a largely unexplored field in cognitive science. Although this situation is beginning to change, existing models of writing only emphasize a small section of this complex problem solving activity. We still do not know what is going on in authors' minds when they progress from "chaos to order" as Brown has characterized this process [Brow86].

The widely cited model of Hayes and Flower [Haye80] emphasizes the problem-solving aspect of writing. Based on the analysis of thinking aloud protocols, it identifies three main subprocesses (planning, translating, and reviewing) and their organization in the overall composing activity. Results from experimental research [Kell87] confirm this distinction and indicate that these processes are not subsequent stages but that they show up during the whole course of writing - though at different times with different frequency.

A model which reflects fundamental differences between novice and expert writers has been proposed by Scardamalia and Bereiter [Scar87]. It emphasizes the role of knowledge in the writing process and distinguishes between a knowledge telling and a knowledge transformation strategy. Knowledge transformation is conceived as an interaction between two problem spaces: the content space and the rhetorical space. While the content space is meant to be the space of generating and structuring the author's knowledge about the domain of the intended document, planning and organization of the document structure takes place in the rhetorical space. This is also the place where e.g. decisions on including, excluding, sequencing and reformulating information are made.

Another theory which will bear on the development of authoring systems stems from van Dijk and Kintsch [Dijk83, Kint88]. For our purposes, we will especially make use of their idea of different levels of text organization (micro- and macrostructure) and the corresponding operations (macrooperators) for mapping transitions between them. Whereas this is basically a semantic organization, we will also adopt a more syntactic differentiation proposed by Collins and Gentner [Coll80] between a global text level, a paragraph level (global sequencing) and the sentence or word level (local sequencing). At the global level we will refer to the concept of superstructures [Dijk83]. An example for such a structure is the organization of a scientific report consisting of hierarchically ordered elements, like introduction, method, results etc.

The case of argumentation

A special case of writing is the creation of argumentative texts. Although it seems pretty obvious to relate models of writing to research on argumentation, this is still lacking. On the other hand, there is a long tradition and a variety of schools of thought on what the basic elements of argumentative structures are [Toul58, Ritt72, Wund80, Kopp85]. Systems which are designed to support argumentation have to adopt a specific argumentation model. The gIBIS-system [Conk87] is based on Rittel´s ideas of Issue Based Information Systems (IBIS)[Ritt72]. Especially geared to computer-aided reasoning is ARL, a special argumentation representation language, proposed by Smolensky et al. [Smol88] which is used as the basis for the development of EUCLID - a system meant to support argumentation. Argumentation has been investigated to some extent - though mostly with focus different from ours. One example is the OpEd-system [Alva86] an implementation of a model of argument comprehension.

For the representation of arguments, we adopt a schema proposed by Toulmin [Toul58]. Figure 1 shows all different elements of a complete argument. While 'datum' and 'claim' are obligatory constituents, 'warrant', 'backing' and ' rebuttal' are optional. The relation 'so' links a datum and a claim, constituting the following argument which states: "The farmer who does without fertilizer and herbicides in the field and without hormones and tranquilizers in the pigsty has to work much harder than a chemistry farmer" --so--> "it is not worthwhile to produce natural food". Since we are dealing with common sense argumentation instead of formal logic reasoning, an argument is more readily accepted if one can provide a 'warrant' which legitimates the 'so' relation via the 'since' relationship. The warrant provides a general rule which justifies the 'so' conclusion. In a further step, this 'warrant' can be backed by a 'backing' giving evidence for the validity of this rule. In order to handle exceptions from the rule one can use the element 'rebuttal' which questions the claim. Although the original version of the Toulmin schema does not account for the concept of a backing for the 'unless' relationship, our analysis shows that this should be included in a complete schema.

Whereas the Toulmin schema provides an analysis at the micro level, we also need a representation of argumentation at the macro level. Kopperschmidt proposes a hierarchical organization of argumentation resulting in different levels of abstractions [Kopp85]. We will adopt this idea but use our own abstraction hierarchy which shares some featureswith the IBIS-approach [Kunz70, Conk87b] and with subsequent refinements by PHIBIS [McCa83]. This approach differentiates between three types of elements: issues, positions, and arguments. An issue describes the initial question to be answered by the argumentation. The main issues can be divided into subissues. For each subissue one can state at least two positions which can be supported or attacked by a number of arguments.

DESIGNING HYPERTEXT SYSTEMS

Cognitive compatibility, externalization, and activity spaces

As indicated before, the idea of cognitive compatibility [Stre87] is our prime principle and guides our system design. This implies that the environment offered to the author corresponds to properties inherent to different cognitive activities and structures of writing. Specifically, we assume that providing different representations which allow easy mapping of internal structures to external task structures and vice versa is a fundamental prerequisite for task-oriented system design [Stre88a]. Second, we adopt the principle of "externalization". Here, we argue that different skills and additional knowledge can be brought to bear on external representations than on internal ones. External representations are open to modification and reinterpretation in more tranparent ways than internal representations. This results in the guideline to provide means which enable the author to externalize as many internal or mental states and intermediary products as possible. Implementing this principle provides the author with different means for structured "thought dumping". Thus, externalization reduces mental load, especially memory load, which results in overcoming the limits of internal representations.

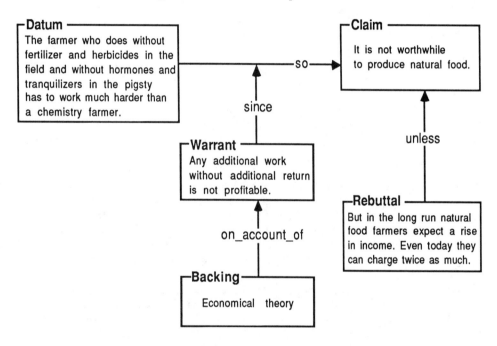

Figure 1. Example of a Toulmin Argumentation Schema

Observation of authors shows for the situation of outlining with paper and pencil that they make extensive use of scribbles and drawings with idiosyncratic notations in order to express part of their internal structures. A standard text editor does not provide a space to do this. There, the author has to write words and sentences - line by line. Usually, something like a scratchpad is not provided. And if one has something like it, it only offers standard graphical tools. But our argumentation is not aiming at providing sophisticated graphic capabilities. It is rather the idea to provide room for specialized notational schemata consisting of elements and relations (leading to node-link hyperstructures) and providing operations on these structures which correspond to generic mental operations of writing and arguing.

This goal is achieved by providing a variety of "activity spaces" realized by dedicated windows which differ in their structural setup and their inherent functionality. The number of activities supported and the extent of this functionality is identified on the basis of cognitive models of writing and task-specific features. Examples are modes for generating and structuring ideas for the content domain (content space), for the type/structure of the target document (rhetorical space), and the style/procedure of argumentation (argumentation space). Our idea of activity spaces originates from Newell's [Newe80] extension of the problem space to be the fundamental organization unit of all cognitive activities and the notion that more than one problem space can be generated during problem solving [Kant84]. Accordingly, we decompose the overall writing activity into a number of specific activities and assign a special space to each of them. Elements of activity spaces are not problem states. Instead, they function as objects of the problem solving activity and are presented to the problem solver who can manipulate them directly. This conceptualization results in a design which has some resemblance to the "Rooms"- metaphor of Card & Henderson an interface which supports fast task switching [Card87]. Furthermore, the idea of activity spaces is similar to the concept of having different windows for different cognitive modes in the WE-system [Smit88]. By distinguishing between network mode, tree mode, edit mode, and text mode, WE focusses mainly on the stages of preparing traditional (linear) documents. Our approach stresses additional cognitive features of the authoring activity, e.g. planning, argumentation, and rhetorical transformations.

Design specifications for activity spaces

Decisions about the number and the functionality of our activity spaces are based on a rationale by integrating results from different models of writing and text production[2]. Details and specifications of these spaces follow therefrom.

First, we adopt the general idea of Scardamelia & Bereiter and distinguish between a "content space" and a "rhetorical space" and corresponding activities [Scar87]. We expand their notion by viewing these spaces as two instantiations of our more general idea of activity specific problem spaces.

Second, we employ Hayes & Flower's analysis of identifying at least three main subprocesses of the writing activity: planning, translating, and reviewing, especially their differentiation of the planning process [Haye80]. Since planning is central to each phase of writing and its results coordinate and guide all other subprocesses, authors need an opportunity for externalization, monitoring and revision of their plans and goals whenever necessary. Therefore, we propose a third space: the planning space.

Third, we have to take into account that our specific activity and document, i.e. argumentation, requires a separate "argumentation space" as a platform for constructing networks of argumentations. This activity is different from generating and structuring elements of the content domain of the intended document and is different from organizing the structure of the document in terms of rhetorical decisions. In summary, our system consists of four spaces which are shown in figure 2.

Although each activity space is defined by its specific characteristics, there are still some common features to all of them. These are derived from our analysis of invariant features of the activities to be supported. First, we provide some generic operations: creating, deleting, copying, naming, renaming nodes and links. Second, it is possible to activate and "open" a node - one way to implement this is the standard use of mouse clicks - which results in the creation of a window to be used for writing and editing the content (e.g. text) of the node. On the other hand, links are also objects which can be activated and edited. The "content" of a link dependends on its type. Example: activating and opening the 'so' link in the argumentation space results in displaying the warrant and backing structure of this link.

---

[2] We are also developing an integrated cognitive model of writing, but there is no space in this paper to give more details of it.

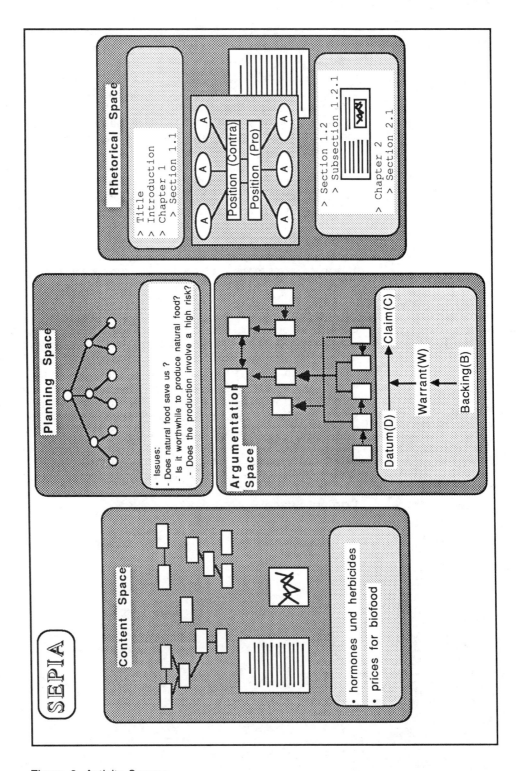

Figure 2. Activity Spaces

Furthermore, we introduce in all spaces the concept of "level". For example, subgraphs of the network in the argumentation space are embedded in a hierarchy thus reflecting different degrees of abstraction which are typical for argumentative texts. On the other hand, there are other relationships within each level so that the total structure is non-linear. The level-concept is motivated for text-like representations by the distinction between micro- and macrostructure proposed by van Dijk & Kintsch [Dijk83] and encompasses also "superstructures" which indicate organizations for larger documents adhering to specific sequencing of chapters and paragraphs.

The following subsections now provide a description of the four spaces: planning, content, argumentation, and rhetorical space. Due to the limited size of this paper, we will only sketch the planning and the content space and rather concentrate on the argumentation and the rhetorical space which are at the center of our current research.

Planning Space

This space serves to support the author in setting up an agenda, in coordinating the whole authoring activity which again requires that the author keeps track of what he is doing (personal monitoring). The function of this space can best be characterized as supporting but also stimulating the authors meta-planning activity. One keystone for the development of a global structure of an argumentative document is the specification of the main issue ("Does natural food save us ?") in a hierarchy of subissues ("Is our food noxious?", " Is it worthwhile to produce natural food?") (see figure 2). These subissues are then taken as topics for working on an argumentation network in the argumentation space. The agenda of interesting questions is not only a planning device for idea generation but at the same time a structured list of topics which can be transformed in the structure of chapters to be used later in the rhetorical space. The planning space functions as a switchboard between the other three spaces. Thus, it contains the overall goal structure and plans for writing. Although the author might stay with his original intentions for quite a while, he is free to change and modify his initial decisions in the sense of what has been called "opportunistic planning" [Haye79].

Content Space

Having identified the domain of the intended document, the author turns - at some point - to the content space. In this space he acquires and collects information about the selected domain which is indicated by the issues identified in the planning space. This can be achieved in two ways. First, the author can start to generate ideas about the domain at a concept level, relate them to each other, e.g. as part-whole relationships, and structure them similar to a semantic network (see figure 2). The purpose here is to obtain a representation of the objects and their mutual relationship involved in the domain of the document.

Second, the author can access additional information which might be documents produced by him before or - sometimes more relevant - which stem from external sources, as e.g. fact and bibliographic data bases, on-line encyclopedias and multi-media knowledge bases. The latter information consists of more or less complete documents where the author can copy parts and use them in the same or in a modified form in his new document. It might also be the case that he receives some stimulation for a new chain of arguments he has not thought of before. Again, this space exhibits different levels ranging from short notes on an idea and sketches of semantic networks to complete multimedia documents which can be viewed and used for inclusion in the intended document. One can think of it as a quarry elements of which are used for further processing by the author.

Argumentation Space

The argumentation space serves as the medium for generating, ordering, and relating arguments for specific issues working at one issue at a time. The representation of the argumentation space in figure 2 provides an impression of the overall structure of this space.

The argumentative activities result in a network having different levels of abstraction. Figure 3 shows an example of an argumentative network with three levels.

The following list provides an overview of possible node and link types as well as of the operations that can be used for their creation and modification in the argumentation network.

> **Nodes:** statements (attributes: name, position, claim, datum, level)
> **Links:**
>> - so (attributes: warrant, backing)
>> - contradicts
>> - contributes_to
> **Operations:**
>> - generate
>> - support
>> - object_to
>> - justify
>> - negate
>> - generalize
>> - specialize

Nodes and links

The nodes of the network represent statements generated by the author during the development of his argumentation. Each node is an object which is characterized by four attributes, we call 'position', 'claim', 'datum', and 'level'. The values of the first three attributes are boolean values relative to the author's subjective representation. Compared to the model of argumentation proposed by Toulmin, datums and claims are both statements but differ in their attributes. In figure 3, 'setbacks' represents a statement at the medium level of the net which is the datum for 'losses' at the same level. Let the content of the first node be 'organic farmers often are victims of disastrous setbacks' and the content of the second 'organic farmers often have to face grave financial losses' then both nodes together with the 'so'-link constitute a simple argument according to Toulmin's model. As can be seen at the lowest level of the net, authors can go beyond such simple arguments by developing argumentative chains the intermediate elements of which simultaniously function as datum and claim, i.e. they can take different roles. At the top *level of the net there are two nodes which represent positions. We consider positions as* general claims like 'it is worthwhile to produce natural food'.

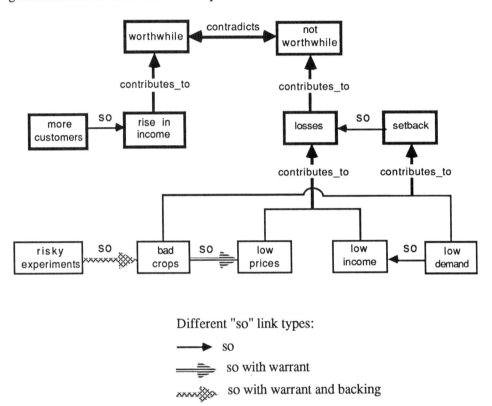

Figure 3. A network resulting from argumentation

Beside the relation 'so', the relation 'contradicts' can be used to connect two statements at each level of the network. But contrary to 'so', this link always connects statements of the same type, i.e. a datum with a datum, a claim with a claim, and a position with a position. It therefore describes the relationship of mutual opposition. For example, in figure 3 the position 'worthwhile' directly contradicts the position 'not worthwhile'.

Relations between different levels of the net are represented by the relation 'contributes_to'. For example, in figure 3 the claim 'losses' contributes to the position 'not worthwhile', which means that the statements 'organic farmers often have to face grave financial losses' contributes to the position 'it is not worthwhile to produce natural food'.

Operations within levels

So far, we have described elements of the argumentative structure but we have not yet specified how this structure is built up. Therefore we have to describe the different operations an author can apply in the course of arguing. To start with, the most basic operation is the generation of a statement. Whenever the author chooses this option a new, unrelated node appears in the argumentation space which has to be named and then can be further processed. For assigning a statement to a new node the author has to use the operation 'edit'. When 'edit' is applied to the node, a text window appears on the screen and the author can write down the intended statement. By default, each node is a claim and functions as a position as long as no other operations have been applied to it.

Statements in the space can be supported by other statements. The operation 'support' results in a new link, i.e. the relation 'so' is established, leading from the supporting to the supported statement. Since the supporting node now serves as a datum its corresponding attribute is changed accordingly. By applying the operation to nodes which are already related to other nodes at the same level an author is able to construct argumentative chains. In figure 3 such a chain is shown at the lowest level.

1) existing "datum --> claim" relation:

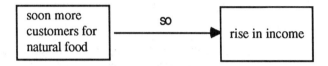

2) attack of "rise in income" results in:

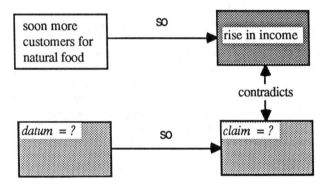

3) edit new datum and claim boxes:

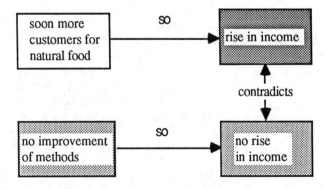

Figure 4. Steps of the operation 'object_to'

If an author wants to indicate that a statement is the direct contradiction of another statement, he can achieve this by using the operation 'negate'. The operation constitutes the relation 'contradict' which connects the two opposite statements. It can be applied at all levels of the network, even at the top.

A more complicated situation arises when the author wants to attack a claim. He can do so by using the operation 'object_to'. Figure 4 shows how the operation works. Suppose the author wants to attack the claim of the argument displayed in part (1) of the figure. When he applies 'object_to' to the claim the system creates two nodes related by 'so' and then connects the claim of this new argument via 'contradict' to the claim under attack. The result is shown in part (2). The author can now formulate his objection by editing the new nodes. This leads to the final structure displayed in part (3) of the figure.

It is obvious that 'object_to' generates a more complicated argument than originally intended by the author. The reason for this is to facilitate further arguing by making the implications of an attack explicit: if a claim can be attacked by a datum the same datum can be interpreted as support for the negation of the claim. Demonstrating this relationship to the author by automatically generating the structure in part (2) should lead to a more complete view of the consequences which are entailed by his argumentation.

The relation 'so' can further be specified by the operation 'justify'. This operation provides the author with the opportunity to formulate a warrant and a backing to cover the relation between datum and claim. When 'justify' is used a new window appears on the screen in which a schema is displayed. The schema shows the model of argumentation proposed by Toulmin and is presented as a template consisting of four slots and three links (see figure 2).

The slots named 'datum' and 'claim' of the schema contain the statements of the two nodes whose connection shall be justified. The author can now fill in the other two slots by generating appropriate statements which function as warrant and backing. The modification of the link leads to a change of its attributes which in turn is indicated in the network by a new symbol for the 'so'-relationship. The 'so' between 'bad crops' and 'low prices' in figure 3 represents a link which is justified by a warrant alone, whereas the connection between 'risky experiments' and 'bad crops' stands for a 'so' which is further covered by a backing.

Operations between levels

All operations described so far serve as means to incrementally develop and expand arguments at a given level of abstraction and we believe that a good deal of the structural characteristics of argumentative documents can be modelled by them. However, in many cases only one level of abstraction is not sufficient for representing the structures which arise in the course of a more complex argumentation. For example, authors often start with a global argument, as indicated at the medium level in figure 3, and then gradually refine it by creating other arguments which are specific instantiations of it. Another way to proceed is to write down several arguments and then draw a specific conclusion by summarizing their claims in a more general position. To support authors in those activities of organizing, the argumenation space provides them with two operations which establish different levels of abstraction in an argumentation. Using the operation 'generalize' an author can create a statement and relate it to one or more statements via a link labeled 'contributes_to'. If the specific statements are situated on level i the more general statement gets located at level i+1. The level of a statement is reflected in its 'level' attribute as well as in its position in the space: general statements appear on a higher level than more specific ones. The counterpart of the operation 'generalize' is 'specify'. It enables the author to create more specific statements and link them to the appropriate general statements.

Both operations can be used in a variety of ways thus creating argumentative structures of different hierarchical complexity. For example, if the author wants to summarize several specific arguments in a more general one, he can accomplish this by first generalizing their datums and claims and then using the operation 'support' to link these generalizations. The left part of figure 3 shows a structure which has been developed this way. On the other hand, the author can first write down a more global argument and then start specifying it by more concrete arguments. Thus the combination of both 'generalize' and 'specify' guarantees a high flexibility in developing, organizing, and structuring a complex argumentation.

Another way of using the two operations lies in the generation or specification of general positions. As described above, a position is a general claim. If the author develops his argumentation in a top down manner he may first generate such a claim and then use the operation 'specify' to create arguments which favour it. On the other hand, if he prefers to argue bottom up he may reach the same goal by starting at a low level and using the operation 'generalize' to join the claims of his specific arguments in a general position. Since both ways are often used the combination of 'specify' and 'generalize' provides authors with a high flexibility with regard to their strategy of argumentation.

The data types (nodes, links) as well as the operations described in this paragraph form a useful basis for supporting authors in their attempt to construct sophisticated argumentations. The operations in the space obey the principle of cognitive compatibility and the proposed network gives a clear view of the argumentative structure preserving the different levels typically found in more complex argumentations. Therefore, we think that this space considerably facilitates the writing of argumentative documents.

Rhetorical Space

In essence, argumentation is always an interaction or at least a dialog. Writing an argumentative document has to account for the absence of the dialog partner. This situation implies that the objections of an opponent have to be anticipated. Therefore, writing an argumentative text, reflections about the reader are more relevant than in other types of text. The author's intention is not only to communicate his ideas, but also to convince others of the validity of those ideas. To increase the persuasiveness of an argumentation, is not only a matter of content and argument structures but above all a matter of discourse and rhetorical structuring.

By considering rhetorical aspects, the author imposes a document structure on his ideas and arguments which he has explicated and elaborated in the content and argumentation space. For this task we propose another separate activity space, called rhetorical space. The problems to be solved in this space require:

- decisions about the global outline of the document
- decisions about the rhetorical reorganization of positions and arguments for each subissue
- decisions about writing coherent sentences

To support authors in making these rhetorical decisions, we distinguis between three modes: an outline mode, an argumentation strategy mode, and a text edit mode (compare figure 2).

Outline mode

In the planning space, the author has already decided on the issue hierarchy. Now he has to decide when and where to deal with these issues. In order to use the tree structure of subissues for the generation of an outline format of the document, the author selects an issue, a subtree or the whole tree and copies it in the outline mode. As a result of this operation, he gets an outline structure which is completely or partially identical with the hierarchy of issues. This means that either a substructure of the issue tree is mapped in a one-to-one correspondence on the hierarchy of chapters or that some selected issues are combined in one chapter or distributed over several chapters.

In most cases, argumentation is embedded in a context. Thus, the document has to include sections which have no direct relation to any of the specified arguments. Therefore, the author can expand the outline structure by creating a new headline with a link to a text node previously generated in the content space. Establishing a context for argumentation can be supported by providing a conventionalized text schema. Van Dijk and Kintsch call such a schema the superstructure of a text [Dijk83]. An example of a superstructure which is relevant for the domain of argumentation is the usual outline of a scientific report. If there exists such a convention for a certain type of document, the system will offer the corresponding superstructure as a guideline for the development of the outline structure.

Argumentation strategy mode

Beyond establishing text coherence at a global level, the author has to arrange positions, counterpositions, and arguments into a convincing form. We call this important rhetorical task the development of an argumentation strategy.

For the development of this strategy the system provides a special environment in a subwindow. The rhetorical reordering starts with a selection of an argumentative subnet to be copied from the argumentation space. The selection of subnets is guided by the selection of positions, which are relevant for a particular subissue. The selected positions are not copied together with all arguments but only with those from the next lower level of the abstraction hierarchy. Now the author has the freedom to reorder the relation of arguments and positions. On the other hand, there are traditional rhetorical schemata, as e.g. the top-town form (pyramid form) with the position slot on top, or the bottom-up form (inverse pyramid form) with the slots for the arguments first and then the supported position (see figure 2). One possibility of support is that a selected argumentation structure is copied into this schema and the slots are filled with the name of a position and its corresponding arguments.

By applying some basic rhetorical operations the author can change the sequence of the statements or delete some elements of the argumentation structure.

delete: Not every statement in a selected argumentation structure is worth to be incorporated in the final document. In order to leave some obvious positions and well known arguments implicit, the author can delete specified elements.

reorder: The order of arguments is very important for the development of an argumentation strategy, because the same arguments may be of different importance for different groups of readers. If an author wants to consider these differences, he can change the order of arguments with the reorder command, thereby adjusting his argumentation to the reader´s profile.

expand: Since the argumentative subnet selected by the author includes only a position and the next lower level of the argumentation hierarchy, the author needs support if he wants to expand this structure. By activating an argument and applying the expand operation, he gets those arguments which are connected to the activated argument on the next lower level This type of expansion is a node expansion. Another form is to expand a link. Activation of a 'so'-link returns warrant and backing justifying the corresponding 'so'-relation as an additional hypertext node.

The results of these operations are demonstrated in figure 5. It represents a section of an article dealing with the main issue "Does natural food save us?" and corresponds to the previously described argumentation net in figure 3. Part 1 of figure 5 shows a section of the issue structure of the article, part 2 describes the rhetorical structure of one of the subissues.

1) Part of an issue structure

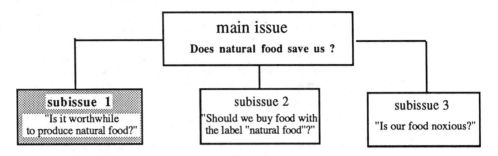

2) A rhetorical structure for subissue 1

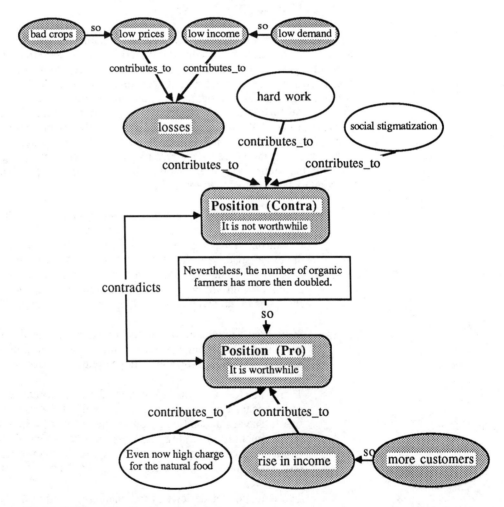

Figure 5. Example of a rhetorical structure

As the rhetorical space provides means to reorganize and enrich selected parts of the argumentative network and to place them in a rhetorically rearranged hierarchy of subissues, different types of documents can be produced on this basis. We only mention two examples: (1) a "guided tour" through the argumentation network. Starting with a selected issue, the recipient is guided through the original line of the author's argumentation leading to a spelled out position. (2) In general, the result of the rhetorical transformations will be a coherent full text document having either a linear or a non-linear structure with respect to the "surface" information about facts and statements. In either case, the document is a hyperdocument providing not only the factual information for the reader but also access to the underlying argumentation structure. Therefore, the reader gets - even while reading a "traditional" document - the exciting possibility to go back to the sources, i.e. to early and intermediate products of the authoring process ("travelling back to the quarry"). This way, the reader can duplicate the author's argumentation at a more detailed level. In a next step of our research, we will specify the functionality necessary for the production of these types of hyperdocuments.

Text edit mode

In every mode, the author has a text editor at his disposal which allows him to create the content of a new node, to edit the content of existing nodes, and to write transitions so that the final document meets the criteria of coherence, connectivity and fluency.

TRAVELLING ACTIVITY SPACES

Empirical research on the writing process of mature authors has shown that production and transformation of knowledge during writing is not done in a linear sequence of stages from idea generation to text generation. There is a constant interaction between levels of text representation as well as between different subtasks. For instance, problems in formulating an argument clearly and convincingly might result in the subgoal "generate an example illustrating this argument". Let us translate this situation into our world of activity spaces. Although the rhetorical space is always the final destination, an author's train of thought is not heading there in a straightforward way. Instead, we expect heavy traffic between the spaces. This resembles the interaction of cognitive processes when locating the solution of different subproblems in different problem spaces which can be mapped to the proposed activity spaces.

> Information flows from the *planning space* to the other three spaces: Issues specified in the planning space set topics for the content space, direct the structuring in the argumentation space, and are transformed into an outline in the rhetorical space. On the other hand, information flows from these three spaces back to the planning space: Operations in each of them might result in new insights leading to the formulation of new goals or to the specification of new subissues in the planning space ("opportunistic planning").

> Structured knowledge, elicited or generated in the *content space* may be translated into argumentative statements in the argumentation space or into a nonargumentative text passage in the rhetorical space.

> There is a close relationship between the *argumentation space* and the rhetorical space because the argumentation space functions as a quarry for the rhetorical space. The argumentation graph or parts of it must be reorganized according to an argumentation strategy in the rhetorical space. In addition, the need for explication of an argument often results in operations in the content space discovering new insights and thus reducing the original fuzzyness.

> The detection of deficits in the *rhetorical space* leads to the formulation or specification of new arguments in the argumentation space. It may also require certain operations in the content space, such as searching for missing knowledge or elaborating facts generated so far.

EMBEDDING ACTIVITY SPACES IN SEPIA

The activity spaces are the environment where authors generate and structure their ideas. But this is not the whole story. As we have mentioned in the introduction, the idea of activity spaces is central but it is only one component of a more comprehensive system called SEPIA: Structured Elicitation and Processing of Ideas for Authoring. Although this paper only addresses the concept and design requirements for activity spaces, we want to place these ideas into a wider perspective. Therefore, we provide in this section an overview of the complete system we are currently developing. Beyond the basic and central functionality of the Generation/Structuring Component, we will realize an active part for the SEPIA-system including the following components (see figure 6).

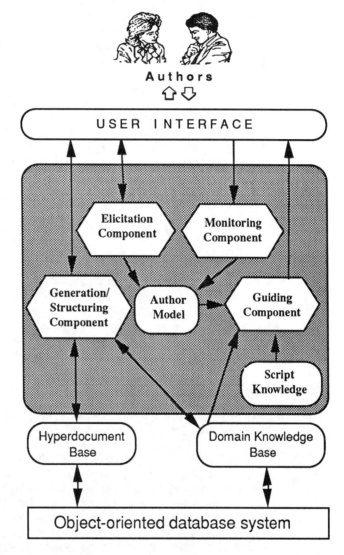

Figure 6. Architecture of the knowledge-based authoring tool SEPIA (Structured Elicitation and Processing of Ideas for Authoring)

First, in order to provide feedback and to react in an author-oriented way the system has to acquire knowledge about the author's original goals and plans, intended topic domain, document type, writing strategy, target group, etc. These data are acquired via a Knowledge Elicitation Component employing an interactive dialog technique. They form the basis of the system's model about the author (the initial author model).

Second, in order to be active at an appropriate point of time, the system has to monitor the author's writing behavior. The Monitoring Component provides protocol data about the author's activities in different windows (= activity spaces). These data are used to update a dynamic part of the author model which obviously has to be distinguished from a rather static part corresponding to the author's initial profile. In order to use this information in a coherent way for guiding we will provide a mechanism which integrates the data coming from different information sources. A future goal for the monitoring component is to make use of results from research on text analysis in order to employ a semantic analysis of the author's input.

Third, a Guiding Component processes the integrated information about the author's activity (i.e. the dynamic author model), compares it to information about the earlier acquired author's profile (on goals and plans, etc.) and to information stored in a script knowledge base. The script knowledge base contains knowledge about document types (e.g. hypertext structures) and argumentation structures. In a more advanced version, the system will also use additional knowledge about the content domain. Thus, the system has "objective" knowledge of rules of discourse (argumentation) and rules and facts of the domain. On the other hand, it has "subjective" knowledge of the author: i.e. of the author's mental model of the domain and the author's mental model of discourse esp. argumentation. Based on the result of the comparison of the objective knowledge to the subjective one the system provides feedback and active support/advice to the author following a specific guiding strategy. Of course, these additional features need much more detailed considerations which will be reported elsewhere.

CONCLUSIONS AND RECOMMENDATIONS

In this section, we summarize our ideas within a more global framework and make some recommendations for the design of future hypertext systems. The availability of innovative technology for the production and reception of electronic documents raises the question of how to improve the quality of these documents. There are at least two aspects to the notion of quality. The first refers to additional multi-media features, as e.g. high-resolution graphics and images, animation and simulation, video including sound, etc.

The second is the extent to which the document contains additional structural information which can be used for further processing. Although multi-media features are of course desirable for hyperdocuments, we want to stress the second aspect.

The current situation is characterized by predominantly linear documents - on paper as well as in electronic format. An additional level of structure can be found in currently produced hyperdocuments. Unfortuately, in most cases it is restricted simple "points_to" links. A general hypertext model should go beyond this and rather employ the full capability of multiple types of nodes and links, including composites as an augmentation of the basic node and link model [Hala88]. The analysis and specification proposal in this paper has identified how one can enrich hyperdocuments with special links and nodes. We have demonstrated this for argumentative and rhetorical structures. The enrichment of hyperdocuments is reached by preserving structural information created and used by the author along his composing activity. The information concerns the final structure of the document as well as that of transient intermediary products. It has to be noted that this additional structure can be accessed by the author as well as the reader. It thus facilitates the comprehension of the intended message. Another advantage of this approach is that these links are also machine processible.

Additional information of this kind is only available if the author is provided with tools which allow him to externalize his internal structures by making them part of the hyperdocument. Since the use of these tools should not result in an additional burden we have to design them in a user-oriented and task-driven fashion in accordance with the principle of cognitive compatibility. In summary, this leads to the conclusion that developers of hypertext systems should focus on the role of authoring more intensively than they do today.

Such a demand is intrinsically linked to the issue of human factors aspects for interface design of hypertext systems. Our approach led to the concept of activity spaces and the heavy utilization of externalizing subjective knowledge structures based on the author's mental models. Activity spaces implemented as dedicated windows with activity specific functionalities can be viewed as a natural metaphor for supporting cognitive processes in any interactive problem solving activity. Thus, this concept is applicable to a wide range of interactive systems and not restricted to hypertext systems.

A further and logical step in the development of authoring tools in hypertext environments is to extend the support by knowledge-based components as given in the description of the SEPIA-system. It has to be pointed out that this kind of support is possible because monitoring of the author's externalized behavior provides the system with information that can be used to guide his subsequent activities.

A final remark

If our argumentation for designing an authoring system this way did not convince you to the extent we hoped it would, this might be due to the circumstance that - unfortunately- the system we propose is still under development and therefore has not been at our disposal for writing this paper.

Acknowledgements

Thanks are due especially to our colleagues Jörg Haake, Werner Rehfeld, Helge Schütt, and Wolfgang Schuler working in the WIBAS-project. The ideas presented in this paper have greatly profited from our dicussions with them and their stimulating comments.

REFERENCES

[Aksc88] Akscyn, R.M., McCracken, D.L. & Yoder. E.A. KMS: A distributed hypermedia system for managing knowledge in organizations. *Communications of the ACM*, 31(7), 1988, 820-835.

[Alva86] Alvarado, S.J., Dyer, M.G., & Flower, M. Editorial comprehension in OpEd through argument units. In: *Proceedings of the 5th National Conference of Artificial Intelligence - AAAI '86* (Vol. 1). Los Altos, CA: Kaufmann, 1986, pp. 250-256.

[Brow86] Brown, J.S. From cognitive to social ergonomics and beyond. In D. Norman, & S. Draper (Eds.), *User-centered system design: New perspectives on human-computer interaction*. Hillsdale, N.J.: Erlbaum, 1986, pp. 457 - 486.

[Brow87] Brown, P.J. Turning ideas into products: The Guide System. In: *Proceedings of the Hypertext '87 Workshop*, Chapel Hill, NC, 1987,.pp. 33-40.

[Card87] Card, S.K., & Henderson, A. A multiple, virtual-workspace interface to support user task switching. In Carroll, J.M., & Tanner, P.P. (Eds.), *Proceedings of the CHI und GI '87 Conference on Human Factors in Computing Systems*, Toronto. New York: ACM, 1987, pp. 53-59.

[Coll80]   Collins, A., & Gentner, D. A framework for a cognitive theory of writing. In L.W. Gregg, & E. Steinberg (Eds.), *Cognitive processes in writing: An interdisciplinary approach* Hillsdale, NJ: Lawrence Erlbaum, 1980, pp. 51-72.

[Conk87a]   Conklin, J. Hypertext: An introduction and survey. *IEEE Computer Magazine*, 20(9), 1987, 17-41.

[Conk87b]   Conklin, J., & Begeman, M.L. gIBIS : A hypertext tool for team design deliberation. In: *Proceedings of the Hypertext '87 Workshop*, Chapel Hill, NC, 1987, pp. 247-251.

[Deli86]   Delisle, N.A., & Schwartz, M.D. Neptune: A hypertext system for CAD applications. In C. Zaniolo (Ed.), *Proceedings of the International Conference on Management of Data - SIGMOD '86*, Washington, D.C. New York, NY: ACM, (1986), pp. 132-143.

[Dijk83]   Dijk, T.A. van, & Kintsch, W. *Strategies of discourse comprehension.* New York, NY: Academic Press, 1983.

[Hala87]   Halasz, F.G., Moran, T.P., & Trigg, R. Notecards in a nutshell. In J.M. Carroll, & P.P. Tanner (Eds.), *Proceedings of the CHI und GI '87 Conference on Human Factors in Computing Systems,* Toronto. New York: ACM,1987, pp. 45-52.

[Hala88]   Halasz, F.G. Reflections on Notecards: Seven issues for the next generation of hypermedia systems. *Communication of the ACM*, 31, 1988, 836-852.

[Haye80]   Hayes, J.R., & Flower, L.S. Identifying the organisation of writing processes. In L.W. Gregg, & E.R. Steinberg (Eds.), *Cognitive processes in writing*. Hillsdale, NJ: Lawrence Erlbaum 1980, pp. 3-30.

[Haye79]   Hayes-Roth, B., & Hayes-Roth, F. A cognitive model of planning. *Cognitive Science*, 3(4), 1979, 275-310.

[Kant84[Kant, E. & Newell, A. Problem solving techniques for the design of algorithms. *Information Processing & Management*, 20(1-2), 1984, 97-118.

[Kell87]   Kellog, R.T. Effects of topic knowledge on the allocation of processing time and cognitive effort to writing processes. *Memory & Cognition*, 15(3), 1987, 256-266.

[Kint87]   Kintsch, W. Foreword. In C. Bereiter, & M. Scardamelia, *The psychology of written composition*. Hillsdale, NJ: Lawrence Erlbaum, (1987), pp. 9-12.

[Kint88]   Kintsch, W. The role of knowledge in discourse comprehension: A construction integration model. *Psychological Review*, 95(2), 1988, 163-182.

[Kopp85]   Kopperschmidt, J. An analysis of argumentation. In T.A. van Dijk (Ed.), *Handbook of discourse analysis: Vol. 2. Dimensions of discourse* London: Academic Press, 1985, pp. 159-168.

[Kunz70]   Kunz, W., & Rittel, H. *Issues as elements of information systems* (Working paper 131). Berkeley, CA: University of California, Center for Planning and Development Research, 1970.

[McCa83]   McCall, R., Schaab, B., & Schuler, W. An information station for the problem solver: system concepts. In C. Keren & L. Perlmutter (Eds.), *Applications of mini- and microcomputers in information, documentation and libraries.* New York: Elsevier, 1983.

[Marc88]   Marchionini, G., & Shneiderman, B. Finding facts versus browsing knowledge in hypertext systems. *IEEE Computer,* 21(1), 1988, 70-81.

[Newe80]   Newell, A. Reasoning, problem solving, and decision processes: The problem space as the fundamental category. In: R. Nickerson (Ed.), *Attention and performance VIII.* Hillsdale, N.J.: Lawrence Erlbaum, 1980, pp. 693-71.

[Scar87]   Scardamalia, M., & Bereiter, C. Knowledge telling and knowledge transforming in written composition. In S. Rosenberg (Ed.), *Advances in applied psycholinguistics: Vol. 2. Reading, writing, and language learning.* Cambridge: Cambridge University Press, 1987, pp. 142-175.

[Smit87]   Smith, J.B., Weiss, S.F., & Ferguson, G.J. A hypertext writing environment and its cognitive basis. In: *Proceedings of the Hypertext '87 Workshop,* Chapel Hill, NC, 1987, pp. 195-214.

[Smit88]   Smith, J.B., & Lansman, M. *A cognitive basis for a computer writing environment.* (Technical Report). Chapel Hill, NC: University of North Carolina, Department of Computer Science, 1988.

[Smol88]   Smolensky, P., Fox, B., King, R., & Lewis, C. Computer-aided reasoned discourse or, how to argue with a computer. In R. Guindon (Ed.), *Cognitive Science and its application for human-computer interaction.* Norwood, NJ: Ablex, 1988, pp.109-162.

[Stre87]   Streitz, N.A. Cognitive compatibility as a central issue in human-computer interaction: Theoretical framework and empirical findings. In G. Salvendy (Ed.), *Cognitive engineering in the design of human-computer interaction and expert systems.* Amsterdam: Elsevier, 1987, pp. 75-82.

[Stre88a]   Streitz, N.A. Mental models and metaphors: Implications for the design of adaptive user-system interfaces. In H. Mandl & A. Lesgold (Eds.), *Learning issues for intelligent tutoring systems.* New York: Springer, 1988, pp. 164 - 186.

[Stre88b]   Streitz, N.A., & Hannemann, J. *Writing is rewriting: A cognitive framework for computer-aided authoring.* Paper presented at the 4th European Conference on Cognitive Ergonomics (ECCE 4), Cambridge (England), 1988.

[Toul58]   Toulmin, S. *The uses of argument.* Cambridge: Cambridge University Press, 1958.

[Trig86]   Trigg, R., & Weiser, M. TEXTNET: A network-based approach to text handling. *ACM Transactions on Office Systems,* 4(1), 1986, 1-23.

[Trig87]   Trigg, R.H., & Irish, P. M. Hypertext habitats: Experience of writers in NoteCards. In: *Proceedings of the Hypertext '87 Workshop,* Chapel Hill, NC, 1987, pp. 89-107.

[Walk87]   Walker, J.H. Document Examiner: Delivery system for hypertext documents. In: *Proceedings of the Hypertext '87 Workshop*, Chapel Hill, NC, 1987, pp. 307-324.

[Will87]   Williams, G. HyperCard. *Byte*, 12, 1987, 109-117.

[Wund80]   Wunderlich, D. *Arbeitsbuch Semantik.* Frankfurt: Athenaeum, 1980.

[Yank85]   Yankelovich, N., Meyrowitz, N., & Dam van, A. Reading and writing the electronic book. *IEEE Computer*, 18(10), 1985, 15-30.

InterNote:
Extending a Hypermedia Framework
to Support Annotative Collaboration

Timothy Catlin, Paulette Bush, and Nicole Yankelovich

Institute for Research in Information and Scholarship (IRIS)
Brown University
Box 1946
Providence, RI 02912

ABSTRACT

Based on three years of user feedback, a design team at IRIS embarked on a project to enhance Intermedia to better support small groups of collaborators, particularly those involved with document review and revision. Towards this end, we defined user-level requirements for the new functionality. The result of this process was the design and implementation of InterNote. One aspect of InterNote involves a fundamental extension to Intermedia's navigational linking paradigm. Instead of simply being able to traverse links, users are now also able to transfer data across the links using a technique we call *warm linking*. In this paper we describe extensions to our hypermedia framework to support annotative collaboration, including the user interface of the new linking functionality and the InterNote extension. Finally, we discuss our plans for future work.

I. INTRODUCTION

Working together to create materials is a familiar activity in a wide range of settings. The evolution of these materials, such as joint research papers, software design documents, or information for use in the classroom, frequently depends on group consensus. Drafts are produced, these drafts are reviewed, and new drafts are produced. We see the *annotative collaboration* process [Trig86] as consisting not only of commenting, questioning, and critiquing others' work, but also of assimilating those "notes" back into the original material to create a new version. It is a process that includes both the review and the revision cycle.

As groups of users begin to develop materials ranging from small information networks to entire on-line books within our Intermedia hypermedia desktop environment, their need for more efficient and effective collaboration tools is apparent. Currently, users are writing papers and developing software design and issues materials jointly within Intermedia. A group at Johns Hopkins University is even importing an entire medical textbook into Intermedia, working together to create the connecting network of links and to revise the text and illustrations. Many working groups link comments to a core set of documents, spawning on-line discussions within the context of the jointly owned materials. Professors creating course materials within Intermedia find that their task is almost always a group effort with student assistants. Text documents, structured graphics figures, timelines, and scanned images (created using InterWord, InterDraw, InterVal and InterPix respectively), and the linkages between them, are prepared and revised incrementally. More detailed descriptions of Intermedia are available in [Garr86, Meyr86 and Yank88].

In the version of Intermedia in use in our field trials, users wishing to attach an annotation to any selection in a document can do so by linking an empty document of any type to the selection and entering the annotation in that document. This process, however, requires multiple user actions. The user must select a portion of the original document, choose the "Start Link" command, open a new document from the "New" application window, enter the annotation content, select a portion of the annotation content, and choose the "Complete Link" command. The multiple-step process for attaching an annotation proves frustrating when a reviewer only wants to attach small, quick annotations. Similarly, to incorporate a change suggested in an annotation, the document author has to use the generic "Copy" and "Paste" commands, copying the desired section from the annotation document and pasting it in the correct location in the original document. This, too, is a multiple-step process. Also there is no way to mark the annotations that have been incorporated so that the author can keep track of which annotations still need to be viewed.

Motivated by the amount of group work currently being done in Intermedia, we decided to investigate and implement tools to better support annotative collaboration in our environment. The first phase of this project resulted in the development of an annotation facility called InterNote. Before we began designing InterNote, we looked at some studies of annotation styles and usage [Brow84, Krau86, Niel84]. We also investigated a number of currently available software products and research prototypes which support annotative collaboration [Brod, Brow82, Cont, Dene, Main, Trig86, Wang]. We found that a number of systems provided varying levels of support for the review process, but no systems supported both review *and* revision. In addition, we found little or no support for annotation management and simultaneous multi-user annotation.

Of the systems that supported the review process, we were specifically interested in the range of tools that could be used to create annotations and the range of document types that could be annotated. We were also interested in the granularity of data with which an annotation could be associated and the level of multi-user support provided. We found that all the systems provide for textual annotations. Some give users the ability to overlay the document being annotated with text, some allow the text to be added in a separate window, and some allow for a combination of both. In addition to textual annotations, some systems provide a palette of graphical mark-up tools, facilities to create "hand-written" annotations with a tablet and "pencil," or even mechanisms to attach voice annotations to a document. In terms of document types that a user can annotate, some systems only allow for the annotation of text documents while others allow users to annotate any type of document.

Most systems that allow the user to annotate any type of document first take an electronic snapshot of the document, creating a bitmap version of it. The reviewer then annotates the snapshot, using one set of annotation tools, regardless of whether the original document was text, graphics, a spreadsheet, etc. While this approach is powerful for the annotator, the author cannot simply copy and paste annotations into the original document. The author can only use the annotated document as a reference, either on-line or printed, for the process of revising the original document. If the author has changed the document since the snapshot was taken, the annotations will reference an out of date version.

The type of elements to which an annotation can be attached defines the annotation granularity. Systems that make a bitmap copy of the document allow annotations to be attached to any coordinate location on the page. The annotation granularity for systems that do not take this approach varied from an entire page to one or more document objects (words, sentences, paragraphs, graphics objects, etc).

A few systems also provide some type of multi-user support. For example, Context [Cont] allows the author to assign a unique identifying tag to each document reviewer, so that each reviewer's comments can be easily identified. MarkUp by Mainstay [Main] allows an author to specify a list of reviewers. A bitmap copy of the document to be marked up can then be sent over a network to each of the reviewers. When the reviewers are finished, the author is able to merge all the comments into a single marked-up version. This version can either be printed or can be viewed electronically, side-by-side with the original. Such a feature is useful because it allows multiple people to review a document simultaneously, but it has limitations. Specifically, reviewers cannot look at each others suggestions, and the author cannot see a reviewer's comments until he or she submits the marked up copy.

From our analysis of current systems and the group work users are currently doing, we established general goals for extensions to Intermedia to support annotative collaboration. These goals were to provide a set of intuitive reviewing tools and to provide, at the same time, integrated revision and annotation management capabilities. With Intermedia as our base, we already had the functionality for creating links between fine-grained selections in multiple document types and the support for multiple users linking to and from a document simultaneously. In addition, we could take advantage of Intermedia's shared desktop folder hierarchy. Intermedia provided us with a powerful framework on which we could build support for annotative collaboration beyond what was available in any one of the existing systems.

In this paper we present our requirements for supporting annotative collaboration, followed by a description of the user interface. We then go on to describe our plans for future research.

II. REQUIREMENTS

Based on our general goals, we identified a set of high-level user requirements that we wanted our design to address. We broke these requirements down into three categories: general requirements, annotator requirements and author requirements. These categories are intended to help organize sets of functionality and are not meant to imply an actual differentiation among users. As with all other Intermedia functionality, no distinction is actually made between types of users. In the course of a single session, one user may be both an annotator and an author, depending on the task they are trying to accomplish.

A. General Requirements

Our most basic requirement was to design a general-purpose annotation facility within the existing Intermedia environment. We believed that the method for creating and viewing annotations had to be identical across all applications, current and future. From this it also followed that users had to be able to create annotations of any document type. For example, an annotator should be able to suggest revisions on a graphics document using graphics editing tools. Regardless of the type of document being annotated, however, we felt it was likely that users would want to add textual commentary alone or in conjunction with the suggested revisions. We found that in our own annotations, we frequently attempted to justify a suggestion with a sentence or a phrase. In other words, we realized that there were two major types of annotations: suggested changes in the same data type as the original document, and textual commentary for notes, comments, non-specific suggestions, and justifications [Niel84]. The annotation functionality, therefore, had to provide a set of text-editing capabilities along with the editing tools of the original document.

Regardless of the way a document is annotated, we wanted to be sure that an author or an annotator could see the source of the annotation and the annotation simultaneously. The author of a document, the annotator or another reviewer also had to be able to either annotate an existing annotation or make a navigational link to or from an existing annotation. In addition, a user had to be able to print the annotations both separately and in conjunction with the document.

Another crucial requirement was that the annotation functionality fit in with Intermedia's existing functionality, especially the linking mechanisms, and be fundamentally integrated into the existing application architecture. We wanted users to learn as few new skills as possible in order to use the new annotation features and we wanted developers to be able to write new applications that would take advantage of the annotation functionality with minimal programming effort. In the Intermedia system, all applications participate in navigational linking by implementing a small linking protocol interface. We wanted to extend the existing linking protocol very slightly so that all applications could also participate in annotation. By implementing this extended protocol, a developer has to be able to easily provide users with the ability to annotate documents created with their new application.

B. Annotator Requirements

As described in the introduction, it was possible, before the addition of annotation features, for users to annotate existing Intermedia documents. The major difficulty involved the number of steps it took to do so. Our major requirement from the annotator's perspective was that the creation of annotations be a one-step process. By making a selection and issuing a single command, an annotator had to be able to enter textual commentary or suggest specific editing changes. These editing changes might include a range of changes from rewording a sentence to resequencing an animation.

Intermedia documents are by definition dynamic. They can be updated at any time by the original author or by any collaborator with the appropriate access rights. We felt it was crucial for the system to provide some facility for contention management. In other words, if the author is updating a document at the same time another user is annotating it, the author may end up with comments and corrections on an out-of-date document. The system had to be able to resolve these types of edit/annotate collisions and allow multiple users to annotate the same document simultaneously.

Since it is often useful for one reviewer to see comments made by a previous reviewer to avoid duplication of effort, we wanted annotators to be able to see other users' annotations [Niel84]. On the other hand, if an annotator preferred working on a clean copy of the document, he or she had to be able to hide the annotations created by others.

C. Author Requirements

The most basic requirement we defined for authors was the ability to automatically incorporate a suggested change, such as a sentence rewording or spelling correction. This mechanism had to be faster and more direct than using the "Copy" and "Paste" commands, particularly as some documents could have literally hundreds of annotations.

We also wanted the system to allow the author to keep track of which annotations had been incorporated. When a document has been reviewed by more than one person, this problem is exacerbated, particularly if the annotations suggest conflicting revisions.

As an author edits a document, the annotations had to stick with the document objects with which they are associated until intentionally deleted. For example, if an author inserts a new sentence before a paragraph that contains annotations, the annotations had to stick with their paragraph.

If more than one person reviews a document, the author had to be able to merge the annotations so that they could be viewed in the order in which they appear in the document. Authors also had to be able sort annotations so that they could view one person's annotations at a time, view annotations by date, or view only the annotations that had not yet been incorporated. An author may want to do a number of things besides incorporating a specific annotation while revising the annotated document. The author may want to delete the annotation, delete the reference to the annotation, but still save it somewhere, or leave the annotation as is.

III. USER INTERFACE

With these high-level user requirements, we were able to design and implement an extension to Intermedia called InterNote. InterNote provides a consistent user interface for annotating all Intermedia document types. For annotators, InterNote provides the "Create Annotation" command, which links an annotation to any selection in an Intermedia document. The command also copies the selection into a "Note" window, so that the annotator can immediately make copy-editing changes or suggest a reordering. Authors use the "Incorporate Annotation" command to revise the document with the suggested changes from the annotation.

When we were designing the "Create Annotation" and "Incorporate Annotation" commands, we decided to extend Intermedia's navigational linking paradigm rather than build a special-purpose annotation and incorporation tool just for InterNote. The extension we designed combines navigation and data transfer into a single action. We call this action *warm linking*. Warm linking allows a user to not only traverse a link from a selection in one document to a selection in another document but also to transport data across the same link. Before explaining the details of the user interface of InterNote, we describe the warm linking user interface in more detail.

A. Warm Linking

The concept of *warm linking* is a variation of the master/instance relationships of computer aided design (CAD). In CAD applications, when a master component is changed, all instances of that component are automatically updated. In integrated software products, such as Lotus' Jazz, the term *Hot View* was introduced to describe this kind of automatic update facility. The user could place a hot view of chart or spreadsheet in a word processing document that would automatically update when the underlying data changed [Jazz85]. In the hypertext arena we have the ability to create links – associative relationships between objects – so it seemed natural to refer to links that provide automatic updating in addition to navigational linking as *hot links*. Purely navigational links, or *cold links*, are at the other end of the spectrum because they do not involve data transfer. *Warm links* fall in the middle ground. Rather than having the system automatically update the data at the other end of a link, the user has to explicitly update the remote data.

In Intermedia, links are made between selections of document objects. These selections are called *link anchors*. Visible markers are placed next to the anchors at both endpoints of the link. To traverse a link, a user selects a marker and picks the "Follow" menu command (or double-clicks on the marker). Similarly, to transfer data across a link, a user selects a link marker and issues one of the warm linking menu commands, either "Push" or "Pull." The "Push" command copies the content of the link anchor associated with the selected link marker and pastes it at the other end of the link, replacing the contents of the remote link anchor. "Pull" has the opposite effect. The command copies the contents of the remote link anchor and replaces the contents of the link anchor associated with the selected marker. In other words, data can be transferred in either direction across a link by asking the system to copy data from one end of a link, traverse the link, and paste the data at the other end of the link. These actions are diagrammed in Figure 1.

Because warm linking has many applications beyond creating and incorporating annotations, we provide the functionality as a system-wide feature. For example, when writing a paper, an author can link the illustrations in an InterWord document to the original versions stored in InterDraw documents. If the author revised an illustration in a previous session, he or she can "Pull" the revised illustration across the link into the InterWord document. Similarly, the author can revise one of the illustrations by following the link from the InterWord document to the InterDraw document and editing the illustration. The author can then "Push" the updated illustration across the link back into the InterWord document.

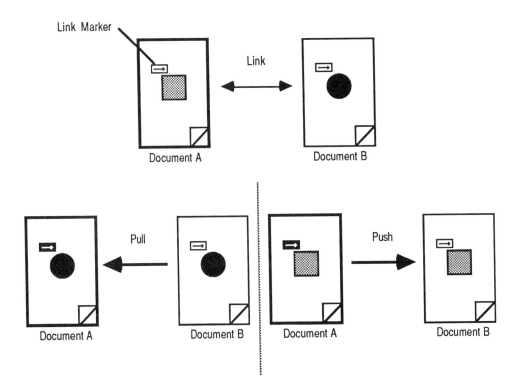

Figure 1. In the top diagram, the square in Document A is linked to the circle in Document B. The existence of the link is indicated by the markers above the circle and the square. Document A is the active document. The other two illustrations show what happens if a user selects the link marker in Document A and issues either the "Pull" or "Push" command.

With the addition of warm linking to Intermedia, all links in the system can be used for both navigation and data transfer. In the following section, we describe the user interface of InterNote and how warm linking is used both to create the content of annotations and to allow authors to incorporate annotations.

B. InterNote

Annotations to Intermedia documents are made using *Notes*. To create a note, the user makes a selection in a document and picks the "Create Annotation" menu command. A document that has been annotated is called a *draft*. All annotations for a particular draft are automatically kept in a *Note Folder* associated with the document. Note Folders are similar to other folders found on the desktop, but they contain additional information specific to annotations, such as the status of each annotation. Note Folders are particularly useful for sorting and organizing annotations. Intermedia allows only one person to edit the content of a document at a time, but any number of people can create links to or from a document simultaneously. Similarly, any number of users can attach Notes to a document at the same time.

Once a document has been annotated by one or more users, the author of the document can incorporate any changes suggested in a Note using the "Incorporate Annotation" command.

Notes

The structure of a Note allows the annotator to make both direct editing changes to a copy of a selection from a draft and to provide textual commentary that might explain or justify the suggested change. For this reason, a Note consists of two frames: the Incorporation Frame and the Commentary Frame, as shown in Figure 2. Figure 3 depicts a sample session with InterNote where the author is viewing three Notes to determine whether or not to incorporate them into the draft of an InterWord document.

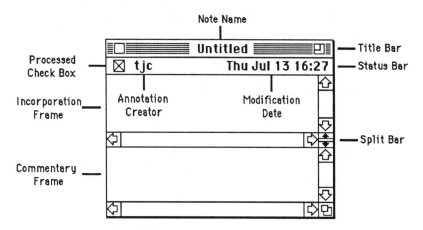

Figure 2. A Note window.

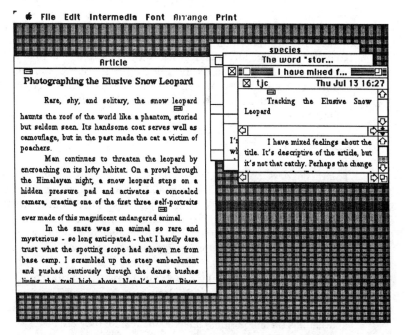

Figure 3. An InterWord document with three Notes attached.

The Incorporation Frame occupies the top portion of the Note window. In this frame, annotators enter specific suggestions to replace a section in the draft. To make a comment or suggest a change in the draft, the annotator selects one or more text, graphics or timeline objects and chooses the "Create Annotation" command. "Create Annotation" performs a number of actions. First, a new Note window is opened and a link is established between the annotator's selection in the draft and an insertion point in the Note's Incorporation Frame. A marker is placed next to both anchors, indicating the existence of a link. Next, the annotator's selection in the draft is "Pulled" across the link into the link anchor in the Incorporation Frame. To the annotator, it appears that the Note window opens with an exact copy of his or her selection linked to the original selection. As with all other links in Intermedia, this link may be followed in both directions. If the annotator wants to add textual commentary without suggesting a change, it is easy to delete the contents of the Incorporation Frame or make an annotation to an insertion point in the draft.

The editing tools available to annotators in the Incorporation Frame correspond to the editing tools available in the draft. For example, if a user is annotating an InterDraw document, the Incorporation Frame of the Note will have a full set of graphics editing tools. By editing the copy of the original selection in the Incorporation Frame, the annotator indicates to the author of the draft that the change can be used as a replacement. The author may then decide to incorporate this change when he or she is revising the document. The process of incorporating annotations is discussed in more detail below in the section *Revising an Annotated Document*.

The Commentary Frame in the lower portion of the Note window is used for textual commentary. This may include general suggestions for revising the draft, specific explanations of the editing changes made in the Incorporation Frame, and so forth. Unlike the contents of the Incorporation Frame, authors cannot automatically incorporate the contents of the Commentary Frame. The author must use the "Copy" and "Paste" commands to include any text from the Commentary Frame in the draft.

Just like any other Intermedia document, a Note itself can be annotated. An annotation may be attached to any selection in a Note window. This allows one annotator to comment on another annotator's suggested revisions or commentary.

After an annotator has created a number of Notes for a document, he or she has the option of saving Notes individually or all at once. Unlike other types of Intermedia documents, Notes are automatically named when they are saved to help simplify the annotator's job. The name is derived from the first line of text in the Commentary Frame. If there is no commentary in a Note, the name is either based on the contents of the Incorporation Frame, if it contains text, or the name of the draft. Annotators can always change the default name.

Note Folders

To prevent desktop clutter, annotations are stored in a special Note Folder which is at the same level in the folder hierarchy as the annotated draft. Each document that has been annotated will have a single Note Folder associated with it, no matter how many people have annotated the document. The Note Folder is automatically created and opened the first time a document is annotated. All subsequent annotations are then stored in the Note Folder, so they may be easily found and organized.

The name of the Note Folder is derived from the draft name. For example, if the draft name is "Proposal," its Note Folder would be named "Proposal Notes." Each individual annotation is represented as a row in the Note Folder. If multi-level annotations (i.e., annotations on annotations) have been created, they are also stored in this Note Folder.

To see the link markers that indicate which elements of a document have been annotated, the Note Folder for that document must be open. Closing a Note Folder hides the annotation markers.

Notes are displayed in the Note Folder in a table format with the column headers: Title, User, Date, Processed, Status, and Order. There is also a Type column, but no header is displayed for this in the table. Each row in the table represents a single annotation. The name of the draft that corresponds to these annotations is shown on the right side of the Note Folder's Status Bar. Figure 4 shows a Note Folder with all its components.

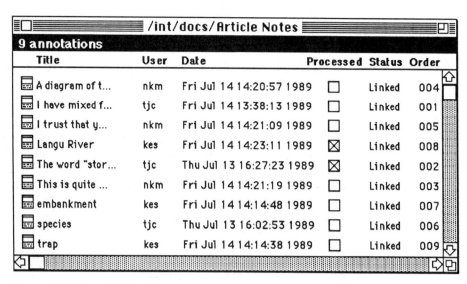

Figure 4. A Note Folder.

The columns of the Note Folder hold the following information:

Type
A small icon representing the type of the annotation (i.e. InterWord, InterDraw, InterVal, etc.). The type is determined by the editor that is used in the Incorporation Frame.

Title
A system-generated title for the annotation taken from the first few words in the Commentary Frame.

User
The user ID of the annotator.

Date
The date and time that the annotation was created. The time is not displayed if the Note Folder window is too narrow.

Processed
The check box contains an "x" if the annotation has been handled by the document author and is blank if it has not. Details on processing annotations are provided below.

Status
The status of an annotation may either be "Held" or "Detached." Details on assigning status to annotations are provided below.

Order
This column contains a number (beginning with 1) that reflects the position of the annotation in the document. For InterWord documents, annotations are numbered in the normal reading order (left to right, then top to bottom). Other logical ordering schemes are used in each of the Intermedia documents.

The rows of a Note Folder can be sorted, using up to three of the column headings. This feature allows the user to group Notes for different purposes. For example, sorting the rows by the "Status" and "Processed" columns, would enable the user to determine which Notes had been "Held" but not "Processed."

Revising an Annotated Document

If a document has been annotated, authors may revise the document based on suggested changes and commentary. The revision process includes reading the annotations, determining whether or not to incorporate the suggested changes, and making editing changes to the document based on the commentary in the attached Notes.

To look at annotations, the author must first open the corresponding Note Folder. This action parallels the opening of a Web View in order to follow links, which is a standard Intermedia action. The Web View is discussed briefly below. Once the Note Folder is open, annotation markers appear in the draft. Notes can be opened by following links from the annotated document or by double-clicking on their names in the Note Folder table. If the author is not certain of the location in the draft referred to by a Note, he or she simply has to follow the link from the Note window to the document. The block of text or graphics at the other end of the link will be highlighted. This highlighted area indicates the extent of text or graphics that will be replaced if the author chooses to incorporate the suggested change from the Note's Incorporation Frame. The author can easily change how much will be incorporated or replaced by changing the block extent either in the annotation or in the draft.

The author can incorporate a suggested change by transferring the data across the link between the annotation and the draft. If a Note is the active window, the author can "Push" the contents of the Incorporation Frame into the original document, thereby replacing the contents of the existing link anchor (the selection the annotator made when creating the annotation). Likewise, if the annotated document is the active window, the author can "Pull" the contents of the Incorporation Frame into the document. The result is identical. So that users do not have to remember the difference between pushing and pulling data, we provide an "Incorporate Annotation" command that either pushes or pulls the data across a link, depending on whether a Note window or a draft window is currently active. The "Incorporate Annotation" command also marks the annotation as "Processed."

When the data from the Incorporation Frame of the Note replaces the data in the document, the link anchor in the draft now consists of the revised data. This is crucial for two reasons. First, the link between the Note and the draft remains intact so that any commentary in the Note window can still be found by following the link. Second, the author may discover that a different annotator has suggested a better revision. If this is the case, the revision of the other annotator can be incorporated, thereby replacing the revision suggested by the first annotator.

The author can always undo the incorporation and return to the original document state by using the "Undo" command one or more times.

Managing Annotations

To accommodate different working styles, we provide authors with a number of facilities for handling annotations. One option is to open an annotation, examine its contents and then close it. In this case, the annotation remains linked to the document and has a status of "Held." All annotations are given a status of "Held" when they are initially created. Another option is to delete the annotation. This is done by selecting the name of the Note in the Note Folder and choosing the "Delete Document" command (the same command used to delete any other Intermedia document). Once an annotation is deleted, it is no longer represented in the Note Folder. At times, however, an author may want to save an annotation, but not have it linked to the draft any longer. In this case, the author has the option of disconnecting it. This is done by using the "Unlink" command (the same command used to disconnect navigational links). When an annotation is disconnected, its status in the Note Folder is changed to "Detached." The last option is to keep some or all of the annotations attached (i.e., "Held"), but indicate the ones that have been dealt with by manually placing an "x" in their Processed Check Box (see the Note diagram above). This box is automatically checked if the author uses the "Incorporate Annotation" command.

One step in managing annotations is for the author to decide on their status as he or she opens, reads, and incorporates them. To aid this process, the author can also organize the Note Folder by sorting the Notes based on any three of the Note Folder column headers. For example, the author may want to sort the annotations by the order in which they appear in the document or sort them based on user ID and the date of creation so that all the annotations created by one person are brought together in the order that they were made.

Annotation Links in the Web View

Since we anticipated that potentially hundreds of Notes would be attached to a single document, we needed to devise a mechanism for viewing Notes in the Intermedia *Web View*. This window displays a history of the user's *path* through a set of linked documents and a *map* showing the current document and all other documents connected to it (for a detailed description of the Web View see [Utti89]). To avoid cluttering the Web View, we decided to compact the annotation information by displaying the Note Folder rather than each individual Note in the map portion of the Web View. If a web is open when a user opens an annotated document, a single icon representing the Note Folder will appear in the map (this feature is not yet implemented). This folder icon is connected to the document's icon, indicating that the document has at least one annotation attached to it, as shown in Figure 5.

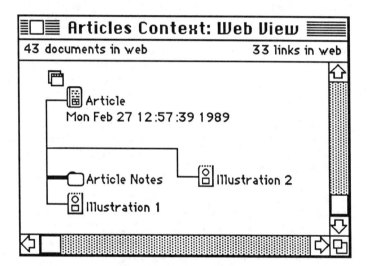

Figure 5. The proposal to use the folder icon to reduce clutter in the Web View is illustrated above. The InterWord document called "Article" is currently active on the user's screen (it is the last item in the path). This document has annotations attached to it as well as two InterDraw documents. The highlighting of the link line to "Article Notes" indicates that the user has selected a marker in the "Article" document that is connected to a Note stored in the "Article Notes" Note Folder.

No differentiation is made between annotation markers and other link markers, because, once created, there is no functional difference between the two. The only way to differentiate between them without following the links is to use the Web View. If a user selects a marker in a draft and an annotation is attached to it, the *link line* to the Note Folder will be highlighted in the Web View. If a user selects a marker and sees that both the link line to the Note Folder and link lines corresponding to other documents are highlighted in the Web View, then the selected marker has both standard and annotation links emanating from it.

With the exception of the Web View, InterNote has been fully integrated into the existing Intermedia environment. While we have been successful in achieving the level of integration we specified in our end-user requirements, we believe there is still a significant amount of additional work necessary to effectively support annotative collaboration. The following section goes on to describe some of our plans for future extensions to Intermedia in this arena.

IV. FUTURE RESEARCH

Informal evaluation of InterNote by a group of early users led us to draw the following conclusions. The "Create Annotation" interface was found to be simple and effective. Annotators tended to make the same number of suggestions for editorial changes; however, they tended to support those suggestions more extensively with commentary. While the interface supported editorial changes and attached commentary, the annotators found it difficult to suggest structural changes, such as reordering whole paragraphs of text.

We recognize that different styles of annotation interfaces might be more appropriate for different types of annotation tasks. For example, text in a separate window, such as a Note, might be best for a two or three paragraph comment, while drawing lines, arrows and circles directly onto the document might be best for suggesting revisions to an architectural drawing. It might also be useful for an author or annotator to switch between the different interfaces with ease and with no loss of information.

We are actively pursuing alternate interfaces for the annotation process. In particular, we have been exploring the notion of "layers of acetate" that an annotator can lay over the draft. The annotator can then make suggestions via lines, arrows and circles for structural changes to the document in addition to using proofreaders' symbols for conventional document markup. Unlike the mark-up implementations that exist today, we believe that it is possible to allow authors to incorporate suggested changes, and with judicious use of color, to view multiple annotators' comments simultaneously. We also believe that it is possible to have the markings on the acetate layer "stick" with the objects to which they refer, even after further editing by the author.

Because users should be able to switch between the different interfaces with ease and with no loss of information, we are trying to develop a *Common Annotation Format* to represent annotations in an interface-independent way. This Common Annotation Format must retain the specific contents for all parts of an annotation in a structure which will be compatible with all implemented interfaces.

Regardless of what interface is used, we feel that authors must be able to print reasonable hard copies of their drafts, complete with annotations. Printing linked documents is, in general, a hard problem in hypertext systems. One possible solution is to print the draft with annotations appearing as foot or end notes. Just as in regular foot/end notes, annotations would be tied to their locations in the draft via corresponding superscripts or textual bracketed labels. This seems feasible when the draft contains text; however, when considering annotated documents of types other than text, it is hard to devise a logical printing layout that is independent of the document type.

Our small trial emphasized the need for a number of communications tools to help groups of annotators and authors coordinate their efforts. It became clear that more than simple electronic mail is necessary. A user should be able to know at any time whether anyone else on the system has a document open for annotation or editing. There should be facilities for synchronously communicating with users currently working on the same task, as well as asynchronously sending messages to users not currently working.

One of our underlying assumptions while designing InterNote was that the focus of a group's editorial efforts is a single source document. In a hypertext environment, this may not always be the case. The group may wish to comment on the existence and placement of links between documents, as well a document's content. We plan to explore the issues of printing annotated documents and annotating the links between documents in the future.

While much work has been accomplished over the years in studying the structure and interactions involved in group work, very little has been done to integrate the notion of groups into desktop environments. We plan to work on developing simple and intuitive interfaces for users to create and modify both permanent or ad hoc work groups [Finh89]. We hope, in the long run, that applications will be developed where the single-user version is considered a special case of a group version where the group size is one.

V. CONCLUSION

For annotation systems to be effective, they must blend into a user's daily working environment, rather than overtake or displace it. If annotation systems, groupware systems, or hypermedia systems work only in a limited domain, they are simply not as useful as they could be.

Assuming that the daily working environment for the remainder of the 1980s and a good part of the 1990s will be based upon the desktop metaphor of multiple applications running simultaneously and generating documents that appear in overlapping windows on a screen, we must make sure that any annotation systems that are created work over the entirety of that environment. Stated succinctly, group annotation functionality must be integrated fundamentally into an already existing application architecture.

Specifically, just as our Intermedia hypermedia philosophy holds that all applications can provide navigational linking by implementing a small linking protocol interface, it follows that all applications should be able to provide annotation facilities by implementing an even smaller annotation interface protocol. By implementing this protocol, a developer can provide users with the ability to annotate documents created with the developer's new application. Similarly, when users obtain a new application, they can be assured that it will have annotation functionality, since annotation is a fundamental part of the environment.

To this end, by extending our existing hypermedia framework to include support for annotative collaboration in the form of warm links and annotation commands, we were able to meet most of our requirements. Most significantly, we were able to provide consistent annotation functionality across all applications within the Intermedia environment, regardless of data type.

ACKNOWLEDGEMENTS

We would like to thank our sponsors, US West and Apple Computer, and all of the people who have helped in the requirements and design phases of InterNote, especially Karen Smith Catlin, Helen DeAndrade, L. Nancy Garrett, Norman Meyrowitz and Murugappan Palaniappan. Thanks also to Mark Sawtelle for his helpful comments on earlier drafts of this paper and the rest of the team at IRIS for their support of this effort.

REFERENCES

[Brod]   Broderbund Software, Inc., *ForComment*, 17 Paul Dr., San Rafael, CA 94903-2101.

[Brow82]   J.S. Brown, "Notes concerning desired functionality issues and philosophy for an *AuthoringLand*," *Xerox PARC CIS working paper*, 1982.

[Brow84]   M. Brown, "A Report on Peer Review and Co-authorship among the Humanities Faculty at Stanford University," *ACIS/IRIS Report,* December, 1984.

[Cont]   Context, *Context,* 8285 S.W. Nimbus, Beaverton, OR 97005.

[Dene]   Deneba Software, *Comment 2.0,* 7855 NW 12th St., Ste. 202, Miami, FL 33126.

[Finh89]   T. Finholt, L. Sproull, S. Kiesler, "Communication and Performance in Ad Hoc Task Groups," to appear in *Intellectual Teamwork: Social and Technical Bases of Collaboration,* edited by Kraut, Galegher, & Egido, Lawrence Earlbaum Assoc., 1989.

[Garr86]   L. Garrett, K. Smith, N. Meyrowitz, "Intermedia: Issues, Strategies, and Tactics in the Design of a Hypermedia Document System," *Proceedings of the Conference on Computer-Supported Cooperative Work (CSCW '86),* Austin, TX, December, 1986.

[Jazz85]   Jazz Handbook, Lotus Development Corporation, Cambridge, MA, 1985.

[Krau86]   R. Kraut, J. Galegher, C. Egido, "Relationships and Tasks in Scientific Research Collaborations," *Proceedings of the Conference on Computer-Supported Cooperative Work (CSCW '86),* Austin, TX, December, 1986.

[Main]   Mainstay, Inc., *MarkUp,* 5311-B Derry Ave., Agoura Hills, CA 91301.

[Meyr86]   N. Meyrowitz, "Intermedia: The Architecture and Construction of an Object-Oriented Hypermedia System and Applications Framework," *Proceedings of OOPSLA '86,* Portland, OR, September, 1986.

[Niel84]   J. Nielsen, "How Readers Annotate Textbooks and Manuals," DAIMI PB - 182, Computer Science Dept., Aarhus University, Denmark, October, 1984.

[Trig86]   R. Trigg, L. Suchman, F. Halasz, "Supporting Collaboration in NoteCards," *Proceedings of CSCW '86,* Austin, TX, December, 1986.

[Utti89]   K. Utting, N. Yankelovich, "Context and Navigation in Hypermedia Networks," *Transactions on Information Systems,* January, 1989.

[Wang]   Wang Laboratories, Inc., *FreeStyle,* One Industrial Ave., Lowell, MA 01851.

[Yank88]   N. Yankelovich, B. Haan, N. Meyrowitz, S. Drucker, "Intermedia: The Concept and Construction of a Seamless Information Environment," *IEEE Computer 21,* 1988.

Panel: Interchanging Hypertexts

Robert Akscyn, Knowledge Systems

Frank Halasz, Xerox PARC

Tim Oren, Apple Computer (chair)

Victor Riley, Brown University

Lawrence Welch, NIST

INTRODUCTION

One of the seminal visions of hypertext is the "docuverse," a seamless carpet of inter-linked text and media components where each additional work can be fluidly linked to pre-existing information, and any user can browse, search, and comment on the entire collection.

The reality of hypertext today is rather different. Driven by the needs of particular applications and by platform and market constraints, a plethora of competing and incompatible hypertext systems have arisen. Their user interfaces vary radically, from the fixed frames of KMS to the multiple scrolling texts of Guide. The data models are equally diverse, from the formalisms of HAM and Intermedia to HyperCard's combination of object structure with procedural links. Many of these systems have already carved out substantial market niches and a growing amount of content is being created within their confines. Indeed, our ability to make global statements of utility for any of these approaches is still quite limited, and there may be no one best way of storing or presenting hypertext which suits all users and applications.

Compounding the problem is the emergence of the academic and commercial computing milieu as a distributed, loosely coupled collection of machines and networks of varying scale and vendor. In this environment, the emergence of a uniform hypertext storage substrate such as Xanadu is problematic and the difficulties of maintaining consistency across a large docuverse are compounded.

If we are not to abandon the vision of grand scale collaboration within the docuverse, some means of interchange and communication between hypertext systems becomes necessary. The requirement is equally pressing for potential publishers of hypertext based content, who must worry about portability of their works between hypertext systems and ensuring their longevity in the face of rapidly changing hardware and software platforms. Loss of either of these applications areas could be permanently crippling to the evolution of hypertext as a medium.

Steps toward interchange, standards, and ultimately distributed open hypertext systems must be founded on an abstract model of hypertext to which existing and future systems can be related. Creation of such a model forces us to go beyond casual references to "links" or "nodes" and to begin defining in a formal fashion the underpinnings of our field, building a *lingua franca* of hypertext.

The opening presentation in this panel describes the beginning of such a hypertext modeling effort at the so-called Dexter Workshops. The three following talks describe interchange experiments undertaken in the areas of hypertext publishing, interchange between remote sites, and interchange of structured documents in a distributed computing environment. Several of these designs have drawn on the Dexter modeling work. The final presentation places the current state of hypertext interchange within the context of the overall standards process.

The formal presentations will be followed by an exchange of issues among the panelists, and then by questions from the floor.

— Tim Oren

THE DEXTER WORKSHOP HYPERTEXT MODEL

Frank Halasz, Xerox PARC

The Dexter Workshops (named for the first meeting location) have brought together a small group of hypertext workers to consider research issues and directions in the field. One of the early realizations of the Workshop was the need for a formal model and vocabulary for hypertext which could replace the "intuitive," but often inconsistent, definitions in current use. This talk will report on the current state and content of the Dexter Hypertext Model.

INTERCHANGE IN THE REAL WORLD

Robert Akscyn, Knowledge Systems

This talk will describe Knowledge Systems' current efforts to interchange KMS-based hypertexts with other hypertext systems such as HyperCard, NoteCards, and Intermedia. The talk will focus on the difficulties encountered (or anticipated) in interchanging hypertexts with each of these particular systems — especially difficulties that stem from differences in the underlying data models of these systems.

DATA INTERCHANGE IN INTERMEDIA

Victor Riley, Brown IRIS

Victor Riley is a senior software engineer at IRIS (Institute for Research in Information and Scholarship) at Brown University. He has developed a hypermedia data interchange protocol specific to the IRIS Intermedia system. This interchange protocol is a definition for data interchange between remote IRIS Intermedia sites.

BUILDING A LAYERED INTERCHANGE FORMAT

Tim Oren, Apple Computer

With the emergence of hypertext and compound documents, needs for inter-application data interchange have outpaced Apple's existing standards. An effort is underway to create MIFF, a media interchange file format. MIFF is a layered specification, including distinct layers for object identify, data chunk storage, links and persistent selection, and time, version, and proxy representations. The design was heavily influenced by the Dexter Workshop model. This talk will describe the layering policy and adaptations for distributed systems made in the MIFF design.

HYPERTEXT INTERCHANGE AND STANDARDS

Lawrence Welsh, National Institute of Standards and Technology

NIST is concerned about the need to integrate standards so that they will work together as opposed to against each other. We perceive hypertext to be an area where such integration/harmonization can occur between database and document processing standards. We believe that the first step toward standardizing hypertext is to develop a standard hypertext reference model. Developing standards for specific aspects of hypertext before there is a reference model could easily result in the type of confusion that currently exists in the document processing world.

Panel: Hypertext, Narrative, and Consciousness

Michael Joyce, Jackson Community College

Nancy Kaplan, Cornell University

John McDaid, New York Institute of Technology

Stuart Moulthrop, Yale University

This panel attempts to initiate a dialogue on the implications of hypertext between information theorists and literary theorists, writers of texts and designers of text systems. Though the panelists base their views on several years of practical work with hypertext in education, they are concerned with broader social and conceptual problems raised by this technology -- its likely effect on the way we teach ourselves and others to understand texts and the way we use those texts to construct an orderly (or disorderly) world. It seems important to raise these issues at Hypertext '89 because hypertext is rapidly being recognized by humanists as a crucial and revolutionary enterprise. This recognition creates an opportunity for humanists and scientists to convene a productive dialogue which could have great significance both for hypertext and for the future of the humanities. We hope for a frank and free-ranging exchange of views and emphasize that this is a forum for questioning and controversy, not a series of monologues. Each panelist will deliver a ten-minute position statement, with the remaining hour of the session devoted to discussion. Abstracts of the three presentations follow.

MICHAEL JOYCE: "A Read/Write Revolution"

Until recently, the term "interactive narrative" looked like an oxymoron. While most storytelling requires involvement and feedback from its audience, fiction as we know it in the west is not spontaneously improvised but asynchronously composed. Homer may have tailored his formulaic performances to different audiences, but it is likely that no one interrupted him to asking to hear "Faithful Penelope" one more time. Under hypertext, electronic systems become virtual storytellers and narrative is no longer disseminated in a single direction from singer to listener or writer to reader. It exists instead as a cycle in which readers become co-authors and artificially intelligent systems "read" their responses. At the moment, most interest centers on the machine side of this cycle, focusing on hypertext systems and intelligent navigators that can structure or generate narratives. But the human side of the cycle deserves equal attention, for it is unlikely that readers of interactive narrative will behave with the same passivity as readers of conventional fiction. This presentation, based on three years of observing encounters with hypertext fiction, suggests that many hypertextual readers will not be satisfied with being co-authors of the narrative, but will want to assume authoring privileges at the system level as well -- a consideration which could be of great importance not only to the aesthetics of interactive literature, but to the development of hypertext systems as well.

STUART MOULTHROP: "Hypertext and the Academy"

This presentation is a reconsideration of Michael Joyce's ideas about the "read/write revolution" of hypertext. What happens when this revolution begins to impinge upon the academic study of literature? How is hypertext likely to be integrated into educational institutions that seek to empower students but necessarily depend on intellectual hierarchies?

Based on experiments with hypertextual media in composition and literature courses at Cornell and Yale, I propose a number of observations about the function of hypertext in literary studies: (1) hypertext can greatly enrich the literary encounter for students whose previous education has alienated them from literature and writing; (2) it also provides a powerful tool for scholars engaged in the study of complex and allusive texts (e.g., Tennyson's *In Memoriam* or Pynchon's *Gravity's Rainbow*); but (3) these applications of hypertext raise questions about the nature of literary authority and the integrity of the text that have yet to be resolved in theory or practice. The hypertext "revolution" is likely to provoke considerable academic controversy in the next decade and may ultimately transform humanistic education.

JOHN McDAID: "Hypertext and Nonlinear Discourse"

Michael Joyce's presentation concerns the present development of hypertext literature; Stuart Moulthrop's addresses the next ten years; my presentation is an attempt to place hypertext and hypermedia in a larger evolutionary context. Following McLuhan and Hofstadter, I take hypertext to be the latest in a series of procedural recursions that have advanced the scope and function of human consciousness. The spoken word folded a single sensory experience back over the unified sensorium of pre-linguistic experience. Writing, in McLuhan's phrase, gave us "an eye for an ear," inscribing the lasting and simultaneous presence of print on the evanscent stream of speech. Hypertext is a third recursion in which a primary system of discourse (the hypertext structure) organizes a secondary system (the text) and hence realizes the polysequentiality latent in print. I believe that, as McLuhan predicted, hypertext and hypermedia lead toward a reunification of the sensorium, a return to human experience of the "many-at-onceness" accessible to the pre-linguistic mind. Such a transformation of consciousness presumes formidable changes in rhetorical, aesthetic, and even social categories. In this presentation I will attempt to indicate the nature of these changes, drawing on the groundwork laid down in Joyce's and Moulthrop's talks.

Panel: Lessons Learned From the ACM Hypertext on Hypertext Project

Bernard Rous, Association for Computing Machinery

Ben Scheiderman, University of Maryland

Nicole Yankelovich, Brown University

Elise Yoder, Knowledge Workshop

INTRODUCTION

In the Fall of 1988 the Association for Computing Machinery (ACM) released its first hypertext product, entitled *Hypertext on Hypertext* [ACM88b]. It contained all of the major articles from the special issue on hypertext of the *Communications of the ACM* (July 1988) [ACM88a].

Three different versions of the product were developed:

- Hyperties version for IBM PC [Marc88] (Ben Shneiderman, editor)
- HyperCard version for Apple Macintosh [Good87] (Nicole Yankelovich, editor)
- KMS version for Sun and Apollo workstations [Aksc88] (Elise Yoder and Robert Akscyn, editors)

The Hypertext on Hypertext project was significant in several ways. ACM is one of the world's largest publishers of computer science information. This project represents ACM's first venture into hypertext publishing [Fox88] and its first experience of the effort required and the results that can be expected. It is also the only commercial project we know of where three groups of experienced hypertext developers independently designed hypertext databases using the same raw materials. This is a rare opportunity to compare their design decisions and their experiences.

DISCUSSION

This panel brings together the editors of the three Hypertext on Hypertext products. The panelists will compare the approaches they took to structuring the hypertext database, formatting the material, and adding links. They'll also recount the more interesting challenges they faced and summarize some of the lessons they learned.

The panelists will also discuss the following issues:

- The problems inherent in translating linear material into a hypertext form: how should the database be structured? How should the material be divided into smaller units?
- The extent to which the particular hypertext system being used influenced (for better or worse) the design of the database.
- The need for more interaction with the original authors, whose material was being significantly changed by dividing it into screen-sized chunks, adding links, and adding substructure.

- The difficulty of creating meaningful links that help the reader make associations between ideas (as opposed to straightforward cross-reference links such as bibliographic references). The role of the editor versus that of the original author(s) in creating links.

- The importance of graphic design and aesthetic issues for published material: how should the hypertext nodes be formatted? how should links be displayed? how should the product be packaged?

- The things that might have been done differently if there had been more time to develop the products.

- The value of small-scale hypertext publishing projects, and the extent to which the experience with this project is applicable to larger-scale projects.

PANELISTS

Bernard Rous, the panel moderator, is Associate Director of Publications at ACM. He was the chief coordinator of the Hypertext on Hypertext project at ACM.

Ben Shneiderman is Professor of Computer Science and Director of the Human Computer Interaction Laboratory at the University of Maryland.

Nicole Yankelovich is a senior member of IRIS (Institute for Research in Information and Scholarship) at Brown University.

Elise Yoder is President of Knowledge Workshop, a hypertext publishing company.

REFERENCES

[Aksc88]   Akscyn, R., McCracken, D., and Yoder, E. KMS: A distributed hypertext system for managing knowledge in organizations. *Communications of the ACM 31*, 7 (July 1988), 820-835.

[ACM88a] Association for Computing Machinery (ACM). *Communications of the ACM 31*, 7 (July 1988).

[ACM88b] Association for Computing Machinery (ACM). *Hypertext on Hypertext*. ACM Press Database and Electronic Products Series, 1988.

[Fox88]   Fox, E. ACM Press Database and Electronic Products--New Services for the Information Age. *Communications of the ACM 31*, 8 (Aug. 1988), 948-951.

[Good87] Goodman, D. *The Complete HyperCard Handbook*. Bantam Books, New York, NY, 1987.

[Marc88] Marchionini, G. and Shneiderman, B. Finding Facts vs. Browsing Knowledge in Hypertext Systems. *IEEE Computer* (Jan. 1988), 70-80.

Panel: Indexing and Hypertext

Mark Bernstein, Eastgate Systems, moderator

James Critz, Hewlett-Packard

Nancy Mulvany, Bayside Indexing Service

Rosemary Simpson, Indexing Unlimited

Mary-Claire van Leunen, Digital Equipment Corporation

INTRODUCTION

The index is one of the oldest information retrieval devices. When the earliest scribe produced a document that could not be easily browsed, the need for an index emerged. Today we find voluminous amounts of text being placed online. While readers have the option of browsing and searching the text, these are not always efficient options for fruitful information retrieval. A navigational aid is needed. The back-of-the-book index offers itself as an excellent starting point for the organization of online information into a cohesive structure. Without a structured mechanism for information retrieval, online information will be lost. Given the amount of material being placed online, it is indeed a frightening prospect to consider the amount of information that is inaccessible due to the lack of a sound retrieval method. This panel will discuss formal indexing methodology and how it has been and might be applied to hypertext design.

NANCY MULVANY - RELATIONS BETWEEN INDEXING AND HYPERTEXT DESIGN

The similarities between sound back-of-the-book index design and sound hypertext design are many. Both offer the opportunity to immediately guide readers to desired information and related information. However, if they are not designed properly, an index and hypertext links can lead readers astray, waste their time, and greatly reduce the accessibility of information. A clear understanding of what an index is and what an index is not is the main theme of this discussion. The criterion for judging an index will be discussed as well as the applicability of this criterion to hypertext design. Particular attention will be devoted to the elements of the traditional back-of-the-book index that are transferable to hypertext design. Accuracy and completeness, a major concern of indexers, will be discussed in relation to book indexing and hypertext.

In traditional publishing the index is usually found at the back of the book. The notion that the index be moved up front in hypertext documents will be advocated. As a familiar and structured information access matrix, an index may very well be the front-end navigation aid that adds coherent structure to hypertext documents.

MARY-CLAIRE VAN LEUNEN - INDEXED HYPERTEXT CASE STUDY

Mary-Claire van Leunen is responsible for maintaining online documentation for operating systems, utilities, and peripheral equipment at DEC's Systems Research Center in Palo Alto, California. The SRC documentation system provides online (hypertext) access and demand printing for some 30 million words, all of which can change without warning at any time. A Boolean search of terms is not adequate because it does not properly handle issues of specificity, centrality, and hierarchy. Concordances to the whole corpus are built automatically, but for the central core of information, access is provided through manual, back-of-the-book style indexing. The automatic and manual tools used to maintain information access to this documentation will be discussed as well as plans for the future.

ROSEMARY SIMPSON - HYPERMEDIA RESOURCE BASE PROJECT

The Hypermedia Resource Base is a comprehensively indexed hypertext covering the activities, people and publications of the hypermedia community. It will include a comprehensive bibliography, abstracts of key papers and books, selected annotations, commentary, biographies, research descriptions, product descriptions, concept maps, and a multi-definition annotated glossary.

The goals of the Resource Base are to: 1) provide information about hypermedia activities to the hypermedia community; and 2) provide a test bed for research into the role of indexing as a hypermedia navigation and management tool. We see indexing as being part of a suite of information access tools. These tools include indexes - alphabetical structures of object-qualifier phrases, hypertext browsing links, table-of-contents partitioning, and trails - both history links and directed trails.

The research issues we are addressing include:

Completeness - the problem of completeness in information retrieval is a serious issue which hypertext systems tend to exacerbate. We are testing the idea that comprehensive, context-oriented indexes can be used as link generators as well as link completeness testors.

Extensibility - information systems are rarely static, and need to address divergent and changing points of view. At the same time, users need controlled vocabularies to aid in finding all related information. Extensible indexing systems accommodate both sets of needs by providing the ability 1) to integrate alternate points of view into an index and 2) to subset and reformulate indexes to more closely model particular retrieval needs.

Portability - hypertext link and document portability is critical if hypertext systems are to be accessible to all who want information. One approach is to divide the problem into two domains - documents and links. Then we can view an index as a link reservoir which can be ported to different systems independently of the issues of document transport. Currently the indexed bibliography subset of Hypermedia Resource Base is available on paper and as an application of HyperGate.

JAMES CRITZ - AUTOMATED INDEXING AND HYPERTEXT

As the volume of material integrated into hypertext and hypermedia systems increases and is more widely shared, there is a need both to develop standards and strategies for hypertext generation, use, and administration and to implement these in intelligent, automated tools. The experience and knowledge of indexers will be crucial to the achievement of this.

However, major obstacles exist to creating tools based on an understanding of indexing skills and knowledge. Current knowledge of psychological and semantic interpretation of textual and visual material is poor; and little has been done to incorporate even this limited knowledge into automated tools. At the same time, indexers have not previously had to grapple so seriously with the problems of indexing multiple texts which are subject to change. In addition, as user needs become more clearly defined there are issues of judgment in indexing possible interpretations as well as the more obvious content.

BIOGRAPHIES

Mark Bernstein, Eastgate Systems, Inc., 134 Main Street, Watertown, MA 02172, (617) 924-9004: Mark Bernstein, chief scientist at Eastgate Systems, Inc., is the principal designer of the HyperGate hypertext system. Bernstein advocates an approach to "deeply intertwingled hypertext" that emphasizes the expressive power of complex networks of finely crafted links. He is co-author (with Erin Sweeney) of the historical hypertext *1912*, was chairman of the AAAI-88 Workshop on AI and Hypertext, and has contributed to journals ranging from ACM SIGOIS to Chemical Physics. A graduate of Swarthmore College, he received his doctorate in 1983 from Harvard University. Bernstein has been an invited lecturer at conferences running the gamut from the Hypertext '87 Workshop to UniForum '89.

James T. Critz, Hewlett-Packard Company, 3155 Porter Drive, MS 28AD, Palo Alto, CA 94305, (415) 857-6225: As a member of the Leading Edge Technologies Education staff of Hewlett-Packard Co., Jim researches new technologies, primarily related to artificial intelligence. He develops education programs to bring recent research quickly to R&D labs where it shows promise for use in future products. After receiving his doctorate in theoretical linguistics from the University of Washington, Seattle, WA in 1976, he was a Fulbright lecturer (1976-1978) at the University of Warsaw, Poland. He has lectured and done research in Europe and Asia as well as in United States. His research and publications have been in the areas of knowledge representation, reasoning, models of thinking, text understanding and abstraction, machine translation, expert systems, and information science.

Nancy Mulvany, Bayside Indexing Service, 265 Arlington Avenue, Kensington, CA 94707, (415) 524-4195: Nancy Mulvany is the owner of Bayside Indexing Service, a provider of small- and large-scale indexing services for technical documentation projects. Bayside is also the U.S. publisher of the MACREX Indexing Program for IBM PCs and compatibles. Mulvany is a specialist in the indexing of computer-related mater-ial. She is currently involved in the development of hypertext systems. She also teaches indexing for the University of California Extensions at Berkeley and Santa Cruz, Writers Connection, *editcetera*, and the Graduate School, USDA. Her teaching activities have expanded beyond the classroom to include on-site training for Silicon Valley firms. As a professional member of the Computer Press Association, Mulvany has written articles for a variety of publications. Mulvany has been active in the American Society of Indexers for several years. She has served as the president of the Golden Gate Chapter, national ASI vice present, editor of the ASI Newsletter and currently serves as national ASI president (1989-1990).

Rosemary Simpson, Indexing Unlimited, 4 Lilac Court, Cambridge, MA 02141, (617) 876-3420: Rosemary Simpson is the president of Indexing Unlimited and the director of the Boston Computer Society Hypermedia Group's Resource Base Project. Her background in computers and information management includes: systems engineering and programming for IBM, teaching DecSystem-10 Monitor Internals for Digital Equipment Corporation, writing systems reference documentation for Prime Computer, and designing and prototyping the Gateway hypermedia system for Lisp Machines, Inc. Her current activities include: book and online documentation system indexing, the design and implementation of LMS - an index-oriented hypermedia system for the Macintosh, and the design and management of the Hypermedia Resource Base project for the BCS Hypermedia Group.

Mary-Claire van Leunen, Digital Equipment Corporation, 130 Lytton Avenue, Palo Alto, CA 94306, (415) 853-2211: Mary-Claire van Leunen worked for twenty-five years as an editor, mostly freelance, mostly on scholarly writing. She did editing in fields from philosophy to neurology, from Latin American studies to statistics and she edited books for more than twenty publishers, including the Oxford University Press, the MIT Press and the University of Chicago Press. She edited both the Harvard Divinity Bulletin and the Yale Research Reports in Computer Science. In 1978 Alfred Knopf published her book, *A Handbook for Scholars*, a distillation of her experience in scholarly editing, which is still in print and sell ten or twenty copies a year. In 1984 she changed careers and joined Digital Equipment Corporation, where she does research on software for professional writers, editors, and indexers. She has designed and built a dictionary server call "random" (for the Random House Dictionary) and a documentation environment called "Luke" (for the Gospel of St. Luke).

Panel: Expert Systems and Hypertext

Michael Bieber - University of Pennsylvania

Steve Feiner - Columbia University

Mark Frisse - Washington University, St. Louis

Phil Hayes - Carnegie Group

Gerri Peper - IBM, Boulder

Walt Scacchi - University of Southern California

INTRODUCTION

The relationships between expert systems and hypertext are many and varied. Expert systems have been proposed as authoring environments and navigational aids for hypertext systems and hypertext systems have been proposed as knowledge representation vehicles and rule editors for expert systems. These interrelationships should come as no surprise given the similarity of intellectual challenges confronting investigators in the two respective disciplines. In each, issues of knowledge representation, control of inference, and computational complexity are central. This panel will attempt to explore some of these overlapping issues from the perspective of both basic research and commercial applications. Although some primary data will be presented, the session will be more one of *making links* between other Hypertext 89 Proceedings presentations and a larger body of work. Audience participation will be strongly encouraged.

THE TOPICS

The panelists will argue that hypertext and expert systems are *companions* and not *competitors*. The panelists will argue this point from a number of perspectives. First, they will discuss with the audience methods for building more personalized and "intelligent" hypermedia systems. Among the many issues in "intelligent" hypertext are rule-based procedures associated with information units and links, domain-specific hypertext editors, and automated methods for optimizing presentation of information. Second, the panelists will explore how hypertext systems can improve the function and performance of more traditional expert systems. In particular, they will discuss how hypertext can enhance knowledge acquisition, knowledge based maintenance, and on-line documentation. Third, the panelists will discuss the knowledge representation issues of granularity and modularity. Finally, the panelists will discuss the relationships between the artificial intelligence industry and the emerging number of groups engaged in professional hypermedia work. They will discuss problems related to the modularity of hypertext and to the transition from small prototype systems to large-scale "industrial" hypertext systems.

The panelists will also respond to a number of issues first raised by Halasz. First, they will explore expert system technology's potential to filter links and to find complex relationships between nodes. Second, they will discuss how artificial intelligence techniques can be used to reason over hypermedia networks. Finally, they will discuss how automated inference programs can be used to create new "virtual structures" which assist in the location and use of what Bush called "the momentarily important item."

THE PARTICIPANTS AND PERSPECTIVES

Michael Bieber - University of Pennsylvania

Michael Bieber will serve as panel co-moderator. He will discuss formalizations necessary to reason about complex hypertext systems. He will explore the notion of "smart links" and intelligent decision support systems.

Steve Feiner - Columbia University

Steve Feiner will discuss the work he and his colleagues are performing at Columbia University. In particular, he will discuss the interrelationships between artificial intelligence and automation of presentation.

Mark Frisse - Washington University, St. Louis

Mark Frisse will serve as panel co-moderator. He will briefly discuss how various investigators use heuristics to facilitate information retrieval from hypertext.

Phil Hayes - Carnegie Group

Phil Hayes will comment further on his Monday afternoon presentation on the Integrated Maintenance Project. He will take the perspective of one who integrates hypertext into large-scale expert systems projects.

Gerri Peper - IBM, Boulder

Gerri Peper will discuss recent work comparing the performance of a hypertext system with that of an expert system when applied to complex diagnostic problems. Through an examination of comparison data, she will argue for the use of hypertext systems in some domains usually associated with expert systems technology.

Walt Scacchi - University of Southern California

Walt Scacchi will discuss the need and potential for incorporating into a software development hypertext system knowledge about users and their tasks.

Panel: Hypertext and Higher Education: A Reality Check

Stephen C.Ehrmann, The Annenberg/CPB Project

Steven Erde, Cornell University Medical College

Kenneth Morrell, Saint Olaf College

Ronald F. E. Weissman, Brown University

This panel discussion will examine the extent to which today's hypermedia systems are actually used and usable in higher education instruction and research. The panel will seek to foster dialog between hypermedia systems developers, corpus authors, and faculty users. A series of questions will be addressed by the panel and audience, including:

How are hypermedia corpuses actually used in classes? How well do today's systems meet the exploratory learning goals so often described as being at the heart of the hypermedia movement? What kinds of assignments make sense pedagogically? Are there system features which tend to discourage or prevent such uses?

What are the difficulties involved in administering a course using hypertext? Are there unusual logistical problems? How does one monitor or manage the annotation and expansion of the corpus during the semester?

Are today's hypermedia environments, tools, and practices proving to be useful for the faculty researcher? the student researcher? For faculty considering a hypertext to organize data, is periodic porting to new hardware and software a safe bet? or does the faculty member risk marooning two years of work inside an obsolete system?

What are the prospects for published hypertext corpuses? What system features are likely to affect the economics of publication and distribution? What are the special problems in creating hypertext materials that can be used on other campuses and in other courses?

Panel: Hypertext and Software Engineering

Robert Balzer, USC Information Sciences Institute

Michael Begeman, MCC

Pankaj K. Garg, Hewlett-Packard Laboratories

Mayer Schwartz, Tektronix Laboratories

Ben Scheiderman, University of Maryland

OVERVIEW

The purpose of this panel is to bring together researchers in software engineering and hypertext and help identify the major issues in the application of hypertext technology and concepts to software engineering and vice versa.

Hypertext for Software Engineering

Software engineering as a discipline strives to improve the process of developing, maintaining, and using large scale software systems. Large scale software systems are programs which necessarily require the coordinated effort of teams of people for their development, use, and maintenance. An approach to mitigating the negative affects of communication and coordination required for this cooperative effort is to provide an active information base through which all cooperative activity in software engineering can be mediated. This way, certain burdens of the communication and coordination can be transmitted to the active information base (from the humans), thereby increasing the effectiveness of the humans in the process.

Hypertext is well suited as a model for this active information base because of its generality and flexibility. It is general in the sense that there is no restriction on the types of information in the nodes of a hypertext. It is flexible in the sense that users of a hypertext can impose their own structure on the hypertext. However, the application of hypertext technology to software engineering information base is a fairly non-trivial effort. This panel will discuss some of the issues which arise in such an effort.

Software Engineering for Hypertext

Software engineering is concerned with the issues involved in the life cycle of large scale software systems. Hypertext systems potentially are large scale software systems; therefore several concepts and tools of software engineering can be applied to the development, use, and maintenance of hypertext systems.

Conceptually, hypertext is a genre of communication which allows immense freedom as to the contents and structure of messages being communicated. However, the technology of a truly "freedom providing" hypertext model is fairly non-trivial. As software engineering research has demonstrated in the past, formal specifications of large scale software systems can lead to better understanding between researchers about the issues involved. Moreover, to ultimately achieve Ted Nelson's vision of a "docuverse", we need to develop hypertext systems which can talk to each other. Just as it is easy to carry a piece of paper, it should be easy to transfer a hypertext from one hypertext system to another. This requires that a consistent hypertext model be followed by all hypertext developers.

This panel will discuss such concepts of software engineering which are applicable to the design, use, and maintenance of hypertext systems.

Categories of Issues

To help guide the panel discussion we have categorized the issues involved into three categories:

1. Requirements from hypertext models for effectively managing software engineering information, e.g., how important is it to support active links in the hypertext?

2. Application of hypertext concepts to manage software engineering information, e.g., how does the concept of trail blazing in hypertext apply to software engineering; and

3. Application of software engineering concepts for designing hypertext systems, e.g., the use of formal specifications for hypertext systems.

Panelists and their Affiliations

Robert Balzer, USC Information Sciences Institute, 4676 Admiralty Way, Marina del Rey, CA 90292.

Michael Begeman, Software Technology Program, MCC, 3500 West Balcones Center Drive, Austin, Texas 78759

Ben Shneiderman, Department of Computer Science University of Maryland, College Park, MD 20742.

Mayer Schwartz, Computer Research Laboratory, Tektronix Labs, Tektronix, Inc., P. O. Box 500, Beaverton, Oregon 97077.

Panel: Cognitive Aspects of Designing Hypertext Systems

Pat Baird, University of Strathclyde,

Dennis Egan, Bellcore

Walter Kinch, University of Colorado

John Smith, University of North Carolina

Norbert A. Streitz, Integrated Publications and Information Systems Institute

INTRODUCTION

The goal of this panel is to discuss those issues of designing hypertext systems which reflect the fact that producing hyperdocuments (writing, authoring role) and using hyperdocuments (reading nonlinear documents, accessing and retrieving information) is a cognitively demanding activity. In order to built systems that provide (intelligent) support for these activities cognitive processes and structures play a crucial role when designing hypertext systems. It can be observed that the construction of hypertext systems is often based on intuition and first-order task analysis. To overcome this situation, we need a user-oriented and task-driven approach to system design utilizing results of cognitive science or stimulating new research topics by looking at these applications.

The range of the topics of the panel will include the role of cognitive models of writing and reading for designing authoring tools in hypertext environments; critical issues of designing support for navigation in large information spaces including browsing and reading for the recipient; questions of how to arrive at cognitive compatibility of mental models of designers and users for the design of appropriate and cognitively adequate user-interfaces; compatibility of authors and readers; strategies of mapping knowledge representations on hyperstructures so that they can be processed later; the organization of multiple tasks extending to cooperative authoring and editing.

Panel: Confessions — What's Wrong with Our Systems

Frank Halasz, Xerox PARC [Notecards]

Don McCracken, Knowledge Systems [KMS]

Norman Meyrowitz, IRIS/Brown University [Intermedia]

Amy Pearl, Sun Microsystems, Inc. [Sun Link Service]

Ben Shneiderman, University of Maryland [Hyperties]

INTRODUCTION

As with any new field, it is typically the successes that are recorded, touted, and hyped, while the failures and deficiencies of systems and experiments are largely ignored. By the time that this panel speaks, attendees of the conference will have been at a two-day World's Fair of progress in hypertext and hypermedia. It is the goal of our panel to present the Dark Side of the Force, by explaining all the things our systems don't do well or don't do at all. By highlighting these problems, we hope to encourage new areas of research that fill the void.

The panel session will begin with *very* brief reviews of the systems that the panelists represent. After this, each panelist will have several chances to remark on problems and deficiencies in their own systems. Next each panelist will have a chance to ask a pithy, pointed, but polite question about some perceived problem in one of the other panelists' systems. Finally, each panelist will identify the most salient features of the other panelists's systems, and end with a prescription for the future.

Index

HYPERTEXT '89
Corporate Sponsors

 Apple Computer, Inc.

IBM

TEXAS
INSTRUMENTS